Preface

The aim of this textbook is to provide detailed coverage of the topics in the new AQA AS and A Level Computer Science specification.

The book is divided into twelve sections and within each section, each chapter covers material that can comfortably be taught in one or two lessons.

In the first year of this course there will be a strong emphasis on learning to program. You will start by learning the syntax of your chosen programming language – that is, the rules of how to write correct statements that the computer can understand. Then you will code simple programs, building up your skills to the point where you can understand and make additions and amendments to a program consisting of several hundred lines of code.

Sections 1 and 2 of this book can be studied in parallel with your practical programming sessions. It will give you practice in the skills you need to master.

In the second year of this course the focus will turn to algorithms and data structures, covered in Sections 7 and 8. These are followed by sections on regular languages, the Internet and databases.

Object Oriented Programming and functional programming are covered in the final section, which describes basic theoretical concepts in OOP, as well as providing some practical exercises using the functional programming language Haskell. Lists, the fact-based model and 'Big Data' are all described and explained.

Two short appendices contain A Level content that could be taught in the first year of the course as an extension to related AS topics.

The OOP concepts covered may also be helpful in the coursework element of the A Level course.

Each chapter contains exercises and questions, some new and some from past examination papers. Answers to all these are available to teachers only in a Teacher's Supplement which can be ordered from our website **www.pgonline.co.uk**.

Approval message from AQA

This textbook has been approved by AQA for use with our qualification. This means that we have checked that it broadly covers the specification and we are satisfied with the overall quality. Full details of our approval process can be found on our website.

We approve textbooks because we know how important it is for teachers and students to have the right resources to support their teaching and learning. However, the publisher is ultimately responsible for the editorial control and quality of this book.

Please note that when teaching the A Level Computer Science course, you must refer to AQA's specification as your definitive source of information. While this book has been written to match the specification, it cannot provide complete coverage of every aspect of the course.

A wide range of other useful resources can be found on the relevant subject pages of our website: www.aqa.org.uk.

Contents

Section 10

Section 11

Section 12

Appendices and Index

Section 1

Fundamentals of programming

In this section:

1

Chapter 1 – Programming basics

Objectives

- Define what is meant by an algorithm and pseudocode
- Learn how and when different data types are used
- Learn the basic arithmetic operations available in a typical programming language
- Become familiar with basic string handling operations
- Distinguish between variables and constants

What is an algorithm?

An algorithm is a set of rules or a sequence of steps specifying how to solve a problem. A recipe for chocolate cake, a knitting pattern for a sweater or a set of directions to get from A to B, are all algorithms of a kind. Each of them has **input**, **processing** and **output**. We will be looking in more detail at properties of algorithms in Section 2 of this book.

Q1: What are the inputs and outputs in a recipe, a knitting pattern and a set of directions?

Ingredients	Method
100g plain flour	Put flour and salt into a large mixing bowl and make a well in the centre.
2 eggs	
300ml milk	Crack the eggs into the middle.
1tbsp oil	Pour in about 50ml milk and the oil.
Pinch salt	Start whisking from the centre, gradually drawing the flour into the eggs, milk and oil, etc.

In the context of programming, the series of steps has to be written in such a way that it can be translated into program code which is then translated into machine code and executed by the computer.

Using pseudocode

Whatever programming language you are using in your practical work, as your programs get more complicated you will need some way of working out what the steps are before you sit down at the computer to type in the program code. A useful tool for developing algorithms is **pseudocode**, which is a sort of halfway house between English and program statements. There are no concrete rules or syntax for how pseudocode has to be written, and there are different ways of writing most statements. We will use a standard way of writing pseudocode that translates easily into a programming language such as Python, Pascal or whatever procedural language you are learning.

This book does not teach you how to program in any particular programming language – you will learn how to write programs in your practical sessions – but it will help you to understand and develop your own algorithms to solve problems.

An introduction to pseudocode statements

Input/output statements

Most programs will have input and output statements to allow the user to enter data and display or print results. Here is the pseudocode for a simple example:

```
OUTPUT "What is your name? "                #display text on the screen
#wait for user input and assign the value to the variable myname
myname ← USERINPUT
OUTPUT "Hello, ",myname
```

This program will ask the user to input their name, and then display "Hello, Jo" or whatever name the user entered. Notice that in this pseudocode, text such as "Hello," will be wrapped in speech marks to distinguish it from variables.

We will also use the pseudocode

```
myname ← USERINPUT "What is your name? "
```

which combines the OUTPUT and USERINPUT statement to display the prompt "What is your name? " and then wait for the user to enter text and press the ENTER key.

Comments

Note also that anything following a **#** will be treated as a **comment** and will have no effect on the running of the program. Comments are very important when you come to code your programs, to document the code (specifying the name, author, date written and purpose of the program, for example) and to explain how any tricky bits of the program work.

Data types

All programming languages have built-in elementary data types. Different data types are held differently in the computer's memory so you need to use the correct data type for the task. The most common data types include:

- integer   a whole number such as -25, 0, 3, 28679

- real/float   a number with a fractional part such as -13.5, 0.0, 3.142, 100.0001

- Boolean   a Boolean variable can only take the value TRUE or FALSE

- character   a letter or number or special character typically represented in ASCII, such as a, A, ? or %. Note that the character "4" is represented differently in the computer from the integer 4 or the real number 4.0

- string   anything enclosed in quote marks is a string, for example "Peter", "123", or "This is a string". Either single or double quotes are acceptable in many languages.

Common arithmetic operations

The symbols +, -, * and / are used for the common arithmetic operations of addition, subtraction, multiplication and division.

e.g. Suppose the bill in a restaurant comes to £20, and you want to divide it equally among 3 or 4 friends.

```
bill ← 20
billBetween4 ← bill/4     will return the value 5
billBetween3 ← bill/3     returns 6.666666667
```

1-1

In pseudocode you can assume that `billBetween3` will be automatically defined as a real variable and will store a value such as 6.666666667, though this may not be the case in every programming language.

The Round function

You can round this number using a function `round`.

```
billBetween3 ← round(billBetween3,2)      #round to 2 decimal places
```

This will return the value 6.67.

The Trunc function

Some languages have a truncate or `trunc` function, which rounds a real number down to the nearest whole number.

Q2: How could you convert this answer to a string variable and assign the answer to billstring?

Exponentiation

If you want to find, for example 2^5, 5 is called the **exponent** and you need to use exponentiation. You can write this operation in pseudocode as:

```
x ← 2**5
```

or, using variables as:

```
x ← y**n
```

1-1

Integer division and finding a remainder

Sometimes you may want to perform **integer division** and find a **remainder**.

For example: Twenty apples are to be divided between 6 people. How many will each receive, and how many will be left over?

In this case you need to use the `div` operator to find the whole number of apples each person will receive. The `mod` operator will find the remainder.

These two operations are coded differently in different programming languages, but in pseudocode you could write the following statements:

```
apples ← 20
applesPerPerson ← 20 div 3          (written applesPerPerson = 20//3 in Python)
```

This will return 6 in `applesPerPerson`.

```
applesRemaining ← 20 mod 3          (written applesRemaining = 20%3 in Python)
```

This will return 2 in `applesRemaining`.

String-handling functions

Programming languages have a number of built-in string-handling methods or functions. Some of the common ones in a typical language are:

`len(string)`	Returns the length of a string
`string.substring(index1,index2)`	Returns a portion of `string` inclusive of the characters at each index position
`string.find(str)`	Determines if `str` occurs in a string. Returns index (the position of the first character in the string) if found, and -1 otherwise. In our pseudocode we will assume that string(1) is the first element of the string, though in Python, for example, the first element is string(0)
`ord("a")`	Returns the integer value of a character (97 in this example)
`chr(97)`	Returns the character represented by an integer ("a" in this example)

Q3: What will be output by the following lines of code?

```
x = "Come into the garden, Maud"
y = len(x)
z = x.find("Maud")
OUTPUT "x= ",x
OUTPUT "y= ",y
OUTPUT "z= ",z
```

1-1

To **concatenate** or join two strings, use the + operator.

e.g. "Johnny" + "Bates" = "JohnnyBates"

String conversion operations

`int("1")`	converts the character "1" to the integer 1
`str(123)`	converts the integer 123 into a string "123"
`float("123.456")`	converts the string "123.456" to the real number 123.456
`str(123.456)`	converts the real number 123.456 to the string "123.456"
`date(year,month,day)`	returns a number that you can calculate with

Converting between strings and dates is usually handled by functions built in to string library modules, e.g. strtodate("01/01/2016").

Example:

```
date1 ← strtodate("18/01/2015")
date2 ← strtodate("30/12/2014")
days ← date1 - date2
OUTPUT date1, date2, days
```

This will output

```
2015-01-18 2014-12-30 19
```

Constants and variables

Some programming languages require you to declare all variables and constants before they are used in the program. For example:

```
var totalMark: integer
const VAT = 20.0
```

Variables are **identifiers** (names) given to memory locations whose contents will change during the course of the program; we have seen plenty of examples of these – e.g. in the statement below, the variable `myname` will change according to what the user enters.

```
myname ← USERINPUT
```

You should always try to use meaningful names for variables, rather than x, y and z, as this helps to make the program easy to follow and update when required.

Some programming languages also allow you to define **constants**, whose value never changes while the program is being run. For example, if your program involved calculating the area of a circle, you could define pi at the start of the program as a constant having the value 3.14159. Or, you might hold the company phone number as a constant, declared at the start of the program as

```
const companyPhone = "01453 123456"
```

Advantages of using constants

The advantage of using a constant is that in a long, complex program there is no chance that a programmer will accidentally change its value by using the identifier for a different purpose. It also means that if the value of a constant (e.g. VAT) changes from say 20.0 to 17.5, the programmer does not have to hunt through the program to find all the lines where the value 20.0 has been used.

In addition, using constants makes programming code more readable than using values.

Some languages such as Python do not require or even allow you to define variables or constants – you just use them as and when required in the program.

Exercises

1. A school keeps data about each of its pupils. State the most suitable data type for each of the following data items:

    Pupil's surname

    A single letter indicating whether they are male or female

    The amount owed for school trips

    The number of school trips they have participated in

    Whether or not the pupil is entitled to free school meals   [5]

2. (a) Write pseudocode for a program which asks the user to enter the total bill for a restaurant meal, and the total number of people who had a meal. The program should add 10% to the bill as a tip, and then calculate and display to the nearest penny what each person owes, assuming the bill is evenly split.   [6]

Exercises continued

(b) Complete the following table showing an additional **two** sets of test data, the reason for each test and the expected result. [6]

Total bill	Number of people	Reason for test	Expected result
100.00	10	Total amount exactly divisible by number of people	11.00

3. (a) Name **two** ways in which you can help to make your programs understandable for another programmer. [2]

(b) Imagine that you have had a stall at the Summer Fayre. At the end of the day you count up the number of each 1p, 2p, 5p, 10p, 20p and 50p coins you have received.

Write a pseudocode algorithm to allow the user to input the number of coins of each value, and to calculate and display the total takings.

Make use of **two** ways of making the program understandable given in your answer to part (a). [6]

1-1

Chapter 2 – Selection

Objectives

- be able to use relational operators
- be able to use Boolean operations AND, OR, NOT, XOR
- be able to use nested selection statements

Program constructs

There are just three basic programming constructs: **sequence**, **selection** and **iteration**.

Sequence is just two or more statements following one after the other, such as

```
OUTPUT "Please enter a number: "
n ← USERINPUT
nsquared ← n * n
```

The last statement is an **assignment** statement in which a value is **assigned** to a variable.

In this chapter and the next, we will look at selection and iteration.

Selection

Selection statements are used to select which statement will be executed next, depending on some condition. Conditions are formulated using **relational operators**.

Relational operators

The following operators may be used in pseudocode for making comparisons:

- \> greater than
- < less than
- \>= greater than or equal
- <= less than or equal
- = equal
- <> not equal

Q1: Are these operators the same as the ones used in the programming language you are learning? If not, how are they different?

Selection statements can take different forms, for example:

```
IF (expression1) THEN
    (do these statements)
ENDIF
```

Expression1 is an expression involving a relational operator such as

```
IF (AGE >=17) THEN
    canDrive ← TRUE
ENDIF
```

1-2

Q2: What type of variable is `canDrive`?

If `expression1` does not evaluate to TRUE, control passes to the next statement after the IF statement.

Alternatively, you can specify what should happen if the condition does not evaluate to TRUE:

```
IF (expression1) THEN
   (do these statements)
ELSE
   (do these statements)
ENDIF
```

For example:

```
IF mark >= 50 THEN
   OUTPUT "Pass"
ELSE
   OUTPUT "Fail"
   OUTPUT "You will have to retake this test."
ENDIF
```

A 'nested' selection statement may have another IF statement inside one or both of the code blocks for the cases of the outer IF :

```
IF (expression1) THEN
   IF (expression2) THEN
      (do these statements)
   ELSE
      (do these statements)
   ENDIF
ELSE
   (do these statements)
ENDIF
```

Example 1

A bank offers different interest rates according to how much is in the account. There are three thresholds of £500, £3,000 and £10,000:

If `amount` less than `500`, rate = 1%

If `amount` greater than or equal £`500` but less than £`3000`, rate = 1.5%

If `amount` greater than or equal £`3000` but less than £`10000`, rate = 2%

If `amount` greater than or equal £`10000`, rate is 3.5%

The selection statement can be written as follows:

```
IF (amount < 500) THEN
   rate ← 0.01
ELSE IF (amount < 3000) THEN
   rate ← 0.015
ELSE IF (amount < 10000) THEN
   rate ← 0.02
ELSE
   rate ← 0.035
ENDIF
```

1-2

The CASE statement

Some programming languages support the use of a CASE statement, an alternative structure to a nested IF statement. It is useful when a choice has to be made between several alternatives.

Example 2

Perform different statements according to an option choice entered by the user.

```
CASE choice of
    1: OUTPUT "You have selected option 1"
       (more statements here)
    2: OUTPUT "You have selected option 2"
       (more statements here)
    3: OUTPUT "You have selected option 3"
       (more statements here)
ELSE
    OUTPUT "You must enter 1, 2 or 3"
ENDCASE
```

Example 3

A statement to calculate the number of days in each month between 2001 and 2099 may be written:

```
CASE month of
    "Jan","Mar","May","Jul","Aug","Oct","Dec": daysInMonth ← 31
    "Apr","Jun","Sep","Nov":                   daysInMonth ← 30
    "Feb":  IF year MOD 4 = 0 THEN
                daysInMonth ← 29
            ELSE
                daysInMonth ← 28
            ENDIF
ENDCASE
```

Boolean operators AND, OR, NOT

More complex conditions can be formed using the Boolean operators AND and OR.

Example 4

```
IF (a > b) AND (a > c) THEN
    max ← a
ELSE IF (b > a) AND (b > c) THEN
    max ← b
ELSE
    max ← c
ENDIF
```

Q4: What does the above algorithm do?

Example 5

Write pseudocode for a program to allow the user to input the day of the week and output "Weekday" or "Weekend".

```
day ← USERINPUT
IF (day = "Saturday") OR (day = "Sunday") THEN
    OUTPUT "Weekend"
ELSE
    OUTPUT "Weekday"
ENDIF
```

Example 6

A tourist attraction has a daily charge for children of £5.00 on a weekday, or £7.50 on a weekend or bank holiday. Adults are charged £8.00 on weekdays and £12.00 on weekends and bank holidays. Write pseudocode to allow the user to calculate the charge for a visitor.

```
OUTPUT "Enter W for weekend, B for bank holiday or D for weekday"
day ← USERINPUT
OUTPUT "Enter A for adult, C for child"
visitor ← USERINPUT
IF ((day = "W") OR (day = "B")) AND (visitor = "A") THEN
    charge ← 12.0
ELSE IF ((day = "W") OR (day = "B")) AND (visitor = "C") THEN
    charge ← 7.5
ELSE IF (visitor = "A") THEN
    charge ← 8.0
ELSE
    charge ← 5.0
ENDIF
```

Notes:

It is important to use brackets and to get them in the correct place to avoid any confusion over which operator is processed first. In standard Boolean logic the precedence rules make NOT highest, then AND, then OR.

The NOT operator

You can usually avoid the use of the NOT operator, replacing it with an appropriate condition.
e.g.

```
NOT (a = b)  is equivalent to  a <> b
NOT (a < b)  is equivalent to  a >= b
```

The XOR operator

XOR stands for **exclusive OR**, so that a XOR b means "either a or b but not both".

This can be implemented with a combination of AND, OR and NOT conditions:

```
(a AND NOT b) OR (NOT a AND b)
```

Note that NOT takes precedence over AND. Add extra brackets if you are in any doubt!

Exercises

1. Below is a segment of an algorithm to determine at what times different members are allowed to use the competition pool at the local Sports Centre.

```
swimTime ← False
IF (Membership = "Premier") THEN
    swimTime ← TRUE
ELSE IF ((Membership = "Adult") AND (Day = "Weekday") AND
        (Time < 1500)) OR
        ((Membership = "Adult") AND (Day = "Weekend")) THEN
    swimTime ← TRUE
ELSE IF (Membership = "Junior") AND (Day = "Weekend") THEN
    swimTime ← TRUE
ENDIF
```

Write down the values of `swimTime` after the segment of the algorithm has executed with the following data:

(i)   Membership: Premier   Day: Weekday   Time: 1700

(ii) Membership: Adult   Day: Weekday   Time: 1100

(iii) Membership: Junior   Day: Weekday   Time: 1000

(iv) Membership: Adult   Day: Weekend   Time: 0900

(v)   Membership: Adult   Day: Weekday   Time: 1530   [5]

2. (a) Write a pseudocode algorithm for a program which calculates the cost of carpeting a room. The carpet is supplied in a roll 4m wide. The cost of the carpet is £10 per square metre. The program should ask the user to enter the longest dimension (length) and shortest dimension (width) of the room, then calculate and display the length and width and cost of carpet that will be supplied.

   You can assume that the width of the room is not more than 4m. If a width of more than 4m is entered, display an error message and quit the program.

   The length could be more or less than 4m.   [5]

   (b) Calculate the expected results for the following room sizes:

   Length = 5,   width = 3

   Length = 5,   width = 4

   Length = 3,   width = 2

   Length = 3.9,   width = 2

   Length = 6,   width = 5   [5]

1-2

Chapter 3 – Iteration

Objectives

- Understand and use three different types of iterative statement WHILE, REPEAT and FOR

- Be familiar with, and be able to use, random number generation

Performing a loop

In the last two chapters we looked at **sequence** and **selection** statements. The third programming construct is **iteration**. Iteration means repetition, so iterative statements always involve performing a loop in the program to repeat a number of statements. There are three different types of loop to be considered, although some programming languages do not implement all three.

- **Indefinite iteration** where the iteration continues until some specified condition is met, includes WHILE ... ENDWHILE loops and REPEAT ... UNTIL loops

- **Definite iteration**, where the number of times the loop is to be executed is decided in advance, is implemented using FOR ... ENDFOR loop

The WHILE ... ENDWHILE loop

A WHILE ... ENDWHILE loop has two properties:

- The expression controlling the repetition of the loop must be of type Boolean – that is, one which evaluates to True or False

- This expression is tested at the **start** of the loop

This is best explained by means of an example. Suppose you wanted to input the daily maximum temperatures for one month, calculate and output the average of these measurements.

The program has to work for any month, so when you have entered all the temperatures you will enter a 'dummy' value -100 to signify that there are no more temperatures to enter.

A first attempt at the pseudocode might look like this:

```
temp ← 0                    #initialise temp
totalTemp ← 0               #initialise total of temperatures
numberOfTemps ← 0           #initialise number of temperatures
WHILE temp <> -100
   OUTPUT "Enter next temperature"
   temp ← USERINPUT
   totalTemp ← totalTemp + temp
   numberOfTemps ← numberOfTemps + 1
ENDWHILE
averageTemp ← totalTemp/numberOfTemps
OUTPUT averageTemp
```

1-3

Test this algorithm with temperatures 8, 12 and -100. We can draw a trace table showing the value of the variables as they change during execution of the program.

totalTemp	numberOfTemps	Temp <> -100	temp	averageTemp
0	0	TRUE	8	
8	1	TRUE	12	
20	2	TRUE		

Q1: Complete the trace table. What is the average temperature calculated by this algorithm?

You should have ended up with 3 temperatures and an average temperature of -26.66667 instead of 10. The problem is that the expression controlling the loop is tested only once each time round, at the beginning of the loop, and not after each statement within the loop as it is executed. Therefore, we have to make sure that as soon as the number -100 is entered, the next thing that happens is that the Boolean expression is tested.

```
totalTemp ← 0                  #initialise total of temperatures
numberOfTemps ← 0              #initialise number of temperatures
OUTPUT "Enter next temperature"
temp ← USERINPUT               #input first temperature
WHILE temp <> -100
    totalTemp ← totalTemp + temp
    numberOfTemps ← numberOfTemps + 1
    OUTPUT "Enter next temperature"
    temp ← USERINPUT
ENDWHILE
averageTemp ← totalTemp/numberOfTemps
OUTPUT averageTemp
```

Note that with a WHILE ... ENDWHILE loop, if the Boolean expression is TRUE at the start, the loop will not be executed at all and control will pass straight to the next statement after ENDWHILE.

Q2: What will happen if the first temperature entered is -100? Alter the algorithm to ensure that the program displays a suitable message.

The REPEAT ... UNTIL loop

This type of loop is very similar to the WHILE ... ENDWHILE loop, with the difference that the Boolean expression controlling the loop is written and tested at the end of the loop, rather than at the beginning. This means that the loop is always performed at least once.

Note:

Python does not support a REPEAT ... UNTIL statement, but the same output can be achieved with a WHILE ... ENDWHILE loop.

Example 1

Write pseudocode for a program which tests someone on the squares of numbers up to 25.

```
#program to test a user on the squares of numbers
#random(a,b) generates a random integer between a and b

REPEAT
   num ← random(1,25)
   numsquare ← num * num
   OUTPUT "What is the square of ", num
   answer ← USERINPUT()
   IF answer = numsquare THEN
      OUTPUT "Correct, well done"
   ELSE
      OUTPUT "No, it is ", numsquare
   ENDIF
   OUTPUT "Another go? Answer Y or N"
   anotherGo ← USERINPUT
UNTIL (anotherGo = "N") OR (anotherGo = "n")
```

Q3: Rewrite this algorithm using a WHILE … ENDWHILE loop. Which loop do you think is preferable for performing this task?

The FOR … ENDFOR loop

This type of loop is useful when you know how many iterations need to be performed. For example, suppose you want to display the two times table:

```
FOR count ← 1 TO 12
   product ← 2 * count
   OUTPUT "2 x ", count, " = ", product
ENDFOR
```

The value of count starts at 1 and is incremented each time round the loop. When it reaches 12, the loop terminates and the next statement is executed.

Nested loops

Loops can be "nested" one inside another. Suppose we want to display all the multiplication tables between 1 and 12. We can do this with two FOR loops, one inside the other.

Example 2

```
FOR table ← 1 TO 12
   FOR count ← 1 TO 12
      product ← table * count
      OUTPUT table, " x ", count, " = ", product
   ENDFOR
ENDFOR
```

Q4: What will be the second line output by this algorithm?

Example 3

Use a random number generator to simulate throwing a die to find out how many throws it takes to get a 6.

```
answer ← "y"
WHILE (answer = "y") or (answer = "Y")
   numberOfThrows ← 0
   throw ← 0
   WHILE throw <> 6
      throw ← random(1,6)
      numberOfThrows ← numberOfThrows + 1
      OUTPUT "You threw a ", throw
   ENDWHILE
   OUTPUT "That took ",numberOfThrows," throws"
   OUTPUT "Another go? (Y or y)"
   answer ← USERINPUT
ENDWHILE
```

Q5: What will happen if the user answers "yes" in answer to the question "Another go? (Y or y)"?

1-3

Example 4

You can count backwards as well as forwards in a FOR … ENDFOR loop. Here is a pseudocode program which uses the 'sleep' method to count down in seconds to blast-off. It uses a function called `sleep` which suspends execution for a given number of seconds:

```
ReadyForCountdown ← USERINPUT "Press enter when you're ready to start"
FOR secs ← 10 TO 0 STEP -1
   OUTPUT secs
   sleep(1)              #suspends execution for 1 second
ENDFOR
OUTPUT "BLAST-OFF!"
```

Exercises

1. Write a pseudocode algorithm to allow the user to input two integers **highestNumber** and **multiplier**. The program should output the results of multiplying integers **2, 3… highestNumber** by **multiplier**.

    For example if the user enters 100 for **highestNumber** and 7 for **multiplier** the program should output the numbers 14, 21 … 700.   [5]

2. Write pseudocode for a program that asks the user which times table they would like to be tested on, and then gives them 5 random questions on this table. The computer should tell them each time whether they got the answer right or wrong.   [5]

Chapter 4 – Arrays

Objectives

- Be familiar with the concept of a data structure
- Use 1- and 2-dimensional arrays in the design of solutions to simple problems

Data structures

A data structure is a collection of **elementary data types** such as **integer**, **real**, **Boolean**, **char**, and built-in methods to facilitate processing in some way. Computer languages such as Python, Pascal and VB have some built-in **structured data types** such as **string**, **array** or **list** and **record**. Other data structures such as stacks and trees can be created by the programmer to suit a specific purpose.

1-dimensional arrays

An array is defined as a finite, ordered set of elements of the same type, such as integer, real or char. **Finite** means that there is a specific number of elements in the array. **Ordered** implies that there is a first, second, third etc. element of the array.

For example, (assuming the first element of the array is `myArray[0]` and not `myArray[1]`):

```
myArray ← [51, 72, 35, 37, 0, 3]
x ← myArray[2]              #assigns 35 to x
```

Example

Every year the RSPB organises a Big Garden Birdwatch to involve the public in counting the number of birds of different types that they see in their gardens on a particular weekend. During 24-25 January 2015, more than 6 million birds were counted and reported.

The scientists add all the sightings together to find out how birds and other wildlife are doing.

Once this has been checked and pieced together, they can monitor trends and understand how different birds and other wildlife are faring.

An array of strings could be used to hold the names of the birds, and an array of integers to hold the results as they come in. As a simple example we will hold the names of 8 birds in an array:

```
birdName ← ["robin", "blackbird", "pigeon", "magpie", "bluetit",
"thrush", "wren", "starling"]
```

We can reference each element of the array using an **index**. For example:

```
birdName[2] ← "pigeon"  #the index here is 2
```

Most languages have a function which will return the length of an array, so that

```
numSpecies ← len(birdName)
```

will assign 8 to `numSpecies`.

To find at which position of the array a particular bird is, we could use the following algorithm:

```
bird ← USERINPUT
birdFound ← FALSE
numSpecies ← len(birdName)
FOR count ← 0 TO numSpecies - 1
    IF bird = birdName[count] THEN
        birdIndex ← count
        birdFound ← TRUE
    ENDIF
ENDFOR
IF birdFound = FALSE THEN
    OUTPUT "Bird species not in array"
ELSE
    OUTPUT "Bird found at", birdIndex
ENDIF
```

We need a second array of integers to accumulate the totals of each bird species observed. We can initialise each element to zero.

```
birdCount ← [0,0,0,0,0,0,0,0]
```

To add 5 to the blackbird count (the second element in the list) we can write a statement

```
birdCount[1] ← birdCount[1] + 5
```

The following algorithm enables a member of the Birdwatch team to enter results as they come in from members of the public.

```
birdName ← ["robin", "blackbird", "pigeon", "magpie", "bluetit",
            "thrush", "wren", "starling"]
birdCount ← [0,0,0,0,0,0,0,0]
OUTPUT "Please input name of bird (x to end): "
bird ← USERINPUT
WHILE bird <> "x"
    birdFound ← FALSE
    FOR count ← 0 TO 7
        IF bird = birdName[count] THEN
            birdFound ← TRUE
            OUTPUT "number observed: "
            birdsObserved ← USERINPUT
            birdCount[count] ← birdCount[count] + birdsObserved
        ENDIF
    ENDFOR
    IF birdFound = FALSE THEN
        OUTPUT "Bird species not in array"
    ENDIF
    OUTPUT "Please input name of bird (x to end): "
    bird ← USERINPUT
ENDWHILE
#now print out the totals for each bird
FOR count ← 0 TO 7
    OUTPUT birdName[count], birdCount[count]
ENDFOR
```

2-dimensional arrays

An array can have two or more dimensions. A two-dimensional array can be visualised as a table, rather like a spreadsheet.

Imagine a 2-dimensional array called `numbers`, with 3 rows and 4 columns. Elements in the array can be referred to by their row and column number, so that `numbers[1][3] = 8` in the example below.

An alternative syntax used in some programming languages is `numbers[1,3]` or `numbers(1,3)`.

	Column 0	**Column 1**	**Column 2**	**Column 3**
Row 0	1	2	3	4
Row 1	5	6	7	8
Row 2	9	10	11	12

Q1: What is the value of `numbers[2][1]`?

Example

Write a pseudocode algorithm for a module which prints out the quarterly sales figures (given in integers) for each of 3 sales staff named Anna, Bob and Carol, together with the total annual sales for all staff. Assume that the sales figures are already in the 2-dimensional array `quarterSales`. The staff names are held in a 1-dimensional array `staff`.

```
staff ← ["Anna","Bob","Carol"]
quarterSales ← [[100,110,120,110],
                [350,355,360,360],
                [200,210,220,220]]
annualSales ← 0
FOR s ← 0 to 2
   #output staff name
   (insert statement here)

   FOR q ← 0 to 3
      OUTPUT "Quarter ",q, quarterSales[s][q]
      annualSales ← annualSales + quarterSales[s][q]
   ENDFOR
ENDFOR
OUTPUT "Annual sales for all staff: ",annualSales
```

Q2: What statement needs to be inserted after the comment `#output staff name` in order to output the staff name?

Arrays of n dimensions

Arrays may have more than two dimensions. An n-dimensional array is a set of elements of the same type, indexed by a tuple of n integers, where a tuple is an ordered list of elements. In a 3-dimensional array x, a particular element may be referred to as `x[4][5][2]`, for example. The first element would be referred to as `x[0][0][0]` (assuming the array indices start at 0 and not 1).

1-4

Exercises

1. Referring to the BirdWatch program given earlier in this chapter:

   (a) Explain why the FOR … ENDFOR loop repeated below is not the most efficient type of loop in this situation. [1]

   ```
   FOR count ← 0 to 7
      IF bird = birdName[count] THEN
         birdFound ← TRUE
         OUTPUT "number observed: "
         birdsObserved ← USERINPUT
         birdCount[count] ← birdCount[count] + birdsObserved
      ENDIF
   ENDFOR
   ```

   (b) Rewrite the algorithm using a different type of loop. [3]

2. The birth weights in grams of 100 babies, which vary between 1500 to 4000 grams, are held in an array `weight`.

   Write pseudocode for an algorithm which calculates the average birth weight, and then prints out the number of babies who are more than 500 grams below the average weight, together with the average weight of these. [5]

3. The marks for 3 assignments, each marked out of 10, for a class of 5 students are to be input into a two-dimensional array `mark` so that `mark[3][1]`, for example, holds the second mark achieved by the 4th student. Any missing assignments are given a mark of zero.

   Draw a table representing this array, and fill it with test data. [2]

   Write a pseudocode algorithm which allows the user to enter the marks for the class. Calculate the average mark for each student, and the class average. [4]

4. In a certain game, treasure is hidden in a 10x10 grid. The grid coordinates are given by `grid[row][col]` where `grid[0][0]` represents the top left hand corner and `grid[9][9]` the bottom right corner. The grid coordinates of the treasure are signified by a 1 at `grid[row][col]`. All other grid elements are filled with zeros.

   What is the purpose of the following pseudocode algorithm? [2]

   ```
   FOR row ← 0 TO 9
      FOR col ← 0 TO 9
         IF grid[row][col] = 1 THEN
            OUTPUT "row", row, "column", col
         ENDIF
      ENDFOR
   ENDFOR
   ```

   Write pseudocode statements to initialise the grid and "hide the treasure" at a random location inside the grid. [5]

Chapter 5 – Subroutines

Objectives

- Be familiar with subroutines, their uses and advantages
- Be able to use subroutines that return values to the calling routine
- Be able to describe the use of parameters to pass data within programs
- Be able to contrast the use of local and global variables

Types of subroutine

A subroutine is a **named block of code** which performs a specific task within a program.

Most high-level languages support two types of subroutine, **functions** and **procedures**, which are called in a slightly different way. Some languages such as Python have only one type of subroutine, namely functions.

All programming languages have 'built-in' functions which you will have already used if you have written any programs. For example, in Python:

```
print("What is your name? ")
myName = input()
print("Hello, ",myName)
age = input("How old are you? ")
```

A subroutine is called by writing its name in a program statement. Some functions return a result, like the `input` function above, and some do not return any result, like the `print` function. Notice that the last statement above combines the **print** and **input** functions; when the statement is executed, the computer will display the question "How old are you?" and wait for the user to input an answer, which will be assigned to the variable `age`.

In languages which distinguish between functions and procedures, a **function** is called like the **input** function above, always assigning a return value to a variable. A **procedure** is called by writing its name but not assigning the result to a variable, like the **print** statement above. However, as we shall see later, a procedure can still pass values back to the calling program if necessary.

In Chapter 1, we listed some string-handling functions, and we can write, for example, pseudocode such as

```
x ← int("567")
```

to call the `int` function, which will convert the string `"567"` into an integer.

Q1: List some other functions you have used in your programs or pseudocode algorithms.

Q2: In some languages, `sqrt` is a function which returns the square root of a number. What value will be assigned to the variable `z` by the statement?

```
z = sqrt(25)
```

User-written subroutines

You can write your own subroutines (functions and/or procedures) and call them from within the program as many times as needed. The subroutine (or subprogram) first needs to be defined, typically above the code in the main program.

Example 1

Using pseudocode, write a subroutine which displays a menu of 4 options in a game.

```
SUB displayMenu                          #declare the subroutine
   OUTPUT "Option 1: Display rules"
   OUTPUT "Option 2: Start new game"
   OUTPUT "Option 3: Quit"
   OUTPUT "Enter 1, 2 or 3: "
ENDSUB
```

To call the subroutine from the main program, you simply write its name:

```
displayMenu
```

This subroutine always produces the same result whenever it is called; it simply displays this menu.

Example 2

Sometimes, you may want a subroutine to return a value to the main program:

```
SUB getChoice
   OUTPUT "Option 1: Display rules"
   OUTPUT "Option 2: Start new game"
   OUTPUT "Option 3: Quit"
   OUTPUT "Enter 1, 2 or 3: "
   choice ← USERINPUT
   RETURN choice
ENDSUB
#main program starts here
option ← getChoice
OUTPUT "You have chosen ", option
```

In this example, when the program is run, the first line to be executed is the first statement in the main program, option ← getChoice. The subroutine is called, it displays the menu, gets the user's choice in choice and returns this to the main program using the statement RETURN choice. Execution continues where it left off, at the statement OUTPUT "You have chosen ", option.

The subroutine is called in a slightly different way from the subroutine displayMenu – compare this to the two different ways in which built-in OUTPUT and USERINPUT subroutines are called.

```
OUTPUT "What is your name?"
myName ← USERINPUT
OUTPUT "Hello, ", myName
```

The OUTPUT subroutine does not return a value, the USERINPUT subroutine does.

Q3: Write pseudocode for a program which

- asks the user "Do you like chocolate?"
- calls a subroutine `getresponse` which ask the user to enter y or n, validates this response and repeats the question until y or n is entered
- prints a suitable comment depending on the answer

Subroutines with interfaces

Frequently, you need to pass values or variables to a subroutine. The exact form of the **subroutine interface** varies with the programming language, but will be similar to the examples below:

```
SUB subroutineName(parameter1, parameter 2,...)
```

There are two mechanisms for passing parameters: by value and by reference. When parameters are passed by value, changing a parameter inside the subroutine will not affect its value outside the subroutine. All parameters are passed this way in Python.

In other languages such as Visual Basic, the programmer can specify whether the parameter is to be passed by value or by reference. When a parameter is passed by reference, the address of the parameter, and not its value, is passed, so any change made to it in a subroutine will be reflected in the calling program.

Example 3

Consider a simple subroutine which calculates the volume of a cylinder. In the main program, the user is asked to enter values for the radius and length of the cylinder. These variables are then passed as **parameters** to the subroutine for use in the calculation.

1-5

The values (or addresses) of the parameters `radius` and `length` in line 11 are passed to the subroutine where they are referred to using the identifiers `r` and `len` respectively. The order in which the parameters are written when calling the subroutine is important: `radius` is passed to `r`, `length` is passed to `len`. The return value `vol` is passed back to the main program, where it is assigned to `volume` in line 11.

```
1    SUB cylinderVolume(r,len)
2        pi ← 3.142
3        vol ← pi*r*r*len
4        RETURN vol
5    ENDSUB
6    #main program
7    OUTPUT "Enter the radius of the cylinder:"
8    radius ← USERINPUT
9    OUTPUT "Enter the length of the cylinder:"
10   length ← USERINPUT
11   volume ← cylinderVolume(radius,length)
12   OUTPUT "The volume of the cylinder is ", volume
```

Q4: Line numbers have been added to each statement of the above pseudocode for reference. Write down the statement numbers in the order in which they are executed.

Q5: Write pseudocode for a program which calls a function `addNumbers(n,m)` to add all the numbers between 5 and 10. The result should be returned to the main program and displayed.

Q6: Write pseudocode for a program which asks the user to enter a name and percentage mark. It then calls a subroutine which assigns a grade to the mark which it passes back to the main program, where it is printed together with the name. Grades are assigned as follows:

mark >= 80:	Distinction
mark between 65-79:	Merit
mark between 50 and 64:	Pass
mark < 50:	Fail

Local and global variables

Variables used in the main program are by default **global variables**, and these can be used anywhere in the program, including within any subroutines. Within a subroutine, **local variables** can be used and these exist only during the execution of the subroutine. They cannot be accessed outside the subroutine and changing them has no effect on any variable outside the subroutine, even if the variable happens to have the same name as the local variable.

Q7: Can you find a local variable in `SUB cylinderVolume(r,len)` in Example 3 above? What would happen if you tried to print its value in the main program?

The ability to declare local variables is very useful because it ensures that each subroutine is completely self-contained and independent of any global variables that have been declared in the main program. The principles of **data hiding** and **encapsulation** of all the variables needed in a subroutine are very important in programming. A subroutine written according to these principles can be tested independently, and used many times in many different programs without the programmer needing to know what variables it uses. Any variable in the calling program which coincidentally has the same name as a local variable declared in the subroutine will not cause an unexpected side-effect.

Example 4

```
1   SUB printNumbers(x)
2       a ← 1
3       b ← 2
4       c ← 3
5       OUTPUT "In the subroutine, a,b,c and x have values ", a,b,c,x
6   ENDSUB

7   #main program
8   a ← 4
9   b ← 5
10  c ← 6
11  x ← 10
12  OUTPUT "In the main program, a,b,c and x have values ", a,b,c,x
13  printNumbers(x)
14  OUTPUT "In the main program, a,b,c and x now have values ", a,b,c,x
```

Q8: Write down the line numbers of the statements in the order in which they are executed.

Q9: What will be the output of the program?

Q10: What will happen when the following program is run?

```
SUB printnum
  y ← 20
  OUTPUT "In sub printnum, y = ", y
ENDSUB
#main program
printnum
OUTPUT "In main program, y = ", y
```

Modular programming

When a program is short and simple, there is no need to break it up into subroutines. With a long, complex program, however, a 'top-down' approach, in which the problem is broken down into a number of subtasks, is generally very helpful in designing the algorithm for reaching a satisfactory solution.

Programming with subroutines

Using subroutines in a large program has many advantages:

- A subroutine is small enough to be understandable as a unit of code. It is therefore relatively easy to understand, debug and maintain especially if its purpose is clearly defined and documented
- Subroutines can be tested independently, thereby shortening the time taken to get a large program working
- Once a subroutine has been thoroughly tested, it can be reused with confidence in different programs or parts of the same program
- In a very large project, several programmers may be working on a single program. Using a modular approach, each programmer can be given a specific set of subroutines to work on. This enables the whole program to be finished sooner
- A large project becomes easier to monitor and control

Example 5

A program is to be written which simulates a dice game in which 2 players take turns. The rules of the game are as follows:

Players take turns to throw two dice. If the throw is a 'double', i.e. two 2s, two 3s, etc., the player's score reverts to zero and their turn ends. If the throw is not a 'double', the total shown on the two dice is added to the player's score. A player may have as many throws as they like in any turn until they either throw a double or pass the dice. The first player to reach a score of 50 wins the game.

We will design the solution in a top-down manner. A first attempt at listing the major tasks to be performed might be:

```
REPEAT
   display the menu (display rules, play game or quit)
   get the user's choice (1 to display rules, 2 to play, 3 to quit)
   call a routine to either display the rules, play the game or quit
UNTIL the user chooses quit
OUTPUT "Goodbye"
```

The major tasks can be split into subroutines, which can each be tested independently.

We need the following subroutines:

```
SUB  menuChoice      #display menu and get user's choice
SUB  displayRules
SUB  playGame
```

Playing the game needs to be broken down further. At this stage we can start writing pseudocode for a subroutine playGame which will do the following:

```
SUB  playGame
   initialise scores of each player (score1 and score2) to zero
   ask for the players' names (player1 and player1)
   WHILE score1 < 50 AND score2 < 50
      score1 ← playerTurn(player1,score1)          # player 1's turn
      IF score1 >= 50 THEN
         OUTPUT "You win!"
      ELSE
         score2 ← playerTurn(player2,score2)        # player 2's turn
         IF score2 >= 50 THEN
            OUTPUT "You win!"
         ENDIF
      ENDIF
   ENDWHILE
ENDSUB
```

Finally, we have to design the subroutine `playerTurn`. This is incorporated into the pseudocode for the whole program, which is given below. In some languages it may be necessary to import a library containing the `random` function.

Q11: Have a go at writing an algorithm for `playerTurn` before you look at it! Alternatively, code the program in a language of your choice.

```
#program to play a 2-player dice game

SUB menuChoice
   OUTPUT "Option 1: Display rules"
   OUTPUT "Option 2: Start new game"
   OUTPUT "Option 3: Quit"
   OUTPUT "What would you like to do?"
   choice ← USERINPUT
   WHILE choice < 1 OR choice > 3
         OUTPUT "That is not a valid choice."
         OUTPUT "Please enter a number between 1 and 3: "
         choice ← USERINPUT
   ENDWHILE
   RETURN choice
ENDSUB
```

```
#subroutine to display rules

SUB displayRules
   OUTPUT "The rules of the game are as follows:
   Players take turns to throw two dice.
   If the throw is a 'double', i.e. two 2s, two 3s, etc.,
   the player's score reverts to zero and their turn ends.
   (etc.)"
ENDSUB


#subroutine for each player to take a turn

SUB playerTurn(player,score)
   OUTPUT "Your turn, ", player
   anotherGo ← "Y"
   scoreThisTurn ← 0
   WHILE anotherGo = "Y" OR anotherGo = "y"
      die1 ← random(1,6)    #call a built-in function
      die2 ← random(1,6)
      OUTPUT "You rolled ", die1," and", die2
      IF die1 = die2
         scoreThisTurn ← 0
         cumulativeScore ← 0
         OUTPUT "Bad luck! Press any key to continue"
         anyKey ← USERINPUT   #accept any keypress from user
         anotherGo ← "N"
      ELSE
         scoreThisTurn ← scoreThisTurn + die1 + die2
         cumulativeScore ← score + scoreThisTurn
         OUTPUT "Your score this turn is ",scoreThisTurn
         OUTPUT player,"Your cumulative score is ", cumulativeScore
         IF cumulativeScore >= 50 THEN
            anotherGo ← "N"
         ELSE
            OUTPUT "Another go? (Answer Y or N)"
            anotherGo ← USERINPUT
         ENDIF
      ENDIF
   ENDWHILE
   RETURN cumulativeScore
ENDSUB
```

1-5

27

```
#subroutine to play game
SUB playGame
   score1 ← 0
   score2 ← 0
   OUTPUT "Enter Player 1's name: "
   player1 ← USERINPUT
   OUTPUT "Enter Player 2's name: "
   player2 ← USERINPUT
   WHILE score1 < 50 AND score2 < 50
      score1 ← playerTurn(player1, score1)
      IF score1 >= 50 THEN
         OUTPUT "You win!"
      ELSE
         score2 ← playerTurn(player2, score2)
         IF score2 >= 50 THEN
            OUTPUT "You win!"
         ENDIF
      ENDIF
   ENDWHILE
ENDSUB

#main program starts here
option ← menuChoice
WHILE option <> 3
   IF option = 1 THEN
      displayRules
   ELSE
      playGame
   ENDIF
   option ← menuChoice
ENDWHILE
OUTPUT "Goodbye!"
```

Exercises

1. Referring to the program code above, answer the following questions.

    (a) Give **one** example of a global variable and **one** example of a local variable used in this program.
        Why is it good practice to use local variables whenever possible?   [4]

    (b) Give **one** example of a parameter in this program. What is the advantage of using subroutines
        with parameters?   [3]

    (c) The first statement in the main program is `option ← menuChoice`

        Explain what this statement does.   [2]

1-5

Chapter 6 – Files and exception handling

Objectives

- define the terms field, record, file

- be able to read from and write to a text file

- understand when and how to use exception handling in a program

Fields, records and files

If you want to store data permanently so that you can read or update it at a future date, the data needs to be stored in a file on disk. The most common way of storing large amounts of data conveniently is to use a database, but sometimes you need to create and interrogate your own files.

Generally, a **file** consists of a number of **records**. A record contains a number of **fields**, each holding one item of data. For example, in a file holding data about students, you might have the following record structure:

ID	Firstname	Surname	DateOfBirth	Class
1453	Gemma	Baines	01/05/2004	2G
1768	Paul	Gerrard	17/11/2003	2G
2016	Brian	Davidson	03/08/2002	3H

The table shows a file containing three records, each record having 5 fields. In some languages, a record structure will be declared in the following manner:

```
Student = Record
   integer ID
   string Firstname
   string Surname
   date DateOfBirth
   string Class
End Record
```

This is an example of a user-defined data type.

Another way of storing a file is to use a **text file,** described below.

Writing to a text file

Suppose that you want to write to a text file containing the names of birds seen and the numbers of each bird reported by an individual participating in the RSPB's Big Garden Birdwatch described in Chapter 4, page 17. You may be starting a new file or appending data to an existing file – there are different 'modes' in which a file can be opened including read, write and append. We will assume that if you open the file in 'append' mode it will create a file if one does not already exist in the folder.

Q1: Assume the user did not know how many records needed to be written to the file. Rewrite the pseudocode below so that it works for any number of records.

Programming languages have different syntax for writing to and reading from a file, but pseudocode for a program to write data to a new file would be something like the following:

1-6

```
OPEN birdFile to append data
OUTPUT "How many records do you wish to write?"
numRecs ← USERINPUT
FOR n ← 1 TO numRecs
   OUTPUT "Enter bird name: "
   birdName ← USERINPUT
   OUTPUT "Enter number of birds reported: "
   birdsReported ← USERINPUT
   WRITELINE (birdFile, birdName + birdsReported)
ENDFOR
CLOSE birdFile
```

Reading from a text file

Some programming languages such as Python will allow you to read an entire text file using just a single statement. You can also read a text file line by line (or record by record). Each record will have a number of fields commonly separated by commas, as in a CSV (comma-separated values) file.

Suppose you want to search `birdFile` for a specific bird name and print out the number of birds. Assume that this file has 8 records.

```
OPEN birdFile for reading
OUTPUT "What bird are you searching for? "
birdNameSearch ← USERINPUT
FOR n ← 1 TO 8
   READLINE (birdFile, n)                  #read the nth record
   Split record into individual comma-separated fields
   birdName ← field[0]
   birdsSeen ← field[1]
   IF birdName = birdNameSearch THEN
      OUTPUT birdName, birdsSeen
   ENDIF
ENDFOR
CLOSE birdFile
```

Q2: What does the following pseudocode do?

```
OPEN birdFile for reading
totalBirdsSeen ← 0
FOR n = 1 TO 8
   READLINE (birdFile, n)                  #read the nth record
   Split record into individual comma-separated fields
   birdsSeen ← int(field[1])               #convert string to integer
   totalBirdsSeen ← totalBirdsSeen + birdsSeen
ENDFOR
OUTPUT "Total birds seen: ", totalBirdsSeen
CLOSE birdFile
```

Overwriting text in an existing file

Sometimes you may want to overwrite existing data; for example, to correct a record in the file. In that case, you can open the record for both reading and writing, search through the file for the record you want, and write a new record in its place.

Binary (non-text) files

It is possible to read and write binary files as well as text files. A binary file can contain records with different types of field such as string, integer, real, Boolean. Each of these fields may occupy a different number of bytes; for example a real number stored as text may occupy 12 bytes for a 12-figure number, but considerably fewer as a pure binary number.

Reading a binary file is language-specific but always involves knowing exactly what each field type in the record is and how many bytes it occupies. The file needs to be opened in a mode which specifies that it is a binary file.

Exception handling

It is a good idea to include in your programs some exception-handling routines to specify what should happen if an error occurs that would normally cause the program to crash. Common errors of this sort include:

- trying to read a non-existent file

- trying to convert a non-numeric string entered by the user, to an integer or a real number

- trying to perform calculations with a non-numeric variable

- division by zero

Most languages provide an easy way of handling exceptions with a `try...except` clause. Here are three examples:

Example 1

```
TRY
   OPEN birdFile for reading
EXCEPT
   OUTPUT ("Sorry, can't find this file")
ENDEXCEPT
```

Example 2

Below is an example of a validation routine that could be used in the program shown in the last chapter to simulate a simple dice game.

Q3: What will be displayed by this subroutine if the user enters the following?
(i) 4   (ii) e

1-6

```
SUB menuChoice
   OUTPUT "Option 1: Display rules"
   OUTPUT "Option 2: Start new game"
   OUTPUT "Option 3: Quit"
   OUTPUT "What would you like to do? "
   choice ← USERINPUT
   WHILE choice < "1" OR choice > "3"
      TRY
         choiceAsInteger ← int(choice) #try to convert string to integer
      EXCEPT
         OUTPUT "That is not an integer!"
      ENDEXCEPT
      # The user entry may be an integer but not between 1 and 3…
      OUTPUT "Please try again… enter a number between 1 and 3: "
      choice ← USERINPUT
   ENDWHILE
   RETURN choiceAsInteger
ENDSUB
```

Example 3

This example shows the use of TRY… EXCEPT… ELSE.

```
n ← 10
TRY
   birdRec = READLINE(birdFile, n)
EXCEPT
   OUTPUT "Attempt to read beyond end of file"
ELSE
   Split record into individual comma-separated fields
   TRY
      birdsSeen ← int(field[1])  #convert string to integer
   EXCEPT
      birdsSeen = 0
      OUTPUT "This is not an integer"
   ELSE
      totalBirdsSeen ← totalBirdsSeen + birdsSeen
   ENDEXCEPT
ENDEXCEPT
```

Exercises

1. Write pseudocode for a program which reads a text file containing the current highest score for a game. Compare the current highest with a variable called `myscore` and if `myscore` is greater than the one on the file, replace the record with the new high score. [5]

2. (a) Explain with the aid of an example, the purpose of exception-handling in programs involving file handling. [2]

   (b) Explain why exception-handling routines are useful for validating data input by the user. [3]

Section 2

Problem solving and theory of computation

In this section:

2

Chapter 7 – Solving logic problems

Objectives

- Define the stages of systems development
- Be able to develop solutions to simple logic problems
- Be able to check solutions to simple logic problems

Stages in software development

Software is the name given to any program written for the computer.

There are several well-defined stages in writing software, once your programs progress past the trivial and become more challenging. The stages are:

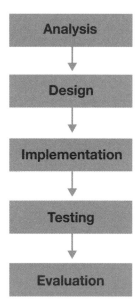

Briefly, the tasks performed at each of these stages are:

- **Analysis:** the requirements and goals of the project must be established, and a data model created. The needs of the end user are considered, and alternative solutions to the problem may be suggested

- **Design:** data structures will be specified, algorithms, user interfaces, screen designs and reports will all be designed

- **Implementation:** the program code is written

- **Testing:** the whole system must be tested for the presence of errors, using selected test data covering normal, boundary and erroneous data

- **Evaluation:** the system is evaluated according to given criteria

It is not necessary or even desirable that one phase is finished before another starts. In an evolutionary prototyping approach, some parts of the design, such as the user interface, may be implemented and shown to the customer, who then gives feedback. If it is not what they wanted, further work is done on the design. Testing may begin on parts of the implementation before other parts are completed. At each stage, it may be necessary to revisit previous stages. Customer feedback at every stage is crucial for successful project development.

We will go through the first four of these stages in this Section, starting with some problem-solving exercises which will get you thinking creatively about how to solve problems – a useful skill for analysing a problem and designing a solution. The types of problems we will be looking at are "computational" rather than "data-processing" problems.

Problem-solving

Solving logic problems is good training for "computational thinking" – basically, the ability to think logically about a problem and apply techniques for solving it. This is closely related to the skill of designing algorithms which can be turned into computer programs.

This chapter is designed to get you thinking about developing and checking solutions to simple logic problems.

(Solutions to the example problems are given at the end of the chapter.)

One type of problem asks you to find a method of solving a problem which has a goal and a set of resources, as in Question 1.

Q1: There are two jugs, A and B. Jug A has a capacity of three litres. Jug B has a capacity of five litres. There are no markings on the jugs, so it is not possible to tell exactly how much is in a jug just by looking at it, unless it is full or empty. There is a sink with a water tap and a drain. How can exactly one litre of water be obtained from the tap using the two jugs?

Tip: *Create a table like the one below with 3 columns headed* **Step, A (3 litres), B (5 litres),** *and several blank rows. Write the contents of each jug after each step.*

Step	A (3 litres)	B (5 litres)
1	3	0
2	etc	

Some problems require you to work out a method of solution and use the clues to find the answer, as in the following problem. An example of this type of problem is shown below.

Q2: The police are interrogating five suspects after a bank robbery. Each of them makes two statements, but it turns out only five of these statements are true.

Can you work out who committed the crime? What strategy will you use to work it out?

Alan said: It wasn't Ben. It was Carl.

Ben said: It wasn't Alan. It was Dave.

Carl said: It wasn't Dave. It wasn't Ben, either.

Dave said: It wasn't Eddie. It was Alan.

Eddie said: It wasn't Carl. It was Derek.

Tip: *What is the key fact given in the statement of the problem?*

Example 3 is a classic logic problem, which has many different variations on the same theme.

Q3: A man has to get a fox, a chicken, and a sack of corn across a river.

He has a rowing boat, which can carry only him and one other thing.

If the fox and the chicken are left together, the fox will eat the chicken.

If the chicken and the corn are left together, the chicken will eat the corn.

How does the man do it?

Strategies for problem solving

There are some general strategies for designing algorithms which are useful for solving many problems in computer science. First of all it is useful to note that there are two types of algorithmic puzzle. Every puzzle has an **input**, which defines an **instance** of the puzzle. The instance can be either **specific** (e.g. fill a magic square with 3 rows and 3 columns), or **general** (n rows and n columns). Even when given a general instance of a problem, it is often helpful to solve a specific instance of it, which may give an insight into solving a more general case.

Exhaustive search

For example, suppose you are asked to fill a 'magic square' with 3 rows and 3 columns with distinct integers 1-9 so that the sum of the numbers in each row, column and corner-to corner diagonal is the same.

This is a **specific** instance of a more **general** problem in which there are n rows and n columns. Some problems can be solved by **exhaustive search** – in this example, by trying every possible combination of numbers. We can put any one of 9 integers in the first square, and any of the remaining 8 in the second square, giving 9x8 = 72 possibilities for just the first two squares. There are 9x8x7x6x5x4x3x2 = 362,880 ways of filling the square. If you are a mathematician you will know that this is denoted by 9!, spoken as "nine factorial".

You might think a computer could do this in a fraction of a second. However, looking at the more general problem, where you have n x n squares, you will find that even for a 5 x 5 square, there are so many different combinations (25! or 25 factorial) that it would take a computer performing 10 trillion operations a second, about 49,000 years to find the answer!

So, to solve this problem we need to come up with a better algorithm. It turns out to be not very difficult to work out that for a 3 x 3 square, each row, column and diagonal must add up to 15 and the middle number must be 5, which considerably reduces the size of the problem. (The details of the algorithm are not discussed here.)

Q4: Fill the magic square to solve the problem.

Divide-and-conquer

To find a particular item in a sorted list, one strategy is to look at every item starting from the beginning until you find what you are looking for (the **exhaustive** search strategy). A far more efficient strategy is to perform a **binary search**:

Step 1: Look at the middle item of the list first. If this is the item being sought, stop searching

Step 2: Otherwise, if the middle item is greater than the one being sought, the item you are looking for must be in the first half of the list so you can discard the second half. Otherwise, discard the first half of the list

Step 3: Repeat with the new list until the item is found.

> **Q5:** Ask a friend to think of a number between 1 and 20. You have a guess and your friend tells you whether it is correct, too low or too high. What is the maximum number of guesses you will need with the best algorithm as described above?
>
> How many guesses, at worst, will you need to find a number between 1 and 1000?
>
> How many guesses, at worst, for a number between 1 and 2^n?
>
> How many guesses, at worst, using the "exhaustive search" strategy?

Sometimes a problem requires a flash of insight to solve. If you have seen the film "The Imitation Game" about Alan Turing and how he cracked the Enigma Code during World War II, you will recall his insight in realising that most messages ended with the words "Heil Hitler". This proved crucial in reducing the exhaustive search algorithm, which could never provide the solution in the 24 hours before the code was changed, to one which the code-breakers used to decode the messages every day.

> **Q6:** You have a bag of 8 coins which all look identical, but one of them is counterfeit and weighs less than a genuine coin.
> You have a two-pan balance, but no weights.
>
> What is the minimum number of weighings needed to identify the fake coin?
>
> **Tip:** The answer is not 3 weighings!

Solutions to examples

> **Q1:** Fill the 3-litre jug and pour it into the 5-litre jug. Then refill the 3-litre jug and pour 2 litres into the 5-litre jug to fill it. What remains in the 3-litre jug is 1 litre.
>
> **Q2:** If Alan did it, that means that 6 of the statements are true. Try out each person in turn. Eddie is the only one who fits the criterion that exactly 5 statements are true. (This is the key fact.)
>
> **Q3:** The man and the chicken cross the river, (the fox and corn are safe together). He leaves the chicken on the other side and goes back across.
>
> The man then takes the fox across the river, and since he can't leave the fox and chicken together, he takes the chicken back with him.
>
> Then, since the chicken and corn can't be left together, he leaves the chicken and he takes the corn across and leaves it with the fox.
>
> He then returns to pick up the chicken and heads across the river one last time.

Solutions to examples continued

Q4: Here is one solution...

2	7	6
9	5	1
4	3	8

Q5: You will need up to 5 guesses; 20 is more than 2^4 and less than 2^5. You will need a maximum of 10 guesses to find a number between 1 and 1000, since 1000 is greater than 2^9 and less than 2^{10}.

Taking the general case, you will need a maximum of n guesses to guess a number between 1 and 2^n.

Q6: Select two groups of three coins each and weigh them against each other. If they weigh the same, weigh the other two and the lighter will be identified. If not, the lighter coin will be among the three in the lighter pan. Weigh two of these. If they are the same, the third is the counterfeit coin. If they do not weigh the same, the lighter one is the counterfeit.

Exercises

2-7

1. Three days ago, yesterday was the day before Sunday. What day will it be tomorrow?

2. There are two married couples who need to cross a river. They have a boat that can hold no more than two people at a time. The husbands insist that at no time can their wives be left alone in the company of the other man. How can they cross the river?

3. You have an 8-pint jug full of water, and two empty jugs of 5- and 3-pint capacity. How can you get exactly 4 pints of water into one of the jugs by completely filling up and/or emptying jugs into others?

4. The following problem has become very popular since it is reputed to have been set to candidates during job interviews at Microsoft.

   A group of four people, who have one torch between them, need to cross a rickety bridge at night. A maximum of two people can cross the bridge at one time, and any party that crosses (either one or two people) must have the torch with them. The torch must be walked back and forth – it cannot be thrown. Person A takes one minute to cross the bridge, person B takes 2 minutes, person C takes 5 minutes and person D takes 10 minutes. A pair must walk together at the rate of the slower person's pace.

   Find the fastest way they can accomplish this task.

Chapter 8 – Structured programming

Objectives

- understand the structured approach to program design and construction
- be able to construct and use hierarchy charts when designing programs
- be able to explain the advantages of the structured approach

The structured approach

The structured programming approach aims to improve the **clarity** and **maintainability** of programs. (See Chapter 5, page 25, "Programming with subroutines".) Using structured programming techniques, only three basic programming structure are used:

- sequence – one statement following another
- selection – IF ... THEN ... ELSE... ENDIF and CASE ... ENDCASE statements
- iteration – WHILE ... ENDWHILE, REPEAT... UNTIL and FOR ... ENDFOR loops

Languages such as Python, Pascal and C# are **block-structured languages** which allow the use of just three types of control structure. They may allow you to break out of a loop, but this is not recommended in structured programming. Each block should have a single entry and exit point.

Block-structured languages

A block is a section of code consisting of one or more statements. For example, a block may be a single IF ... ENDIF statement, with the beginning of the block denoted by, for example, the keyword IF or an opening curly bracket, and the end denoted by either the end of indented code, (as in Python), a curly bracket or a keyword such as END or ENDIF.

2-8

A block may also be a subroutine such as a **function** or **procedure**. Another important aspect of structured programming is to keep subroutines independent of the program which calls them, which means that they should not make use of global variables. Any variable declared in the main program should be passed as a parameter to a subroutine if it is needed.

Q1: Why is it important for clarity not to use global variables in subroutines?

Designing structured programs

Top-down design is the technique of breaking down a problem into the major tasks to be performed; each of these tasks is then further broken down into separate subtasks, and so on until each subtask is sufficiently simple to be written as a self-contained **module** or subroutine. Remember that some programs contain tens of thousands, or even millions, of lines of code, and a strategy for design is absolutely essential. Even for small programs, top-down design is a very useful method of breaking down the problem into small, manageable tasks.

Q2: A computer scientist named Tom Harbron stated: "The Fundamental Principle of Structured Programming is that at all times and under all circumstances, the programmer must keep the program within his intellectual grasp. The well-known methods for achieving this can be briefly summarised as follows: 1) top-down design and construction, 2) limited control structures, and 3) limited scope of data structures." Discuss what he meant by this statement.

Advantages of structured (modular) programming

The advantages of thes structured approach may be stated as:

- Individual modules can be separately tested
- Modules can be kept in a module library and reused in other programs
- Large programs can be split into modules that are easier to read, debug and maintain
- Several programmers in a team can work on separate modules, thus shortening development time for a large project

Hierarchy charts

A hierarchy chart is a tool for representing the structure of a program, showing how the modules relate to each other to form the complete solution. The chart is depicted as an upside-down tree structure, with modules being broken down further into smaller modules until each module is only a few lines of code (never more than a page).

Example 1

Draw a hierarchy chart for a program which calculates and prints a customer's monthly gas bill.

This can be broken down into several steps.

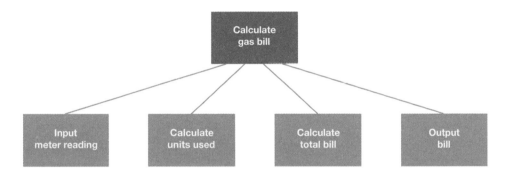

'Calculate units used' and *'Calculate total bill'* may now be further broken down.

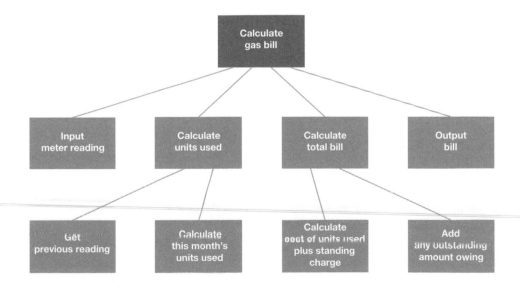

Limitations of a hierarchy chart

Note that a hierarchy chart does not show the detailed program structures required in each module – for example, it does not show selection and iteration. A greater level of detail may be shown in a **structure chart** but these are not covered here.

Example 2

Draw a hierarchy chart for a program which asks the user which times table they would like to be tested on, and then displays five questions, getting the user's answer each time and telling them whether they were right or wrong. If they are wrong, the correct answer is displayed.

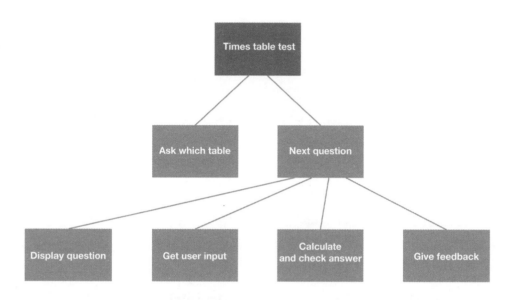

Q3: Draw a hierarchy chart for the program given in Q11 in Chapter 5, page 26.

Exercises

1. Using local rather than global variables in subroutines is one way of helping to make a program easy to maintain.

   (i) Explain why this is the case. [3]

   (ii) Describe briefly **three** other ways in which a program can be made easy to understand and maintain. [6]

2. Draw a hierarchy chart for a quiz program which does the following:

   • asks the user 10 random multiple-choice questions from a bank of 100 questions held in a file

   • if the user gives the correct answer, gives feedback and adds 1 to the user's score

   • if they give the wrong answer, gives feedback and displays the correct answer

   • at the end of the questions, gives the score out of 10

   • asks if they want another 10 questions [6]

Chapter 9 – Writing and interpreting algorithms

Objectives

- To understand the term 'algorithm'
- To learn how to write and interpret algorithms using pseudocode

Properties of an algorithm

A recipe for chocolate cake, a knitting pattern for a sweater or a set of directions to get from A to B, are all algorithms of a kind.

Computational algorithms

The definition of an algorithm is:

- It has clear and precisely stated steps that produce the correct output for any set of valid inputs
- It must always terminate at some point

A good algorithm also has the following properties:

- It should allow for invalid inputs
- It should execute efficiently, in as few steps as possible
- It should be designed in such a way that other people will be able to understand it and modify it if necessary

What kinds of problem are solved by algorithms?

There are thousands of different practical applications of algorithms. Some of the best-known applications include:

- **Internet-related algorithms**. Algorithms are used to manage and manipulate the huge amount of data stored on the Internet. How does a search engine find all the pages on which particular information resides in a fraction of a second?
- **Route-finding algorithms**. Given two locations, how does a route-finder determine the shortest or best route between the two points? There may be thousands of possible routes. This type of algorithm is used not only for driving a vehicle from A to B, but also for many other applications, for example, finding the best route to transmit packets of data from A to B over a network.
- **Compression algorithms**. These are used to compress data files so that they can be transmitted faster or held in a smaller amount of storage space. For example, MP3 files are compressed so that you can hold thousands of tracks on a mobile phone.
- **Encryption algorithms**. When someone purchases something over the Internet and sends their credit card number and other personal details to the store, the data needs to be encrypted so that even if it is intercepted, it cannot be read.

Q1: Who else uses encryption algorithms?

A simple computational algorithm

Suppose you are given the square of an integer and you need to find the integer itself (i.e. the square root of the given number). Your calculator can add, subtract, multiply and divide but it does not have a square root function.

Here is one way of finding the square root of the integer `number`:

```
1  n ← 0                          ;initialise n
2  nsquared ← n*n
3  Is nsquared = number?
4  If yes, output n. If no, add 1 to n and repeat from step 2
```

When you start to program, it is tempting to get straight to the computer and type in some code to solve a given problem. However, it will generally save time to figure out the steps needed using paper and pencil before you start coding using **pseudocode**.

Pseudocode is a way of expressing the solution in a way that can easily be translated into a programming language.

Q2: Write pseudocode for the above algorithm to find the square root of an integer, when you know that the answer is an integer. Write and test the program for the integer 19321.

Q3: Which of the properties of a good algorithm, stated at the start of the chapter, does this algorithm not satisfy?

The algorithm described will do the job, but a better solution is based on the well-known binary search algorithm, which we looked at briefly in Chapter 7, Question 5.

2-9

A "Divide and Conquer" algorithm

This algorithm uses the "Divide and Conquer" strategy to halve the search area every time a guess is made. It goes like this:

1. Set `low ← 1, high ← number, guess ← (low + high)/2` and `nsquared ← guess²`

2. If `nsquared > number`, set `high ← guess` to eliminate the top half of the range, otherwise set `low ← guess` to eliminate the bottom half of the range

3. Set `guess ← (low + high)/2` and `nsquared ← guess²`

4. Repeat steps 2 and 3 until `nsquared = number`

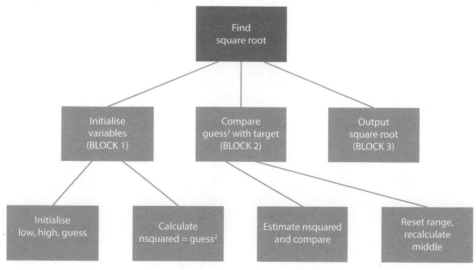

The chart represents the blocks of program code that we will use to solve the problem. The solution is short, so it's not necessary to put each block in a separate subroutine.

```
number ← 19321
low ← 1
high ← number
guess ← int((low + high) / 2)
nsquared ← guess ** 2                          BLOCK 1 SEQUENCE
```

```
WHILE nsquared <> number
   IF nsquared > number THEN
      high ← guess
   ELSE
      low ← guess
   ENDIF
   guess ← int((low + high) / 2)
   nsquared ← guess ** 2                        BLOCK 2 - ITERATION
ENDWHILE
```

```
OUTPUT "Square root is ",guess                  BLOCK 3 - SEQUENCE
```

2-9

Q4: Add statements to calculate and print the number of guesses it took to find the answer.

Try writing and running the program for different values of xsquared.

Is there a formula for calculating how many guesses it should take to find the square root?

Sorting algorithms

Sorting is a very common task in data processing, and frequently the number of items may be huge, so using a good algorithm can considerably reduce the time spent on the task. There are many efficient sorting algorithms such as quicksort and merge sort but you will not be required to use these in this course, so we will look at a simple but rather inefficient sort algorithm as an example.

Bubble sort

The Bubble sort is one of the most basic sorting algorithms and the simplest to understand. The basic idea is to bubble up the largest (or smallest) item, then the second largest, then the third largest and so on until no more swaps are needed.

Suppose you have an array of n items:

- Go through the array, comparing each item with the one next to it. If it is greater, swap them.

- The last item in the array will be in the correct place after the first pass

- Repeat n - 1 times, reducing by one on each pass, the number of items to be examined

Q5: How do you swap two items in an array?

Example 1

Write pseudocode for a bubble sort to sort the numbers 45, 62, 13, 98, 9, 50 into ascending sequence. Print the numbers after each of the 6 passes through the list.

```
numbers ← [45,62,13,98,9,50]
numItems ← len(numbers)        #get number of items in the array
FOR i ← 0 TO numItems - 2
    FOR j ← 0 TO numItems - i - 2
        IF numbers[j] > numbers[j + 1] THEN
            # Swap the numbers in the array
                temp ← numbers[j]
                numbers[j] ← numbers[j + 1]
                numbers[j + 1] ← temp
        ENDIF
    ENDFOR
    OUTPUT numbers
ENDFOR
```

If you run this program, the output is

[45, 13, 62, 9, 50, 98]

[13, 45, 9, 50, 62, 98]

[13, 9, 45, 50, 62, 98]

[9, 13, 45, 50, 62, 98]

[9, 13, 45, 50, 62, 98]

2-9

Q6: Describe how you could modify this algorithm to make it more efficient when there is a large number of items to be sorted.

Interpreting programs

A useful skill is to be able to look at someone else's program and decide what it does and how it works. Of course, if the programmer has put in lots of useful comments, used meaningful variable names and split a complicated program into separate modules, that should not be too difficult!

Strategy for interpreting programs

Here are some tips, which may seem fairly obvious.

1. Read the comments in the program

2. Look at the variable names to see if they give any clues

3. Follow the steps in the program – the one below starts with the statement `shift ← 3`

4. Try a "dry run" with some test data

Evaluating a program

When two programs written to solve the same problem are not the same, is one program better than the other? It may be that one program is well documented with comments, uses meaningful variable names and properly indented code, does not contain statements that are not needed, and uses a more efficient algorithm. Once a program has been written and tested, you need to be able to:

- articulate how it works

- produce test data and results to show that it works correctly

- get user feedback to show that nothing has been omitted, that it performs all the required tasks and does so efficiently

Q7: What will be the output from the algorithm below if the user inputs "Hi, Jo!"

Explain briefly the purpose of the algorithm.

```
SUB code(message, shift)
   message ← lowercase(message)
   codedMessage ← ""
   FOR x IN message
      IF x IN "abcdefghijklmnopqrstuvwxyz" THEN
         num ← ord(x)                    # convert to ASCII value
         num ← num + shift
         IF num > ord("z") THEN          # wrap if necessary
            num ← num - 26
         ENDIF
         char ← chr(num)                 # convert back to character
         codedMessage ← codedMessage + char
      ELSE
         codedMessage ← codedMessage + x
      ENDIF
   ENDFOR
   RETURN codedMessage
ENDSUB


# main program
shift ← 3
OUTPUT("Enter your message: ")
msg ← USERINPUT
codedMessage ← code(msg,shift)
OUTPUT("The encoded message is: ", codedMessage)
```

Exercises

1. (a) Three types of programming constructs are sequence, selection and iteration.

Describe what is meant by each of these. [6]

(b) A computer program contains the following instructions:

```
X ← 10
Y ← 20
X ← Y
OUTPUT X, Y
```

   (i) State which of the constructs in part (a) has been used. [1]

   (ii) What will be output by this code? [1]

2. In a football league, the results of each match are input to the computer, which updates each team's points.

In the case of a draw, each team (Team A and Team B) gets one point.

If Team A wins, then Team A gets 3 points and Team B gets no points.

The algorithm for updating points in the case of a draw is:

```
IF TeamAGoals = TeamBGoals THEN
    TeamAPoints ← TeamAPoints + 1
    TeamBPoints ← TeamBPoints + 1
ENDIF
```

Write an algorithm for updating the points if there is a winner. [3]

2-9

3. Expert jugglers learn new juggling patterns according to certain rules represented by numbers. In this example, the rules for patterns of three numbers are:

Rule 1: the total value of the numbers in the list must be a multiple of 3

Rule 2: No number must be one less than the previous number, even if the pattern is repeated indefinitely.

Here are some valid patterns of three numbers:

7 4 4

4 4 1

Here are some examples of invalid patterns with three numbers:

4 2 1   (4 + 2 + 1 = 7, which is not a multiple of 3, so does not obey rule 1)

6 5 1   (5 is one less than the previous number, so this does not obey rule 2)

6 2 7   (when this is repeated, 6 2 7 6 2 7 6 2 7... 6 is one less than the previous number, so this does not obey rule 2)

(a) State why the following lists of 3 numbers are not valid patterns of numbers.

   (i) 5 1 6 [1]

   (ii) 4 4 2 [1]

(b) Write pseudocode for a program which:

   • Prompts the user to enter 3 numbers, one after the other

   • Outputs "INVALID PATTERN" if the sequence of numbers does not obey the two rules. [7]

Chapter 10 – Testing and evaluation

Objectives

- Understand the purpose of testing

- Devise a test plan

- Select test data covering normal (typical), boundary and erroneous data

- Check an algorithm by completing a dry run

- Know the criteria for evaluating a system

The purpose of testing

We have looked briefly at problem-solving strategies and the design of solutions using structured programming techniques. You will have implemented several algorithms in your practical sessions. **Testing** your solutions for correctness can be a complex and time-consuming task, but one that needs to be done thoroughly and systematically.

The purpose of testing is not to show that your program usually works correctly, if the user is careful when entering input data. ***The purpose of testing is to try and uncover undetected errors.***

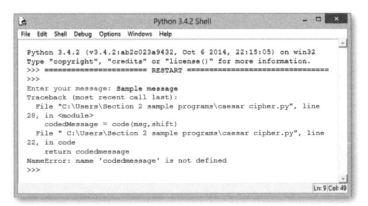

Devising a test plan

Your program should work correctly whatever data is input. If invalid data is entered, the program should detect and report this, and ask the user to enter valid data. Some data may be valid, but may nevertheless cause the program to crash if you have not allowed for particular values.

We need to choose test data that will test the outcome for any user input. To do this, we need to select **normal**, **boundary** and **erroneous** data.

- **normal** data is data within the range that you would expect, and of the data type (real, integer, string, etc.) that you would expect. For example, if you are expecting an input between 0 and 100, you should test 1 and 99

- **boundary** data is data at the ends of the expected range or just either side of it – for example -1, 0, 1, 99, 100, 101. Test 0 and 100 to make sure that these give the expected results if the valid range is between 0 and 100

- **erroneous** data is data that is either outside an expected range, e.g. -1, 101 or is of the wrong data type – for example, non-numeric characters when you are expecting a number to be input

For each test, you should specify the purpose of the test, the expected result and the actual result.

Example 1

The following program is intended to calculate and print the average mark for each student in a class, for all the tests they have attempted:

```
OUTPUT "How many students? "
students ← USERINPUT
FOR n ← 1 TO students
    OUTPUT "Enter student name"
    name ← USERINPUT
    OUTPUT "Enter total marks for ", name
    totalMarks ← USERINPUT
    OUTPUT "How many tests has this student taken? "
    numTests ← USERINPUT
    averageMark ← ROUND(totalMarks/numTests)
    OUTPUT "Average mark ",averageMark
ENDFOR
```

The test plan will look something like this:

Test number	Test data	Purpose of test	Expected result	Actual result
1	Number of students = 4 for tests 1-4 Jo: total marks 27, tests 3	Normal data, integer result	9	9
2	Tom: total marks 31, tests 4	Normal data, non-integer result rounded up	8	8
3	Beth: total marks 28, tests 3	Normal data, result rounded down	9	9
4	Amina: total marks 0, tests 0	No tests taken	0	Program crashes
5	Number of students abc	Test invalid data	Program terminates	

You can probably think of some other input data that would make the program crash. For example, what if the user enters 31.5 for the total marks? The program should validate all user input, so some amendments will have to be made.

Q1: Devise a test plan for the program in Q7, page 46.

Dry-running a program

A useful technique to locate an error in a program is to perform a **dry run**, with the aid of a **trace table**. As you follow through the logic of the program in the same sequence as the computer does, you note down in the trace table when each variable changes and what its value is. Examples of this are given in the exercises below.

Evaluating a computer system

Once a system has been written and thoroughly tested, the final stage is **evaluation**. This will take place over a period of time, during which the user may run the new system in parallel to an old one. The criteria that may be used for evaluation include:

- Does it meet the performance criteria:

    o Can it handle the amount of data or users that it needs to in a live environment?

    o Is the speed of operation satisfactory?

- Does it always perform as expected?

- Is the system reliable or does it crash at intervals?

- Is the system easy to use?

- Is the interface pleasant to work with, all spellings correct, navigation simple and not 'clunky'?

- Has all the functionality documented in the original specification been implemented, or has one or more of the requirements been overlooked?

- Has it been well documented?

- Will it be easy to maintain?

- How far has the system been 'future-proofed' - will it be easy to upgrade or add new features in the future?

- How cost effective is the system - will it increase income, decrease costs, or both?

2-10

Exercises

1. Complete the trace table below to show how each variable changes when the algorithm is performed on the text data given.

```
x ← 0
y ← 0
z ← 0
w ← USERINPUT
REPEAT
    x ← x + w
    y ← y + 1
    w ← USERINPUT
UNTIL w < 0
z ← x / y
OUTPUT z
```

Test data: 5 7 2 2 4 -1   [5]

w	x	y	z
	0	0	0
5	5	1	0

2. Explain what is meant by an *algorithm*.   [2]

   One way of checking that an algorithm is correct is to complete a dry run. Dry run the algorithm below by completing the table below.   [6]

   Assume that x has a value of 7. The MOD operator calculates the remainder resulting from an integer division.

```
Answer ← True
FOR Count ← 2 to (x-1) DO
    Remainder ← x MOD Count
    IF Remainder = 0 THEN
        Answer ← False
    ENDIF
ENDFOR
```

Answer	Count	Remainder
True	–	–
	2	1

What is the purpose of this algorithm?   [1]

AQA Comp 1 Qu 5 June 2010

2-10

Chapter 11 – Abstraction and automation

Objectives

- Describe the skills involved in computational thinking

- Understand the concept of abstraction

- Give examples of different types of abstraction

- Describe the process of automation for solving problems

Computational thinking

By this time, you are probably fairly clear about the idea of an algorithm and a problem which involves computation. But what is **computational thinking**? It is not about following an algorithm in one's head to carry out a mathematical task like adding two numbers. Rather, it is about thinking how a problem can be solved. This involves two basic steps:

- Formulate the problem as a computational problem – in other words, state it in such a way that it is potentially solvable using an algorithm

- Try to construct an algorithm to solve the problem

A computational thinker will not be satisfied with any old algorithm, though; it must be a 'good' solution – that is, a *correct* and *efficient* solution. A programmer needs to be able to show that a solution is correct and efficient by using logical reasoning, test data and user feedback.

Clearly, then, computational thinking is a vital skill for a programmer, and in fact it is not possible to be a programmer without it. It includes the ability to think logically and to apply the tools and techniques of computing to thinking about, understanding, formulating and solving problems.

Computing has been called the **automation of abstractions**, so let's move on to talk about abstraction.

Abstraction

Representational abstraction can be defined as *a representation arrived at by removing unnecessary details.*

Here are some examples of abstraction.

- Any computer model, say of the environment, a new car or a flight simulator, is an abstraction.

- If you are planning to write a program for a game involving a bouncing ball, you will need to decide what properties of the ball to take into account. If it's bouncing vertically rather than, say, on a snooker table, gravity needs to be taken into account. How elastic is the ball? How far and in what direction will it bounce when it hits an edge? What you are required to do is build an abstract model of a real-world situation, which you can simplify; remembering, however, that the more you simplify, the less likely it becomes that the model will mimic reality.

- A builder who is planning to build 100 houses on a new estate may use a physical model of the new estate, or in the first instance, a plan on paper or on a computer screen. In either case the model will be greatly simplified. All the houses may appear identical in the model. They may lack windows, doors or chimneys. All the trees in the model may be of identical size, colour and shape.

- The map of the London Underground is a simple model of the actual geography of the Tube stations. The map tells you what line each station is on and which other lines each station is connected to. It is very useful for a person travelling around London, but of very little use to an engineer who is planning where to dig tunnels for a proposed new line.

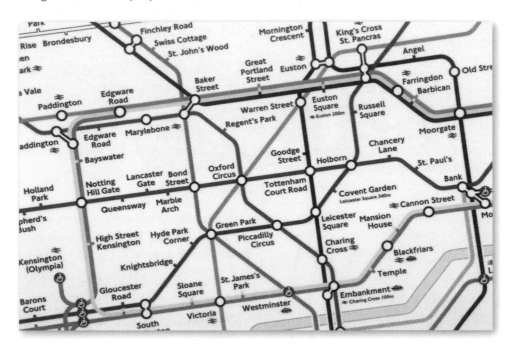

Abstraction applied to high level programming languages

Abstraction is the most important feature of high level programming languages such as Python, C#, Java and hundreds of other languages written for different purposes. To understand why, we need to look at different generations of programming language.

- The first generation of language was **machine code** – programmers entered the binary 0s and 1s that the computer understands. Writing a program to solve even a short, simple problem was a tedious, time-consuming task largely unrelated to the algorithm itself.

- The second generation was an improvement; mnemonic codes were used to represent instructions. But as you will see in later chapters in Sections 4 and 5, it was still an enormously complex task to write an assembly language program and what's more, if you wanted to run the program on a different type of computer, it had to be completely rewritten for the new hardware.

- The third generation of languages, starting with BASIC and FORTRAN in the 1960s, used statements like X = A + 5, finally freeing the programmer from all the tedious details of where the variables X and A were stored in memory, and all the other fiddly implementation details of exactly how the computer was going to carry out the instruction.

Finally, programmers could focus on the problem in hand rather than worrying about irrelevant technological details, and that is a good example of what abstraction is all about.

Abstraction by generalisation

There is a famous problem dating back more than 200 years to the old Prussian city of Königsberg. This beautiful city had seven bridges, and the inhabitants liked to stroll around the city on a Sunday afternoon, making sure to cross every bridge at least once. Nobody could figure out how to cross each bridge once and once only, or alternatively prove that this was impossible, and eventually the Mayor turned to the local mathematical genius Leonhard Euler.

The map of 18th century Königsberg

Euler's first step was to remove all irrelevant details from the map, and come up with an abstraction:

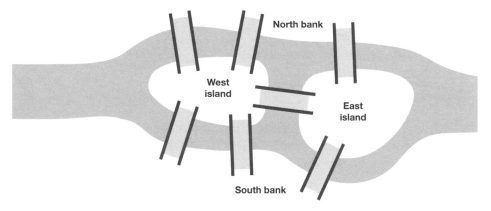

To really simplify it, Euler represented each piece of land as a circle and each bridge as a line between them.

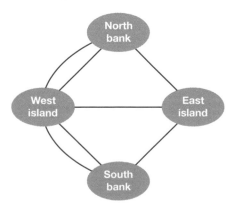

What we now have is a **graph**, with **nodes** representing land masses and **edges** (lines connecting the nodes) representing the bridges. Now that Euler had his graph, how could he solve the problem?

2-11

He did not want to try every possible solution; he realised that this was just a particular instance of a more general problem and he wanted to find a solution that was applicable to similar problems. He noticed a critical feature of the puzzle: since each bridge could be crossed only once, each node had to have an even number of connections, because you must enter and leave a node by a different edge. The only exceptions are the start and end node, since you don't have to enter a start node or leave the end node.

All the nodes in this graph have an odd number of nodes, so it is therefore impossible!

Euler had laid the foundation of graph theory, which you will come back to in the second year of this course.

By abstracting the problem, Euler made possible the solution of innumerable related problems. Not only does it apply to different cities with different numbers of bridges, it applies to many other problems with similar requirements.

Abstraction by generalisation, as illustrated above, is a grouping by common characteristics to arrive at a hierarchical relationship of the "is a kind of" type. Thus Euler's problem is a particular instance of graph theory.

This type of abstraction is very common in object-oriented programming. A class of object, say an Animal, will be defined with its own attributes such as gender and whether it is carnivore or vegetarian, and its own behaviours, methods or procedures such as move, sleep, eat, etc. Other objects such as Dog, Cat, Mouse and so on may be defined as sub-classes of Animal - they all share common characteristics which are defined in the Animal class, but have their own attributes and behaviours as well. In other words Dog "is a kind of" Animal, as are Cat and Mouse.

Q1: Use abstraction by generalisation to continue the sequence 1,4,9,16... What is the 50th number in the sequence?

2-11

Procedural abstraction

Computer science is, in broad terms, the study of problem-solving, and as such, is also the study of **abstraction**. As we have seen, abstraction allows us to separate the **physical** reality of a problem from the **logical** view. Thus, for example, you can send an email, play music or download an image without knowing any of the detail of how these things are actually done. On the other hand, the computer engineers, technicians and system administrators who enable these things to happen have a very different view. They need to be able to control the low-level details that users are not even aware of.

Procedural abstraction means using a procedure to carry out a sequence of steps for achieving some task such as calculating a student's grade from her marks in three exam papers, buying groceries online or drawing a house on a computer screen.

Consider, for example, how you could code a program to create the plan for an estate of 100 new houses. You could use a procedure which will draw a triangle of certain dimensions and colour at a particular place on the screen. The colour and dimension are passed as arguments to the procedure, for example:

```
procedure drawTriangle(colour, base, height)
```

This may be called using the statement

```
drawTriangle("red", 4.5,2.0)
```

The programmer does not need to know the details of how this procedure works. She simply needs to know how the procedure is called and what arguments are required, what data type each one is and what order they must be written in. This is called the **procedure interface**.

Similarly, there may be a procedure to build a rectangle that is defined by parameters colour, height and width, which are passed as arguments:

```
drawRectangle ("beige", 4.0, 5.0)
```

To draw a house at a given position on the screen, the programmer may write a procedure `buildHouse()` which uses the `drawTriangle()` and `drawRectangle()` procedures, aligns them and positions the house at a particular position on the screen. All these variables will be passed as arguments to the procedure.

Several houses could be combined to make a street. Several streets could be drawn to represent the estate.

Then, if the builder of the new estate decides to make all the houses larger, the procedure for drawing the house does not need to be changed - it is simply called with new arguments.

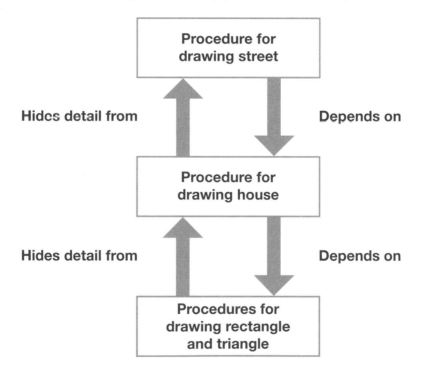

Functional abstraction

A function is called to return the result of a particular problem. For example,

```
x = sqrt(17)
```

The computation method is of no concern to the user and is hidden.

Functional abstraction, then, is a mapping from one set of values to another. The result of this mapping is unique to a given set of inputs, and a value must always be returned.

Q2: List some other functions that you can call in a high level programming language without having to worry about the details of how they work.

2-11

Data abstraction

A similar idea is that of **data abstraction**.

The details of how data are actually represented are hidden. For example, when you use integers or real numbers in a program, you are not interested in how these numbers are actually represented in the computer.

In a higher level language, it is possible to create **abstract data types** such as queues, stacks and trees. The abstract data type, for example a queue, is a logical description of how the data is viewed and the operations that can be performed on it. For example, elements can be added to the rear of the queue and removed from the front. The queue may have a maximum size that cannot be exceeded. The programmer using this data structure, however, is concerned only with the operations such as `AddToQueue` or `RemoveFromQueue` and does not need to know how the data structure is implemented using, for example, an array and pointers to the front and rear of the queue.

Information hiding

Information hiding is where data is not directly accessible and can only be accessed through defined procedures/functions. This is most commonly seen in object-oriented programming, for example in a class where the data or attributes of the class are private and can only be accessed through public functions.

Decomposition and Composition

Decomposition is breaking down a complex problem into a number of sub-problems, each of which performs an identifiable task. **Composition** is the opposite – combining procedures to form compound procedures (e.g. BuildHouse, BuildStreet). It can also mean combining objects to form compound data, for example records or a data structure such as a queue, tree or list.

Problem abstraction

2-11

Problem abstraction involves removing details until the problem is represented in a way that it is possible to solve because it reduces to one that has already been solved. For example, the problem of how to find your way through a maze can be reduced to a problem of traversing a graph, for which there is an algorithm - something you will be studying in the second year of this course! (See Chapter 47 of the A Level textbook.)

Consider the following problem:

There are four knights on a 3x3 chessboard: the two white knights are at the bottom two corners, and the two black knights are at the two upper corners. The goal is to switch the knights in the minimum number of moves so that the white knights are in the upper corners and the black knights are in the bottom corners. (A knight can only move in the following manner: one or two squares horizontally or vertically, followed by two squares or one square at right angles, moving 3 squares in total.)

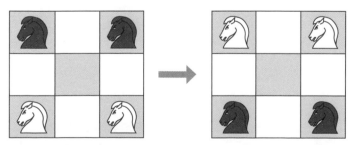

We can abstract this problem by first numbering the squares of the chessboard. 1 to 9. Now we can draw lines from 1 to 6 and 1 to 8 representing the two possible moves from square 1. Do the same for each square in turn, and you end up with the graph shown in (b). (Square 5 can't be reached with a knight's move so it is omitted from this graph.)

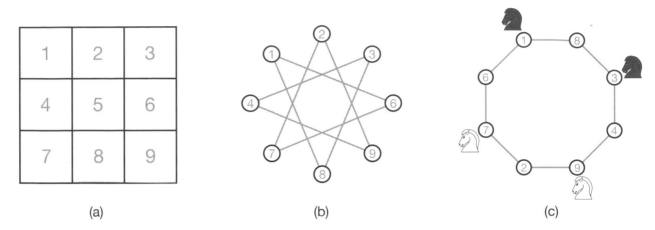

(a)   (b)   (c)

Figure (b) is not much help in solving the problem. Now imagine that all the vertices are joined by a single string, and now rearrange the string so that the vertices form a circle – this gives us a much more revealing picture. There are only two ways to solve the puzzle in the minimum number of moves; move the knights along the edges in either a clockwise or a counter-clockwise direction until each of the knights reaches the diagonally opposite corner for the first time.

This can be seen as a **'graph unfolding'** problem, equivalent to a general problem that has already been solved in the same way, so is a **reduction** of the more general problem.

Q3: What is the total number of moves required to switch the knights to the opposite side of the board?

2-11

Automation

Automation in computer science deals with building and putting into action models to solve problems. For example, you could model the financial implications of running an ice-cream stand at a given venue for a week or a longer period. You have to decide on what has to be included in the model and what assumptions you are going to make. Then you have to create and implement the algorithms and execute and test the results.

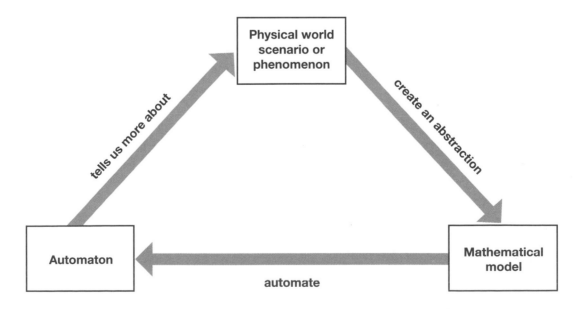

Automating the abstraction may in fact tell us more about the reality that we are modelling.

Exercises

1. "Representational abstraction is a representation arrived at by removing unnecessary details."

   Describe what this means in relation to a computer program which allows the user to enter a starting address **A** and a destination address **B** and returns a map of the route, the number of miles and the estimated journey time it will take to travel by car from **A** to **B**. [5]

2. Explain how **information hiding** and **procedural abstraction** could be used in a game program in which the player has to collect treasure in a cave and avoid being eaten by a monster. [5]

3. Describe briefly **three** ways in which computer scientists make use of the concept of **abstraction** in solving problems. [6]

4. The goal in this problem is to place as many coins as possible at points of the 8-pointed star depicted below, according to the following rules:

   - Each coin must first be placed on an unoccupied point and then moved along a line to an unoccupied point

   - Once a coin has been positioned, it cannot be moved again.

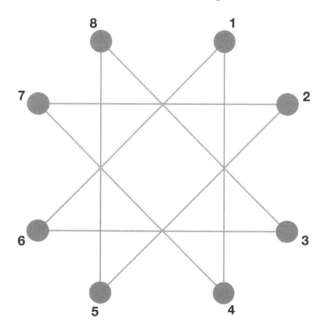

   For example, you could make the following sequence of moves: 1 → 4, 2 → 5, 3 → 6, 7 → 2, 8 → 3 which places 5 coins.

   What is the maximum number of coins that can be placed? [1]

   Tip: Use the "graph unfolding" method of solution explained on the previous page.

Chapter 12– Finite state machines

Objectives

- Understand what is meant by a finite state machine

- List some of the uses of a finite state machine

- Draw and interpret simple state transition diagrams for finite state machines with no output

- Draw a state transition table for a finite state machine with no output and vice versa

What is a finite state machine?

A finite state machine is a model of computation used to design computer programs and sequential logic circuits. It is not a "machine" in the physical sense of a washing machine, an engine or a power tool, for example, but rather an abstract model of how a machine reacts to an external event. The machine can be in one of a finite number of states and changes from one state to the next state when triggered by some condition or input (say, a signal from a timer).

In a finite state machine:

- The machine can only be in one state at a time

- It can change from one state to another in response to an event or condition; this is called a **transition**. Often this is a switch or a binary sensor.

- The Finite State Machine (FSM) is defined by a list of its states and the condition for each transition

There can be outputs linked to the FSM's state, but in this chapter we will be considering only FSMs with no output.

Example 1

Draw an FSM to model the states and transitions of a door. The door can be open, closed or locked. It can change from the state of being open to closed, from closed to locked, but not, say, from locked to open. (It has to be unlocked first.)

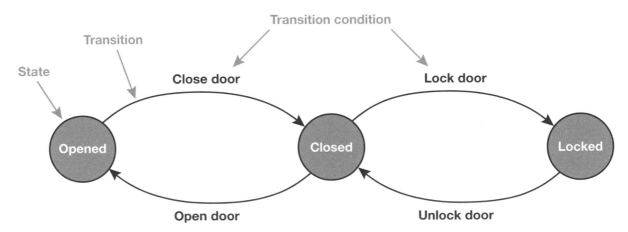

Example 2

Draw an FSM to represent a light switch. When the button is pressed, the light goes on. When the button is pressed again, the light goes off.

There is just one input B to this system: Button pressed (B=1) or Button not pressed (B=0).

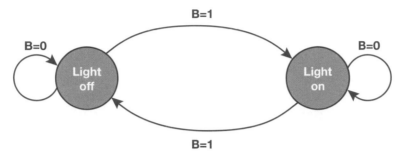

Notice that in each state, both the transitions B=0 and B=1 are drawn. If the light is off, the transition B=0 has no effect so the transition results in the same state. Likewise, if the light is on, as long as the button is not pressed, the light will stay on.

Usage of finite state machines

FSMs are widely used in modelling the design of hardware digital systems, compilers and network protocols. They are also used in the definition of languages, and to decide whether a particular word is allowed in the language.

A finite state machine which has no output is also known as a **finite state automaton**. It has a start state and a set of accept states which define whether it accepts or rejects finite strings or symbols. The finite state automaton accepts a string $c_1, c_2...c_n$ if there is a path for the given input from the start state to an accept state. The language recognised by the finite state automaton consists of all the strings accepted by it.

If, when you are in a particular state, the next state is uniquely determined by the input, it is a **deterministic final state automaton**. All the examples which follow satisfy this condition.

Notation

Symbol	Meaning
	State
	Start state
	Accept state
	Transition

2-12

Example 3

Use an FSM to represent a valid identifier in a programming language. The rules for a valid identifier for this particular language are:

- The identifier must start with a lowercase letter
- Any combination of letters and lowercase numbers may follow
- There is no limit on the length of the identifier

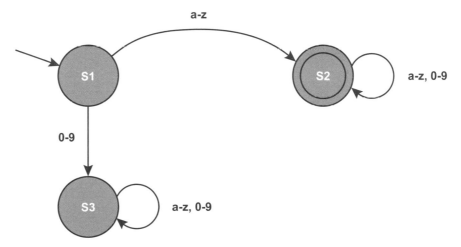

In this diagram, the **start state** S1 is represented by a circle with an arrow leading into it.

The **accept state** S2 is denoted by a double circle.

S3 is a "dead state" because having arrived here, the string can never reach the accept state.

Each character of the input string is input sequentially to the FSM and if the last character reaches the final state S2 (the **accept** state), the string is valid and is accepted. If it ends up anywhere else the string is invalid.

Note that there can only be one starting state but there may be more than one accept state (or no accept states).

Q1: Which of the following strings is valid and accepted by this finite state machine?
(i) a (ii) bba (iii) abbaa (iv) bbbb

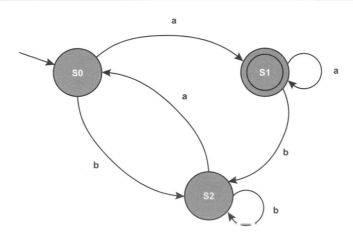

2-12

Example 4

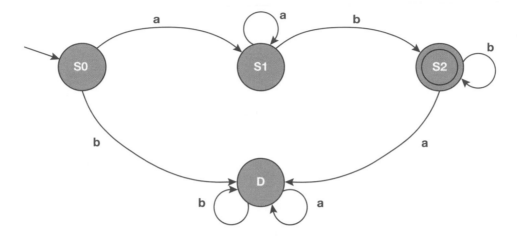

This FSM takes a string, e.g. aaabb, baa, aba. If after reading the whole string, you reach the accept state, the string is valid.

The first of these strings is accepted. What about the other two?

Q2: Can you formulate a rule for a valid string in this language?

State transition tables

2-12

An alternative representation of an FSM is a **state transition table**. This shows the current state and the next state for each input. The table below corresponds to the finite state diagram in Example 4 above.

Current state	Next state	
	Input = a	**Input = b**
S0	S1	D
S1	S1	S2
S2	D	S2
D	D	D

Example 5

Draw the state transition diagram and the equivalent state transition table for a language in which an empty string or a string of any length in the form *ababab* is accepted, and any other string is rejected.

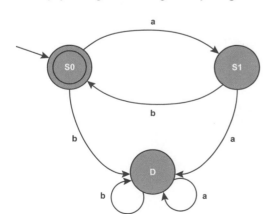

Current state	Next state	
	Input = a	**Input = b**
S0	S1	D
S1	D	S0
D	D	D

Exercises

1. Figure 2 shows the state transition diagram of a finite state machine (FSM) used to control a vending machine.

   The vending machine dispenses a drink when a customer has inserted exactly 50 pence.

   A transaction is cancelled and coins returned to the customer if more than 50 pence is inserted or the reject button (R) is pressed. The vending machine accepts 10, 20 and 50 pence coins. Only one type of drink is available.

   The only acceptable inputs for the FSM are 10, 20, 50 and R.

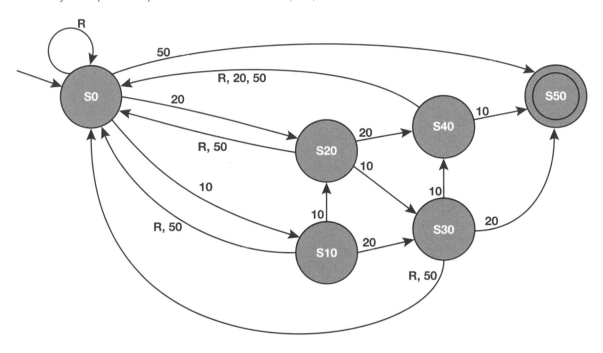

Figure 2

   An FSM can be represented as a state transition diagram or as a state transition table. Table 2 is an incomplete state transition table for part of Figure 2.

   (a) Complete the missing sections of the four rows of Table 2.

Original state	Input	New state
S0	10	S10
S0		
S0		
S0		

   Table 2 [3]

   There are different ways that a customer can provide **exactly three** inputs that will result in the vending machine dispensing a drink. Three possible permutations are "20, 10, 20", "10, R, 50" and "10, 50, 50".

   (b) List **four** other possible permutations of **exactly three** inputs that will be accepted by the FSM shown in Figure 2. [4]

   AQA Comp1 Qu 4 June 2012

2-12

Exercises continued

2. Figure 2 shows a Finite State Automaton (FSA). The FSA has input alphabet {0, 1} and five states, S1, S2, S3, S4 and S5.

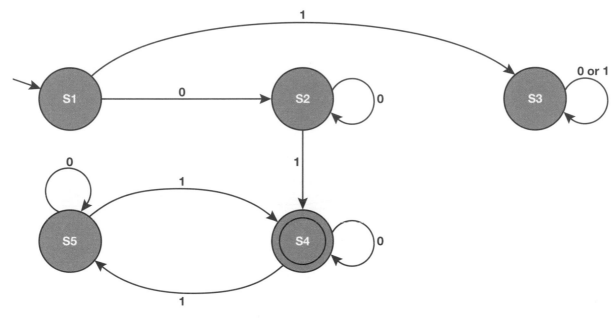

Figure 2

(a) Complete the transition table below for the FSA in Figure 2.

Current state	S_1	S_1	S_2	S_2	S_3	S_3	S_4	S_4	S_5	S_5
Input symbol	0	1	0	1	0	1				
Next state	S_2	S_3	S_2	S_4	S_3	S_3				

[1]

(b) The state S4 is a special state. This is indicated by the double circle in the diagram.

What does the double circle signify? [1]

(c) Write Yes or No in each row of the table below to indicate whether or not each of the four input strings would be accepted by the FSA in Figure 2. [2]

Input string	String accepted? (Yes/No)
101	
000	
010001101	
0100011011	

(d) Describe the language (set of strings) that the FSA will accept. [2]

AQA Comp 3 Qu 4 June 2011

2-12

Exercises continued

3. (a) A **state transition diagram** models the operation of a hotel lift. A program is written to simulate the behaviour of the lift in a hotel.

Describe **three** states that should be present in this diagram. [3]

(b) Figure 1 shows a state transition diagram for a problem which has two states S1 and S2.

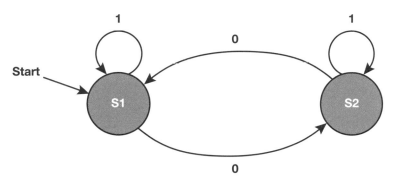

Figure 1

Table 1 is a state transition table for Figure 1. The **Next State** column is incomplete. Complete the table.

Input	Current state	Next state
0	S1	S2
0	S2	
1	S1	
1	S2	

Table 1 [3]

AQA Comp 1 Qu 3 June 2009

2-12

Section 3

Data representation

In this section:

3

Chapter 13– Number systems

Objectives

- Define a natural number, an integer and a real number

- Explain the difference between a rational and irrational number by example

- Understand and use ordinal numbers in context

- Convert between binary, decimal and hexadecimal number systems

Number types

On the number line, any whole number, for example, -10, -4, 0, 7, 1076 or 130793879 is an **integer**.

A **natural** number is a whole number that is used in counting. For example, *five gold rings*, *four* calling birds, *three* French hens. The (infinite) set of natural numbers, including zero, is referred to as $\mathbb{N}$ in mathematics. Thus $\mathbb{N} = \{0, 1, 2, 3, \ldots\}$

A **rational** number is any value that can be expressed as a ratio, or fraction. This includes all integer values since each can simply be expressed as 7/1 or 1076/1, to use the examples above.

An **irrational** number such as **pi** is one that cannot be expressed as a fraction and which has an endless series of non-repeating digits. Pi (π) can be expressed as 3.141592…. but not as a fraction. 22/7 gets close, but it's not correct. An irrational number cannot be correctly represented using a finite number of digits, and therefore a rounding error will occur.

Number	Ratio or fraction	Rational or irrational?
1.75	7/4	Rational
0.3333333 recurring	1/3	Rational
$\sqrt{2}$	Cannot be expressed as a fraction	Irrational

In mathematics, the set of integers is referred to as $\mathbb{Z}$ and the set of rational numbers is expressed as $\mathbb{Q}$. All integers are rational numbers, so $\mathbb{Z} = \{\ldots, -3, -2, -1, 0, 1, 2, 3, \ldots\}$

A real number is any natural, rational or irrational number. The set $\mathbb{R}$ of real numbers is defined as 'the set of all possible real world quantities'. This includes, for example, -10, -6.456, 0.4, 6.0, $\sqrt{2}$ and π. It does not include 'imaginary' numbers such as $\sqrt{-1}$, or infinity (∞). In programming languages, the data type 'real' has a slightly different meaning and is defined simply as a number with a decimal point.

The set of real numbers is represented by the symbol $\mathbb{R}$. While natural numbers are used for counting, real numbers are commonly used for measurement.

Ordinal numbers

Ordinal numbers describe the numerical position of objects: *first* in a race, *second* turn on the left. They are used as pointers to a particular element in a sequence, or to define the position of something in a list, for example, an array pointer. Characters and integers are examples of ordinal data types.

Number bases

Our familiar **decimal** (or **denary**) number system uses the digits 0 through 9 and therefore has a base of 10. Binary uses only the digits 0 and 1 and has a base of 2. **Hexadecimal** uses a base of 16 with digits 0-9 and letters A to F. A number's base can be written as a subscript to denote its value in the correct number system. For example 11_{10} denotes the number eleven in decimal. 11_2 would denote a binary value, (with a decimal equivalent of three) and 11_{16} would denote a hexadecimal value. (17 in decimal.)

The binary number system

In order to better understand the simplicity of the binary number system, it is best to examine how our familiar decimal number system works. Columns, right-to-left, represent units, tens and hundreds etc. We mentally multiply the values with their column value and add the totals together.

1000s	100s	10s	1s		
5	**0**	**7**	**4**		
5000		+ 70	+ 4	=	**5074**

The principle is exactly the same in the binary number system. As we move from right to left, each digit is worth twice as much as the previous one, instead of ten times as much.

128	64	32	16	8	4	2	1	
1	**1**	**0**	**0**	**1**	**0**	**1**	**1**	
128	+ 64			+ 8		+ 2	+ 1	= **203**

The minimum and maximum values that can be represented using unsigned binary for n bits are 0 and $2^n - 1$ respectively.

3-13

> **Q1**: Convert the binary numbers 0011 1001 and 1111 1111 into decimal.

Converting from decimal to binary

To convert a decimal number to binary, first write headings from right to left of 1, 2, 4, 8 … 128. (If the number given is greater than 255, continue writing headings).

To convert a number, for example 73, to binary, write a 1 under the largest heading less than 73 (i.e. 64). You now have 73 – 64 = 9 remaining, to be converted to binary. 9 = 8 + 1 so put 1 under 8 and under 1. Fill the spaces with zeros. The binary number representing 73 is 01001001.

128	64	32	16	8	4	2	1
0	**1**	**0**	**0**	**1**	**0**	**0**	**1**

> **Q2:** Convert the decimal numbers 37 and 100 into binary.

The hexadecimal number system

The hexadecimal system, often referred to as simply 'hex', uses a base of 16 as follows:

Decimal	Hexadecimal	Binary
0	0	0
1	1	1
2	2	10
3	3	11
4	4	100
5	5	101
6	6	110
7	7	111
8	8	1000
9	9	1001
10	A	1010
11	B	1011
12	C	1100
13	D	1101
14	E	1110
15	F	1111
16	10	10000

Converting from binary to hexadecimal and vice versa

To convert a binary number to hexadecimal, split the binary number into groups of 4 binary digits.

Binary	0011	1010	1111	1001	
Hex	3	A	F	9	= 3AF9

3-13

To convert from hex to binary, perform this operation in reverse by grouping the bits in groups of 4 and translating each group into binary. For example, to convert the number 23_{16} to binary

Hex	2	3	
Binary	0010	0011	= 00100011

> **Q3:** Convert the hexadecimal number A7 into binary.
>
> **Q4:** What is 1111 1111 in hexadecimal?

Converting from hexadecimal to decimal and vice versa

To convert from hexadecimal to decimal, remember that the left column now represents 16s and not tens. For example, to convert 27_{16} to decimal:

	16s	1s	
Hex	2	7	$= 2 \times 16 + 7 = 39$

To convert a decimal number to hex, the easiest way is to first convert the decimal number to binary and then from binary to hex. For example, to convert 75_{10} to hex:

	128	64	32	16	8	4	2	1
Binary	0	1	0	0	1	0	1	1
Hex		4				B		

Therefore $75_{10} = 4B_{16}$ (75/16 = 4 remainder 11, or 4B, since 11 is B in hexadecimal).

Q5: Convert the decimal numbers 37 and 100 into hexadecimal.

Q6: Convert the hexadecimal numbers 3B and 14 into binary.

Why the hexadecimal number system is used

The hexadecimal system is used as a shorthand for binary since it is simple to represent a byte in just two digits, and fewer mistakes are likely to be made in writing a hex number than a string of binary digits. It is easier for technicians and computer users to write or remember a hex number than a binary number. Colour codes in images often use hexadecimal to represent the RGB values, as they are much easier to remember than a 24-bit binary string. In the example below #364DB2 represents 36_{16} for Red, $4D_{16}$ for Green and $B2_{16}$ for Blue values, which can be displayed or printed in the Colour Picker window more compactly.

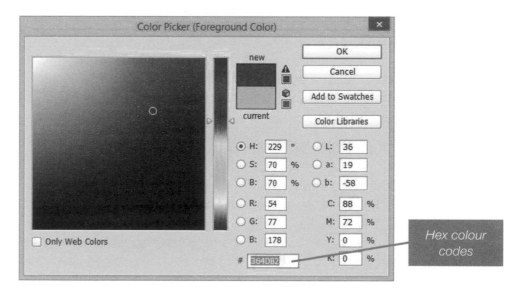

3-13

Exercises

1. Represent the decimal number 123 in binary using 8 bits. [1]

2. How many different decimal numbers can be represented using 8-bit binary? [1]

3. What is the hexadecimal equivalent of the decimal number 123? [1]

4. Why are bit patterns often displayed using hexadecimal instead of binary? [2]

1	0	1	0	0	1	1	1

Figure 1

5. Figure 1 shows the contents of a memory location. What is the decimal equivalent of the contents of this memory location if it represents an unsigned binary integer? [1]

6. What is the hexadecimal equivalent of the binary pattern shown in Figure 1? [1]

7. Convert the hexadecimal number DA to decimal. [1]

8. Give **one** example of a natural number and **one** example of an irrational number. [2]

9. Which of the following, if any, are **not** part of the set ℝ of real numbers?
   -12.75, 0, 22/7, 58, $\sqrt{2}$ [1]

Chapter 14 – Bits, bytes and binary

Objectives

- Define a bit as a 1 or a 0, and a byte as a group of eight bits
- Know that 2^n different values can be represented with *n* bits
- Use names, symbols and corresponding powers of 2 for binary prefixes e.g. Ki, Mi, Gi, Ti
- Differentiate between the character code of a decimal digit and its pure binary representation
- Describe ASCII and Unicode coding systems and explain why Unicode was introduced
- Describe methods used for error-checking and correction

Bits and bytes

A **bit** is the fundamental unit of information in the form of either a single 1 or 0. 1 and 0 are used to represent the two electronic states: on and off, or more accurately a switch that is closed (to complete a circuit) or open (to break it). A **byte** is a set of eight bits, for example 0110 1101. A set of four bits is referred to as a **nibble**.

Q1: Why is the on/off symbol designed like this:

The number of values that can be represented with *n* bits is 2^n. Two bits can represent 4 different values: 00, 01, 10 and 11. Three bits can represent 8 values and four bits can represent 16 different values, since 2 x 2 x 2 x 2 = 16.

Unit nomenclature

Although we frequently refer to 1024 bytes as a kilobyte, it is, in fact a **kibibyte**. To avoid any confusion between references to 1024 bytes rather than 1000 bytes, an international collaboration between standards organisations decided in 1996 that kibi would represent 1024, and kilo would represent 1000. Kibi is a combination of the words **ki**lo and **bi**nary. The same is true of the other familiar names Mega, Giga and Tera being replaced by mebi, gibi and tebi. The table below outlines the nomenclature for increasing quantities of bytes, in which a **KiB** is a **kibibyte** and a **MiB**, a **mebibyte**.

Name	Symbol	Power	Value		Name	Symbol	Power
kibi	Ki	2^{10}	1024		Kilo	K or k	10^3
mebi	Mi	2^{20}	1,048,576		Mega	M	10^6
gibi	Gi	2^{30}	1,073,741,824		Giga	G	10^9
tebi	Ti	2^{40}	1,099,511,627,776		Tera	T	10^{12}
pebi	Pi	2^{50}	1,125,899,906,842,624		Peta	P	10^{15}
exbi	Ei	2^{60}	1,152,921,504,606,846,976		Exa	E	10^{18}
zebi	Zi	2^{70}	1,180,591,620,717,411,303,424		Zetta	Z	10^{21}
yobi	Yi	2^{80}	1,208,925,819,614,629,174,706,176		Yotta	Y	10^{24}

The ASCII code

Historically, the standard code for representing the characters on the keyboard was ASCII (American Standard Code for Information Interchange). This uses seven bits which form 128 different bit combinations, more than enough to cover all of the characters on a standard English-language keyboard. The first 32 codes represent non-printing characters used for control such as **backspace** (code 8), the **Enter** or **Carriage Return** key (code 13) and the **Escape** key (code 27). The **Space** character is also included as code 32 and **Delete** as code 127.

ASCII	DEC	Binary	ASCII	DEC	Binary	ASCII	DEC	Binary	ASCII	DEC	Binary
NULL	000	000 0000	space	032	010 0000	@	064	100 0000	`	096	110 0000
SOH	001	000 0001	!	033	010 0001	A	065	100 0001	a	097	110 0001
STX	002	000 0010	"	034	010 0010	B	066	100 0010	b	098	110 0010
ETX	003	000 0011	#	035	010 0011	C	067	100 0011	c	099	110 0011
EOT	004	000 0100	$	036	010 0100	D	068	100 0100	d	100	110 0100
ENQ	005	000 0101	%	037	010 0101	E	069	100 0101	e	101	110 0101
ACK	006	000 0110	&	038	010 0110	F	070	100 0110	f	102	110 0110
BEL	007	000 0111	'	039	010 0111	G	071	100 0111	g	103	110 0111
BS	008	000 1000	(	040	010 1000	H	072	100 1000	h	104	110 1000
HT	009	000 1001	)	041	010 1001	I	073	100 1001	i	105	110 1001
LF	010	000 1010	*	042	010 1010	J	074	100 1010	j	106	110 1010
VT	011	000 1011	+	043	010 1011	K	075	100 1011	k	107	110 1011
FF	012	000 1100	,	044	010 1100	L	076	100 1100	l	108	110 1100
CR	013	000 1101	-	045	010 1101	M	077	100 1101	m	109	110 1101
SO	014	000 1110	.	046	010 1110	N	078	100 1110	n	110	110 1110
SI	015	000 1111	/	047	010 1111	O	079	100 1111	o	111	110 1111
DLE	016	001 0000	0	048	011 0000	P	080	101 0000	p	112	111 0000
DC1	017	001 0001	1	049	011 0001	Q	081	101 0001	q	113	111 0001
DC2	018	001 0010	2	050	011 0010	R	082	101 0010	r	114	111 0010
DC3	019	001 0011	3	051	011 0011	S	083	101 0011	s	115	111 0011
DC4	020	001 0100	4	052	011 0100	T	084	101 0100	t	116	111 0100
NAK	021	001 0101	5	053	011 0101	U	085	101 0101	u	117	111 0101
SYN	022	001 0110	6	054	011 0110	V	086	101 0110	v	118	111 0110
ETB	023	001 0111	7	055	011 0111	W	087	101 0111	w	119	111 0111
CAN	024	001 1000	8	056	011 1000	X	088	101 1000	x	120	111 1000
EM	025	001 1001	9	057	011 1001	Y	089	101 1001	y	121	111 1001
SUB	026	001 1010	:	058	011 1010	Z	090	101 1010	z	122	111 1010
ESC	027	001 1011	;	059	011 1011	[	091	101 1011	{	123	111 1011
FS	028	001 1100	<	060	011 1100	\	092	101 1100	|	124	111 1100
GS	029	001 1101	=	061	011 1101	]	093	101 1101	}	125	111 1101
RS	030	001 1110	>	062	011 1110	^	094	101 1110	~	126	111 1110
US	031	001 1111	?	063	011 1111	_	095	101 1111	DEL	127	111 1111

3-14

Character form of a decimal digit

Although numbers are represented within the code, the number character is not the same as the actual number value. The ASCII value 0110111 will print the character '7', even though the same binary value equates to the decimal number 55. Therefore ASCII cannot be used for arithmetic and would use unnecessary space to store numbers. Numbers for arithmetic are stored as pure binary numbers.

'7' + '7' (i.e. 0110111 + 0110111 in ASCII) would be 77, not 14 or 1110.

The development of ASCII

ASCII originally used only 7 bits, but an 8-bit version was developed to include an additional 128 combinations to represent symbols such as æ, © and ƒ. You can try holding down the ALT key and typing in the code number using the number pad to type one of these symbols. For example, ALT+130 will produce é, as used in *café*. The 7-bit ASCII code is compatible with the 8-bit code and simply adds a leading 0 to all binary codes.

Unicode

By the 1980s, several coding systems had been introduced all over the world that were all incompatible with one another. This created difficulty as multilingual data was being increasingly used and a new, unified format was sought. As a result, a new 16-bit code called Unicode (UTF-16) was introduced. This allowed for 65,536 different combinations and could therefore represent alphabets from dozens of languages including Latin, Greek, Arabic and Cyrillic alphabets. The first 128 codes were the same as ASCII so compatibility was retained. A further version of Unicode called UTF-32 was also developed to include just over a million characters, and this was more than enough to handle most of the characters from all languages, including Chinese and Japanese.

However, Unicode encodings take more storage space than ASCII, significantly increasing file sizes and transmission times.

3-14

Error checking and correction

Bits can change erroneously during transmission owing to interference. Computers use a variety of systems to verify that the data they receive is actually the same as the data that was sent.

Parity bits

A parity bit is an additional bit that is used to check that the other bits transmitted are likely to be correct. Using 7-bit ASCII with an 8-bit system meant that there was an extra bit available. This was used as a parity bit.

Computers use either odd or even parity, and the parity bit is used to ensure that the total number of 1s in each byte, including the parity bit, equals an odd or even number. For example an R is represented by 1010010 in 7-bit ASCII:

0	1	0	1	0	0	1	0

Using odd parity, the parity bit above is the most significant bit, and becomes 0 to make the total number of 1s an odd number – in this case, 3. Using even parity, the parity bit would have been set to 1.

Q4: What would be the parity bit value for 0010110 using odd parity?

Majority voting

Majority voting is a system that requires each bit to be sent three times. If a bit value is flipped erroneously during transmission over a noisy line, the recipient computer would use the majority rule and assume that the two bits that have not changed were therefore correct.

0			0			1			0			0			1			1			0		
0	0	**1**	0	0	0	1	1	**0**	0	0	0	**1**	0	0	1	1	1	1	**0**	1	0	0	0

In the example above, each bit was sent three times. 00100110 was sent as 000 000 111 000 000 111 111 000 and received as 001 000 110 000 100 111 101 000. In the 1st, 3rd, 5th and 7th bits a transmission error changed one of the bits. Since the majority (two) of the bits were 0, in the case of the 1st bit, 0 was interpreted by the recipient as the intended bit value. The recipient computer can then reassemble the correct values, i.e. 00100110, although you may have realised that the problem with this system is a tripling in the volume of data that is sent.

Q5: Assuming 010 011 110 010 000 110 111 100 is received, what value would be accepted?

Checksums (A Level only)

A checksum is a mathematical algorithm that is applied to a 'unit' or packet of data, for example a block of 256 bytes. The data in the block is used to create a checksum value which is transmitted with the block. The same algorithm is applied to the block after transmission and if the two checksums match, the transmission is deemed to have been successful. If they do not match, an error must have occurred during transmission and the block should be transmitted again.

A simple example of a checksum algorithm is to add together all of the numerical values of each byte in the block. If any bits change, it is likely, but not guaranteed, to change the checksum, and the block should be resent. In this short block of 3 bytes, the checksum would be 114, i.e. 51+43+20.

0	0	1	1	0	0	1	1	0	0	1	0	1	0	1	1	0	0	0	1	0	1	0	0
51								43								20							
114																							

Check digits

A check digit is similar to a checksum, and is an additional digit at the end of a string of other numbers designed to check for mistakes in input or transmission. Printed books and other products have a unique ISBN (International Standard Book Number) or EAN (European Article Number), a 13-digit number which includes the calculated check digit and is printed with the barcode. The first 12 digits are the unique item number, the 13th is the check digit. This can be calculated using the Modulo 10 system.

ISBN 978-0956143051

9 780956 143051

For example, the ISBN or EAN of 978095614305 has a check digit of 1. This is calculated as follows:

ISBN	9	7	8	0	9	5	6	1	4	3	0	5	1
Weight	1	3	1	3	1	3	1	3	1	3	1	3	
Multiplication	9	21	8	0	9	15	6	3	4	9	0	15	
Addition	*Add all the numbers*												99
Remainder	*Find the remainder when divided by 10*												9
Subtraction	*Subtract the result from 10*												1

The ISBN or EAN digits are given weights of 1 and 3 alternatively. Each value is multiplied by its weight. The multiplied values are added together and divided by 10 to get a remainder of 9. The remainder is subtracted from 10 to give a check digit of 1. The published check digit is read by a barcode scanner, an algorithm to check the check digit is performed and if, as in this case, the digits match, the barcode is deemed, with almost 100% accuracy, to have been read accurately. A similar system works with credit card numbers.

> **Q6:** Use the Modulo 10 system to check the check digit on a product or book barcode.

3-14

Exercises

1. The ASCII system uses 7 bits to represent a character. The ASCII code in decimal for the numeric character '0' is 48; other numeric characters follow on from this in sequence.
    (a) Using 7 bits, what is the ASCII code for the character '2' in binary? [1]
    (b) How many different characters can be represented using ASCII? [1]

2. One character encoding scheme is Unicode. An alternative character encoding scheme is ASCII.
    (a) State one difference between Unicode and ASCII. [1]
    (b) State one advantage and one disadvantage of using ASCII rather than Unicode for representing characters. [2]

3. How many times greater is the storage capacity of a 1 terabyte hard disk drive than that of a 256 megabyte hard disk drive?
    Show each stage of your working. [2]

4. A 'majority voting' system of error checking is used to transmit data, with each bit being sent three times.
    (a) What will be the final bit pattern received by the user if the following bit pattern is transmitted? [2]

0	0	1	0	0	0	0	0	0	0	1	1	1	0	1	1	1	1	1	0	0	0	1	0

    (b) Name one disadvantage of the 'majority voting' system for transmitting data. [1]
    (c) Assuming the transmission represents a decimal number, what number does it represent? [1]

5. Explain, with the aid of an example, how an even parity system of error checking works when transmitting data. [3]

Chapter 15 – Binary arithmetic and the representation of fractions

Objectives

- Be able to add and multiply together two unsigned binary numbers
- Convert between signed binary and decimal and vice versa
- Represent positive and negative numbers in two's complement and specify the range of n bits
- Perform subtraction using two's complement
- Understand how numbers with a fractional part can be represented in binary
- Use fixed point binary form to represent a real number in a given number of bits

Binary addition

Binary addition works in a similar way to decimal addition. If two numbers added together are equal to or greater than the base value, (in the case of decimal, 10) then the 'tens' are carried. In binary, an addition that equals 2 or more results in a carry over to the next column.

In binary, the rules for addition are as follows:

1. $0 + 0 = 0$
2. $0 + 1 = 1$
3. $1 + 0 = 1$
4. $1 + 1 = 0$ Carry 1 (This is 2 in decimal or 10 in binary.)
5. $1 + 1 + 1 = 1$ Carry 1 (This is 3 in decimal or 11 in binary.)

Use the following worked example as a guide to where and how each of the rules is implemented.

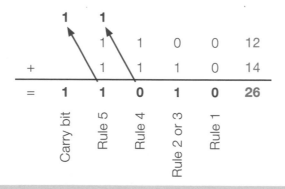

Q1: Calculate 00100111 + 00011001.

3-15

Overflow

In the following example, 8 bits are used to store the result of an addition. The result of the addition is greater than 255, and an overflow error occurs where a carry from the most significant bit requires a ninth bit.

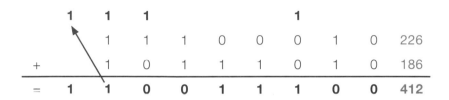

		1	1	1				1			
			1	1	1	0	0	0	1	0	226
+			1	0	1	1	1	0	1	0	186
=		1	1	0	0	1	1	1	0	0	412

Binary multiplication

Multiplication also works in a similar way to our decimal system. In decimal, moving a number one place value to the left multiplies it by 10, and shifting it 2 places to the left multiplies it by 100.

In binary, shifting a number one place to the left multiplies it by 2. Shifting it 2 places to the left multiplies it by 4, shifting it 3 places to the left multiplies it by 8, and so on.

There are several methods of doing binary multiplication, one of them being to use a combination of shifts and addition, best shown by the example below. However, you may find the second method, using long multiplication and shown on the next page, easier to understand and apply.

For example, to multiply 22 by 2:

												Answer columns								
	128	64	32	16	8	4	2	1			128	64	32	16	8	4	2	1		
Multiplicand	0	0	0	1	0	1	1	0	22	Answer	0	0	1	0	1	1	0	0	44	
Multiplier	0	0	0	0	0	0	1	0	2				(Multiplicand shifted left one place)							

To multiply 22 by 3, you need to add the multiplicand (multiplied by 1) to the multiplicand multiplied by 2.

												Answer columns								
	128	64	32	16	8	4	2	1			128	64	32	16	8	4	2	1		
Multiplicand	0	0	0	1	0	1	1	0	22		0	0	0	1	0	1	1	0	22	
Multiplier	0	0	0	0	0	0	1	1	3	+	0	0	1	0	1	1	0	0	44	
										Answer	0	1	0	0	0	0	1	0	66	

To multiply 22 by 10, add the multiplicand multiplied by 2 to the multiplicand multiplied by 8

												Answer columns								
	128	64	32	16	8	4	2	1			128	64	32	16	8	4	2	1		
Multiplicand	0	0	0	1	0	1	1	0	22		0	0	1	0	1	1	0	0	44	
Multiplier	0	0	0	0	1	0	1	0	10	+	1	0	1	1	0	0	0	0	176	
										Answer	1	1	0	1	1	1	0	0	220	

3-15

This is effectively exactly the same as performing a long multiplication sum. Compare a long multiplication in decimal with one in binary:

Decimal	Binary	
3101	10010	18
x 102	x 101	x 5
6202	10010	18
+ 0000	+ 00000	+ 0
+ 3101	+ 10010	+72
316302	**1011010**	**90 Answer**

Q2: Calculate 10111 x 1001.

Signed and unsigned binary numbers

An **unsigned** representation of a binary number can only represent positive numbers. A **signed** representation can represent both positive and negative numbers. Two's complement, described below, is one representation of a signed binary number.

Two's complement

Two's complement binary works in a similar way to numbers on an analogue counter. Moving the wheel forwards one, will create a reading of 0001; turn back one, and the reading will become 9999. 9999 is interpreted as -1.

3-15

In binary:

11111101	=	-3
11111110	=	-2
11111111	=	-1
00000000	=	0
00000001	=	1
00000010	=	2
00000011	=	3

Calculating the range

The range that can be represented with two's complement using n bits is given by the formula:

$$-\left(2^{(n-1)}\right) \ldots 2^{(n-1)} - 1$$

With eight bits, the maximum decimal range that can be represented is -128 to 127 because the leftmost bit is used as a sign bit to indicate whether a number is negative. If the leftmost number is a 1, it is a negative number. Thus 10000000 represents -128

Q3: What is the range that can be represented using 16 bits?

Converting a negative decimal number to binary

Start by working out the positive equivalent of the number, flip all of the bits and add 1. For example, to convert the decimal number -9 to binary:

		-9
Positive binary	:	00001001
Flip the bits	:	11110110
Add one	:	**1**
		11110111

Converting a negative two's complement binary number to decimal

The same method works the other way. Flip all of the bits and add 1. Then work out the result in decimal using the normal method. For example, to convert the binary number 11100101 to decimal:

		11100101
Flip the bits	:	00011010
Add one	:	**1**
Convert	:	-00011011
		-27

Binary subtraction using two's complement

Binary subtraction is best done by using the negative two's complement number and then adding the second number. For example decimal 17-14 would be:

14	=	00001110
-14	=	11110010
17	=	00010001
17 + (-14)	=	**(1)00000011**

The carry on the addition is ignored, and the correct answer is given.

Fixed point binary numbers

Fixed point binary numbers can be a useful way to represent fractions in binary. A binary point is used to separate the whole place values from the fractional part on the number line:

In the binary example above, the left hand section before the point is equal to 5 (4+1) and the right hand section is equal to ½ + ¼ (¾), or 0.5 + 0.25 = 0.75. So, using four bits after the point, 0101 1100 is 5.75 in decimal. A useful table with some decimal fractions and their equivalents is given below:

Q4: How is 19.25 represented using a single byte with 3 bits after the point?

Binary fraction	Fraction	Decimal fraction
0.1	1/2	0.5
0.01	1/4	0.25
0.001	1/8	0.125
0.0001	1/16	0.0625
0.00001	1/32	0.03125
0.000001	1/64	0.015625
0.0000001	1/128	0.0078125
0.00000001	1/256	0.00390625

Converting a decimal fraction to fixed point binary

To convert the fractional part of a decimal to binary, you can employ the same technique as you would when converting any decimal number to binary. Take the value and subtract each point value from the amount until you are left with 0. Take the example 3.5625 using 4 bits to the right of the binary point:

Subtract 0.5:	0.5625 – 0.5 = 0.0625	**1**
Subtract 0.25 from 0.0625:	Won't go	**0**
Subtract 0.125 from 0.0625:	Won't go	**0**
Subtract 0.0625 from 0.0625:	0.0625 – 0.0625 = 0	**1**

3 = 0011 in binary. 0.5625 = 1001. So 3.5625 = 0011 1001

It is worth noticing that in this system, some fractions cannot be represented at all. 0.2, 0.3 and 0.4, for example, will require an infinite number of bits to the right of the point. The number of fractional places would therefore be truncated and the number will not be accurately stored, causing rounding errors. In our decimal system, two decimal places can hold all values between .00 and .99. With the fixed point binary system, 2 digits after the point can only represent 0, ¼, ½, or ¾ and nothing in between.

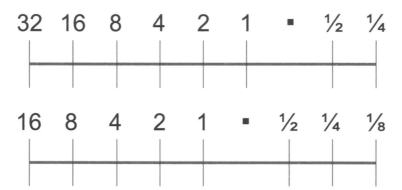

The range of a fixed point binary number is also limited by the fractional part. For example, if you have only 8 bits to store a number to 2 binary places, you would need 2 digits after the point, leaving only 6 bits before it. 6 bits only gives a range of 0-63. Moving the point one to the left to improve accuracy within the fractional part also serves to half the range to just 0-31. Even with 32 bits used for each number, including 8 bits for the fractional part after the point, the maximum value is only about 8 million. Another format called floating point binary may be used, but this is not examined at AS Level.

3-15

Exercises

1. Represent the decimal value -19 as an 8-bit two's complement binary integer. [2]

2. What is the largest positive decimal value that can be represented using 8-bit two's complement binary? [1]

3. Describe how 8-bit two's complement binary can be used to subtract one number from another number. In your answer show how the calculation 25 – 49 would be completed using the method that you have described. [2]

4. A computer stores the current temperature of a supermarket delivery van.
The temperature in °C is stored as a two's complement integer using a single byte.

   (a) Convert the freezer temperature value of -19 into binary. [2]

   (b) State the range of temperature values that can be stored using 8 bits. [1]

5. A memory location contains the value 10101011. What is its decimal equivalent if it represents a two's complement binary integer? [2]

6. Using 1 byte to hold each number, with an imaginary binary point fixed after the fourth digit, convert the following decimal numbers to binary:

   (a) (i) 4.25   (ii) 7.1875   (iii) 6.875 [3]

   (b) Convert the following binary numbers to decimal, assuming four bits after the point:
   (i) 0000000001101000   (ii) 0000000000110010 [2]

   (c) What are the largest and smallest positive numbers that can be stored in two bytes assuming four bits after the binary point? [2]

Chapter 16 – Bitmapped graphics

Objectives

- Understand how bitmapped images are represented in terms of size in pixels, resolution and colour depth

- Be able to calculate storage requirements for a bitmap image

- Be aware that images contain metadata and be able to describe typical metadata

Representation of bitmapped images

A bitmap (or **raster**) image contains many picture elements or pixels, that make up the whole image. A pixel is the smallest identifiable area of an image. Each pixel is attributed a binary value which represents a single colour.

Resolution

The resolution of an image can be expressed as the **width in pixels x height in pixels**. This does not determine the size of the image, simply the number of pixels within it. Assuming an image's physical dimensions remain the same, then the greater the number of pixels it contains, the sharper the image, as the pixels must become smaller to fit inside its boundaries.

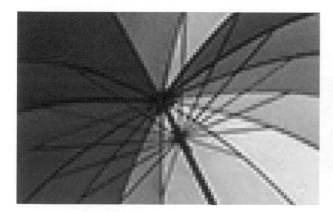

100 x 67 pixels

1000 x 670 pixels

Sometimes resolution is expressed as the number of pixels per inch or **PPI**. This indicates the density of the pixels, rather than the actual image dimensions. 72PPI is a standard screen resolution, and images with a resolution greater than this will not appear any better on screen. Print quality requires images at 300PPI to print in photographic quality. DPI (or Dots Per Inch) is a printing term relating to the number of ink dots per inch on a page and is often confused with PPI.

Some newer screens, including smartphones, can have a screen resolution of up to 400PPI. This makes pixels so small that they can no longer be easily distinguished by the human eye without the aid of a microscope.

Colour depth

Each pixel in an image has a binary value attributed to it. The number of bits determines the number of combinations (as n bits gives 2^n combinations), and this determines the number of colours that a pixel can represent. Each binary value represents a single colour, and the number of bits per pixel is referred to as the **colour depth**.

A simple black and white image will only require one bit per pixel, 0 to represent black and 1 to represent white.

1	1	1	0	1	1	1
1	0	1	0	1	0	1
1	1	0	0	0	1	1
0	0	0	0	0	0	0
1	1	0	0	0	1	1
1	0	1	0	1	0	1
1	1	1	0	1	1	1

This icon image has a resolution of 7x7 pixels, with 49 pixels in total. If each pixel is represented by one bit, the total image file size (ignoring metadata) will be 49 bits.

Once we begin to introduce colour, or increase the number of colours in the image, the number of bits that each pixel will need must be increased to allow for a greater number of combinations.

11	11	11	01	11	11	11
11	10	11	01	11	10	11
11	11	10	01	10	11	11
01	01	01	00	01	01	01
11	11	10	01	10	11	11
11	10	11	01	11	10	11
11	11	11	01	11	11	11

This image, although identical in size, has four colours, and will therefore require two bits per pixel to offer four combinations. The file size (ignoring metadata) will therefore double to 98 bits, with 2 bits x 49 pixels.

One byte per pixel will offer 256 different colours, 16 bits will give 65,536 colours and 24 bits will allow for over 16 million colours – approaching the number that the human eye can detect. This has become the current standard with 256 colour values (8 bits) per channel: red, green and blue. Where 32 bits are used, the last 8 bits are either ignored or used for an alpha channel to control transparency.

Q1: Given an image with a resolution of 1024 x 1024, what would the file size be if 256 colours are to be represented?

Metadata

Metadata is best described as data about data. In the case of image metadata, details such as the image **width in pixels**, **height in pixels** and **colour depth**.

3-16

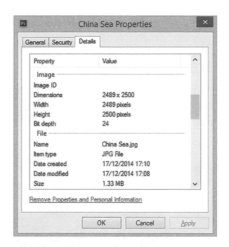

The storage of this additional data with the file helps to explain why your calculated image size may not equal exactly what the computer shows as the image size. Another reason is compression which can dramatically reduce the size of an image.

Vector graphics (A Level only)

Vector graphics are represented quite differently. Rather than storing information on each individual pixel and building an image from them, vector images are made up of **geometric shapes** or **objects** such as lines, curves, arcs and polygons. A vector file stores only the necessary details about each shape in order to redraw the object when the file loads.

Q2: In order to draw a square exactly as someone else intended, what information would you need to know?

3-16

To recreate an image of a circle, a computer must store its **properties**, including the **position** of its centre within the image, its **radius**, **fill** colour, **line colour** and **line weight**.

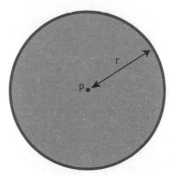

Vector drawing lists

These properties are stored in a **drawing list** which specifies how to redraw the image. If the image is resized on screen, the computer will adjust the position and dimensions of the image properties and redraw the image perfectly every time. A bitmapped image will pixelate.

The drawing list item for the circle above might appear in a drawing list like this:

Vector drawing list
Circle (centre = x,y, radius = r, fill = blue, stroke = red, weight = 3px)
Rectangle (position = x,y, width = 20, height = 60, fill = yellow, stroke = none)
Line (start = x,y, end = x,y, stroke = green, weight = 1px)

Regardless of how large these shapes are drawn, the image will always be sharp, and the amount of data required to store the image will not change.

Vector graphics versus bitmapped graphics

A **vector** image usually has a much smaller file size and will scale perfectly, regardless of how large or small you make it. A logo is often best created as a vector graphic since the company is then able to print it crisply on anything from a business card to a billboard.

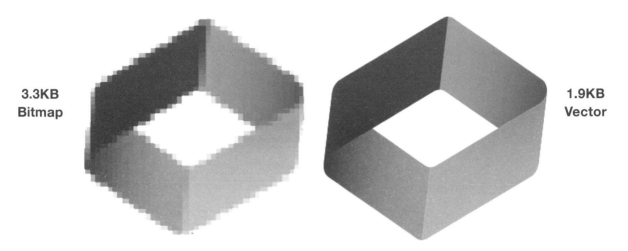

**3.3KB
Bitmap**

**1.9KB
Vector**

3-16

Since they are often smaller files, vectors use less memory and storage space, transmit faster and often load more quickly. Why then, are bitmap images used at all? A vector image cannot easily replicate an image with continuous areas of changing colour such as a photograph, taken with a digital camera. Take this image below, with a vectorised equivalent. Theoretically, if you created a vector image with squares of solid colour, each 1 pixel in size, you would be able to replicate a bitmap exactly; but your file would need to store a single list item for each pixel – far more than a short binary value. Note the difference in file size and quality here:

84KB – Original bitmap   *1.2MB – Vectorised version*

Individual pixels can be manipulated within a bitmap image – useful in the case of photo retouching, for example. With a vector image, individual objects are easily manipulated, but individual pixels cannot be changed.

Exercises

1. Images are often represented in a computer's main memory using bitmapped graphics. Bitmapped images consist of **pixels**. A pixel is the smallest addressable part of an image.

    (a) What is meant by the **resolution** of a bitmapped graphic image? [2]

    (b) What is meant by the **colour depth** of a bitmapped graphic image? [2]

    An image has 10 x 10 pixels. It is stored in an image format that is limited to 16 colours.

    (c) Calculate the image size in bytes. [2]

    Instead of using bitmapped graphics, images may be represented in a computer's main memory using vector graphics.

    (d) State **one** advantage of vector graphics compared with bitmapped graphics. [1]

    AQA Comp 1 Qu 3 June 2011

2. A bitmapped image consists of pixels. The figure below shows a bitmapped representation of an image of a winking, happy face consisting of red, blue, black and white pixels only.

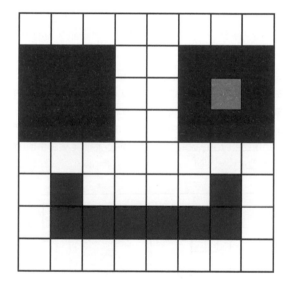

3-16

    (a) Why must at least two bits be used to represent each pixel? [1]

    The second line of pixels (from the top) has been represented in a computer's memory as the bit pattern 1111 1100 0011 1111. A black pixel is coded as 11.

    (b) Suggest a suitable 16-bit bit pattern that could be used to represent the third row of pixels. [2]

    (c) What, in bytes, is the minimum file size for the bitmapped image? [3]

    Instead of representing the face as a bitmapped image, vector graphics could have been used.

    (d) State **three** items of data that would need to be stored about an eye object, similar to those shown in the image in the above figure, if it is to be represented using vector graphics. [3]

    (e) Describe **two** advantages of using vector graphics instead of bitmaps to represent an image. [2]

    AQA Comp 1 Qu 5 June 2012

Chapter 17 – Digital representation of sound

Objectives

- Describe the digital representation of sound in terms of sampling rate and resolution
- Describe the principles of operation of an analogue to digital converter and a digital to analogue converter
- Understand and apply the Nyquist theorem
- Calculate sound sample sizes in bytes
- Describe the purpose of MIDI and the use of event messages
- Describe the advantages of using MIDI files for representing music

Sound sampling and resolution

Sound waves are naturally in a continuous, analogue form. To represent sound in a computer, the (**continuous**) analogue sound waves have to be converted to a (**discrete**) digital format. This can be done by measuring and recording the amplitude of the sound wave at given time intervals (several thousand times per second). The more frequently the samples are taken, the more accurately the sound will be represented. The frequency at which samples are taken is measured in **hertz (Hz)**, a unit of frequency equal to one cycle per second.

In addition, in the same way that an image's quality is improved with a more precise representation of colour enabled by a greater colour depth, the accuracy of a sound recording increases with a greater audio bit depth. Increasing the number of points of amplitude (represented on the y axis below) increases the accuracy at which you can record a sound's amplitude (or wave height) at a given point in time.

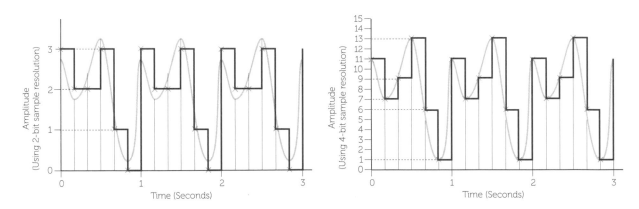

> **Q1:** Which of the graphs above represents a more accurate recording? Why?

Sample rate

The **sampling rate** is the frequency with which you record the amplitude of the sound. The more often you take a sample, the smoother the playback will sound. The disadvantage of this, is that every time you take a sample, at a resolution of say 16 bits, you need to store another 2 bytes of data. A typical CD recording is made at 44,100Hz, or 44,100 times per second. This means that for every second of sound, 2 bytes x 44,100 = 88,200 / 1000 = 88.2KB is required and for every minute, approximately 5.3MB is required. For stereo sound, this is doubled to provide samples for left and right channels.

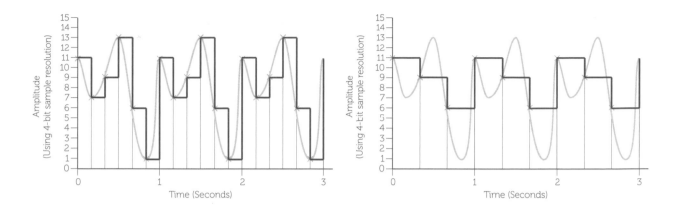

Calculating sound sample sizes

To calculate the byte size of a sample, you must multiply:

the number of samples per second x the number of bits per sample x the length of the sample in seconds

A sample of one minute taken at a resolution of 16 bits at 20KHz would be calculated as follows:

$$20,000 \text{ x } 16 \text{ x } 60 = 19,200,000 \text{ bits } \textbf{or } 2,400,000 \text{ bytes } \textbf{or } 2.4MB$$

If the sample is recorded in stereo, a sample for each channel is taken and therefore the sample size will double.

3-17

Q3: Calculate the kbit/s of a radio jingle recorded in stereo at 10KHz using 8 bits per sample.

Analogue and digital signals and data

The differences are shown in the table below.

	Analogue	**Digital**
Signal	A continuous signal which represents physical measurements	Discrete time signals generated by digital modulation
Representation	Uses a continuous range of values to represent information	Uses discrete or discontinuous values to represent information
Example	Human voice, mercury thermometer, tape recorder, analogue watch	Computers, CDs, DVDs, digital watch
Data	In analogue technology, a wave is recorded in its original form; for example, a signal from a microphone can be copied onto a tape, then read, amplified and sent to a speaker to produce the sound	In digital technology, analogue waveforms are sampled at intervals, turned into a limited set of numbers and stored on a digital device
Quantifying	Continuously varying quantities are measured	Quantities are counted rather than measured.

Analogue to digital conversion

During the process of converting an **analogue** sound into a **digital** recording, a microphone converts the sound energy into electrical energy. The analogue to digital converter (ADC) samples the analogue data at a given frequency, measuring the amplitude of the wave at each point and converting it into a binary value according to the resolution or audio bit depth being used for each sample.

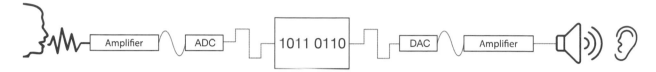

To output a sound, the binary values for each sample point are translated back into analogue signals or voltage levels and sent to an amplifier connected to a speaker.

ADCs are used with analogue sensors such as a microphone and the most common use for a DAC is to convert a digital audio signal to an analogue signal.

Interpreting frequency

The **frequency** of a sound is determined by the speed of oscillation or vibration of a wave. This controls the pitch and is measured in **Hertz**, (Hz). By looking at a simple graph, you can interpret the frequency or pitch of the sound.

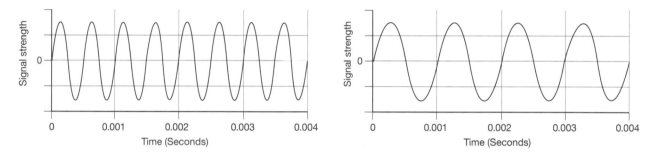

In the first example above, the wave is oscillating (from peak to trough) twice every 0.001 seconds. That equates to 2,000 oscillations per second, and would therefore have a frequency of 2,000 Hz or 2KHz. The second example would be a lower pitched sound with a frequency of 1KHz.

Nyquist's theorem

Harry **Nyquist** discovered in 1928 that in order to produce an accurate recording, the sampling rate must be at least double that of the highest frequency in the original signal. His theory was later proven in 1949 by Claude Shannon.

This means that a sound with a frequency of 10,000Hz must be sampled at a minimum of 20,000Hz in order to accurately reproduce the original. The human ear can hear frequencies between approximately 20Hz and 20,000Hz and some individuals are able to hear frequencies a little beyond that. For that reason, CDs are sampled at 44,100Hz in order for recorded sound to be reproduced accurately enough for there to be no audible distinction from the original – at least to most of us. What your dog might make of hearing a CD versus the original is another matter!

Q4: A sample is played with a maximum frequency of 12KHz. What is the minimum sampling rate that must be used when recording this sample in order to accurately replicate the sound?

Musical Instrument Digital Interface (MIDI)

MIDI is a technical standard that describes a protocol, digital interface and connectors which can be used to allow a wide variety of electronic musical instruments, computers and other related devices to connect and communicate with one another. A midi **controller** carries **event messages** that specify pitch and duration of a note, timbre, vibrato and volume changes, and synchronize tempo between multiple devices.

The ability to specify an instrument for a note makes it possible for a computer and only a few skilled musicians with a synthesiser to recreate the music of a much larger ensemble.

A **MIDI** file is not a recording of a live source. It is a list of instructions that tell it to **synthesise** a sound based on pre-recorded digital samples and synthesised samples of sounds created by different sources of instruments. A MIDI file can use 1,000 times **less disk space** than a conventional recording at an equivalent quality. The music created is also easily manipulated and the 'instructions' to play a specific song can also be passed on to other digital instruments or played in a different key

Exercises

1. To record sound a computer needs to convert the analogue sound signal into a digital form. During this process samples of the analogue signal are taken. Figure 1 shows part (0.02 seconds) of an analogue sound wave.

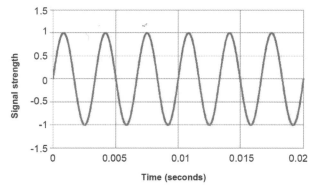

Figure 1

The frequency of an analogue sound wave is determined by how many waves of oscillation occur per second and is measured in Hertz (Hz) – the number of waves of oscillation per second.

(a) If the part of the analogue sound shown in Figure 1 is the highest frequency in the entire sound to be sampled, what is the minimum sampling rate (in Hz) that should be used? [2]

(b) Describe clearly the steps taken by an ADC (analogue-to-digital converter) in the conversion of an analogue sound wave to an equivalent digital signal. [3]

MIDI is an alternative method for storing sound digitally that does not use sound waves; instead, information about each musical note is stored.

(c) State one advantage of using the MIDI representation for storing sound digitally. [1]

(d) State an item of data, other than the note itself, that might be stored about a musical note in a MIDI file. [1]

AQA Comp 1 Qu 3 June 2012

3-17

Exercises continued

2. A performance by a music band is to be recorded and distributed on CD.

   The figure below shows three samples stored in a computer's memory that have been taken from an analogue signal as part of the recording process. A sampling rate of 44,000Hz (Hertz) has been used.

   1Hz is one sample per second.

0000 0001 1000 1110
0000 0001 1000 1110
0000 0001 1000 0011

   (a) What sampling resolution has been used?   [1]

   (b) If the original analogue signal lasts 100 seconds, how many bytes of storage will be required to store all the samples taken in the recording process?   [3]

   The average human can hear frequencies up to 20,000Hz (Hertz).

   (c) Explain why a sampling rate of 44,000Hz has been chosen for the recording.   [2]

   The CD recording is processed to create a version of the performance that can be downloaded from the band's website. The sound quality of the version of the recording stored on the web server is not as good as the sound quality of the CD version.

   (d) State one possible cause of this reduction in sound quality.   [1]

   AQA Comp 1 Qu 3 June 2013

3-17

3. To record sound a computer needs to convert the analogue sound into a digital form. During this process samples of the sound have to be taken. Figure 2 shows 6 samples that have been stored in a computer's memory. These samples have been taken from the analogue signal over a period of one hundredth of a second.

Sample 6	01101100
Sample 5	01101100
Sample 4	01100000
Sample 3	00001101
Sample 2	00001000
Sample 1	00011011

   Figure 2

   Look at the digital representation, shown in Figure 2, of the analogue sound.

   One Hertz (Hz) is one sample per second.

   (a) What sampling rate, in Hertz, has been used?   [2]

   (b) What sampling resolution has been used?   [1]

   (c) State Nyquist's theorem.   [2]

   AQA Comp 1 Qu 3 June 2010

Chapter 18 – Data compression and encryption algorithms

Objectives

- Know why sound and images are often compressed
- Understand how other files can be compressed
- Understand the difference between lossless and lossy compression
- Explain the advantages and disadvantages of different compression techniques
- Explain run length encoding and dictionary based compression
- Define encryption by use of examples
- Be able to encrypt and decrypt a message using the Caesar cipher
- Understand the flaws of the Caesar cipher with reference to substitution and brute force methods
- Explain the function of the Vernam cipher by example
- Explain why the Vernam cipher is considered to have perfect security
- Compare the Vernam cipher with others that depend on computational security

Why use compression?

File compression techniques were developed to reduce the storage space of files on disk. With disk storage becoming larger and cheaper, this is less important these days, but the reduction of file size has become even more important in the sharing and transmission of data. Internet Service Providers (ISPs) and mobile phone networks impose limits and charges on bandwidth. Images on websites need to be in a compressed format to enable a web page to load quickly – even on a fast connection, music and video streaming must take advantage of compression in order to reduce buffering. (In streaming audio or video from the Internet, buffering refers to downloading a certain amount of data to a temporary storage area or buffer, before starting to play a section of the music or movie.)

Compression can be either **lossy**, where unnecessary information is removed from the original file, or **lossless**. Lossless compression retains all information required to replicate the original file exactly.

Lossy compression

Lossy compression works by removing non-essential information. The two **JPG** images overleaf are clearly identifiable as the same thing, but one has been heavily compressed, displaying untidy and blocky compression artefacts as a consequence. Nevertheless, we can make out the subject of the image well, but the degree to which they are compressed comes at the cost of quality.

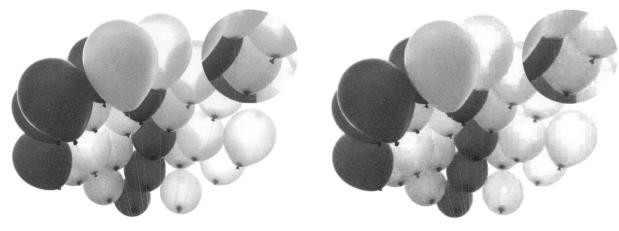

Original image 310KB   *Heavily compressed image 5.7KB*

The compression of sound and video works in a similar way. **MP3** files use lossy compression to remove frequencies too high for most of us to hear and to remove quieter sounds that are played at the same time as louder sounds. The resulting file is about 10% of original size, meaning that 1 minute of MP3 audio equates to roughly 1MB in size.

Voice is transmitted over the Internet or mobile telephone networks using lossy compression and although we have no problem in understanding what the other person is saying, we can recognise the difference in quality of a voice over a phone rather than in person. The apparent difference is lost data.

3-18

Lossless compression

Lossless compression works by recording patterns in data rather than the actual data. Using these patterns and a set of instructions on how to use them, the computer can reverse the procedure and reassemble an image, sound or text file with exact accuracy and no data is lost. This is most important with the compression of program files for example, where a single lost character would result in an error in the programming code. A pixel with a slightly different colour would not be of huge consequence in most cases. Lossless compression usually results in a much larger file than a lossy file, but one that is still significantly smaller than the original.

> **Q1:** What type of compression is likely to be used for the following: a website image, a zipped file of long text documents and images, an instruction manual in PDF format?

Run Length Encoding (RLE)

If you were ordering food from a takeaway restaurant for a group of five friends, it is likely that you might ask for "5 pizzas" rather than "one pizza, and another pizza, and another pizza etc." **Run Length Encoding** exploits the same principle. Rather than recording every pixel in an image, for example, it records its value and the number of times it repeats.

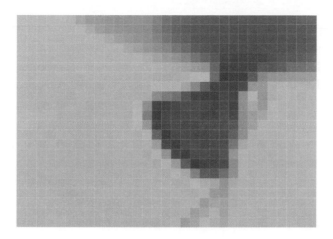

For this section of the balloon image, the encoding for the first row might crudely translate to: 6 green, 8 yellow and 17 orange, using one binary value for the colour value and another for the number of contiguous matching pixels in the run. This would reduce the data necessary to store this row to 6 bytes (00000110 00000001 00001000 00000010 00010001 00000011) rather than 31 bytes assuming a bit depth of 8 and values for each colour of 00000001, 00000010 and 00000011.

6▨ 8▨ 17▨

Dictionary-based compression techniques

Suppose that instead of sending a complete message, a copy of the Oxford English Dictionary was sent alongside a coded message using the page number and the position of the word on that page. The word 'pelican' falls on page 249 as the 7th word on that page. This could be send as 249,7 – using only 2 bytes; considerably fewer than the 7 bytes it would take to send the complete word. (Ignore, for now, the additional space that it would take to send the dictionary with it!)

Dictionary based compression works in a similar way. The compression algorithm searches through the text to find suitable entries in its own dictionary (or it may use a known dictionary) and translates the message accordingly.

Number	Entry	Binary
1	Do	000
2	_unto	001
3	_others	010
4	_as	011
5	_you	100
6	_would	101
7	_have	110
8	_do	111

Using the dictionary table above, the saying **"Do unto others as you would have others do unto you"** would be compressed as **1 2 3 4 5 6 7 3 8 2 5** or in binary using only **33 bits**. This compares to 51 characters or 51 bytes – a reduction of 92%. This still ignores the fact that the dictionary must also be stored with the text, but with a longer body of text to be compressed, a dictionary becomes quite insignificant in size compared with the original, and the original message can still be reassembled perfectly.

What is encryption?

Encryption is the transformation of data from one form to another to prevent an unauthorised third party from being able to understand it. The original data or message is known as **plaintext**. The encrypted data is known as **ciphertext**. The encryption method or algorithm is known as the **cipher**, and the secret information to lock or unlock the message is known as a **key**.

The Caesar cipher and the Vernam cipher offer polar opposite examples of security. Where the Vernam offers perfect security, the Caesar cipher is very easy to break with little or no computational power. There are many others methods of encryption – some of which may take many computers, many years to break, but these are still breakable and the principles behind them are similar.

The Caesar cipher

Julius Caesar is said to have used this method to keep messages secure. The **Caesar cipher** (also known as a **shift cipher**) is a type of **substitution cipher** and works by shifting the letters of the alphabet along by a given number of characters; this parameter being the key. Below is an example of a shift cipher using a key of 5. (An algorithm for this cipher is given as an example on page 46.)

A	B	C	D	E	F	G	H	I	J	K	L	M	N	O	P	Q	R	S	T	U	V	W	X	Y	Z
↓	↓	↓	↓	↓	↓	↓	↓	↓	↓	↓	↓	↓	↓	↓	↓	↓	↓	↓	↓	↓	↓	↓	↓	↓	↓
F	G	H	I	J	K	L	M	N	O	P	Q	R	S	T	U	V	W	X	Y	Z	A	B	C	D	E

Q2: Using the table above, what is the ciphertext for 'JULIUS CAESAR' using a shift of 5?

Q3: What word can be translated from the following ciphertext, which uses a key of −2: ZYBECP

You will no doubt be able to see the ease with which you might be able to decrypt a message using this system.

DGYDQFH WR ERUGHU DQG DWWDFN DW GDZQ

Even if you had to attempt a brute force attack on the message above, there are only 25 different possibilities (since a shift of zero means the plaintext and the ciphertext are identical). Otherwise you might begin by guessing the likelihood of certain characters first and go from there. Using cryptanalysis on longer messages, you would quickly find the most common ciphertext letter and could start by assuming this was an E, for example, or perhaps an A. *(Hint.)*

Cryptanalysis and perfect security

Other ciphers that use non-random keys are open to a cryptanalytic attack and can be solved given enough time and resources. Even ciphers that use a computer-generated random key can be broken since mathematically generated random numbers are not actually random; they just appear to be so. A truly random sequence must be collected from a physical and unpredictable phenomenon such as white noise, the timing of a hard disk read/write head or radioactive decay. A truly random key must be used with a Vernam cipher to ensure it is mathematically impossible to break.

The Vernam cipher

The **Vernam cipher**, invented in 1917 by the scientist Gilbert Vernam, is one implementation of a class of ciphers known as **one-time pad ciphers**, all of which offer perfect security if used properly. All others are based on **computational security** and are theoretically discoverable given enough time, ciphertext and computational power. Frequency analysis is a common technique used to break a cipher.

One-time pad

To provide perfect security, the encryption key or **one-time pad** must be equal to or longer in characters than the plaintext, be truly random and be used only once. The sender and recipient must meet in person to securely share the key and destroy it after encryption or decryption. Since the key is random, so will be the distribution of the characters meaning that no amount of cryptanalysis will produce meaningful results.

The bitwise exclusive or XOR

A Boolean XOR operation is carried out between the binary representation of each character of the plaintext and the corresponding character of the one-time pad. The XOR operation is covered in Chapter 23 and you may want to refer to this to verify the output for any combination of 0 and 1. Use the ASCII chart on page 73 for reference.

Plaintext: M	Key: +	XOR: f
1	0	1
0	1	1
0	0	0
1	1	0
1	0	1
0	1	1
1	1	0

Q4: Using the ASCII chart and the XOR operator, what ciphertext character will be produced from the letter E with the key w?

Using this method, the message "**Meet on the bridge at 0300 hours**" encrypted using a one-time pad of **+tkiGeMxGvnhoQ0xQDlllVdT4slJm9qf** will produce the ciphertext:

$$f◀🏳g\#X3♂H\#Y6!i(=vTg^J Ci"_┐L^{⊔}$$

The encryption process will often produce strange symbols or unprintable ASCII characters as in the above example, but in practice it is not necessary to translate the encrypted code back into character form, as it is transmitted in binary. To decrypt the message, the XOR operation is carried out on the ciphertext using the same one-time pad, which restores it to plaintext.

Exercises

1. Explain the difference between lossy and lossless data compression. [2]

2. Run-length encoding (RLE) is a pattern substitution compression algorithm.
   Data is stored in the format (colour,run) where 0 = White, 1 = Black.
   ```
   (0,1),(1,5),(0,1),
   (1,7),
   (1,1),(0,2),(1,1),(0,2),(1,1),
   (1,7),
   (0,1),(1,1),(0,1),(1,1),(0,1),(1,1),(0,1),
   (0,1),(1,1),(0,1),(1,1),(0,1),(1,1),(0,1),
   (0,1),(1,1),(0,3),(1,1),(0,1)
   ```

3-18

Exercises continued

(a) Reassemble the encoded sequence above to form a 7x7 web icon image in the grid below.

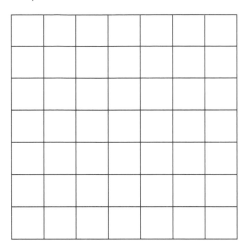

[3]

(b) RLE encoding is a lossless compression method. Give one disadvantage of lossless compression over lossy methods for the compression of images. [1]

(c) Explain why compression is considered necessary for images on the web. [2]

3. a) Explain why lossy compression techniques would not be suitable for use with files containing large bodies of text. [1]

(b) Suggest a suitable lossless method for compressing text. [1]

4. The Vernam cipher uses a one-time pad.

(a) Explain what is meant by a one-time pad. [1]

(b) Using the section of ASCII code below, apply the one-time pad *£]FL* to the word ***exam*** to encrypt it using the Vernam method. [4]

ASCII	DEC	Binary	ASCII	DEC	Binary	ASCII	DEC	Binary
space	032	010 0000	E	069	100 0101	`	096	110 0000
!	033	010 0001	F	070	100 0110	a	097	110 0001
"	034	010 0010	G	071	100 0111	b	098	110 0010
£	035	010 0011	K	075	100 1011	c	099	110 0011
$	036	010 0100	L	076	100 1100	d	100	110 0100
%	037	010 0101	M	077	100 1101	e	101	110 0101
&	038	010 0110	[	091	101 1011	m	109	110 1101
'	039	010 0111	\	092	101 1100	n	110	110 1110
(	040	010 1000	]	093	101 1101	x	120	111 1000
)	041	010 1001	^	094	101 1110	y	121	111 1001
?	063	011 1111	_	095	101 1111	z	122	111 1010

(c) A student claims that "All ciphers are breakable given enough time and ciphertext". Explain why the Vernam cipher disproves this statement. [2]

Section 4

Hardware and software

In this section:

4

Chapter 19 – Hardware and software

Objectives

- Define the terms hardware and software and understand the relationship between them
- Explain what is meant by system software and application software
- Understand the need for, and attributes of, different types of software
- Understand the functions of operating systems, utility programs, libraries and translators

Hardware and software

There is a very simple distinction between computer **hardware** and **software**. Hardware is the term used to describe the electrical or electro-mechanical parts of a computer and its input, output and storage devices.

Software comprises all the programs that are written to make computers function.

In the early days of computing, pioneers like von Neumann (1903-1957) and other (mostly male) engineers, who were figuring out the extremely complex task of how to how to build a computer, thought that the actual coding of programs using binary numbers to represent instructions, and setting the appropriate switches on the machines was a relatively simple task which could be left to young women with suitable secretarial skills and some aptitude for mathematics.

They were soon disabused of this notion. Maurice Wilkes (1913-2010), a computer scientist in the 1940s, recalls:

"As soon as we started programming, we found out to our surprise that it was not as easy to get programs right as we had thought. I can remember the exact instant when I realised that a large part of my life from then on was going to be spent in finding mistakes in my own programs."

Q1: Explain the difference between hardware and software and suggest two examples for each.

Classification of software

Software can be broadly classified into **system software** and **application software**.

System software

System software is the software needed to run the computer's hardware and application programs. This includes the operating system, utility programs, libraries and programming language translators.

Operating system

An operating system is a set of programs that lies between applications software and the computer hardware. It has many different functions, including:

- resource management – managing all the computer hardware including the CPU, memory, disk drives, keyboard, monitor, printer and other peripheral devices
- provision of a user interface (e.g. Windows) to enable users to perform tasks such as running application software, changing settings on the computer, downloading and installing new software.

Operating systems are covered in the next chapter.

Utility programs

Utility software is system software designed to optimise the performance of the computer or perform tasks such as backing up files, restoring corrupted files from backup, compressing or decompressing data, encrypting data before transmission, providing a firewall, etc.

For example, a **disk defragmenter** is a program that will reorganise a hard disk so that files which have been split up into blocks and stored all over the disk will be recombined in a single series of sequential blocks. This makes reading a file quicker. The software utility *Optimise Drives*, previously called *Disk Defragmenter*, runs automatically on a weekly schedule on the latest versions of Windows. You can also optimise drives on your PC manually.

A **virus checker** utility checks your hard drive and depending on the level of protection offered, incoming emails and internet downloads, for viruses and removes them. Windows 8.1 comes with built-in virus protection called Windows Defender.

Several utility programs such as the disk defragmenter, software uninstaller, backup and restore programs and screensavers are supplied as part of the operating system. Other utility programs such as WinZip for compressing and sharing files have to be purchased from independent suppliers.

4-19

Libraries

Library programs are ready-compiled programs which can be run when needed, and which are grouped together in software libraries. In Windows these often have a .dll extension. Most compiled languages have their own libraries of pre-written functions which can be invoked in a defined manner from within the user's program.

Q2: What library programs or routines have you used in any of the programs you have written? How is the library invoked by the program?

Translators

Programming language translators fall into three categories: compilers, interpreters and assemblers. All of them translate program code written by a programmer into machine code which can be run by the computer.

Translators are covered in Chapter 22.

Application software

Application software consists of programs that perform specific user-oriented tasks. It can be categorised as general purpose, special-purpose or custom-written (bespoke) software.

General-purpose software such as a word-processor, spreadsheet or graphics package, can be used for many different purposes. For example, a graphics package may be used to produce advertisements, manipulate photographs, draw vector or bit-mapped images.

Special-purpose software performs a single specific task or set of tasks. Examples include payroll and accounts packages, hotel booking systems, fingerprint scanning systems, browser software and hundreds of other applications. Software may be bought "**off-the-shelf**", ready to use, or it may be specially written by a team of programmers for a particular organisation. If, say, a hotel wants to buy some visitor booking software, they may be able to find a ready-made package that is quite suitable, or they may want a **bespoke** software package that will satisfy their particular requirements. It will almost certainly be cheaper to buy a ready-made package, even if it contains a lot of features which they will never use, since the cost is shared among all the other people buying the package. It will also have the advantages that it is ready to be installed immediately, and is likely to be well-documented, well-tested and bug-free.

Exercises

1. (a) Software can be classified as either **system** or **application software**. What is meant by

    (i) system software? [1]

    (ii) application software? [1]

  (b) Give an example of each type of software. [2]

4-19

2. A company sells widgets via an online web store. The process of updating the website and processing sales involves many different types of software.

Below is a list of software:

    Operating system, Utility software, Special-purpose software, General purpose application software, Bespoke software

Complete the table below by writing one software category beside each use. You should not use a category more than once.

Software	Category
Firewall software installed on the web server	
Store's own online ordering system designed for their products and systems	
Graphics software to crop product images suitable for uploading to the site	
Online payment verification software	

[4]

3. Give **two** reasons why a company might choose to purchase a special purpose software package rather than a suite of programs written specifically for their needs. [2]

Chapter 20 – Role of an operating system

Objectives

- Understand that the role of the operating system is to hide the complexities of the hardware from the user

- Know that the OS handles resource management, managing hardware to allocate processors, memories and I/O devices among competing processes

What is an operating system?

An operating system is a program or set of programs that manages the operations of the computer for the user. It acts as a bridge between the user and the computer's hardware, since a user cannot communicate with hardware directly.

The operating system is held in permanent storage, for example on a hard disk. A small program called the **loader** is held in ROM. When a computer is switched on, the loader in ROM sends instructions to load the operating system by copying it from storage into RAM.

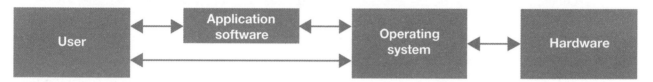

Functions of an operating system

4-20

Regardless of whether the operating system is embedded within an mp3 player or is the latest version of Windows installed on a desktop computer, all operating systems share the same basic functions.

An operating system disguises the complexities of managing and communicating with its hardware from the user via an **Application Programming Interface (API)**. Through this interface, a user can naively tap away to complete their tasks, (loading, saving or printing for example), oblivious to the actual operations taking place behind the scenes to support their actions.

Apart from providing a user interface, the operating system has to perform the following functions:

- memory management

- processor scheduling

- backing store management

- management of all input and output

We will look at what each of these functions involve.

Q1: A PC is a multitasking machine. What does this mean? Is it the same thing as multiprocessing?

Memory management

A PC allows a user to be working on several tasks at the same time. You may be listening to music via a streaming site such as Spotify, entering a Python program, checking your emails every so often and running Word so that you can document your program design. Meanwhile, a virus checker may be running in the background.

Each program, open file or copied clipboard item, for example, must be allocated a specific area of memory whilst the computer is running. Should a user wish to switch from one application to another in a separate window, each application must be stored in memory simultaneously. The allocation and management of space is controlled by the operating system.

In some cases, the computer's RAM may not be not large enough to store all these programs simultaneously, so the hard disk is used as an extension of memory – called **virtual** memory. MS Word may be open on your desktop but if you are not actually using it at a particular time, the operating system may copy the Word software and data to hard disk to free up RAM for the browser software, the Pascal compiler or whatever you as the user have requested. When you switch back to Word, the operating system will reload it into memory.

> **Q2:** Do you notice that response time slows down on your PC when you have a lot of programs running? What would be the effect of installing more RAM on your computer? Why?

Processor scheduling

With computers able to run multiple applications simultaneously, the operating system is responsible for allocating processor time to each one as they compete for the CPU. While one application is busy using the CPU for processing, the OS can queue up the next process required by another application to make the most efficient use of the processor. A computer with a single-core processor can only process one instruction at a time, but by carrying out small parts of multiple larger tasks in turn, the processor can give the appearance of carrying out several tasks simultaneously. This is what is meant by **multi-tasking**.

The **scheduler** is the operating system module responsible for making sure that processor time is used as efficiently as possible. Of course, this is a much more complex task on a large multi-user system where many users may, for example, be accessing the same database or running different applications on an application server. The objectives of the scheduler are to:

- maximise throughput
- be fair to all users on a multi-user system
- provide acceptable response time to all users
- ensure hardware resources are kept as busy as possible

> **Q3:** There are several different "scheduling algorithms" used by different operating systems. Suggest an algorithm that would achieve the objectives of the scheduler.

Backing store management

When files and applications are loaded, they are transferred from backing storage into memory. The operating system is required to keep a directory of where files are stored so that they can be quickly accessed. Similarly, it needs to know which areas of storage are free so that new files or applications can be saved. The file management system that comes with your desktop operating system enables a user to move files and folders, delete files and protect others from unauthorised access.

> **Q4:** What happens to file access times as the disk becomes very full? Why? What action needs to be taken?

Peripheral management

Different applications will require different input or output devices throughout their operation. If you send a file to print, the operating system will need to communicate with the printer to check that it is switched on and online, check that it is a printer and not, say, the keyboard and begin communication to send it the correct data to print. The operating system also ensures that peripherals are allocated to processes without causing conflicts.

Interrupt handling

An interrupt is a signal from a peripheral or software program that causes the operating system to stop processing its current list of instructions and think what to do next. Should an error occur such as a software crash or 'out of paper' message from a printer, the OS is responsible for detecting the interrupt signal and displaying an appropriate error message for the user if appropriate. It is because a processor can be interrupted that **multi-tasking** can take place.

Q5: What other events could cause an interrupt?

Exercises

1. Explain the purpose of the operating system. [2]

2. An operating system is designed to hide the complexities of the hardware from the user and to manage the hardware and other resources.

   Give **three** different types of management of either hardware or other resources that are performed by an operating system. [3]

   AQA Comp 3 Qu 1 June 2013

4-20

Chapter 21 – Programming language classification

Objectives

- Be aware of the development of programming languages and their classification into low- and high-level languages

- Describe low-level languages: machine-code and assembly language

- Explain the term 'imperative high-level language' and its relationship to low-level programming

- Understand the advantages and disadvantages of machine-code and assembly language programming compared with high-level programming

Early programmable computers

The first computers were conceived in the 1940s during the Second World War for military purposes – famously, Alan Turing and others at Bletchley Park cracked the Enigma Code used by the Germans with the aid of Colossus, one of the very first programmable computers. By the late 1940s, there was still only a handful of computers in existence but a few large companies were becoming interested in using them for commercial purposes such as payroll; one of the first major computer applications. They discovered that a computer could work out employees' pay about 1000 times faster than a human being.

The Colossus computer

These early computers had very limited memory (with each memory cell made out of a vacuum tube the size of a lightbulb). As well as a collection of memory cells, typically consisting of 16 bits, they had an **accumulator** – a special memory location in which all calculations were carried out – and a **control unit** that decoded instructions. There was only one way of programming a computer; entering the binary digits that the computer could understand. This was called **machine code**.

Machine code

In machine code, a typical instruction holds an operation code (opcode) in the first few bits and an operand in the rest of the memory cell. For example, in an 8-bit instruction set, the first 4 bits might hold the opcode and the other 4 bits will hold the operand (the data to be operated on, or the address where the data is held). In reality, at least 32 bits would usually be used to hold an instruction.

Q1: How many different instructions are possible with 4 bits being used for the op code?

For example, some of the machine code instructions in the instruction set for this imaginary computer might take the form given by the following table:

Instruction	Meaning
0000	Load the value stored in memory location specified by the operand into the accumulator
0001	Store the value in the accumulator in memory location specified by the operand
0010	Add the value specified in the operand to the value in the accumulator
0011	Compare the contents of the accumulator with the contents of the location specified by the operand
0100	Jump to the address held in the operand if the accumulator held the lesser value in the last comparison
0101	Jump to the address held in the operand if the accumulator held the greater value in the last comparison
0110	Jump to the address held in the operand
1000	Stop

Now we can write a machine code program!

Example 1

Lines 1-7 below are part of a machine code program to swap the two numbers held in locations 8 and 9.

```
1  0000 1000
2  0001 1010
3  0000 1001
4  0001 1000
5  0000 1010
6  0001 1001
7  1000 0000
8  0001 1001
9  0001 0111
```

4-21

Q2: Fill in a trace table to show the contents of the accumulator and memory locations 8, 9, 10. The first line has been done. The initial contents of location 10 are unknown.

Accumulator	Location 8	Location 9	Location 10
25	25	23	25
etc.			

It's very easy to see how extremely difficult, tedious and error-prone it was to program in machine code. The same operation can be done in Python, for example, with the statement:

```
x,y = y,x
```

This is a good example of **abstraction** – you really don't want to know all the details of how the computer actually achieves the swap, as it distracts from the task to be performed – and you certainly don't want to have to write out and debug all the machine code instructions. In the Python version, all the details have been abstracted away, leaving you free to concentrate on the algorithm (which could be, for example, a sorting algorithm).

Machine code is called a **low-level programming language**, because the code reflects how the computer actually carries out the instruction – it is dependent on the actual architecture of the computer.

Assembly language

The next stage in the development of programming languages was assembly language, another **low-level language**. This had two major improvements:

1. Each opcode was replaced by a mnemonic which gave a good clue to what the operator was actually doing.
2. The operand was replaced by a decimal (or hexadecimal) number.

The program to swap two numbers now looks like this:

```
1  LDA 8      ;load the contents of location 8 into accumulator
2  STO 10     ;store the contents of the accumulator in location 10
3  LDA 9      ;load the contents of location 9 into accumulator
4  STO 8      ;store the contents of the accumulator in location 8
5  LDA 10     ;load the contents of location 10 into accumulator
6  STO 9      ;store the contents of the accumulator in location 9
7  STOP
8  25         ;data
9  23         ;data
```

This was a major improvement on machine code but still involved coding every step that the computer needed to perform to accomplish each task. The set of mnemonics looked something like this:

Instruction	Meaning
LDA	Load the value stored in memory location specified by the operand into the accumulator
STO	Store the value in the accumulator in memory location specified by the operand
ADD	Add the value specified in the memory location specified by the operand to the value in the accumulator
CMP	Compare the contents of the accumulator with the contents of the location specified by the operand
BLT	Jump to the address held in the operand if the accumulator held the lesser value in the last comparison
BGT	Jump to the address held in the operand if the accumulator held the greater value in the last comparison
JMP	Jump to the address held in the operand
STOP	Stop

Q3: Write an assembly language program to add the two numbers in locations 8 and 9 and store the result in location 10.

High-level programming languages

In the 1960s, John Backus and his team at IBM made a hugely significant breakthrough in the development of programming. Backus saw that what was needed was a programming language that enabled programmers to write programs in the same way that they wrote algorithms or mathematical formulae. The first high-level language was born, and they called it **FORTRAN**, short for FORmula TRANslation. Other languages such as ALGOL, BASIC and COBOL soon followed.

In a high-level language, programmers could write statements such as

```
X = (B - C) * D
```

These languages are all examples of **imperative high-level languages**, so-called because each instruction is basically a command to perform some step in the program, which consists of the step-by-step instructions needed to complete the task. They are **high-level** because they enable programmers to think and code in terms of algorithms, without worrying about how each tiny step will be executed in machine code and where each item of data will be stored. Each instruction in a high level language is translated into several low-level language instructions.

The advantages of high-level languages compared to a low-level language include the following:

- They are relatively easy to learn
- It is much easier and faster to write a program in a high-level language
- Programs written in high-level languages are much easier to understand, debug and maintain
- Programs written in a high-level language are not dependent on the architecture of a particular machine – they are machine independent
- There are many built-in library functions available in most high-level languages
- Different high-level languages are often written specifically for a particular class of problem; for example SQL is tailor-made for querying and manipulating databases

The assembly language program on the previous page to swap two numbers would be written using high-level language as:

```
a ← 25
b ← 23
c ← a
a ← b
b ← c
```

Assembly language is still used when the program needs to execute as fast as possible, occupy as little space as possible or manipulate individual bits and bytes. Examples include embedded systems, real-time systems, sensors, mobile phones, device drivers and interrupt handlers.

Exercises

1. (a) A machine code instruction can be split into an opcode part and an operand part.

    (i) What does an opcode represent? [1]

    (ii) What does an operand represent? [1]

  (b) State **two** advantages of writing a program in assembly language over writing a program in machine code. [2]

AQA Comp 2 Qu 2 June 2012

4-21

Chapter 22 – Programming language translators

Objectives

- Understand the role of an assembler, compiler and interpreter

- Explain the difference between compilation and interpretation, and describe situations when both would be appropriate

- Explain why an intermediate language such as bytecode is produced as the final output by some compilers and how it is subsequently used

- Understand the difference between source and object (executable) code

Assembler

In the last chapter we looked at machine code and assembly language. Both of these are **low-level languages**, with each instruction in assembly language almost always being equivalent to one machine code instruction. The machine code instructions that a particular computer can execute (the **instruction set**) are completely dependent on its hardware, and therefore each different type of processor will have a different instruction set and a different assembly language.

Before an assembly language program can be executed, it must be translated into the equivalent machine code. This is done by a program called an **assembler**. The assembler program takes each assembly language instruction and converts it to the 0s and 1s of the corresponding machine code instruction. The input to the assembler is called the **source code** and the output (machine code) the **object code**.

Compiler

A compiler is a program that translates a high-level language such as Visual Basic, C#, Python etc. into machine code. The code written by the programmer, the **source code**, is input as data to the compiler, which scans through it several times, each time performing different checks and building up tables of information needed to produce the final object code. Different hardware platforms will require different compilers, since the resulting object code will be hardware-specific. For example, Windows and the Intel microprocessors comprise one platform, Apple and ARM processors another, so separate compilers are required for each.

The object code can then be saved and run whenever needed without the presence of the compiler.

INPUT	PROCESS	OUPUT
Source code e.g. Python program	Compile	Object code (executable machine code)

Interpreter

An interpreter is a different type of programming language translator. The interpreter software itself contains subroutines to carry out each high-level instruction. Once the programmer has written and saved a program, and instructs the computer to run it, the interpreter looks at each line of the source program, analyses it and, if it contains no syntax errors, calls the appropriate subroutine within its own program code to execute the command.

For example, the following Python program contains an error at line 5.

```
1  a = 1
2  b = 2
3  c = a + b
4  print ("a + b = ", c)
5  e = a - n
6  print ("a - b = ", e)
7  print ("goodbye")
```

When the program runs, it produces the following output:

```
a + b = 3
Traceback (most recent call last):
  File "C:/Users/A Level sample programs/prog1.py", line 5, in <module>
    e = a - n
NameError: name 'n' is not defined
```

The program produces output at line 4, gets as far as line 5 and then crashes.

However, it is not always quite that simple. If we modify the program to introduce a syntax error at line 6, (missing closing bracket) the interpreter does not attempt to run any of the program until this is fixed.

```
1  a = 1
2  b = 2
3  c = a + b
4  print ("a + b = ", c)
5  e = a - b
6  print ("a - b = ", e
7  print ("goodbye")
```

When the program runs, it does not execute any of the code but produces the following output:

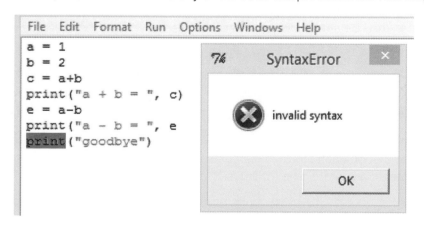

From this we can deduce that the translator has scanned through the whole program checking for certain types of error before executing any of it.

Bytecode

Interpreting each line of code just before executing it has become much less common. Most interpreted languages such as Python and Java use an intermediate representation which combines compiling and interpreting. The resulting **bytecode** is then executed by a **bytecode interpreter**.

The bytecode may be compiled once and for all (as in Java) or each time a change in the source code is detected before execution (as in Python).

A big advantage of bytecode is that you can achieve **platform independence**; any computer that can run Java programs has a **Java Virtual Machine (JVM)**, a piece of software which masks inherent differences between different computer architectures and operating systems. The JVM understands bytecode and converts it into the machine code for that particular computer.

A second advantage of using, for example, Java bytecode is that it acts as an extra security layer between your computer and the program. You can download an untrusted program and you then execute the Java bytecode interpreter rather than the program itself, which guards against any malicious programs.

It is also possible to compile from Python into Java bytecode (using the Jython compiler) and then use the Java interpreter to interpret and execute it.

Advantages and uses of compilers and interpreters

A compiler has many advantages over an interpreter:

- the object code can be saved on disk and run whenever required without the need to recompile. However, if an error is discovered in the program, the whole program has to be recompiled
- the object code executes faster than interpreted code
- the object code produced by a compiler can be distributed or executed without having to have the compiler present
- the object code is more secure, as it cannot be read without a great deal of 'reverse engineering'

A compiler would therefore be appropriate when a program is to be run regularly or frequently, with only occasional change. It is also appropriate when the object code produced by the compiler is going to be distributed or sold to users outside the company that produced the software, since the source code is not present and therefore cannot be copied or amended.

> **Q1:** Why would a company or an individual programmer not want to distribute the source code when they sell a software package?

An interpreter has some advantages over a compiler:

- it is useful for program development as there is no need for lengthy recompilation each time an error is discovered
- it is easier to partially test and debug programs

However, the program may run slower than a compiled program, because each statement has to be translated to machine code each time it is encountered. So if a loop of 10 statements is performed 20 times, all 10 statements are interpreted 20 times.

An interpreter may, for example, be used during program development and when the program is complete and correct, it can be compiled for distribution or regular use within the company. An interpreter may also be used in a student environment when students are learning code, as they can test parts of a program before coding it all.

Exercises

1. A programmer is asked to write a program and can choose between using a low-level language or a high-level procedural language.

   Outline the major difference between these two types of languages, naming an example of each.

   For each language explain:

   • advantages and disadvantages of each one compared to the other

   • what translation software would be used, if applicable

   • a situation when each one would be the most appropriate choice   [10]

2. Explain why an intermediate language such as bytecode is produced as the final output by some compilers and how it is subsequently used.   [5]

3. (a) The high-level language statement

         A := B + 5

   is to be written in assembly language.

   Complete the following assembly language statements, which are to be the equivalent of the above high level language statement. The `Load` and `Store` instructions imply the use of the accumulator register.

   ```
   Load    ............................
   ........................................# 5
   Store   ..........................
   ```
         [3]

   (b) (i) What type of translator is required to translate assembly language statements into machine code?   [1]

   (ii) What type of translator is required to translate a high-level language statement into machine code?   [1]

   AQA Comp2 Qu 3 January 2009

4-22

Chapter 23 – Logic gates

Objectives

- Construct truth tables for a variety of logic gates
- Be familiar with drawing and interpreting logic gate circuit diagrams involving multiple gates
- Complete a truth table for a given logic gate circuit
- Write a Boolean expression for a given logic gate circuit
- Draw an equivalent logic gate circuit for a given Boolean expression

Binary logic

At the most elementary level, an electronic device can only recognise the presence or absence of current or voltage. Either electricity is present or it isn't. This is a switch – on or off, true or false, 1 or 0. With a computer's semiconductor, the voltage at the input and output terminals is measured and is either high or low; 1 or 0. Computers comprise billions of these switches and manipulating these sequences of Ons and Offs can change individual bits.

Electronic logic gates can take one or more inputs and produce a single output. This output can become the input to another gate and a complicated cascaded sequence of logic gates can be implemented to form a circuit in, for example, the CPU.

Simple logic gates and truth tables

4-23

There are a number of different logic gates that are each designed to perform a different operation in terms of output. These are: NOT, AND, OR, XOR, NAND and NOR gates. Each of these gates can be represented by a truth table showing the output given for each possible input or combination of inputs. The first three gates are shown below. Inputs are usually given algebraic letters such as A, B and C and output is usually represented by P or Q.

NOT gate

The NOT gate is represented by the symbol below and inverts the input. The small circle denotes an inverted input.

Using 1s and 0s as inputs to a gate, its operation can summarised in the form of a **truth table**.

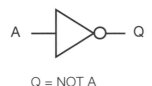

Q = NOT A

Input A	Output Q
0	1
1	0

The Boolean algebraic expression is written: Q = $\overline{A}$ where the overbar ‾ represents NOT.

AND gate

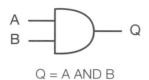

$Q = A \text{ AND } B$

Input A	Input B	Output Q
0	0	0
0	1	0
1	0	0
1	1	1

The Boolean expression for AND is written: $Q = A \cdot B$ where $\cdot$ represents AND.

The truth table reflects the fundamental property of the AND gate: the output of A AND B is 1 only if input A and input B are both 1.

OR gate

$Q = A \text{ OR } B$

Input A	Input B	Output Q
0	0	0
0	1	1
1	0	1
1	1	1

The Boolean expression for OR is written: $Q = A + B$ where $+$ represents OR.

Creating logic gate circuits

Multiple logic gates can be connected to produce an output based on multiple inputs.

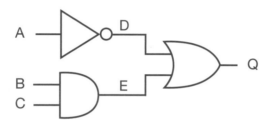

4-23

This circuit can be represented by Q = (NOT A) OR (B AND C) or $Q = \overline{A} + (B \cdot C)$ and shown using the truth table below:

Input A	Input B	Input C	D = NOT A	E = B AND C	Output Q = (NOT A) OR (B AND C)
0	0	0	1	0	1
0	0	1	1	0	1
0	1	0	1	0	1
0	1	1	1	1	1
1	0	0	0	0	0
1	0	1	0	0	0
1	1	0	0	0	0
1	1	1	0	1	1

Q1: Draw a truth table for the following circuit:

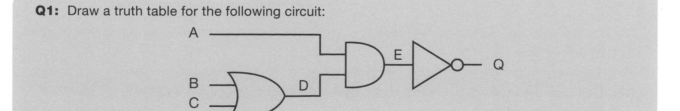

The XOR, NAND and NOR gates

XOR gate

The XOR (*pronounced ex-or*) gate stands for exclusive OR, meaning that the output will be true if one or other input is true, but not both. Compare this to the OR gate, which outputs true if either or both inputs are true.

Q = A XOR B

Input A	Input B	Output Q
0	0	0
0	1	1
1	0	1
1	1	0

The Boolean algebraic expression is written: $Q = A \oplus B$ where the $\oplus$ represents XOR, and is the equivalent of $Q = (A \cdot \overline{B}) + (\overline{A} \cdot B)$. This gate is similar to the OR gate but excludes the condition where A and B are both true. For this reason the OR gate is sometimes referred to as an inclusive OR.

Q2: Show, by drawing a truth table for $P = (A \cdot \overline{B}) + (\overline{A} \cdot B)$, that P = Q, where $Q = A \oplus B$.

The XOR gate performs the function of an addition of the two inputs and combined with an AND gate, will output the carry bit value as well.

NAND gate

The NAND gate is an amalgamation of the AND and NOT gates, which inverts the output of the AND gate. Having a single type of NAND gate that can perform two separate functions can help to reduce development costs if a NAND gate is cheaper than separate AND and NOT gates.

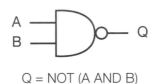

Q = NOT (A AND B)

Input A	Input B	Output Q
0	0	1
0	1	1
1	0	1
1	1	0

The Boolean algebraic expression is written: $Q = \overline{A \cdot B}$.

NOR gate

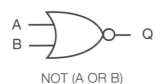

NOT (A OR B)

Input A	Input B	Output Q
0	0	1
0	1	0
1	0	0
1	1	0

The Boolean algebraic expression is written: $Q = \overline{A + B}$. This gate only produces an output of true when both inputs are false.

Q3: Compare the truth table outputs of the AND and NAND gates, and the OR with the NOR. How do these differ?

Q4: Draw a logic circuit for the expression Q = NOT ((A XOR B) AND C), i.e. $Q = \overline{(A \oplus B) \cdot C}$

Exercises

1. (a) Complete the following truth tables for the NAND, NOR and XOR logic gates.

NAND gate

Input A	Input B	Output Q
0	0	
0	1	
1	0	
1	1	

[1]

NOR gate

Input A	Input B	Output Q
0	0	
0	1	
1	0	
1	1	

[1]

XOR gate

Input A	Input B	Output Q
0	0	
0	1	
1	0	
1	1	

[1]

(b) Draw logic circuits for the following Boolean expressions:

   (i) $Q = A \oplus B + \overline{B}$ [3]

   (ii) $Q = \overline{A} \cdot B + C$ [3]

   (iii) $Q = \overline{A + B} + (A \cdot C)$ [3]

2. The figure below shows a logic circuit.

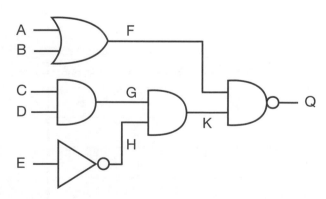

(a) Write the equivalent Boolean expression. [3]

(b) What are the values of F, G, H, K and Q if A, B, C and D and E are all equal 1? [5]

Chapter 24 – Boolean algebra

Objectives

- Be familiar with the use of Boolean identities and De Morgan's laws to manipulate and simplify Boolean expressions

- Write a Boolean expression for a given logic gate circuit, and vice versa

De Morgan's laws

Augustus de Morgan (1806-1871) was a Cambridge Mathematics professor who formulated two theorems or laws relating to logic. These laws can be used to manipulate and simplify Boolean expressions. Although his theoretical work had little practical application in his lifetime, it became of major significance in the next century in the field of digital electronics, in which TRUE and FALSE can be replaced by ON and OFF or the binary numbers 0 and 1.

Using de Morgan's laws, any Boolean function can be converted to one which uses only NAND functions or only NOR functions, and these can be further converted to an expression using all NAND functions or all NOR functions.

Thus, any integrated circuit can be built from just one type of logic gate. This is an advantage in manufacturing where costs can be kept down by using only one type of gate.

De Morgan's first law

$$\overline{A + B} = \overline{A} \cdot \overline{B}$$

The truth of this is clear from the Venn diagram on the right. Suppose we have a variable X defined by

$$X = \overline{A + B}$$

Looking at the Venn diagram, A + B is represented by the white area. Since X is not in A + B, it consists of all the shaded area. This can be defined as everything not in A and not in B, i.e.

$$X = \overline{A} \cdot \overline{B}$$

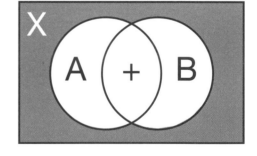

Q1: Complete the following truth table to show that $\overline{A + B} = \overline{A} \cdot \overline{B}$

A	B	$\overline{A}$	$\overline{B}$	A + B	$\overline{A + B}$	$\overline{A} \cdot \overline{B}$
0	0					
0	1					
1	0					
1	1					

De Morgan's second law

$$\overline{A \cdot B} = \overline{A} + \overline{B}$$

Again, looking at the Venn diagram on the right, if

$$X = \overline{A \cdot B}$$

X cannot be in the white area, so must be in the red, orange, or shaded areas. That is, X is either not in A, or not in B, or not in either. This is the definition of

$$X = \overline{A} + \overline{B}$$

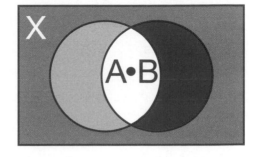

Q2: Complete the following truth table to show that $\overline{A \cdot B} = \overline{A} + \overline{B}$

A	B	$\overline{A}$	$\overline{B}$	A · B	$\overline{A \cdot B}$	$\overline{A} + \overline{B}$
0						
0						
1						
1						

To implement each of de Morgan's laws to find $\overline{A + B}$, or $\overline{A \cdot B}$, follow the three steps:

1. Complement both terms in the expression, e.g. A, B
2. Change AND to OR and OR to AND
3. Invert the result

Drawing circuits using NAND and NOR gates

We saw in the last chapter that a NAND gate is equivalent a combination of an AND gate and a NOT gate.

Q = NOT (A AND B), which is the same as $Q = \overline{A \cdot B}$

Likewise, a NOR gate is a combination of an OR gate and a NOT gate.

Q = NOT (A OR B), which is the same as $Q = \overline{A + B}$

Q3: Using only NAND and NOR gates and with the aid of de Morgan's laws, draw circuits for

(i) $Q = \overline{A} + \overline{B}$

(ii) $Q = \overline{A} \cdot \overline{B}$

4-24

Rules of Boolean algebra

In addition to de Morgan's laws, there are several identities or "rules" which will help you to simplify Boolean expressions. The most useful are listed below.

General rules

1. $X \cdot 0 = 0$
2. $X \cdot 1 = X$
3. $X \cdot X = X$
4. $X \cdot \overline{X} = 0$
5. $X + 0 = X$
6. $X + 1 = 1$
7. $X + X = X$
8. $X + \overline{X} = 1$
9. $\overline{\overline{X}} = X$

Commutative rules

10. $X \cdot Y = Y \cdot X$
11. $X + Y = Y + X$

Associative rules

12. $X \cdot (Y \cdot Z) = (X \cdot Y) \cdot Z$
13. $X + (Y + Z) = (X + Y) + Z$

Distributive rules

14. $X \cdot (Y + Z) = X \cdot Y + X \cdot Z$
15. $(X + Y) \cdot (W + Z) = X \cdot W + X \cdot Z + Y \cdot W + Y \cdot Z$

Absorption rules

16. $X + (X \cdot Y) = X$
17. $X \cdot (X + Y) = X$

Note: $X \cdot Y$ can be written as XY and vice versa.

Example 1

Use de Morgan's laws and the rules of Boolean algebra to simplify the following Boolean expression:

$Q = \overline{\overline{(X \cdot \overline{Y})} \cdot \overline{(\overline{Y} + Z)}}$

Answer:	$Q = (X \cdot \overline{Y}) + \overline{(\overline{Y} + Z)}$	(using de Morgan's second law)
	$= (X \cdot \overline{Y}) + (Y \cdot \overline{Z})$	(using de Morgan's first law)

This is an acceptably simplified answer. It could also be expressed as:

$Q = X \cdot \overline{Y} + Y \cdot \overline{Z}$

Example 2

Use de Morgan's laws to simplify $A \cdot B + \overline{A} + \overline{B}$

Answer:	The expression is equivalent to:	
	$A \cdot B + \overline{A \cdot B}$	(using de Morgan's first law)
	$= 1$	(using rule 8 above)

Q4: Use de Morgan's laws to simplify $\overline{A} + \overline{B} + \overline{(A + B)}$

Example 3

Use Boolean algebra to show that $(A + B) \cdot (A + C) = A + B \cdot C$

Answer: $(A + B) \cdot (A + C) = A \cdot A + B \cdot A + B \cdot C + A \cdot C$ (distributive rule)

                 $= A + B \cdot A + B \cdot C + A \cdot C$ (since A.A = A for rule number 3)

                 $= A + A \cdot B + A \cdot C + B \cdot C$ (commutative rule)

                 $= A \cdot (1 + B + C) + B \cdot C$ (distributive rule)

                 $= A + B \cdot C$ (rules 2 and 6)

The final line makes use of the fact that anything OR'd with 1 is 1.

Q5: Draw a truth table to show that $(A + B) \cdot (A + C) = A + B \cdot C$

Q6: Use Boolean algebra and de Morgan's laws to show that: $A \cdot (A + B) = A$

Example 4

A single output Q is produced from three inputs X, Y and Z. Q is 1 only if X and Y are 1, or Z is 1 and Y is 0.

Write the Boolean expression to represent this circuit.

Answer: There are three separate logic gates involved here: X AND Y, Z AND (NOT Y). The output from these three gates are input to an OR gate.

$Q = (X \cdot Y) + (Z \cdot \overline{Y})$

Represent this equation diagrammatically using a combination of AND, OR and NOT gates.

Answer:

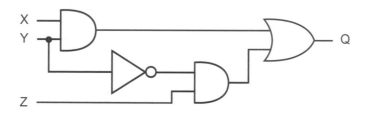

Example 5

Write the Boolean expression corresponding to the following logic circuit.

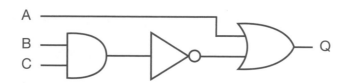

Answer: $A + \overline{(B \cdot C)}$

Q7: Replace two of the gates in the above circuit with a single gate.

Q8: The NAND gate is a universal gate. Can you work out how to make combinations of NAND gates act like NOT, AND and OR gates? (Look up "universal NAND gate" on Google for help!)

Exercises

1. Figure 1 below shows a logic circuit.

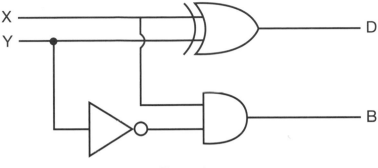

Figure 1

(a) Write a Boolean expression for **D**. [1]

(b) Write a Boolean expression for **B**. [1]

(c) Figure 2 below shows a different logic circuit.

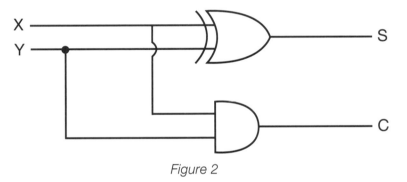

Figure 2

(i) Complete the truth table for the logic circuit shown in Figure 2.

Inputs		Outputs	
X	**Y**	**C**	**S**
0	0		
0	1		
1	0		
1	1		

[2]

(ii) What arithmetic function does the logic circuit in **Figure 2** perform? [1]

(d) Without using a truth table, simplify the Boolean expression below.

$(X + Y) \cdot (X + \overline{Y})$

Show the stages of your working. [3]

AQA Comp 2 Qu 2 January 2012

4-24

Exercises continued

2. (a) Complete the truth tables for the following logic gates. [2]

AND gate			XOR gate		
Input X	Input Y	Output Q	Input X	Input Y	Output Q
0	0		0	0	
0	1		0	1	
1	0		1	0	
1	1		1	1	

(b) A line-following robot has three sensors. It moves along a black line on a white background whilst the following conditions are met:

• the ultrasonic sensor U does not detect any obstacle

• either, but not both, of the infrared sensors L and R are on the black line.

Sensor U returns 1 if it detects an obstacle and 0 if the path is clear.

Sensors L and R each return 1 if they detect black and 0 if they detect white.

A logic circuit will process the input from the sensors and produce an output M.

M should be 1 if the robot is to move and 0 if the robot should stop.

(i) Represent the output M as a Boolean expression. [3]

(ii) The following symbols are used to represent logic gates:

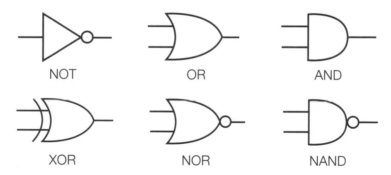

Using a combination of any of the above logic gates draw a logic circuit for this system in the box below. You will not need to use all of the different types of logic gates.

[3]

(c) Apply de Morgan's laws to the following expression and simplify the result.

$$Q = \overline{\overline{A} + \overline{(B \cdot A)}}$$

Show the stages of your working. [3]

AQA Comp 2 Qu 8 June 2012

3. (a) State the names of the logic gates represented by each of the three truth tables below.

Input A	Input B	Output
0	0	0
0	1	0
1	0	0
1	1	1

Logic gate name:

Input A	Input B	Output
0	0	1
0	1	0
1	0	0
1	1	0

Logic gate name:

Input A	Input B	Output
0	0	0
0	1	1
1	0	1
1	1	0

Logic gate name: [3]

(b) Simplify the following Boolean expressions.

    (i) $B \cdot (A + \overline{A})$ [1]

    (ii) $A \cdot B + B$ [1]

    (iii) $\overline{B} \cdot \overline{(\overline{A} + \overline{B})}$ [2]

4-24

(c) Draw a logic circuit for the following Boolean expression:

$$Q = A \oplus B \cdot B$$

You will need to make use of the symbols below when drawing your logic circuit.

[2]

AQA Comp 2 Qu 6 June 2013

Section 5

Computer organisation and architecture

In this section:

5

Chapter 25 – Internal computer hardware

Objectives

- List the basic internal components of a computer system

- Understand the role of the processor, main memory, buses and I/O controllers and how they relate to each other

- Understand the need for, and the means of communication between components

- Explain the difference between von Neumann and Harvard architectures and describe where each is typically used

- Understand the concept of addressable memory

- Describe the stored program concept

Introduction

A computer system has both **internal components** – those within the Central Processing Unit (CPU) – and **external components** such as input/output and storage devices. This chapter describes the internal components. These include:

- processor

- main memory

- address bus, control bus, data bus

- I/O controllers

A simplified block diagram of these components is shown below.

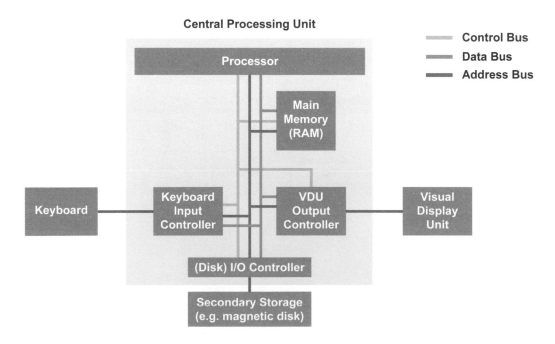

The internal components of a computer

The Processor

The processor responds to and processes the instructions that drive the computer. It contains the **control unit**, the **arithmetic/logic unit (ALU)** and **registers**.

The control unit coordinates and controls all the operations carried out by the computer. It operates by repeating three operations:

Fetch – causes the next instruction to be fetched from main memory

Decode – decodes the instruction

Execute – causes the instruction to be executed

The ALU can perform different sorts of operations on data. **Arithmetic** operations include addition, subtraction, multiplication and division. **Logical** operations consist of comparing one data item with another to determine whether the first data item is smaller than, equal to or greater than the second data item. Bitwise logical operations (AND, OR etc.) and shift operations can manipulate individual bits.

Registers are special memory cells that operate at very high speed. All arithmetic and logical operations take place within registers.

Buses

A bus is a set of parallel wires connecting two or more components of a computer.

The processor is connected to main memory by three separate **buses**. When the CPU wishes to access a particular main memory location, it sends this address to memory on the **address bus**. The data in that location is then returned to the CPU on the **data bus**. Control signals are sent along the **control bus**.

In the figure below, you can see that data, address and control buses connect the processor, memory and I/O controllers. These three buses are known collectively as the **system bus**. Each bus is a shared transmission medium, so that only one device can transmit along a bus at any one time.

Data and control signals travel in both directions between the processor, memory and I/O controllers. Addresses, on the other hand, travel only one way along the address bus: the processor sends the address of an instruction, or of data to be stored or retrieved, to memory or to an I/O controller.

5-25

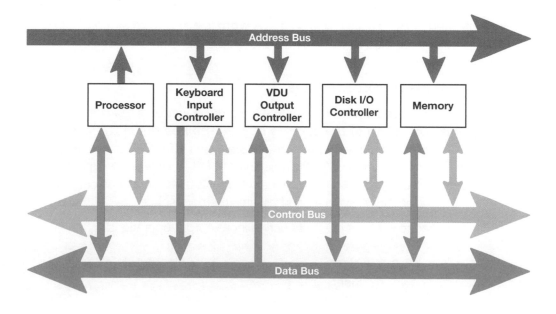

Direction of transmission along the buses

> **Q1:** Which of the data buses in the figure above are uni-directional? Explain why this is the case. What direction does data flow to/from (i) a mouse controller? (ii) a touchscreen controller?

Control bus

The control bus is a bi-directional bus, meaning that signals can be carried in both directions. The data and address buses are shared by all components of the system. Control lines must therefore be provided to ensure that access to and use of the data and address buses by the different components of the system does not lead to conflict.

The purpose of the control bus is to transmit command, timing and specific status information between system components.

Control lines include:

- *Memory Write:* causes data on the data bus to be written into the addressed location
- *Memory Read:* causes data from the addressed location to be placed on the data bus
- *Interrupt request:* indicates that a device is requesting access to the CPU
- *Bus Request:* indicates that a device is requesting the use of the data bus
- *Bus Grant:* indicates that the CPU has granted access to the data bus
- *Clock:* used to synchronise operations
- *Reset:* initialises all components

5-25

Data bus

The data bus, typically consisting of 8, 16, 32 or 64 separate lines provides a bi-directional path for moving data and instructions between system components. ***The width of the data bus is a key factor in determining overall system performance.*** For example, if the data bus is 8 bits wide, and each instruction is 16 bits long, then the processor must access the main memory twice just to fetch the instruction.

Address bus

Memory is divided up internally into units called words. A **word** is a fixed size group of digits, typically 8, 16, 32 or 64 bits, which is handled as a unit by the processor, and different types of processor have different word sizes.

Each word in memory has its own specific address.

When the processor wishes to read a word of data from memory, it first puts the address of the desired word on the address bus. ***The width of the address bus determines the maximum possible memory capacity of the system.*** For example, if the address bus consisted of only 8 lines, then the maximum address it could transmit would be (in binary) 11111111 or 255, giving a maximum memory capacity of 256 (including address 0). A system with a 32-bit address bus can address 2^{32} (4,294,967,296) memory locations giving an addressable memory space of 4GiB.

The address bus is also used to address I/O ports during input/output operations.

> **Q2:** A 64-bit computer with a 64-bit address bus could theoretically address 16.8 million tebibytes. Is this a practical proposition? Justify your answer.

No of address lines, m	Maximum no of addressable cells	Maximum no of addressable cells expressed as a power of two, 2^m
1	2	2^1
2	4	2^2
3	8	2^3
4	16	2^4
8	256	2^8
16	65536	2^{16}
20	1048576	2^{20}
24	16777216	2^{24}
.	.	.
.	.	.
.	.	.
32	4,294,967,296	2^{32}

Relationship between number of address lines m and maximum number of addressable memory cells

I/O Controllers

An I/O controller is a device which interfaces between an input or output device and the processor. Each device has a separate controller which connects to the control bus. I/O controllers receive input and output requests from the processor, and then send device-specific control signals to the device they control. They also manage the data flow to and from the device.

The controller is an electronic circuit board consisting of three parts:

- an interface that allows connection of the controller to the system or I/O bus

- a set of data, command and status registers

- an interface that enables connection of the controller to the cable connecting the device to the computer

An **interface** is a standardised form of connection defining such things as signals, number of connecting pins/sockets and voltage levels that appear at the interface. An example is a Universal Serial Bus (USB) connection, which can be used with many different peripherals.

Memory and the stored program concept

Computers as we know them were first built in the 1940s, and two of the early pioneers were Alan Turing and John von Neumann. The **von Neumann architecture** specifies the basic components of the computer and processor in which a shared memory and bus is used for both data and instructions.

The **stored progam concept** can be defined as follows: *machine code instructions are fetched and executed serially by a processor that performs arithmetic and logical operations*.

- A program must be resident in main memory to be executed

- The machine code instructions are fetched from memory one at a time, decoded and executed in the processor

Virtually all computers today are built on this principle, and so the general structure as shown in the figure below is sometimes referred to as the **von Neumann machine**.

5-25

Memory

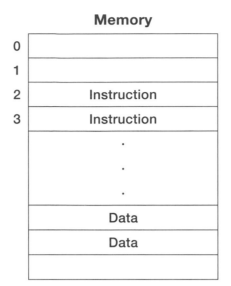

The von Neumann machine

Harvard architecture

The Harvard architecture is a computer architecture with physically separate memories for instructions and data. Harvard architecture is used extensively with embedded **Digital Signal Processing** (DSP) systems.

The two different memories can have different characteristics; for example, in **embedded systems** instructions may be held in read-only memory while data memory requires read-write memory. In some systems, there is much more instruction memory than data memory so the instruction addresses and address bus are wider than the data addresses and data bus. **Embedded systems** include special-purpose computers built in to devices often operating in real time, such as those used in navigation systems, traffic lights, aircraft flight control systems and simulators.

Harvard architecture can be faster than von Neumann architecture because data and instructions can be fetched in parallel instead of competing for the same bus.

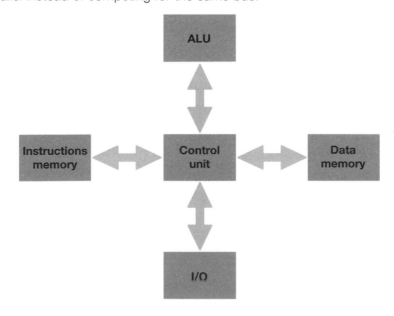

Harvard architecture

Exercises

1. The data bus, control bus and address bus are three important parts of a modern computer.

   (a) In this context, explain what is meant by the term *bus*. [2]

   (b) Fill in the gaps in the paragraph below.

   The data bus can be used to transfer data and .... between the main memory and the processor. The control bus carries control signals. An example of a control signal is ....

   (c) **Figure 1** shows some of the internal components of a computer system.

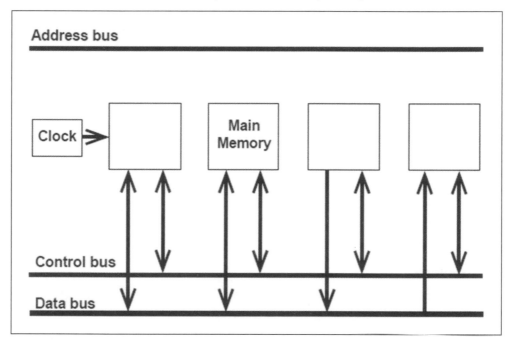

Figure 1

   On **Figure 1** label the following components.

   Processor, Keyboard controller, Graphics controller

   Draw **all** the connections between the address bus and the components. Make sure that you **clearly** show the direction of each connection. [5]

   AQA Comp2 Qu 2 January 2013

2. The program below is written in a low-level language.

```
AB1C  ;Load value 1C into accumulator
BD3E  ;Store contents of accumulator at address 3E
E405  ;Add 5 to the accumulator
BDFF  ;Store contents of accumulator at address FF
AC42  ;Load accumulator with contents of address 42
BD3F  ;Store contents of accumulator at address 3F
```

   (a) What is the name of this language? [1]

   (b) The machine for which this program is written has limited addressing capability.

   What are the highest and lowest memory addresses that can be addressed by this machine? [2]

   (c) What is the width of the address bus in this machine? [1]

Chapter 26 – The processor

Objectives

- Explain the role and operation of the processor and its major components

- Describe the Fetch-Execute cycle

- Describe the factors affecting processor performance

Components of the processor

The processor components were briefly described in the last chapter – here their operation is described in more detail.

Arithmetic Logic Unit (ALU)

The ALU performs arithmetic and logical operations on the data. It can perform instructions such as ADD, SUBTRACT, MULTIPLY, DIVIDE on fixed or floating point numbers. It can also perform shift operations, shifting bits to the left or right within a register. It can carry out Boolean logic operations, comparing two values and using operators such as AND, OR, NOT, XOR.

Control Unit

The Control Unit controls and coordinates the activities of the CPU, directing the flow of data between the CPU and other devices. It accepts the next instruction, breaks down its processing into several sequential steps such as fetching addresses and data from memory, manages its execution and stores the resulting data back in memory or registers.

The system clock

The system clock generates a series of signals, switching between 0 and 1 billions of times per second and synchronising CPU operations. A 3GHz processor's clock ticks three billion times per second. Each CPU operation starts as the clock changes from 0 to 1 (or in some systems from 1 to 0), and the CPU cannot perform operations faster than the clock cycle (the time the clock takes to go from 0 to 1 and back to 0). Some CPU operations take multiple clock cycles.

General-purpose registers

There are typically up to 16 general purpose registers in the CPU. All arithmetic, logical or shift operations take place in registers, which are very fast memory numbered, for example, R0 to R15.

For example, instructions to add the value held in location 164 to the number held in location 150 and store the result in location 170 might take the form:

Load contents of 150 into R1

Add contents of 164 to R1

Store contents of R1 in 170

An **accumulator** is another word for a general purpose register, generally only used when there is just a single register in which to store the result of each calculation or logical expression. Although most modern computers have many registers, some special-purpose processors still use a single accumulator, in order to simplify the design.

Dedicated registers

These include:

- the **program counter (PC)**, which holds the address of the next instruction to be executed. This may be the next instruction in a sequence of instructions, or, if the current instruction is a branch or jump instruction, the address to jump to, (copied from the current instruction register to the PC).

- the **current instruction register (CIR)**, which holds the current instruction being executed.

- the **memory address register (MAR)**, which holds the **address** of the memory location from which data (or an instruction) is to be fetched or to which data is to be written.

- the **memory buffer register (MBR)**, which is used to temporarily store the **data** read from or written to memory. It is also sometimes known as the **memory data register**.

- the **status register (SR)**, which contains bits that are set or cleared depending on the result of an instruction. For example, one bit will be set if an overflow has occurred, other bits will indicate whether the result of the last instruction was negative, zero or caused a carry.

The following block diagram shows these components.

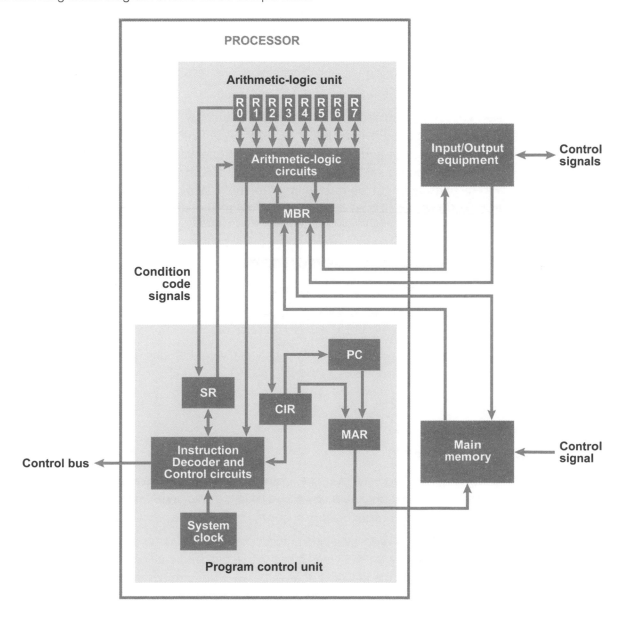

5-26

The Fetch-Execute cycle

The sequence of operations involved in executing an instruction can be divided into three phases – **fetching**, **decoding** and **executing** it. This cycle is repeated over and over as each instruction of the program is executed.

How the registers are used in the Fetch-Execute cycle

(Fetch phase)

1. The address of the next instruction is copied from the program counter (PC) to the memory address register (MAR). The address is sent via the address bus to main memory.

2. The instruction held at that address is returned along the data bus to the memory buffer register (MBR). Simultaneously, the content of the PC is incremented so that it holds the address of the next instruction.

3. The contents of the MBR are copied to the current instruction register (CIR).

(Decode phase)

4. The instruction held in the CIR is decoded. The instruction is split into opcode and operand and the opcode is used to determine the type of instruction and what hardware to use to execute it. Additional data is fetched if necessary, and passed to the registers.

(Execute phase)

5. The instruction is executed, using the ALU if necessary, and results are stored in the accumulator, general purpose register or memory.

Q1: Draw a flowchart showing the steps in the fetch-execute cycle.

Q2: Assume that each machine code instruction is held in one word of memory. When a sequence of instructions is performed, at Step 2 of the Fetch phase above, the PC is incremented by 1 to point to the instruction in the next word of memory. When would the PC not simply be incremented by 1 in order to hold the address of the next instruction?

Factors affecting processor performance

The main factors affecting processor performance are:

- The number of **cores** linked together on a single chip
- The amount and type of cache memory
- Clock speed
- Word length
- Address bus width
- Data bus width

Number of cores

In a traditional computer (von Neumann machine) instructions are fetched and executed one at a time in a serial manner. However, many computers nowadays have multiple cores, having for example, a **dual-core** or **quad-core** processor.

Each core is theoretically able to process a different instruction at the same time with its own fetch-execute cycle, making it two or even four times faster with a quad-core chip. However, although a dual-core processor has twice the power, it does not always perform twice as fast, because the software may not be able to take full advantage of both processors.

5-26

Amount and type of cache memory

Cache is a very small amount of expensive, very fast memory inside or very near to the CPU. When an instruction is fetched from main memory it is copied into the cache so if it is needed again soon after, it can be fetched from cache, which is much quicker than going back to main memory. As cache fills up, unused instructions or data still being held are replaced with more recent ones.

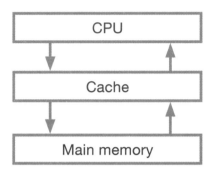

There are different "levels" of cache:

- Level 1 cache is extremely fast but small (between 2-64KB)
- Level 2 cache is fairly fast and medium-sized (256KB-2MB)
- Some CPU's also have Level 3 cache

Clock speed

All processor activities begin on a clock pulse, although some activities may take more than one clock cycle to complete. One clock cycle per second = 1 Hertz (Hz), and clock speed is measured in Gigahertz (GHz), 1 billion cycles per second. Typical speeds for a PC are between 2 and 4 GHz. The greater the clock speed, the faster instructions will be executed.

5-26

Word length

The word size of a computer is the number of bits that the CPU can process simultaneously. Bits may be grouped into 8-, 16-, 32-, 64- or 128-bit 'words', and processed as a unit during input and output, arithmetic and logic instructions. A processor with a 32-bit word size will operate faster than a processor with a 16-bit word size, and word size is a major factor in determining the speed of a processor. Typical word lengths are 32 or 64 bits.

Address bus and data bus width

Both the addresses of data and instructions, and the data and instructions themselves, are transmitted along buses. The width of the address bus determines the maximum memory address that can be directly referenced. For example, if the width of the address bus is 16 bits, the maximum address that can be transmitted is 11111111 11111111 in binary which is 2^{16} - 1 or 65,535. In all, 65,536 addresses, from 0 to 65,535, can be referenced. In order to send larger addresses, say up to 2^{32} - 1, the address needs to be sent in two groups of 16 bits, which has a detrimental effect on performance. Increasing the width of the address bus would allow more memory locations to be accessed.

The width of the data bus determines how many bits can be transferred simultaneously. This is usually but not always the same as the word size of the computer. Not all processors with a 32-bit word for example have a 32-bit data bus, and so the data may have to be fetched in two groups of 16 bits. Increasing the bus size to 32 bits will therefore increase performance.

The role of interrupts (A Level only)

An **interrupt** is a signal sent by a software program or a hardware device to the CPU. A software interrupt occurs when an application program terminates or requests certain services from the operating system. A hardware interrupt may occur, for example, when an I/O operation is complete or an error such as 'Printer out of paper' occurs.

When the CPU receives an interrupt signal, it suspends execution of the running program or process and puts the values of each register and the program counter onto the system stack, while an **Interrupt Service Routine** is called to deal with the interrupt. Depending on the type of interrupt, a particular routine will be run in order to service it. Once the interrupt has been serviced, the original values of the registers are retrieved from the stack and the fetch-execute cycle resumes from the point that it left off. A test for the presence of interrupts is carried out at the end of each instruction cycle.

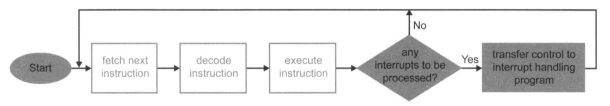

Exercises

1. (a) State the full names of two of the special purpose registers that are used in the fetch part of the fetch-execute cycle.

Register 1 ....

Register 2 .... [2]

(b) Figure 1 below is an incomplete diagram of the fetch-execute cycle.

Describe the missing steps 1, 2b and 4 using either register transfer notation or written description. Steps 2a and 2b occur at the same time.

Figure 1

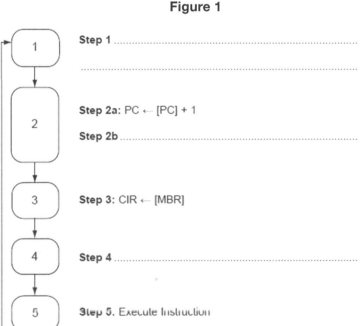

Step 1 ....

....

Step 2a: PC ← [PC] + 1

Step 2b ....

Step 3: CIR ← [MBR]

Step 4 ....

Step 5. Execute Instruction

[3]

AQA Comp 2 Qu 2 June 2013

5-26

Exercises continued

2. **Figure 2** below shows an incomplete diagram of the components of a processor.

Figure 2

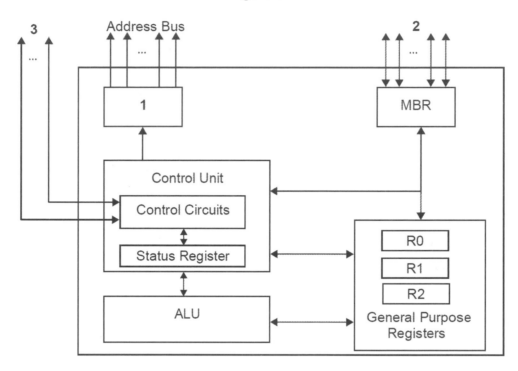

(a) Provide full names for the components numbered 1 to 3 in Figure 2 by completing the table below.

Component number	Component name
1	
2	
3	

[3]

(b) What is the role of the Control Unit?   [1]

(c) State the full name of the processor component that would perform subtraction and comparison operations.   [1]

(d) What is meant by the term *register*?   [1]

(e) State **one** example of when the status register might have a bit set.   [1]

AQA Comp 2 Qu 3 January 2012

5-26

Chapter 27 – The processor instruction set

Objectives

- Understand the term 'processor instruction set'

- Learn that instructions consist of an opcode and one or more operands, where an operand could be a value, a memory address or a register

- Understand and apply immediate and direct addressing modes

The processor instruction set

Each different type of processor has its own instruction set, comprising all the instructions which are supported by its hardware. The instruction set of a typical computer includes the following types of instructions:

- **Data transfer** such as LOAD, STORE

- **Arithmetic operations** such as ADD, SUBTRACT

- **Comparison operators** to compare two values

- **Logical operators** – AND, OR, NOT, XOR

- **Branching** – conditional and unconditional

- **Logical** – shift bits right or left

- **Halt**

Format of a machine code instruction

The basic structure of a machine code instruction may take the format shown below:

Operation code		Operand(s)							
Basic machine operation						Addressing mode			
0	1	0	0	0	1	0	1	0	0	0	0	0	0	1	1

The number of bits allocated to the **operation code** (opcode) and the **operand** will vary according to the architecture and word size of the particular processor type. The above example shows an instruction held in one 16-bit word. In this particular machine, all operations are assumed to take place in a single register called the **accumulator**.

In more complex architectures, each machine code instruction may occupy up to 32 bits and allow for two operands, for example specifying that:

- a number stored at address 578 is to be loaded into register 3

- the number stored at address 580 is to be added to the contents of register 1

- the number in register 6 is to be stored in address 600

5-27

Addressing modes

The operation code (**opcode**) consists of binary digits representing the basic operation such as ADD or LOAD, and a 2-digit code representing the **addressing mode**. We will show examples of just two addressing modes – **immediate** and **direct** addressing. These two addressing modes could be indicated by, for example, 00 or 01 in the two 'addressing mode' bits. (Note that real processors have more than two addressing modes so two or more bits would be required.)

In **immediate addressing**, the operand is the **actual value** to be operated on, say 3 or 75.

In **direct addressing**, the operand holds the **memory address** of the value to be operated on.

Example: Suppose that the operation code 010001, with addressing mode 00, means "Load the operand into the accumulator".

The instruction below with addressing mode 00, in this example meaning **immediate** addressing, will result in the actual value 3 being loaded into the accumulator.

0	1	0	0	0	1	0	0	0	0	0	0	0	0	1	1

Q1: Suppose that the opcode 010000 means STORE and the addressing mode 01 indicates direct addressing.

Describe the operation that will be performed by the following machine code instruction:
010000 01 00100001

5-27

A simple model

In this course, a simple model will be used in which the addressing mode is incorporated into the bits allocated to the opcode. The opcode will therefore define both the basic machine code operation and the addressing mode.

For example, in this model an 8-bit instruction will be represented as follows:

Opcode		Operand
Basic machine operation	**Addressing mode**	
001	0	0110

Assuming that the code 001 means ADD, and addressing mode 0 means immediate addressing, the above instruction means "Add the number 6 to the contents of the accumulator".

Q2: Suppose that the opcode 010 means LOAD and the addressing mode 1 indicates direct addressing.

Describe the operation that will be performed by the following machine code instruction:
0101 1100

Q3: What is the maximum value of the operand that can be represented in 4 bits?

Q4: How many different opcodes incorporating an addressing mode can be represented in 4 bits?

Assembly language instructions

Machine code was the first "language" used to enter programs by early computer programmers. The next advance in programming was to use mnemonics instead of binary codes, and this was called **assembly code** or **assembly language**. Each assembly language instruction translates into one machine code instruction.

Different mnemonic codes are used by different manufacturers, so there are several versions of assembly language.

Typical statements in machine code and assembly language are:

Machine code	Assembly code	Meaning
0100 1100	LDA #12	Load the number 12 into the accumulator
0010 0010	ADD #2	Add the number 2 to the contents of the accumulator
0111 1111	STO 15	Store the result from the accumulator in location 15

The # symbol in this assembly language program signifies that the immediate addressing mode is being used.

Q5: Write a statement in a high level language which performs an operation equivalent to the three statements in the above machine code program, with the result being stored in a location called TOTAL.

Q6: Write a machine code program, and an equivalent assembly language program, to add the contents of locations 10 and 11 and store the result in location 14.

5-27

Exercises

1. A computer with a 16-bit word length uses an instruction set with 6 bits for the opcode, including the addressing mode.

    (a) What is an *instruction set*? [1]

    (b) How many instructions could be included in the instruction set of this computer? [1]

    (c) What is the largest number that can be used as data in the instruction? [1]

    (d) What would be the effect of increasing the space allowed for the opcode by 2 bits? [2]

    (e) What would be the benefits of increasing the word size of the computer? [2]

2. The high-level language statement

        X = Y + 6

    is to be written in assembly language.

    Complete the following assembly language statements, which are to be the equivalent of the above high level language statement. The LOAD and STORE instructions imply the use of the accumulator register.

        LOAD ....
        ....#6
        STORE ....

    [3]

Exercises continued

3. **Figure 1** and **Figure 2** show different versions of the same program.

Figure 1			Figure 2		
(x)	(y)	(z)	(x)	(y)	(z)
200	LOAD	7	200	01010110	00000111
201	ADD	3	201	11010000	00000011
202	ADD	6	202	11010000	00000110
203	STORE	255	203	11110000	11111111

(a) What type of programming language is shown in Figure 2? [1]

(b) In both figures there is a column labelled **(x)**

What would be a suitable heading for this column? [1]

(c) In both figures the instruction is split into two parts.

What are the names of the instruction parts in columns **(y)** and **(z)**? [2]

(d) What is the relationship between the instructions in **Figure 1** and **Figure 2**? [1]

AQA Comp 2 Qu 4 June 2011

5-27

Chapter 28 – Assembly language

Objectives

- Use basic machine code operations expressed in mnemonic-form assembly language

- Understand and apply immediate and direct addressing modes

Assembly language

Assembly language uses mnemonics to represent the operation codes and addresses. Typically, 2-, 3- or 4-character mnemonics are used to represent all the machine code instructions. The **assembler** then translates the assembly language program into machine code for execution.

The following table shows typical mnemonics for data transfer, arithmetic, branch and compare instructions in the instruction set of a particular computer.

LDR Rd, <memory ref>	Load the value stored in the memory location specified by <memory ref> into register d.
STR Rd, <memory ref>	Store the value that is in register d into the memory location specified by <memory ref>.
ADD Rd, Rn, <operand>	Add the value specified in <operand> to the value in register n and store the result in register d.
SUB Rd, Rn, <operand>	Subtract the value specified by <operand> from the value in register n and store the result in register d.
MOV Rd, <operand>	Copy the value specified by <operand> into register d.
CMP Rn, <operand>	Compare the value stored in register n with the value specified by <operand>.
B <label>	Always branch to the instruction at position <label> in the program.
B<condition> <label>	Conditionally branch to the instruction at position <label> in the program if the last comparison met the criteria specified by the <condition>. Possible values for <condition> and their meaning are: EQ: Equal to, NE: Not equal to, GT: Greater than, LT: Less than.
HALT	Stops the execution of the program.

Table 1

<operand> can be interpreted in two different ways, depending on whether the first symbol is a # or an R:

- # – use the decimal value specified after the #, e.g. #27 means use the decimal number 27

- Rn – use the value stored in register n, e.g. R6 means use the value stored in register 6.

- Assume the available registers that the programmer can use are numbered 0 to 7.

Q1: Write two instructions to

(i) compare the value held in register 1 with the integer 100.

(ii) branch to the instruction labelled .loop1 if register 1 does not contain 100.

Examples

All the examples below use instructions from Table 1.

Data transfer and arithmetic operations

Add 12 to the number stored in memory location 52 and save the result in memory location 53.

```
LDR R0, 52      ;Load the contents of location 52 into R0
ADD R0, R0, #12 ;Add 12 to R0
STR R0, 53      ;Store the result in location 53
```

Compare and branch instructions

The value in a memory location can be compared with the value in a register using a CMP (compare) instruction. The code can then be made to conditionally branch to a given label in the program depending on whether the number held in the register was Equal to (BEQ), Not Equal to (BNE), Greater Than (BGT) or Less Than (BLT) the number held in the memory location.

Example: Compare the two numbers held in memory locations 35 and 40. If the value in location 35 is greater than the value in location 40, branch to the instruction labelled next, where the program will halt.

```
        LDR R1, 35
        LDR R2, 40
        CMP R1, R2
        BGT next
        ...
        ...
next:   HALT
```

Example: Write the assembly language equivalent of the following high-level language instructions, explaining each assembly language instruction used.

```
A ← 0
repeat
   A ← A + 1
until A = 99
```

Assembly language code:

```
    MOV R0, #0      ;Load the initial value of A into Register 0
loop:
    ADD R0, R0, #1  ;Add 1 to Register 0
    CMP R0, #99     ;Compare R0 with the value 99
    BNE loop        ;Branch if not equal to label loop.
```

Q2: Register 1 holds the value 200 in the 8-bit operand. The format of the ADD instruction is:

ADD Rd, Rn, <operand>	Add the value specified in <operand> to the value in register n and store the result in register d.

What will be the bit pattern held in R2 after execution of the following statement?

ADD R2, R1, 64

What other register will be changed? (Hint: Look back at the **dedicated registers** on page 133.)

5-28

Logical bitwise operators

Assembly language instructions for logical operations are shown in Table 2 below.

`AND Rd, Rn, <operand>`	Perform a bitwise logical AND operation between the value in register n and the value specified by `<operand>` and store the result in register d.
`ORR Rd, Rn, <operand>`	Perform a bitwise logical OR operation between the value in register n and the value specified by `<operand>` and store the result in register d.
`EOR Rd, Rn, <operand>`	Perform a bitwise logical exclusive or (XOR) operation between the value in register n and the value specified by `<operand>` and store the result in register d.
`MVN Rd, <operand>`	Perform a bitwise logical NOT operation on the value specified by `<operand>` and store the result in register d.
`LSL Rd, Rn, <operand>`	Logically shift left the value stored in register n by the number of bits specified by `<operand>` and store the result in register d.
`LSR Rd, Rn, <operand>`	Logically shift right the value stored in register n by the number of bits specified by `<operand>` and store the result in register d.
`HALT`	Stop the execution of the program.

Table 2

The instructions OR, NOT, AND and XOR (exclusive OR) produce the following results:

		OR	NOT	AND	XOR
Inputs	A	1010	1010	1010	1010
	B	1100		1100	1100
Result		1110	0101	1000	0110

The NOT function can be used to find the two's complement of a number:

A	0110 0111
NOT A	1001 1000
Add 1	1
2's complement	1001 1001

The assembly language instructions to carry out this operation with B indicating a binary, rather than a decimal value, would be something like:

```
MVN R1, #01100111B    ;perform NOT operation, store result in R1
ADD R1, R1, #1        ;add 1 to result in R1
```

The OR function can be used to set certain bits to 1 without affecting the other bits in the binary code. For example, a system has eight lights that can be turned on (output 1) or off (output 0), controlled by an 8-bit binary code. At present, lights 1 to 4 are on. We now wish to turn on lights 5 and 7 as well.

Light numbers	1	2	3	4	5	6	7	8
Present output	1	1	1	1	0	0	0	0
OR with	0	0	0	0	1	0	1	0
Result	1	1	1	1	1	0	1	0

5-28

The assembly language code for this operation could be:

```
LDR R2, LIGHT                   ;load contents of LIGHT into R2
ORR R3, R2, #00001010B          ;OR with binary 00001010 and store in R3
STR R3, LIGHT                   ;Store result back in LIGHT
```

The AND function can be used to mask out certain bits of a number. For example, if we input the ASCII character 3 at the keyboard, the ASCII pattern 00110011 is input. In order to change this to a pure binary digit, we need to mask out the first 4 bits.

```
LDR R2, NUM                     ;load ASCII digit from NUM into R2
AND R3, R2, #00001111B          ;AND with binary 00001111 and store in R3
STR R3, NUM                     ;Store result back in NUM
```

Q3: Write an instruction to clear bit 2 in register 3 and store the result in register 4.
(Bit 2 is the second bit from the left.)

Logical shift operations

A logical shift right causes the least significant bit to be shifted into the **carry** bit and a zero moves in to occupy the vacated space.

Suppose R1 contained the following bit pattern:

| 0 | 1 | 0 | 0 | 0 | 1 | 1 | 1 | | 0 | (carry bit) |

After the instruction

LSR R2, R1, #1   ;Logically shift right the value in R1 by 1 place, store in R2

R2 will hold the bit pattern

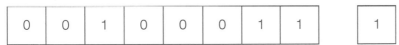

| 0 | 0 | 1 | 0 | 0 | 0 | 1 | 1 | | 1 |

This can be used for examining the least significant bit of a number. After the operation, the carry bit can be tested and a conditional branch instruction executed.

Q4: Where is the carry bit to be found? (Hint: Look back at the **dedicated registers** on page 133.)

Q5: Register 2 holds the following bit pattern.

| 0 | 1 | 0 | 1 | 0 | 0 | 1 | 1 |

What will be the contents of R2 and R3 after execution of the following instruction?

LSL R3, R2, #3   ; *(add a description of the instruction here)*

5-28

Exercises

1. Memory locations FIRST, SECOND and THIRD each contain an integer. With the aid of the following trace table, explain what the following assembly code does.

    ```
            LDR R0, FIRST
            LDR R1, SECOND
            LDR R2, THIRD
            CMP R0, R1
            BGT label1
            LDR R0, SECOND
    label1:
            CMP R0, R2
            BGT label2
            LDR R0, THIRD
    label2:
            STR R0, M
    ```
    [3]

    Trace table:

FIRST	SECOND	THIRD	R0	R1	R2	M
17	25	19				

    The following mnemonic codes have been used:

LDR Rd, <memory ref>	Load the value stored in the memory location specified by <memory ref> into register d.
STR Rd, <memory ref>	Store the value that is in register d into the memory location specified by <memory ref>.
CMP Rn, <operand>	Compare the value stored in register n with the value specified by <operand>.
B<condition> <label>	Conditionally branch to the instruction at position <label> in the program if the last comparison met the criteria specified by the <condition>. Possible values for <condition> and their meaning are: EQ: Equal to, NE: Not equal to, GT: Greater than, LT: Less than.

2. (a) In a particular machine code, the opcode is stored in 6 bits and the operand is stored in 12 bits. What is the maximum number of operations in the machine's instruction set? [1]

    (b) Explain, with the aid of examples, the difference between immediate and direct addressing. [4]

Exercises continued

3. A single accumulator microprocessor supports the assembly language instructions:

```
LOAD    memory reference
ADD     memory reference
STORE   memory reference
```

An example instruction is:

```
                    LOAD  4
```

which would copy the contents of the referenced memory location 4 into the accumulator register.

(a) (i) Identify which part of the instruction is the *operand* and which part is the *opcode* by writing the words operand and opcode in the two boxes below.

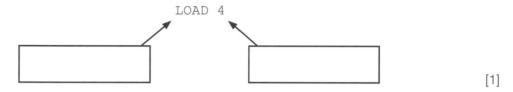

[1]

   (ii) The accumulator is a general purpose register.

   What is a *register*?   [1]

(b) Using the assembly language instructions, write an assembly language program that adds together the values stored in memory locations 12 and 13, storing the resulting total in memory location 14.   [3]

AQA Comp 2 Qu 5 January 2010

5-28

4. A process can only begin if bits 0, 3, 5 and 6 of an 8-bit accumulator are set to 1.
   The status of the other bits has no effect on the process. Write the key assembly language instructions to check whether the process can take place.   [3]

Chapter 29 – Input-output devices

Objectives

- Learn the main characteristics and principles of operation of:
  - Barcode reader
  - Digital camera
  - Laser printer
  - RFID

- Understand the purposes and suitability of these devices

Barcodes

Barcodes first started appearing on grocery items in the 1970s, and today, they are used for identification in thousands of applications from tracking parcels, shipping cartons, passenger luggage, blood, tissue and organ products around the world to the sale of items in shops and the recording of the details of people attending events.

A handheld barcode scanner used for scanning medical samples

There are two different types of barcode: Linear barcodes such as the one shown above and 2D barcodes such as the **Quick Response (QR)** code, which can hold more information than the 1D barcode.

A 2D barcode

2D barcodes are used for example in ticketless entry to concerts, or access through gates to board a Eurostar train or passenger airline. They are also used in mobile phone apps which enable the user to take a photo of the code which may then provide them with further information such as a map of their location, product details or a website URL.

5-29

Barcode readers

There are four different barcode readers available, each using a slightly different technology for reading and decoding a barcode. The four types are pen-type readers, laser scanners, CCD readers and camera-based readers.

Pen-type readers

In a pen-type reader, a light source and a photo diode are placed next to each other in the tip of a pen. To read a barcode, the tip of the pen is dragged across all the bars at an even speed. The photo diode measures the intensity of the light reflected back from the light source and generates a waveform that is used to measure the widths of the bars and spaces in the barcode. Dark bars in the barcode absorb light and white spaces reflect light so that the voltage waveform generated by the photo diode, once converted from analogue to digtal, is an exact duplicate of the bar and space pattern in the barcode. The simplest encoding translates areas of light and dark as 1s and 0s. These can be used to create ASCII character codes for an alphanumeric string, which may be, for example, a product code or library book number.

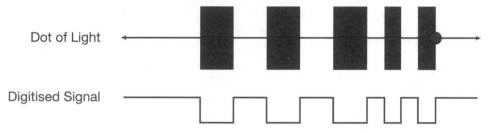

Digital representation of a barcode

5-29

Q1: Using 7-bit the ASCII code on page 73, how would the digital wave pattern above be translated, assuming a black bar equated to a 1 and a white space, a 0?

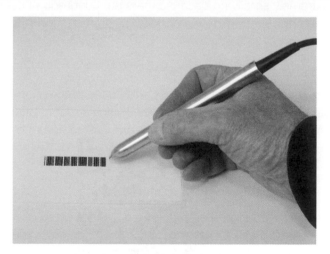

A pen or wand barcode scanner

Because of their simple design, the pen-type scanner is the most durable type of barcode scanner, and can be tightly sealed against dust, dirt, and other environmental hazards. However, their applications are limited because they must come into direct contact with a barcode to read it.

Because of their small size and low weight, this type of barcode scanner is ideally suited for use with portable (laptop) computers or very low volume scanning applications.

Laser scanners

Laser scanners work in the same way as pen scanners except they use a laser beam as the light source. The laser reflects off a moving mirror which allows the barcode to be read in many different positions. They are available in a variety of forms, the most familiar being the in-counter units in supermarkets. They are reliable and economical for low-volume applications.

Laser scanner

5-29

CCD (Charge-Coupled Device) readers

CCD readers use an array of hundreds of tiny light sensors lined up in a row in the head of the reader. Each sensor measures the intensity of the light immediately in front of it. Each individual light sensor in the CCD reader is extremely small and because there are hundreds of sensors lined up in a row, a voltage pattern identical to the pattern in a barcode is generated in the reader by sequentially measuring the voltages across each sensor in the row.

Camera-based readers

A camera-based **imaging scanner** uses a camera and image processing techniques to decode a 1D or 2D bar code. An imaging scanner can read a barcode on any surface, printed or onscreen, and can also read a code that is damaged or poorly printed. Image processing has to be carried out by the software as the barcode might be at any rotation or variety of distances from the scanner. They are used in multiple applications such as:

- age verification by scanning an individual's driving licence

- couponing – a 2D barcode coupon is emailed to a customer, which can be scanned from their phone screen at the POS (Point of Sale). Unique codes for each customer and promotion can be stored in the bar code, so that tracking coupon usage is easy

- event ticketing – tickets can be issued electronically and then scanned off a phone screen

Consumers can use a cell phone to scan a QR code which can, for example:

- display a catalogue of movies or DVDs

- play an MP3 when scanned

- display nutrition information about a product

Digital cameras

A digital camera uses a **CCD** or **CMOS** (Complementary Metal Oxide Semiconductor) sensor comprising millions of tiny light sensors arranged in a grid. When the shutter opens, light enters the camera and projects an 'image' onto the sensor at the back of the lens. Like the CCD barcode reader, each sensor measures the brightness of each pixel, turns light into electricity and stores the amount of charge as binary data. The image on the camera's screen is a greyscale representation of what the sensors are 'seeing'. To record colour, the sensors are often placed under a mosaic of red, green and blue filters to separate out the different colour wavelengths. The processor can then approximate binary values for the three RGB channels of each individual pixel based on the values of neighbouring pixels. The binary data is recorded onto the camera's memory card so that the image can be reproduced using suitable software.

A CCD sensor tends to produce higher quality images and they are used in higher end cameras. They are also more reliable since the technology has been around for much longer. This however, is at the cost of power consumption, using up to 100 times that of a CMOS sensor.

> **Q2:** Suggest a suitable sensor type for use in a mobile phone camera and give a reason why.

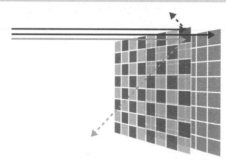

Bayer colour filter applied to a sensor array

5-29

Radio Frequency Identification (RFID)

In much the same way as barcodes, RFID tags are increasingly being used to identify and track everything from household products and cars to bank cards and animals. The difference however, is that an RFID tag can be read without line of sight and from up to 300 metres away. They can also pass stored data from the tag to the receiver and vice versa. An RFID chip consists of a small microchip transponder and an antenna. The microchip at the centre of the image below can be manufactured to be less than 1mm in size but the antenna must be larger in order for it to communicate with a base unit. This can increase the size of the smallest tags to about that of a large grain of rice. These can be embedded in special capsules and injected under the skin for the identification of pets.

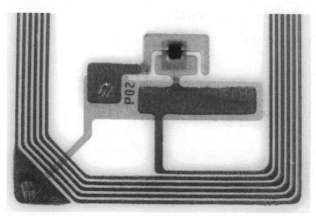

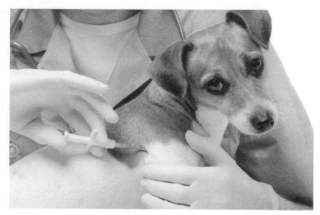

Passive and active tags

Active tags are physically larger as they include a battery to power the tag so that it actively transmits a signal for a reader to pick up. These are used to track things likely to be read from further away, such as cars as they pass through a motorway toll booth or runners in a marathon as they pass mile markers. Passive tags are much cheaper to produce as they do not have a battery. They rely on the radio waves emitted from a reader up to a metre away to provide sufficient electromagnetic power to the card using its coiled antenna. Once energised, the transponder inside the RFID tag can send its data to the reader nearby. These are most common in tagging items such as some groceries, music CDs, and for smart cards such as Transport for London's Oyster Card or a contactless bank card.

Laser printer

Laser printers offer high-quality, high-speed printing. Their function is similar to that of a photocopier, using powdered ink called toner. The printer generates a bitmap image of the printed page and using a laser unit and mirror, 'draws' a negative, reverse image onto a negatively charged drum. The laser light causes the affected areas of the drum to lose their charge. The drum then rotates past a toner hopper to attract charged toner particles onto the areas which have not been lasered. The particles are transferred onto a sheet of paper and then bonded onto it using pressure and heat.

Laser printers are becoming increasingly affordable and are frequently used as home printers, in businesses and in professional printing services. Colour laser printers are far more expensive to run than black and white versions. They contain four toner cartridges (Cyan, Magenta, Yellow and Black or CMYK) and the paper must go through a similar process to the black-only printer four times; once for each colour. The usage of laser printers for print jobs other than text is limited by the quality of the print produced, which at about 1200 dpi makes photorealistic prints impossible and best left to inkjet printers.

5-29

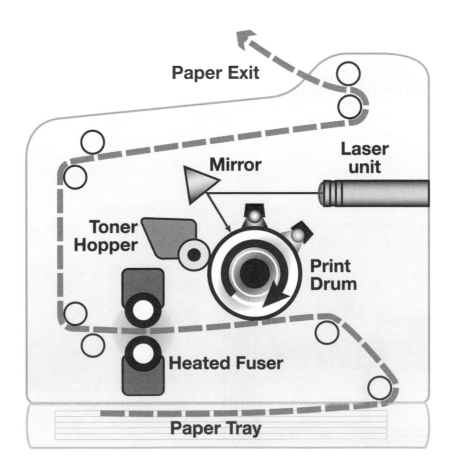

Exercises

1. A supermarket uses a computerised stock control system. Each product is identified by a unique product code which is printed on the product as a bar code. The bar codes are input into the stock control system at the till using a bar code reader. One of the digits in the bar code is a check digit.

   (a) Describe the principles of operation of a bar code reader, **excluding** the use of the check digit. [4]

   (b) Explain the purpose of the check digit. [1]

   (c) Some unpackaged items such as loose fruit and vegetables do not have a product code printed on them.

   Name an input device that the till operator could use to enter details of these items. [1]

   AQA Comp 2 Qu 9 January 2010

2. A Radio Frequency Identification (RFID) system is made up of a transponder built into an RFID tag and an interrogator or reader. One example of use is to detect unauthorised removal of library books from a library.

   Explain the principles of operation of this RFID system. [2]

   AQA Comp 2 Qu 11 January 2009

3. Some countries have introduced electronic passports for their citizens. The passport stores data about the passport holder using a Radio Frequency Identification (RFID) tag.

   Explain how the RFID tag could be read at passport control in an airport. [2]

5-29

Chapter 30 – Storage devices

Objectives

- Explain the need for secondary storage within a computer system
- Know the main characteristics and principles of operations of:
  - Hard disk
  - Optical disk
  - Solid-state disk (SSD)
- Understand the purposes and suitability of these devices

The need for secondary storage

A computer's primary store is Random Access Memory. Unlike RAM, secondary storage is not directly accessible to the processor and has slower access speeds. Secondary storage, however, has the advantage that it retains its contents when the computer's power is turned off. This includes the computer's internal hard disk, optical media and solid state disks.

How storage devices store data

Hard disks, optical disks and solid state disks all use different methods to store data, but in each case, use a technique which allows them to create and maintain a toggle state without power to represent either a 1 or a 0.

Hard disk

A hard disk uses rigid rotating platters coated with magnetic material. Ferrous (iron) particles on the disk are polarised to become either a north or south state. This represents 0 and 1. The disk is divided into tracks in concentric circles, and each track is subdivided into sectors. The disk spins very quickly at speeds of up to 10,000 RPM. Like an old record player, a drive head (like the needle on a record player) moves across the disk to access different tracks and sectors. Data is read or written to the disk as it passes under the drive head. The head, however, is not in contact with the disk, but floats a fraction of a millimetre above it. When the drive head is not in use, it is parked to one side of the disk in order to prevent damage from movement. A hard disk may consist of several platters, each with its own drive head.

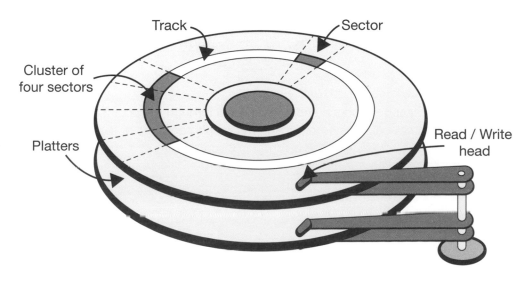

Although hard disks are less portable than optical or solid state media, their huge capacity makes them very suitable for desktop purposes. Smaller, denser surface areas spinning under the read-write heads mean that newer 3.5 inch disks have capacities of up to several terabytes.

Optical disk

Optical disks come in three different formats: read-only (e.g. CD-ROM), recordable (e.g. CD-R) and rewritable (e.g. CD-RW). An **optical** disk works by using a high powered laser to "burn" (change the chemical properties of) sections of its surface, making them less reflective. A laser at a lower power is used to read the disk by shining light onto the surface and a sensor is used to measure the amount of light that is reflected back. A read-only CD-ROM disk pressed during manufacture has pits in its surface. Those areas that have not been pitted, are called lands. At the point where a pit starts or ends, light is scattered and therefore not reflected so well. Reflective and non-reflective areas are read as 1s and 0s. There is only one single track on an optical disk, arranged as a tight spiral.

A **CD-ROM** holds about 650MB of data, whereas a **Blu-Ray** disk (designed to supersede the DVD disk) can hold 50GB. Although these disks do not vary in size, their added capacity is owing to the shorter wavelength in the laser they use. This creates much smaller pits, enabling a greater number to fit in the same space along the track and also means that the track can be more tightly wound, and therefore much longer.

Recordable disks use a reflective layer with a transparent dye coating that becomes less reflective when a spot laser "burns" a spot in the track.

Rewriteable compact disks use a laser and a magnet in order to heat a spot on the disk and then set its state to become a 0 or a 1 using the magnet before it cools again. A **DVD-RW** uses a phase change alloy that can change between amorphous and crystalline states by changing the power of the laser beam.

5-30

Pits and Lands

Spiral track

Optical storage is very cheap to produce and easy to send through the post for distribution purposes. Disks are also used for small backups or for storing music, photographs or films. Disk data can however be corrupted or damaged easily by excessive sunlight or scratches.

Solid-state disk (SSD)

Solid state disks are packaged to look like hard disk drives, rectangular in shape and sized to match industry-standard dimensions for hard drives, typically 2.5 and 3.5 inches.

A 480 GB solid state drive

Inside, however, instead of platters and a read-write head, there is an array of chips arranged on a board. These components are put into the standard size "housing" so that they fit into existing laptops and desktop PCs. Solid state memory comprises millions of **NAND** flash memory cells, and a controller that manages pages and blocks of memory. Each cell works by delivering a current along the bit and word lines to activate the flow of electrons from the source towards the drain. The current on the word line however is strong enough to force a few electrons across an insulated oxide layer into a floating gate. Once the current is turned off, these electrons are trapped. The state of the NAND cell is determined by measuring the charge in the floating gate. No charge (with no electrons) is considered a 1 and some charge is considered a 0.

Data is stored in pages (typically 4KiB each), grouped into blocks of say, 512KiB. NAND flash memory cannot overwrite existing data. The old data must be erased before data can be written to the same location, and although data can be written in pages, the technology requires the whole block to be erased. As writing to a specific block of NAND cells cannot be done directly, a separate block is created to mirror the data to be transferred to the solid state memory and the data is then written to the new block. The contents of the original block are marked as "invalid" or "stale" and are erased when the user wants to write new data to the drive.

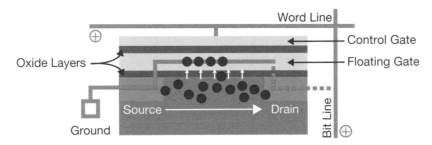

Although capacity is still relatively low, solid state media have faster access speed than hard disks. With no need to move a read-write head across the disk, one piece of data can be accessed just as quickly as any other, even if they are not close together.

SSDs consume far less power than traditional hard drives, meaning that in a laptop, for example, battery life is extended and they stay cooler. In addition, they are less susceptible to damage.

They are also silent in operation, lighter and highly portable – all considerable advantages in personal devices such as mobile phones and MP3 players for example.

Q1: Look up some specifications and prices for hard drives and SSDs.

Exercises

1. (a) Describe how data is written to and read from a CD-R disk.   [3]

    (b) A school has archived all its students' reports on to CD-R. Some years later, a copy of
         a particular student's reports is requested. Unfortunately it is found that the documents
         cannot be opened.

         Give **two** reasons why this may be the case.   [2]

2. In 1995, a high capacity hard disk drive had a storage capacity of 512 mebibytes. In 2012,
    a typical hard disk drive of the same physical size had a capacity of 1 tebibyte.

    (a) Describe the principles of operation of a hard disk drive.   [4]

    (b) How many times greater is the storage capacity of a 1 tebibyte hard disk drive than that
         of a 512 mebibyte hard disk drive?

         Show each stage of your working.   [1]

         Final answer: _____   [1]

    (c) Give **one** development in the design of hard disk drives that has enabled this increase in
         storage capacity.   [1]

    (d) If you are considering purchasing a high-end desktop or laptop you might be offered the
         option of a solid-state drive (SSD) rather than a traditional hard disk drive.

         A solid-state drive is a data storage device that uses solid-state memory, similar to that
         in USB flash drives (memory sticks), to store data that is accessed in a similar way to a
         traditional hard disk drive.

         Ignoring any differences in price and assuming that both drives have the same capacity,
         state **two** reasons why you might choose the solid-state drive.   [2]

AQA Comp 2 Qu 5 January 2013

5-30

Section 6

Communication: technology and consequences

In this section:

6

Chapter 31 – Communication methods

Objectives

- Define serial and parallel transmission methods and discuss the advantages of serial over parallel transmission

- Define and compare synchronous and asynchronous data transmission

- Describe the purpose of start and stop bits in asynchronous data transmission

- Define baud rate, bit rate, bandwidth, latency, protocol

- Differentiate between baud rate and bit rate

- Understand the relationship between bit rate and bandwidth

Electronic data communication

Data communication involves sending and receiving data from one computer or device to another. Data communication applications include e-mail, supermarket EPOS (electronic point of sale) terminals, cash dispensers, cell phones and VOIP (Voice Over Internet Protocol).

Data communication also takes place within the CPU and between the CPU and its peripheral devices; for example, data and addresses are transmitted along the data bus and address bus between the processor and memory, and data is transferred between memory and storage and other peripheral devices.

Serial and parallel data communication

Data can be sent in one of two ways: serial or parallel.

Using **serial data transmission**, bits are sent via an interface one bit at a time over a single wire from the source to the destination. Very high data transfer rates can be achieved – for example using fibre-optic cable, data transfer rates ranging from around 50 Megabits per second (Mbs) to 100 Gigabits per second (Gbs) can be achieved.

Serial transmission

Using **parallel data transmission**, several bits are sent simultaneously over a number of parallel wires.

Parallel communication is used in integrated circuits and within random access memory (RAM).

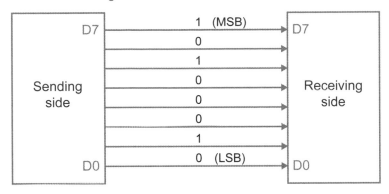

Parallel transmission

When parallel transmission is used, each individual wire has slightly different properties, there is a possibility that bits could travel at slightly different speeds over each of the wires. This produces a problem known as skew. Parallel transmission is only reliable over short distances.

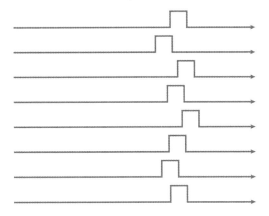

Skew developing in parallel wires

Advantages of serial over parallel transmission

The advantages of serial over parallel links are summarised below.

- The significant reduction in the size and complexity of connectors in serial transmission results in much lower associated costs. Designers of devices such as smartphones use connectors that are small, durable and still produce acceptable performance.

- "Crosstalk" creates interference between parallel lines, and can result in corrupted words which then need to be retransmitted. This is more pronounced as the signal frequency increases, and worsens with the length of the communication link.

- Serial links are reliable over much greater distances than parallel links.

- Because of the lack of interference at higher frequencies, signal frequency can be much higher with serial transmission, resulting in a higher net data transfer rate even though less data is transmitted per cycle. (See bit rate and baud rate below.)

6-31

Bit rate and baud rate

The speed at which data is transmitted serially is measured in bits per second (**bit rate**). The **baud rate** is the rate at which the signal changes.

In baseband mode, only two voltage levels are most commonly used, one to represent zero and the other to represent one. In this case the bit rate and the baud rate are the same.

bit rate of channel = (baud rate) x (number of bits per signal)

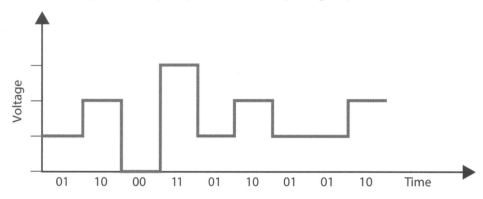

One signal encoding 2 bits: bit rate is twice the baud rate

In the figure above, (a simplified version of reality), four different "voltage levels" on the vertical scale represent four different bit patterns, so 00, 01, 10 or 11 can be encoded at each signal.

With eight different voltage levels or frequencies, each signal can encode 3 bits. Thus, for example, a baud rate of 1 MBd (megabaud) = 3 Mbit/s or 3,000,000 bits per second.

Bandwidth

Bandwidth is the range of frequencies that a transmission medium can carry. The larger the range, the greater the amount of data that can be transmitted in a fixed amount of time. It is usually expressed in bits per second (bps), since **there is a direct relationship between bandwidth and bit rate**. Think of a pipe carrying water – the larger the width of the pipe, the more water can be sent along it.

Modern networks typically have speeds measured in millions of bits per second (Mbps).

Q1: Carry out a speed test on your PC. (Try http://www.speedtest.net/) Why is the upload speed different from the download speed?

Latency

Latency is the time delay between the moment that transmission of the first byte or packet of a communication starts and when it is received at its destination. It is primarily a function of how long it takes information to travel from source to destination.

When satellite links are involved, the distance travelled can be more than 100,000 kilometers, and the result is often seen on live TV when a presenter in a studio talks to a reporter in a distant place.

6-31

Parity

Computers use either even or odd parity. In an even parity machine, the total number of 'on' bits in every byte (including the parity bit) must be an even number. When data is transmitted, the parity bit is set at the transmitting end and parity is checked at the receiving end, and if the wrong number of bits are 'on', an error has occurred. In the diagram below the parity bit is the most significant bit (MSB).

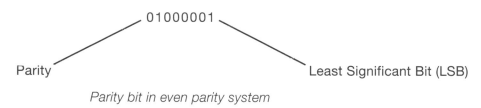

Parity bit in even parity system

> **Q2:** The ASCII codes for P and Q are 1010000 and 1010001 respectively. In an even parity transmission system, what will be the value of the parity bit for the characters P and Q?

Synchronous transmission

Using **synchronous transmission**, data is transferred at regular intervals that are timed by a clocking signal, allowing for a constant and reliable transmission for time-sensitive data, such as real-time video or voice. Parallel communication typically uses synchronous transmission – for example, in the CPU, the clock emits a signal at regular intervals and transmissions along the address bus, data bus and control bus start on a clock signal, which is shared by both sender and receiver.

6-31

Asynchronous transmission

Using **asynchronous transmission**, one byte at a time is sent, with each character being preceded by a start bit and followed by a stop bit.

The start bit alerts the receiving device and synchronises the clock inside the receiver ready to receive the character. The baud rate at the receiving end has to be set up to be the same as the sender's baud rate or the signal will not be received correctly. The stop bit is actually a "stop period", which may be arbitrarily long. This allows the receiver time to identify the next start bit and gives the receiver time to process the data before the next value is transmitted.

A parity bit is also usually included as a check against incorrect transmission. Thus for each character being sent, a total of 10 bits is transmitted, including the parity bit, a start bit and a stop bit. The start bit may be a 0 or a 1, the stop bit is then a 1 or a 0 (always different). A series of electrical pulses is sent down the line as illustrated below:

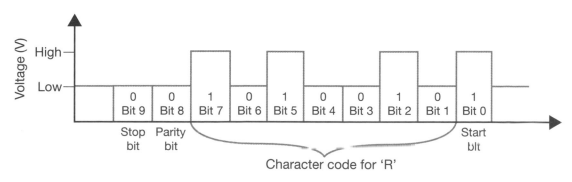

Asynchronous transmission

This type of transmission is usually used by PCs, and is economical for relatively small amounts of data. The main advantage is that there does not need to be a way of sharing the clock signal.

Protocol

Protocol: a set of rules relating to communication between devices.

In order to allow equipment from different suppliers to be networked, a standardised set of rules (protocols) has been devised covering standards for physical connections, cabling, mode of transmission, speed, data format, error detection and correction. Any pieces of equipment which use the same communication protocol can be linked together.

Exercises

1. Data is being transmitted along a serial link using asynchronous data transmission and odd parity.

    (a) Explain what *serial data transmission* is and how it differs from *parallel data transmission*.   [2]

    (b) The figure below shows a byte of data being transmitted along the serial link using odd parity.

    Write the missing values of the Stop bit, Parity bit and Start bit on the figure.

		1	0	0	1	1	0	0	
Stop bit	Parity bit	Byte of data							Start bit

    Direction of data transmission   [2]

    (c) Explain what asynchronous data transmission is.   [1]

    AQA Comp 3 Qu 3 June 2013

2. (a) Explain the terms *bit rate* and *baud rate* and the relationship between the two.   [3]

    (b) What is *latency* in the context of data communications?   [2]

3. (a) What is meant by a *communications protocol*?   [1]

    (b) Why is a communications protocol necessary when communicating over a network?   [1]

    (c) Name **five** items that are commonly covered by a communications protocol.   [5]

6-31

Chapter 32 – Network topology

Objectives

- Describe the star and bus topologies for a local area network
- Differentiate between physical and logical network topologies
- Explain the operation of these network topologies
- Give the advantages and disadvantages of each

Local area networks

A local area network (LAN) consists of a number of computing devices on a single site or in a single building, connected together by cables. The network may consist of a number of PCs, other devices such as printers and scanners, and a central server. Users on the network can communicate with each other, as well as sharing data and hardware devices such as printers and scanners.

LANs can transmit data very fast but only over a short distance.

Physical bus topology

A LAN can use different layouts or topologies. In a **bus** topology, all computers are connected to a single cable. The ends of the cable are plugged into a terminator.

6-32

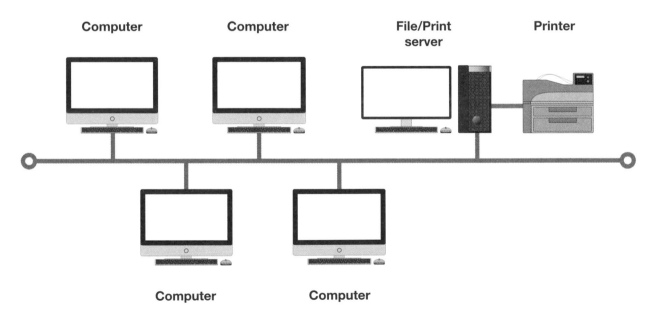

Advantage of a bus topology

- Inexpensive to install as it requires less cable than a star topology and does not require any additional hardware

Disadvantages of a bus topology

- If the main cable fails, network data can no longer be transmitted to any of the nodes
- Performance degrades with heavy traffic
- Low security – all computers on the network can see all data transmissions

Physical star topology

A **star** network has a central node, which may be a switch or computer which acts as a router to transmit messages.

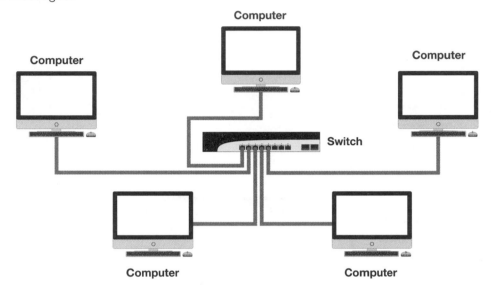

Advantages of a star topology

- If one cable fails, only one station is affected, so it is simple to isolate faults
- Consistent performance even when the network is being heavily used
- Higher transmission speeds can give better performance than a bus network
- No problems with 'collisions' of data since each station has its own cable to the server
- The system is more secure as messages are sent directly to the central computer and cannot be intercepted by other stations
- Easy to add new stations without disrupting the network

Disadvantages of a star network

- May be costly to install because of the length of cable required
- If the central device goes down, network data can no longer be transmitted to any of the nodes

Operation of a star network

In a star network, each node is connected to a central device, typically a switch. A switch keeps a record of the unique MAC address of each device on the network and can identify which particular computer on the network it should send the data to.

6-32

Physical vs logical topology

The **physical** topology of a network is its actual design layout, which is important when you select a wiring scheme and design the wiring for a new network.

The **logical** topology is the shape of the path the data travels in, and describes how components communicate across the physical topology. The physical and logical topologies are independent of each other, so that a network physically wired in star topology can behave logically as a bus network by using a bus protocol and appropriate physical switching.

For example, any variety of Ethernet uses a logical bus topology when components communicate, regardless of the physical layout of the cable.

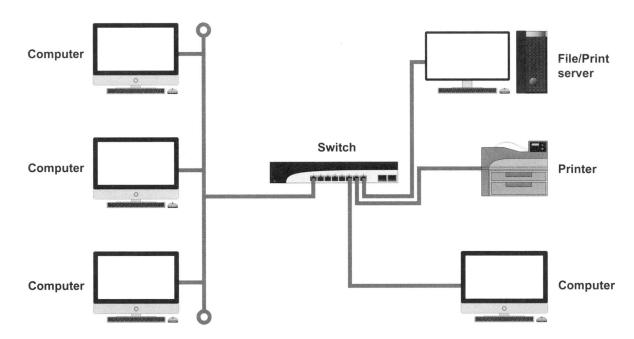

In the diagram, the computers on the left are connected with a single cable coming from the switch, in a physical bus configuration. The computers on the right hand side are each separately connected to the switch, in a physical star configuration. Logically, however, the network on the right can be arranged as a bus network and data will be sent to each computer in turn, as on the left. Each individual cable between the switch and the device will act as a bus and the Ethernet bus protocol will be used to control access to the cable, even though there are only two devices (the switch and the device at the other end of the individual cable) which could attempt to put data onto the cable simultaneously.

Operation of a logical bus network

Data cannot be simultaneously transmitted in both directions, i.e. duplex transmission is not possible. Every station receives all network traffic, and the traffic generated by each station has equal transmission priority. A device wanting to communicate with another device on the network sends a broadcast message onto the wire that all other devices see, but only the intended recipient actually accepts and processes the message.

MAC address

Every computer device, whether it's a PC, smartphone, laptop, printer or other device which is capable of being part of a network, must have a **Network Interface Card (NIC)**. Each NIC has a unique **Media Access Control address (MAC address)**, which is assigned and hard-coded into the card by the manufacturer and which uniquely identifies the device. The address is 48 bits long, and is written as 12 hex digits, for example:

00-09-5D-E3-F7-62

Because they are unique, MAC addresses can be used to track you. When you walk around, your smartphone scans for nearby Wi-Fi networks and broadcasts its MAC address.

Q1: A company named Renew London used rubbish bins in the City of London with Wi-Fi monitoring equipment installed in them to track people's movements around the city. What are the implications for personal privacy of such capabilities? How could advertisers use tracking information? Who else might use it?

You can find out the MAC address of your PC by selecting **Command Prompt** from the **Start** menu in Windows, and then typing `ipconfig /all`. This will display the physical address, i.e. MAC address.

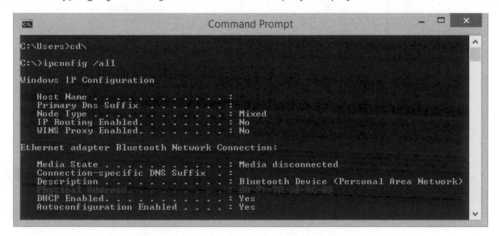

6-32

Displaying your computer's MAC address

Q2: Do some research to find out whether you can change the MAC address of your PC. Why might someone want to do this?

Exercises

1. (a) Draw diagrams representing physical **star** and **bus** topologies. [4]

    (b) Describe **three** advantages of a physical star topology over a bus topology, and **one** disadvantage of the star topology. [4]

    (c) Describe how a network wired in a star topology can behave logically as a bus network. [2]

2. A student claims that "an individual piece of hardware may be tracked and identified by its MAC address".

    (a) What is a MAC address? [1]

    (b) Explain briefly how a MAC address is used and state whether you agree with the statement above. [3]

Chapter 33 – Client-server and peer-to-peer

Objectives

- Explain client-server networking
- Explain peer-to-peer networking
- Describe situations when each of these might be used

Client-server networking

In a client-server network, one or more computers known as **clients** are connected to a powerful central computer known as the **server**. Each client may hold some of its own files and resources such as software, and can also access resources held by the server. In a large network, there may be several servers, each performing a different task.

6-33

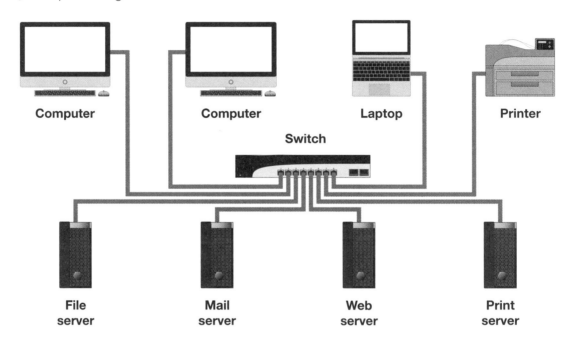

- File server holds and manages data for all the clients
- Print server manages print requests
- Web server manages requests to access the Web
- Mail server manages the email system
- Database server manages database applications

In a client-server network, the client makes a request to the server which then processes the request.

Advantages of a client-server network

- Security is better, since all files are stored in a central location and access rights are managed by the server

- Backups are done centrally so there is no need for individual users to back up their data. If there is a breakdown and some data is lost, recovery procedures will enable it to be restored

- Data and other resources can be shared

Disadvantages of a client-server network

- It is expensive to install and manage

- Professional IT staff are needed to maintain the servers and run the network

Peer-to-peer networks

In a peer-to-peer network, there is no central server. Individual computers are connected to each other, either locally or over a wide area network so that they can share files. In a small local area network, such as in a home or small office, a peer-to-peer network is a good choice because:

- it is cheap to set up

- it enables users to share resources such as a printer or router

- it is not difficult to maintain

Peer-to-peer networks are also used by companies providing, for example, video on demand. The problem arises when thousands of people simultaneously want to download the latest episode of a particular TV show. Using a peer-to-peer network, hundreds of computers can be used to hold parts of the video and so share the load.

6-33

The downside of peer-to-peer networking

Peer-to-peer networking has been widely used for online piracy, since it is impossible to trace the files which are being illegally downloaded. In 2011, the US Chamber of Commerce estimated that piracy sites attracted 53 billion visits each year. The analyst firm *NetNames* estimated that in January 2013 alone, 432 million unique Web users actively searched for content that infringes copyright.

Case study: Piracy sites

In January 1999, 19-year-old Shawn Fanning and Sean Parker created the Napster software, which enabled the peer-to-peer "sharing" of music – in actual fact, the theft of copyright music. Instead of storing the MP3 files on a central computer, the songs are stored on users' machines. When you want to download a song using Napster, you are downloading it from another person's machine, which may be next door or on the other side of the world.

All you need is a copy of the Napster utility and an Internet connection.

Napster was sued for copyright infringement in 2000 but argued that they were not responsible for copyright infringement on other people's machines. However, they lost the case and were pushed into bankruptcy, but the service has since reinvented itself on a legitimate, subscription basis.

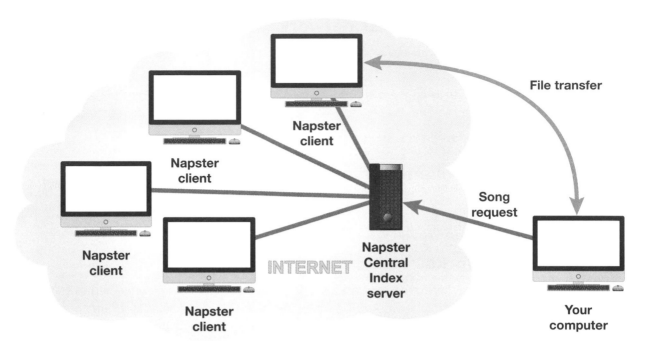

How Napster worked

The consequences of piracy

6-33

In 2014, Popcorn Time was launched, allowing a decentralised peer-to-peer service for illegal streaming of movies. Popcorn Time has already been translated into 32 languages and has been described as a "nightmare scenario" for the movie industry. The more movies that are stolen and illegally downloaded online, the fewer resources moviemakers have to invest in new films. In 2013 there was a 21% drop in the 18-24 age group buying tickets to watch movies, and numbers may plummet further in the next few years.

A 2011 report by the London-based International Federation of the Phonographic Industry (IFPI) estimated that 1.2 million European jobs would be destroyed by 2015 in the music, movie, publishing and photography industries because of online piracy.

> **Q1:** Look up the **Copyright, Designs and Patents Act 1988**. What types of work are protected by this Act? For what period of time is a work protected by copyright?

Exercises

1. Explain the difference between client-server and peer-to-peer networking, and give an example of where each might be used. [6]

2. Why is it illegal to download music from some Internet sites? [1]

   Describe the consequences to the individual artists and to society as a whole, of online piracy. [5]

Chapter 34 – Wireless networking, CSMA and SSID

Objectives

- Explain the purpose of Wi-Fi
- Describe the components required for wireless networking
- Explain how wireless networks are secured
- Explain the wireless protocol CSMA/CA
- Describe the purpose of Service Set Identifier (SSID)

Wi-Fi

Wi-Fi is a local area wireless technology that enables you to connect a device such as a PC, smartphone, digital audio player, laptop or tablet computer to a network resource or to the Internet via a **wireless network access point (WAP)**. An access point has a range of about 20 metres indoors, and more outdoors.

Laptop computer

Wireless access point

Printer

A laptop connected wirelessly to a printer

In 1999, the Wi-Fi Alliance was formed to establish international standards for interoperability and backward compatibility. The Alliance consists of a group of several hundred companies around the world, and enforces the use of standards for device connectivity and network connections.

Components required

In order to connect to a wireless network, a computer device needs a **wireless network adaptor**. The combination of computer and interface controller is called a **station**. All stations share a single radio frequency communication channel, and each station is constantly tuned in on this frequency to pick up transmissions. Transmissions are received by all the stations within range of the wireless access point.

To connect to the Internet, the WAP usually connects to a **router**, but it can also be an integral part of the router itself.

Securing a wireless network

Wi-Fi Protected Access (WPA) and **Wi-Fi Protected Access II (WPA2)**, which has replaced it, are two security protocols and security certification programs used to secure wireless networks. WPA2 is built into wireless network interface cards, and provides strong encryption of data transmissions, with a new 128-bit key being generated for each packet sent.

Each wireless network has a Service Set Identification (SSID) which is the informal name of the local network – for example, HOME-53C1. The purpose of the SSID is to identify the network, and if, for example, you visit someone else's house with a laptop and wish to connect to their Wi-Fi network in order to use the Internet, when you try to log on to the Internet the computer will ask you to enter the name of the network.

Your computer may be within the range of several networks, so having chosen the correct SSID you will then be asked for the password or security key - an identifier of up to 32 bytes, usually a human-readable string. SSIDs must be locally unique.

It is possible to disable the broadcast of your SSID to hide your network from others looking to connect to a named local network. However, this will not hide your network completely.

Whitelists

6-34

Some network administrators set up **MAC address whitelists** (the opposite of blacklists) to control who is allowed on their networks. (The MAC address is a unique identifier assigned to a network interface card by the manufacturer: see page 167.)

> **Q1:** Research some of the applications of "location-based services" such as *Presence Orb*. What are some of the benefits and some of the drawbacks to individuals of tracking software?

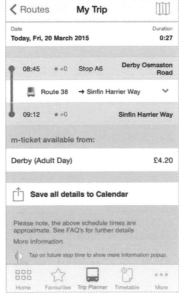

Arriva's Bus App

CSMA/CA

CSMA/CA (Carrier Sense Multiple Access/Collision Avoidance) is a protocol for carrier transmission in wireless local area networks.

This protocol attempts to avoid collisions occuring on a data channel, but due to the 'hidden nodes' problem described below, cannot always do so. It has to rely on acknowledgments to know that data has arrived successfully.

Prior to transmitting, a node first listens for signals on the wireless network to determine whether another node is transmitting. If a signal is detected, it waits for a random period of time for the node to stop transmitting and then listens again.

It is still possible that data will collide using this system as two nodes might transmit at the same time as they both sense the channel is idle. This is detected because the receiver would not send an acknowledgment back to the sender that the data is received. RTS/CTS, explained below, is an attempt to overcome this as well as the problem of "hidden nodes".

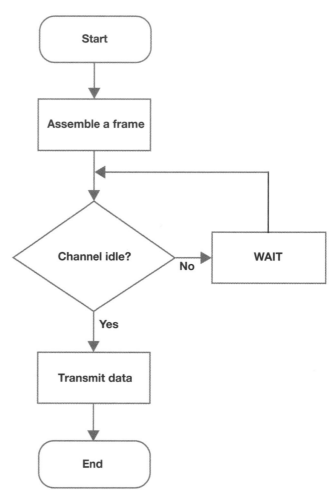

CSMA/CA with RTS/CTS

Having determined that no other node is transmitting, the station wanting to transmit sends a **Request to Send (RTS)** signal, and the WAP sends a **Clear to Send (CTS)** signal back if and when the channel is idle. This counteracts the problem of "hidden nodes", i.e. a node that can be heard by the WAP but not by the node trying to transmit. This is shown in the figure below, in which nodes A and C can each communicate with the WAP at B, but are hidden from each other.

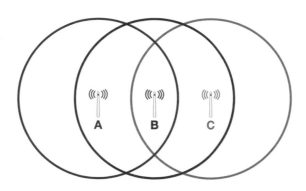

The revised algorithm now looks like this:

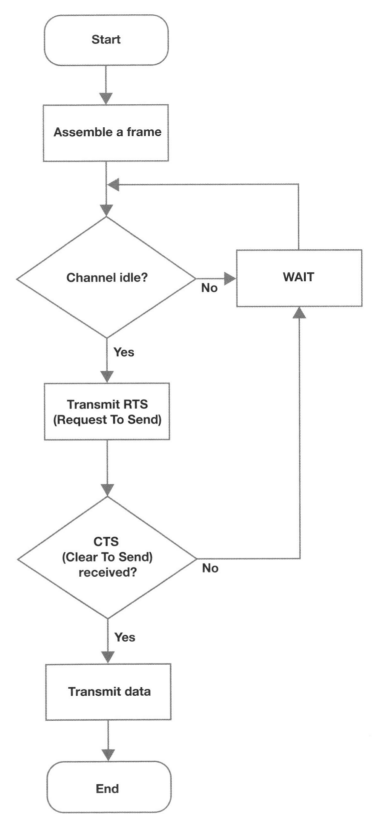

CSMA/CA using RTS/CTS

6-34

Exercises

1. (a) What components are required for wireless networking? [2]

   (b) Explain **two** measures that may be taken to make a wireless network secure from hackers. [4]

   (c) Explain the **CSMA/CA** with **Request to Send/Clear to Send (RTS/CTS)** protocol. [4]

   (d) How does the **RTS/CTS** system reduce the possibility of a data transmission being corrupted? [2]

2. *Wi-Fi location-based technology* is increasingly being used by retailers to maximise sales to potential customers. Describe briefly how this works. What are the benefits of this technology to the retailers and their customers? What are the potential dangers to individuals of widespread use of this technology? [8]

6-34

Chapter 35 – Communication and privacy

Objectives

- To understand that developments in digital technologies have enabled massive transformations in the capacity of organisations to monitor behaviour, amass and analyse personal information

- To understand the issue of scale, and the potential for individual computer scientists and software engineers to produce great good, but also great harm

- Discuss the challenges facing legislators in the digital age

Case Study 1: Edward Snowden

In April 2013, Guardian journalist Glenn Greenwald and Academy Award-winning documentary film director and producer Laura Poitras met in the Marriott Hotel in New York to discuss an initial contact with an anonymous "whistle-blower". Seated in the hotel restaurant, Laura Poitras asked Glenn to either remove the battery from his cell phone or leave it in the hotel room. "It sounds paranoid," she said, "but the government has the capability to activate cell phones and laptops remotely as eavesdropping devices. Turning off the phone or laptop does not defeat the capability; only removing the battery does."

The anonymous source had refused to email any details of what material he had to offer until Glenn installed PGP on his computer. PGP, which stands for "Pretty Good Privacy" is a sophisticated tool to prevent online communications from being hacked. The encryption codes are so lengthy and random that it would take years to decrypt a communication. But it was complicated to install and it took Glenn several months to get round to it, before he was eventually talked through the process online by his anonymous contact. Only then did he receive information from his source about a program called PRISM, which allowed America's National Security Agency (NSA) to collect private communications from the world's largest Internet companies, including Facebook, Google, Yahoo, Microsoft, Apple, YouTube, AOL and Skype.

The first document that Glenn opened was a training manual to teach analysts about the new surveillance capabilities. It told analysts how they could query, for example, particular email addresses or telephone numbers and what data they would receive in response.

What did the source hope to achieve by exposing the secret surveillance practices of the NSA?

"I want to spark a worldwide debate about privacy, Internet freedom, and the dangers of state surveillance," he stated. "I'm not afraid of what will happen to me. I've accepted that my life will be over from my doing this. I'm at peace with that. I know it's the right thing to do."

The next step was for Glenn and Laura to travel to Hong Kong to meet the whistleblower – Edward Snowden, a 29-year-old who had worked since 2005 as a technical expert for the CIA, NSA and its sub-contractors, making around $200,000 in salary and bonuses. He had travelled to Hong Kong in May, staying in a hotel under his own name, figuring he was safer there than staying in the US when news of the leaked documents broke.

"I watched NSA tracking people's Internet activities as they typed. I became aware of just how invasive US surveillance capabilities had become. I realised the true breadth of this system. And almost nobody knew it was happening."

"For many kids, the Internet is a means of self-actualisation. It allows them to explore who they are and who they want to be, but that works only if we're able to be private and anonymous, to make mistakes without them following us. I worry that mine will be the last generation to enjoy that freedom. I do not want to live in a world where we have no privacy and no freedom, where the unique value of the Internet is snuffed out."

On 6th June 2013, the first of many articles was published by the Guardian.

NSA collecting phone records of millions of Verizon customers daily

Exclusive: Top secret court order requiring Verizon to hand over all call data shows scale of domestic surveillance under President Obama.

The order, signed by Judge Roger Vinson, compels Verizon to produce to the NSA electronic copies of "all call detail records or 'telephony metadata' created by Verizon for communications between the United States and abroad" or "wholly within the United States, including local telephone calls".

As journalist Glenn Greenwald painstakingly sifted through the mountain of information provided by Snowden, he was shocked at the extent of the American surveillance operation. It included the NSA's tapping of Internet servers, satellites, underwater fibre-optic cables, local and foreign telephone systems and personal computers. A list of individuals targeted for particularly invasive forms of spying included suspected terrorist and criminal suspects, democratically elected leaders of many countries in Europe including France and Germany, and ordinary American citizens.

6-35

The documents leaked by Snowden revealed that the literal aim of the US Government was to collect, store, monitor and analyse metadata (for example, number called, date, time and duration of call) about all electronic communications by everybody in the world. In one month in 2013, the unit collected data on more than 97 billion emails and 124 billion phone calls from around the world.

Case study 2: Cyber-attacks

Estonia suffers a cyber-attack

Way back in 2007, Estonia suffered a series of cyber-attacks which swamped websites of organisations including The Estonian Parliament, banks, ministries, newspapers and broadcasters. This was one of the largest cases of state-sponsored cyber warfare ever seen, sponsored by Russia in retaliation for the relocation of the Bronze Soldier of Tallinn, an elaborate Soviet-era grave marker, and war graves in Tallinn.

In 2008, an ethnic Russian Estonian national was charged and convicted of the crime.

Sony Pictures is hacked

Sony's film *The Interview*, is an action comedy film in which two journalists are instructed to assassinate North Korean leader Kim Jong-un, and in which the leader is shown in an unflattering light. In June 2014, the North Korean government threatened merciless action against the United States if the film's distributor released the film. Columbia delayed the release from October to December, editing it to make it more acceptable to North Korea. However, in November, Sony Pictures computers were hacked by the "Guardians of Peace", a group the FBI believes was linked to the North Korean Government. Several other forthcoming films and other sensitive information was leaked, and threats of terrorist attacks against cinemas which showed the film were threatened.

Case study 3: Google Street View

Google Street View was integrated into Google Earth in 2008. It provides panoramic street-level views and users can view selected streets in villages, towns and cities in hundreds of countries in every continent throughout the world, including 99% of UK streets. Photos previously taken by a camera mounted on an automobile are stored with the software and users can view the street from any direction and at a variety of angles.

The photos, featuring passers-by without their consent as well as the cars on the street, are freely available to anyone, worldwide. What are the ethical issues involved here? Does the 'principle of informed consent' apply? Google Street View brings convenience to people's lives, but some would say it is a dangerous invasion of privacy. On the one hand, it enables people to check out places they are intending to visit, such as the location of a hotel or a friend's house. On the other hand, it could enable criminals to 'case the joint' that they are intending to burgle, from the privacy of their own home, determine the location of security cameras, locate utility boxes for power or gas, and check out the types of gates, doors and windows.

Google has taken some measures to protect privacy. People's faces and car number plates are blurred out, and individuals and organisations can request that certain images be blurred or removed. However, in some instances, individuals can still be recognisable even with pixelated faces.

6-35

> **Q1:** Imagine you are a Google Project Manager and have been asked to evaluate a proposal to bring Google Street View technology to a remote African village. What questions should be asked? Who should be consulted? What benefits, risks and safeguards should be considered?

Exercises

1. Do you think Edward Snowden was right to reveal the secret documents to which he had access, being legally forbidden to do so under the US Espionage Act 1917? Justify your answer. [4]

2. The FBI and NSA have been protesting about losing surveillance capabilities—through greater encryption of the Internet—since the 1990s. In China, the manufacture, use, sale, import, or export of any item containing encryption without prior government approval may lead to administrative fines, the seizure of equipment, confiscation of illegal gains, and even criminal prosecution.

   Give arguments for and against a policy of making it illegal for individuals and organisations to use strong encryption in their online communications. [4]

3. Among the papers exposed by Edward Snowden was President Barack Obama's presidential directive to prepare offensive cyber-operations.

   Describe some of the possible reasons for this directive. [4]

Chapter 36 – The challenges of the digital age

Objectives

- Discuss how developments in computer science have enabled massive transformations in the capacity to distribute, publish, communicate and disseminate personal information

- Understand that software and their algorithms embed moral and cultural values

- Understand the real and potential impact that digital technology has on employment, the distribution of wealth and the lives of millions of people

The economic impact of the Internet

The Internet has its origins in the 1960s with ARPANET, the first North American wide area network. In 1974, two engineers called Bob Kahn and Vint Cerf devised a protocol for linking up individual networks into what they termed the Internet – the "internetworking of networks".

In the 1980s Tim Berners-Lee, working for CERN in Geneva, invented, or designed, the World Wide Web. He wrote his initial Web proposal in March 1989 and in 1990 built the first Web browser, called WorldWideWeb. His vision was that "all the bits of information in every computer in CERN, and on the planet, would be available to me and to anyone else. There would be a single global information space."

Berners-Lee had little interest in money and gave away his technology for nothing, but one of the most significant consequences of his invention was a complete reshaping of the economy throughout the world. Has it created jobs, or simply created the "1% economy" in which the top Internet companies like Google, Amazon, Facebook, Instagram and others have accumulated huge wealth at the expense of thousands of workers?

6-36

Amazon

Amazon started as an online bookstore in 1994 but soon diversified into DVDs, software, video games, toys, furniture, clothes and thousands of other products. In 2013 the company turned over $75 billion in sales. It now accounts for 65% of all digital purchases of book sales, but in Britain, for example, there are now fewer than 4,000 bookstores, one third less than in 2005. Where a bookshop employs 47 people for every $10 million in sales, Amazon employs 14 to generate the same revenue.

eBay

eBay, essentially an electronic platform bringing together buyers and sellers of goods, grew from a user base of 41,000 trading goods worth $7.2 million in 1995, to 162 million users trading goods worth $227.9 billion in 2014.

Google

In 1996, Larry Page and Sergey Brin, two Stanford University Computer Science postgraduate students, created Google. There were already several successful search engines like Yahoo and AltaVista on the market, but Page and Brin came up with a game-changing algorithm, which they called PageRank, for determining the relevance of a Web page based on the number and quality of its incoming links. The idea was that you could estimate the importance of a Web page by the number and status of other web pages that link to it. Every time you make a search, the Google search engine becomes more knowledgeable and thus more useful. Even more valuable to Google is the fact that Google learns more about you every time you search.

By 1998, Google was getting 10,000 queries every day. By 1999, they were getting 70 million daily requests. Their next step was to figure out how to make money out of their free technology, and they came up with AdWords, which enabled advertisers to place keyword-associated ads down the right hand side of the page. The image below shows what comes up when a user in Dorchester searches for "Paintball", with the nearest companies, sponsored advertisements and a map with their locations.

6-36

By 2014, Google had joined Amazon as a winner-takes-all company, with 1.5 billion daily searches and revenues of $50 billion.

The destruction of jobs

A 2013 paper by Carl Benedikt Frey and Michael Osborne entitled *"The Future of Employment: how susceptible are jobs to computerisation?"* estimates that 47% of total US employment is at risk. They examine the impact of future computerisation on more than 700 individual occupations, and note the shifting of labour from middle-income manufacturing jobs to low-income service jobs which are less susceptible to computerisation. At the same time, with falling prices of computing, problem-solving skills are becoming relatively productive, explaining the substantial employment growth in occupations involving cognitive tasks where skilled, well-educated labour has a comparative advantage.

The disappearance of middle-income occupations has caused a polarization of labour, with growing employment in high-income cognitive jobs and low-income manual labour. Driverless cars developed by Google are an example of how computerisation is no longer confined to routine manufacturing tasks. The possibility of drones delivering your parcels is no longer in the realms of science fiction. In the 10 jobs that have a 99% likelihood of being replaced by software and automation within the next 25 years, Frey and Osbourne include tax preparers, library assistants, clothing factory workers, and photographic process workers.

In fact, jobs in the photographic industry have already all but vanished. In 1989, when Tim Berners-Lee invented the Internet, Kodak employed 145,000 people in research labs, offices and factories in Rochester US and had a market value of $31 billion. In 2013 the company filed for bankruptcy and Rochester became virtually a ghost town.

Meanwhile, in 2010, a young entrepreneur called Kevin Systrom started up Instagram, which enabled users to create photos on their smartphones with filters to give them, for example, a warm and fuzzy glow.

An Instagram moment

Twenty-five thousand iPhone users downloaded the app when it launched on 6th October 2010. A month later, Systrom's Instagram had a million members. By early 2012, it had 14 million users and by November, 100 million users, with the app hosting 5 billion photos. When Systrom sold Instagram to Facebook for a billion dollars in 2012 (less than two years after the startup), Instagram still only had thirteen full-time employees working out of a small office in San Fransisco. It is a good example of a service that is not providing any jobs at all in the winner-takes-all economics of the digital marketplace.

6-36

User-generated content

In his book "The Cult of the Amateur", Andrew Keen argues that *"MySpace and Facebook are creating a youth culture of digital narcissism; open-source knowledge-sharing sites like Wikipedia are undermining the authority of teachers in the classroom, the YouTube generation are more interested in self-expression than in learning about the outside world; the cacophony of anonymous blogs and user-generated content is deafening today's user to the voices of informed experts and professional journalism; kids are so busy self-broadcasting themselves on social networks that they no longer consume the creative work of professional musicians, novelists, or filmmakers."*

Keen asserts that a thriving music, video and publishing economy is being replaced by the multi-billion dollar monopolist YouTube. The traditional copyright-intensive industries accounted for almost 510 billion Euros in the European Union during the period 2008-2010, and generated 3.2% of all jobs, amounting to more than 7 million jobs. What will happen if large numbers of these jobs disappear?

Trolls on the Internet

Trolls, cyber-bullying and misogyny have become a fact of everyday life on the Internet. It wasn't supposed to be this way – the Internet was going to inspire a generation to voice a broad diversity of opinion and empower those who traditionally had no voice.

After the 2010-11 Arab Spring, many people argued that the social media networks were helping to overthrow dictatorships and empower the people. But the Arab Spring deteriorated into vicious religious and ethnic civil wars, culminating in the rise of the so-called ISIS, which uses social networks to post atrocities and radicalise young Muslims.

Feminist writers and journalists, academics like Mary Beard and political campaigner Caroline Criado-Perez, who petitioned the Bank of England to create a bank note featuring a woman's face, receive hundreds of death threats and rape threats for no other reason than that they are women who have dared to appear on the media. Thousands of other women and teenage girls are victims of similar trolling on the Internet. Savage bullying on various social networking sites has led to several tragic cases of suicide.

The Internet has brought great benefits, but all of us have a responsibility to use it wisely and well.

Algorithms and ethics

Computer scientists and software engineers who devise the multitude of algorithms used by YouTube, Facebook, Amazon and Google, and by organisations from banks and Stock Exchanges to the Health Service and the police, have significant power and therefore the responsibility that goes with it. In some US cities, algorithms determine whether you are likely to be stopped and searched on the street. Banks use algorithms to decide whether to consider your application for a mortgage or a loan. Algorithms are applied to decision-making in hiring and firing, healthcare and advertising. It has been reported, for example, that some algorithms which decide what advertisements are shown on your browser screen classify web users into categories which include "probably bipolar", "daughter killed in car crash", "rape victim", and "gullible elderly".[i] Did the programmer who wrote that algorithm have any qualms about his work?

When algorithms prioritise, they "bring attention to certain things at the expense of others".[ii] Facebook's 'News Feed' product filters posts, stories and activities undertaken by friends. Content for the Newsfeed is selected or omitted according to a ranking algorithm which Facebook, with its billion-plus user base, continually develops and tests to show users the content they will be most interested in. But it has been suggested that these social interactions may influence people's emotions and state of mind; the emotions expressed by friends via online social networks may influence our own moods and behaviour.[iii] Clearly, then, those who devise the ranking algorithms potentially have the ability to influence the emotional state of people using Facebook.

Should computer scientists consider the institutional goals of a prospective employer, or the social worth of what they do, before accepting a job? Phillip Rogway, Professor of Computer Science at the University of California, found that on a Google search of deciding among job offers, not one suggested that this was a factor. [iv]

The Internet of things

As digital technologies are used in more and more areas of our lives, spreading into our offline environments through the so-called 'Internet of things', previously inert objects are expected to become networked and start making decisions for us. Algorithms will allow the refrigerator to decide what food needs replacing, a door will decide who to let in. Should your door call the police if the door is opened by someone without a tracking device? Should your house report a child, who screams excessively, to the Social Services?

Driverless cars

The prospect of large numbers of self-driving cars on our roads raises ethical questions about the morality of different algorithms which could be used in the face of causing "unavoidable harm" - who gets harmed and who gets spared. [v]

6-36

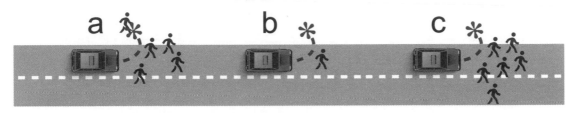

(a) The car can stay on course and kill several pedestrians, or swerve and kill one passer-by

(b) The car can stay on course and kill one pedestrian, or swerve and kill its passenger

(c) The car can stay on course and kill several pedestrians, or swerve and kill its passenger

The MIT Technology Review asked: "Should different decisions be made when children are on board, since they both have a longer time ahead of them than adults, and had less say in being in the car in the first place? If a manufacturer offers different versions of its moral algorithm, and a buyer knowingly chose one of them, is the buyer to blame for the harmful consequences of the algorithm's decisions?"

One of the commonly held principles that form a commonly held set of pillars for moral life is the obligation not to inflict harm intentionally; in medical ethics, the physician's guiding principle is "Do no harm". Going further, the moral duties of all scientists, including computer scientists, should also include trying to promote the common good.

(i)   *Naughton, John, The Guardian (2015, December 6) "Algorithm writers need a code of conduct" www.theguardian.com/commentisfree/2015/dec/06/algorithm-writers-should-have-code-of-conduct*

(ii)   *Centre of Internet & Human Rights (2015) "The ethics of Algorithms: from radical content to self-driving cars". Retrieved from www.gccs2015.com/sites/default/files/documents/Ethics_Algorithms-final%20doc.pdf*

(iii)   *Kramer, Adam et al (2014, March 25) "Experimental evidence of massive-scale emotional contagion through social networks". Retrieved from http://www.pnas.org/content/111/24/8788.full*

(iv)   *Rogway, Phillip (2015, December 12) "The Moral Character of Cryptographic Work". Retrieved from http://web.cs.ucdavis.edu/~rogaway/papers/moral-fn.pdf*

(v)   *Owano, Nancy (2015 October 24) "When self-driving cars drive the ethical questions". Retrieved from http://techxplore.com/news/2015-10-self-driving-cars-ethical.html*

6-36

Challenges facing legislators in the digital age

Legislation relating to privacy can be broadly categorised into laws intended to protect personal privacy and those which have been passed in the interests of national security, crime detection or counter-terrorism.

Some laws relate specifically to computing, for example:

• the Data Protection Act (1998) which is designed to ensure that personal data is kept accurate, up-to-date, safe and secure and not used in ways which would harm individuals.

• the Computer Misuse Act, which makes it an offence to access computer material without permission, or to modify it without permission.

Other laws such as the Copyright, Designs and Patents Act (1988) have a more general application, covering the intellectual property rights of many types of work including books, music, art, computer programs and other original works.

The rapidly changing field of computing and worldwide communications poses particular challenges to legislators.

- Countries have different laws, and it is sometimes hard to prove in which country an offence was committed, and equally hard to trace the offender or to prosecute.

- New applications in Computing are constantly being invented and with them, new ways of committing offences for which there is no legislation.

Legislators have to balance the rights of the individual with the need for security and protection from terrorist or criminal activity. Many countries, for example, have enacted legislation restricting or banning the use of strong cryptography.

> **Q1:** How concerned are you about misuse of your personal data? Are you aware of how your social profile may be used by future employers?
>
> Find some examples of the application of the Computer Misuse Act (e.g. www.computerevidence.co.uk/Cases/CMA.htm)

Exercises

1. Networking sites frequently feature angry, violent or inaccurate content.

   Should Facebook, Twitter, Ask.com and others take responsibility for content posted on their sites? What sort of content should not be allowed? Would it be possible to develop software to facilitate such a task? Discuss. [5]

2. Some of the jobs likely to disappear over the next decade owing to computerisation include manufacturing jobs, clerical jobs and even service jobs, where people will be replaced by robots. Give examples of other jobs which may be lost owing to computerisation. What will be the social effects of the job losses? [5]

3. In September 2015, the Environmental Protection Agency (EPA) found that many VW cars being sold in America had a "defeat device" embedded in the software that could detect when diesel engines were being tested, changing the performance accordingly to improve results. The German car giant has since admitted cheating emissions tests in the US. In October 2015, the company posted its first loss for 15 years, of 2.5 billion euros. In 2016 VW will recall millions of cars and in addition to the cost of doing this, could face fines from the EPA of up to $18 billion.

   Research this case and find answers to some the questions this case raises. For example:

   - Who is responsible for wilfully using "defeat devices" in the software used in the emissions tests?
   - What was the motivation of the perpetrators?
   - Who in the company is ultimately responsible for this situation?
   - Do you consider that the software engineers involved "caused great harm"? If so, in what way?

4. Decisions are often made about us on the basis of algorithms of which we may be completely unaware.

   Car insurance premiums are calculated based largely on your age, experience, address, occupation and vehicle details. Health insurance premiums are affected by age, occupation, personal and parental medical histories. Are the algorithms that calculate these premiums fair? Discuss how the algorithms used embed moral and/or cultural values. State with reasons who benefits from the decisions made by these algorithms and whether anyone is harmed. [4]

6-36

References

The following books have been useful in writing Sections 1 to 6 of this book and will provide interesting and illuminating background reading for this course, for both teachers and students.

Beecher, Karl, "Brown dogs and barbers – What's Computer Science all about?", 2014

Greenwald, Glen, "No Place to Hide: Edward Snowden, the NSA and the Surveillance State", McLelland and Stewart, 2014

Harding, Luke, "The Snowden files: The Inside Story of the World's Most Wanted Man", Vintage Books, 2014

Hey, Tony and Pápay, Gyuri, "The Computing Universe", Cambridge University Press, 2015

Keen, Andrew, "The Cult of the Amateur", Nicholas Brealey Publishing, 2007, 2008

Keen, Andrew, "The Internet is not the Answer", Atlantic Books, London, 2015

Levitin, Anany and Levitin, Maria, "Algorithmic puzzles", Oxford University Press, 2011

Section 7

Data structures

In this section:

7

Chapter 37 – Queues

Objectives

- Understand the concept of an abstract data type

- Be familiar with the concept and uses of a queue

- Describe the creation and maintenance of data within a queue (linear, circular, priority)

- Describe and apply the following to a lincar, circular and priority queue

  o   add an item

  o   remove an item

  o   test for an empty queue

  o   test for a full queue

Introduction to data structures

Programming languages such as Python, Visual Basic or Java all have built-in **elementary data types** such as integer, real, Boolean and char, and some built-in **composite data types** such as string, array or list, for example.

Abstract data types such as queues, stacks, trees and graphs can easily be shown in graphical form, and it is not hard to understand how to perform operations such as adding, deleting or counting elements in each structure. However, programming languages require data types to represent them. An abstract data type (**ADT**) is a logical description of how the data is viewed and the operations that can be performed on it, but how this is to be done is not necessarily known to the user. It is up to the programmer who creates the data structure to decide how to implement it, and it may be built in to the programming language. This is a good example of **data abstraction**, and by providing this level of abstraction we are creating an **encapsulation** around the data, hiding the details of implementation from the user. This is called **information hiding**.

As a programmer, you will be quite familiar with this concept. When you call a built-in function such as `random` to generate a random number, or `sqrt` to find the square root of a number, you are not at all concerned with how these functions are implemented.

Queues

A queue is a **First In First Out (FIFO)** data structure. New elements may only be added to the end of a queue, and elements may only be retrieved from the front of a queue. The sequence of data items in a queue is determined, therefore, by the order in which they are inserted. The size of the queue depends on the number of items in it, just like a queue at traffic lights or at a supermarket checkout.

Queues are used in a variety of applications:

- Output waiting to be printed is commonly stored in a queue on disk. In a room full of networked computers, several people may send work to be printed at more or less the same time. By putting the output into a queue on disk, the output is printed on a first come, first served basis as soon as the printer is free.

- Characters typed at a keyboard are held in a queue in a keyboard buffer.

- Queues are useful in simulation problems. A simulation program is one which attempts to model a real-life situation so as to learn something about it. An example is a program that simulates customers arriving at random times at the check-outs in a supermarket store, and taking random times to pass through the checkout. With the aid of a simulation program, the optimum number of check-out counters can be established.

Operations on a queue

The abstract data type **queue** is defined by its structure and the operations which can be performed on it. It is described as an ordered collection of items which are added at the rear of the queue, and removed from the front.

When Eli leaves the queue, the front pointer is made to point to Jason; the elements themselves do not move. When Adam joins the queue, the rear pointer points to Adam. Think of a queue in a doctor's surgery – people leave and join the queue, but no one moves chairs.

The following queue operations are needed:

- enQueue(item)   Add a new item to the rear of the queue
- deQueue()   Remove the front item from the queue and return it
- isEmpty()   Test to see whether the queue is empty
- isFull()   Test to see whether queue is full

7-37

Q1: Complete the following table to show the queue contents and the value returned by the function or **method**. The queue is named **q**.

Queue operation	Queue contents	Return value
q.isEmpty()	[]	True
q.enQueue("Blue")	["Blue"]	(none)
q.enQueue("Red")	["Blue", "Red"]	
q.enQueue("Green")		
q.isFull()		False
q.isEmpty()	["Blue", "Red", "Green"]	
q.deQueue()		
q.enQueue("Yellow")		

Dynamic vs static data structures

A **dynamic data structure** refers to a collection of data in memory that has the ability to grow or shrink in size. It does this with the aid of the **heap**, which is a portion of memory from which space is automatically allocated or de-allocated as required.

Languages such as Python, Java and C support dynamic data structures, such as the built-in `list` data type in Python.

Dynamic data structures are very useful for implementing data structures such as queues when the maximum size of the data structure is not known in advance. The queue can be given some arbitrary maximum to avoid causing memory overflow, but it is not necessary to allocate space in advance.

A **static data structure** such as a static array is fixed in size, and cannot increase in size or free up memory while the program is running. An array is suitable for storing a fixed number of items such as the months of the year, monthly sales or average monthly temperatures. The disadvantage of using an array to implement a dynamic data structure such as a queue is that the size of the array has to be decided in advance by the programmer, and if the number of items added fills up the array, then no more can be added, regardless of how much free space there is in memory. Python does not have a built-in `array` data structure. A further disadvantage is that memory which has been allocated to the array cannot be reallocated even if most of it is unused. However, an advantage of a static data structure is that no pointers or other data about the structure need to be stored, in contrast to a dynamic data structure.

Implementing a linear queue

There are basically two ways to implement a linear queue in an array or list:

1. As items leave the queue, all of the other items move up one space so that the front of the queue is always the first element of the structure, e.g. q[0]. With a long queue, this may require significant processing time.

2. A linear queue can be implemented with pointers to the front and rear of the queue. An integer holding the size of the array (the maximum size of the queue) is needed, as well as a variable giving the number of items currently in the queue. However, clearly a problem will arise as many items are added to and deleted from the queue, as space is created at the front of the queue which cannot be filled, and items are added until the rear pointer points to the last element of the data structure.

> **Q2:** The queue of names pictured above containing Jason, Milly, Bob and Adam has space for six names. What will be the situation when Jason and Milly leave the queue, and Jack joins it? How many names are now in the queue? How many free spaces are left?

A circular queue

One way of overcoming the limitations of implementing a queue as a linear queue is to use a **circular queue** instead, so that when the array fills up and the rear pointer points to the last element of the array, say q[5], it will be made to point to the first element, q[0], when the next person joins the queue, assuming this element is empty. This solution requires some extra effort on the part of the programmer, and is less flexible than a dynamic data structure if the maximum number of items is not known in advance.

Q3: A circular queue is implemented in a fixed size array of six elements, indexed from 0. Show the contents of the queue and the front and rear pointers for a circular queue of 6 items when

(a) it is empty

(b) Ali, Ben, Charlie, Davina, Enid, Fred join the queue. Ali, Ben and Charlie leave, and Greg joins the queue.

Pseudocode for implementing a circular queue

To initialise the queue:

```
SUB initialise
    front ← 0
    rear ← -1
    size ← 0
    maxSize ← size of array
ENDSUB
```

To test for an empty queue:

```
SUB isEmpty
    IF size = 0 THEN
        RETURN True
    ELSE
        RETURN False
    ENDIF
ENDSUB
```

To test for a full queue:

```
SUB isFull
    IF size = maxSize THEN
        RETURN True
    ELSE
        RETURN False
    ENDIF
ENDSUB
```

To add an element to the queue:

```
SUB enqueue(newItem)
    IF isFull THEN
        OUTPUT "Queue full"
    ELSE
        rear ← (rear + 1) MOD maxSize
        q[rear] ← newItem
        size ← size + 1
    ENDIF
ENDSUB
```

7-37

Q4: In what respect is a circular queue an example of **abstraction**?

To remove an item from the queue:

```
SUB dequeue
    IF isEmpty THEN
        OUTPUT "Queue empty"
        item ← Null
    ELSE
        item ← q[front]
        front ← (front + 1) MOD maxSize
        size ← size - 1
    ENDIF
    RETURN item
ENDSUB
```

Priority queues

In some situations where items are placed in a queue, a system of priorities is used. For example an operating system might schedule jobs in order of priority, or a printer may give shorter print jobs priority over longer ones.

A **priority queue** acts like a queue in that items are dequeued by removing them from the front of the queue. However, the logical order of items within the queue is determined by their priority, with the highest priority items at the front of the queue and the lowest priority items at the back. It is therefore possible that a new item joins the queue at the front, rather than at the rear.

Q5: In what circumstances would an item join a priority queue at the front? In what circumstances would the item join the queue at the rear?

Such a queue could be implemented by checking the priority of each item in the queue, starting at the rear and moving it along one place until an item with the same or lower priority is found, at which point the new item can be inserted.

An example of how to do this is included in the next chapter on Lists.

Exercises

1. (a) Explain why a queue may be implemented as a **circular queue**. [2]

   (b) Explain what is meant by a **dynamic data structure** and why an inbuilt dynamic data structure in a programming language may be useful in implementing a queue.

   Include an explanation of what is meant by the **heap** in this context. [4]

   (c) Print jobs are put in a queue to be printed. The queue is implemented in an array, indexed from 0, as a circular queue which can hold 5 jobs. Jobs enter the queue in the sequence Job1, Job2, Job3, Job4, Job5. Pointers **front** and **rear** point to the first and last items in the queue respectively.

   (i) Draw a diagram to show how the print jobs are stored. Include pointers in your diagram. [3]

   (ii) Two jobs are printed and leave the queue. Another job, Job6 joins the queue.

   Draw a diagram representing the new situation. [2]

2. A computer program is being developed to play a card game on a smartphone. The game uses a standard deck of 52 playing cards, placed in a pile on top of each other.

The cards will be dealt (ie given out) to players from the top of the deck.

When a player gives up a card it is returned to the bottom of the deck.

(a) Explain why a queue is a suitable data structure to represent the deck of cards in this game. [1]

(b) The queue representing the deck of cards will be implemented as a **circular** queue in a fixed size array named DeckQueue. The array DeckQueue has indices running from 1 to 52.

Figure 1 shows the contents of the DeckQueue array and its associated pointers at the start of a game. The variable QueueSize indicates how many cards are currently represented in the queue.

Figure 1

DeckQueue

Index	Data
[1]	10 - Hearts
[2]	2 - Spades
[3]	King - Hearts
[4]	Ace - Clubs
.	
.	
.	
[52]	8 - Diamonds

FrontPointer = 1

RearPointer = 52

QueueSize = 52

(i) Ten cards are dealt from the top of the deck.

What values are now stored in the FrontPointer and RearPointer pointers and the QueueSize variable? [1]

(ii) Next, a player gives up two cards and these are returned to the deck.

What values are now stored in the FrontPointer and RearPointer pointers and the QueueSize variable? [1]

(iii) Write a pseudo-code algorithm to deal a card from the deck.

Your algorithm should output the value of the card that is to be dealt and make any required modifications to the pointers and to the QueueSize variable.

It should also cope appropriately with any situation that might arise in the DeckQueue array whilst a game is being played. [6]

AQA Unit 3 Qu 5 June 2014

Chapter 38 – Lists

Objectives

- Explain how a list may be implemented as either a static or dynamic data structure
- Show how items may be added to or deleted from a list

Definition of a list

In computer science, a **list** is an abstract data type consisting of a number of items in which the same item may occur more than once. The list is sequenced so that we can refer to the first, second, third,… item and we can also refer to the last element of the list.

A list is a very useful data type for a wide variety of operations, and can be used, for example, to implement other data structures such as a queue, stack or tree. Some languages such as Python have a built-in list data type, so that for example a list of numbers could be shown as

$$[45, 13, 19, 13, 8]$$

Q1: In a programming language which does not include the list data type, how could a list be implemented?

Operations on lists

Some possible list operations are shown in the following table. The list a is assumed to hold the values [45, 13, 19, 13, 8] initially, with the first element referred to as a[0].

List operation	Description	Example	list contents	Return value
isEmpty()	Test for empty list	a.isEmpty()	[45, 13, 19, 13, 8]	False
append(item)	Add a new item to list to the end of the list	a.append(33)	[45, 13, 19, 13, 8, 33]	
remove(item)	Remove the first occurrence of an item from list	a.remove(13)	[45, 19, 13, 8, 33]	
search(item)	Search for an item in list	a.search(22)	[45, 19, 13, 8, 33]	False
length()	Return the number of items	a.length()	[45, 19, 13, 8, 33]	5
index(item)	Return the position of item	a.index(8)	[45, 19, 13, 8, 33]	3
insert(pos,item)	Insert a new item at position pos	a.insert(2,7)	[45, 19, 7, 13, 8, 33]	
pop()	Remove and return the last item in the list	a.pop()	[45, 19, 7, 13, 8]	33
pop(pos)	Remove and return the item at position pos	a.pop(1)	[45, 7, 13, 8]	18

> **Q2:** Assume that list names holds the values James, Paul, Sophie, Holly, Nathan.
>
> What does the list hold after each of the following consecutive operations?
>
> (i)   `names.append("Tom")`
>
> (ii) `names.pop(3)`
>
> (iii) `names.insert(1, "Melissa")`

Using an array

It is possible to maintain an ordered collection of data items using an array, which is a static data structure. This may be an option if the programming language does not support the `list` data type and if the maximum number of data items is small, and is known in advance.

The programmer then has to work out and code algorithms for each list operation. The empty array must be declared in advance as being a particular length, and this could be used, for example, to hold a priority queue.

Inserting a new name in the list

If the list needs to be held in sequential order in the array, the algorithm will first have to determine where a new item has to be added, and then if necessary, move the rest of the items along in order to make room for it.

The steps are as follows:

```
Test for list already full, print message if it is and quit
Determine where new item needs to be inserted
Starting at the end of the list, move other items along one place
Insert new item in correct place
```

> **Q3:** Suggest a different algorithm for adding a new element to a sequenced list.
>
> **Q4:** How could the given algorithm be adapted to insert an item in a priority queue?

Deleting a name from the list

Suppose the name Ken is to be deleted from the list shown below. The names coming after Ken in the list need to be moved up to fill the gap.

Holly	James	Ken	Nathan	Paul	Sophie	

> **Q5:** Why not simply leave the array element names[2] blank after deleting *Ken*?

First, items are moved up to fill the empty space by copying them to the previous spot in the array:

Holly	James	Nathan	Paul	Sophie	Sophie	

7-38

Finally the last element, which is now duplicated, is replaced with a blank.

Holly	James	Nathan	Paul	Sophie		

Using a dynamic data structure to implement an ordered list

Programming languages such as Python have a built-in dynamic `list` data structure which is internally implemented using a **linked list**. Functional abstraction hides all the details of how all the associated functions and methods are implemented, making the programmer's task much easier! As items are added to the list, the pointers are adjusted to point to new memory locations taken from the heap. When items are deleted, pointers are again adjusted and the freed-up memory is de-allocated and returned to the heap.

As new nodes are added, new memory locations can be dynamically pulled from the **heap**, a pool of memory locations which can be allocated or deallocated as required. The pointers then need to be changed to maintain the correct sequence.

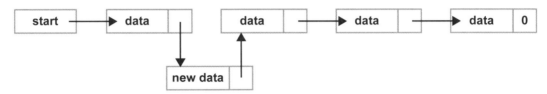

The following shows an interactive session in Python:

```
>>> names = ['James', 'Paul', 'Sophie', 'Holly', 'Nathan']
>>> names
['James', 'Paul', 'Sophie', 'Holly', 'Nathan']
>>> len(names)
5
>>> names.append('Tom')
>>> names
['James', 'Paul', 'Sophie', 'Holly', 'Nathan', 'Tom']
>>> names.pop(3)
'Holly'
>>> names
['James', 'Paul', 'Sophie', 'Nathan', 'Tom']
>>> names.insert(1,'Melissa')
>>> names
['James', 'Melissa', 'Paul', 'Sophie', 'Nathan', 'Tom']
```

Note that `append`, `pop` and `insert` are **methods** on a list object, while `len()` is a **function** that takes the list as an argument.

7-38

Exercises

1. A list data structure can be represented using an array.

The pseudocode algorithm in Figure 1 can be used to carry out one useful operation on a list.

Figure 1

```
p ← 1
If ListLength > 0 Then
    While p <= ListLength And List[p] < New Do
       p ← p + 1
    EndWhile
    For q ← ListLength DownTo p Do
       List[q + 1] ← List[q]
    EndFor
EndIf
List[p] ← New
ListLength ← ListLength + 1
```

(a) The initial values of the variables for one particular execution of the algorithm are shown in the trace table below, labelled Table 1.

Complete the trace table for the execution of the algorithm.

Table 1

ListLength	New	p	q	List [1]	[2]	[3]	[4]	[5]
4	38	–	–	9	21	49	107	

[4]

(b) Describe the purpose of the algorithm in Figure 1. [1]

(c) A list implemented using an array is a static data structure. The list could be implemented using a linked list as a dynamic data structure instead.

(i) Describe one difference between a static data structure and a dynamic data structure. [1]

(ii) If the list were to be implemented as a dynamic data structure, explain what the heap would be used for. [1]

AQA Unit 3 Qu 10 June 2010

Chapter 39 – Stacks

Objectives

- Be familiar with the concept and uses of a stack

- Be able to describe the creation and maintenance of data within a stack

- Be able to describe and apply the following operations: push, pop, peek (or top), test for empty stack, test for full stack

- Be able to explain how a stack frame is used with subroutine calls to store return addresses, parameters and local variables

Concept of a stack

A **stack** is a Last In, First Out (**LIFO**) data structure. This means that, like a stack of plates in a cafeteria, items are added to the top and removed from the top.

Applications of stacks

A stack is an important data structure in Computing. Stacks are used in calculations, and to hold return addresses when subroutines are called. When you use the **Back** button in your Web browser, you will be taken back through the previous pages that you looked at, in reverse order as their URLs are removed from the stack and reloaded. When you use the **Undo** button in a word processing package, the last operation you carried out is popped from the stack and undone.

Implementation of a stack

A stack may be implemented as either a **static** or **dynamic** data structure.

A static data structure such as an **array** can be used with two additional variables, one being a pointer to the top of the stack and the other holding the size of the array (the maximum size of the stack).

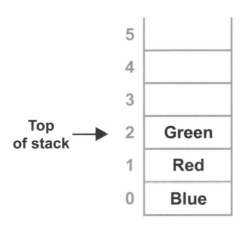

7-39

Operations on a stack

The following operations are required to implement a stack:

- push(item)   adds a new item to the top of the stack
- pop()   removes and returns the top item from the stack
- peek()   returns the top item from the stack but does not remove it
- isEmpty()   tests to see whether the stack is empty, and returns a Boolean value
- isFull()   tests to see whether the stack is full, and returns a Boolean value

Stack operation	Stack contents	Return value
s.isEmpty()	[]	True
s.push('Blue')	['Blue']	
s.push('Red')	['Blue', 'Red']	
s.push('Green')	['Blue', 'Red', 'Green']	
s.isEmpty	['Blue', 'Red', 'Green']	False
s.peek()	['Blue', 'Red', 'Green']	'Green'
s.pop()	['Blue', 'Red']	'Green'

The following pseudocode implements four of the stack operations using a fixed size array.

```
SUB isEmpty
   IF top = -1 THEN
      RETURN True
   ELSE
      RETURN False
   ENDIF
ENDSUB

SUB isFull
   IF top = maxSize THEN
      RETURN True
   ELSE
      RETURN False
   ENDIF
ENDSUB

SUB push(item)
   IF isFull THEN
      OUTPUT "Stack is full"
   ELSE
      top ← top + 1
      s(top)← item
   ENDIF
ENDSUB
```

7-39

```
SUB pop
   IF isEmpty THEN
      OUTPUT "Stack is empty"
   ELSE
      item ← s(top)
      top ← top - 1
      RETURN item
   ENDIF
ENDSUB
```

> **Q1:** Write pseudocode for a "peek" subroutine.
>
> **Q2:** Show the state of the stack and stack pointer after the following operations have been performed on the stack containing ('Blue', 'Red'):
>
> (i) Pop
>
> (ii) Pop
>
> (iii) Push('Yellow')

Some languages, such as Python, make it very easy to implement a stack using the built-in dynamic `list` data structure, with the top of the stack being the last element of the list.

The function `len(s)` can be used to determine whether the stack is empty, and if it is not, `pop()` will remove and return the top (last) element. The built-in method `append(item)` will append or push an item onto the top of the stack (the last element of the list).

7-39

Overflow and underflow

A stack will always have a maximum size, because memory cannot grow indefinitely. If the stack is implemented as an array, a full stack can be tested for by examining the value of the stack pointer. An attempt to push another item onto the stack would cause **overflow** so an error message can be given to the user to avoid this. Similarly, if the stack pointer is -1, the stack is empty and **underflow** will occur if an attempt is made to pop an item.

Functions of a call stack

A major use of the stack data structure is to store information about the active subroutines while a computer program is running. The details are hidden from the user in all high level languages.

Holding return addresses

The **call stack** keeps track of the address of the instruction that control should return to when a subroutine ends (the **return address**). Several subroutines may be nested, so that the stack may contain several return addresses which will be popped as each subroutine completes. For example, a subroutine which draws a robot may call subroutines `drawCircle`, `drawRectangle` etc. Subroutine `drawRectangle` may in turn call a subroutine `drawLine`.

A recursive subroutine may contain several calls to itself, so that with each call, a new item (the return address) is pushed onto the stack. When the recursion finally ends, the return addresses that have been pushed onto the stack each time the routine is called are popped one after the other, each time the end of the subroutine is reached. If the programmer makes an error and the recursion never ends, sooner or later memory will run out, the stack will overflow and the program will crash.

Holding parameters

Parameters required for a subroutine (such as, for example, the centre coordinates, line colour and thickness for a circle subroutine) may be held on the call stack. Each call to a subroutine will be given separate space on the call stack for these values.

Local variables

A subroutine frequently uses local variables which are known only within the subroutine. These may also be held in the call stack. Each separate call to a subroutine gets its own space for its local variables. Storing local variables on the call stack is much more efficient than using dynamic memory allocation, which uses **heap** space.

The stack frame

A call stack is composed of **stack frames**. Each stack frame corresponds to a call to a subroutine which has not yet terminated.

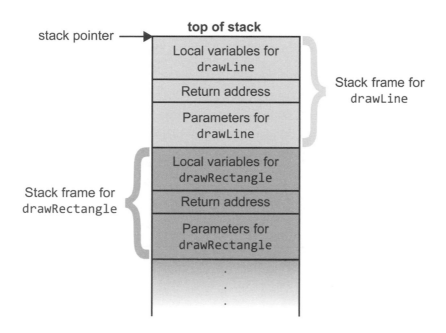

Exercises

1. A Last In, First Out (LIFO) data structure has a pointer called **top**.

   (a) What is this type of data structure known as?   [1]

   (b) Name and briefly describe one type of error that could occur when attempting to add a
       data item or remove a data item from the data structure.   [2]

   (c) Describe briefly one use of this type of data structure in a computer system.   [2]

   (d) Write a pseudocode procedure for reversing the elements of a queue with the aid of a stack.   [6]

Chapter 40 – Hash tables and dictionaries

Objectives

- Be familiar with a hash table and its uses

- Be able to apply simple hashing algorithms

- Know what is meant by a collision and how collisions are handled using rehashing

- Be familiar with the concept of a dictionary

- Be familiar with simple applications of a dictionary

Hashing

Large collections of data, for example customer records in a database, need to be accessible very quickly without having to look through all the records. This can be done by holding an **index** of the physical address on the file where the data is held. But how is the index created?

The answer is that a **hashing algorithm** is applied to the value in the key field of each record to transform it into an address. Normally there are many more possible keys than actual records that need to be stored. For example, suppose 300 records are to be stored, each having a unique 6-digit identifier or key, and 1000 free spaces have been allocated to store the records.

One common hashing algorithm is to divide the key by the number of available addresses and take the remainder as the address. Using the algorithm (address = key mod 1000):

    453781   would be stored at address 781

    447883   would be stored at address 883

    134552   would be stored at address 552

What will happen when the record with key 631552 is to be stored? This will hash to the same address as 134552 and is called a **synonym**. Synonyms are bound to occur with any hashing algorithm, and two record keys hashing to the same address is referred to as a **collision**.

A simple way of dealing with collisions is to store the item in the next available free space. Thus 134552 would be stored at address 553, assuming this space is unoccupied.

Hash table

A hash table is a collection of items stored in such a way that they can quickly be located. The hash table could be implemented as an array or list of a given size with a number of empty spaces. An empty hash table that can store a maximum of 11 items is shown below, with spaces labelled 0,1, 2,...10.

0	1	2	3	4	5	6	7	8	9	10
Empty	Empty	Empty	Empty	Empty	Empty	Empty	Empty	Empty	Empty	Empty

Now assume we wish to store items 78, 55, 34, 19 and 29 in the table using the method described above, using division by 11 and taking the remainder. Collisions are stored in the next available free slot.

First of all, calculate the hash value of each item to be stored.

Item	Hash value
78	1
55	0
34	1
19	8
29	7

Each of these items can now be inserted into their location in the hash table.

0	1	2	3	4	5	6	7	8	9	10
55	78	34	Empty	Empty	Empty	Empty	29	19	Empty	Empty

Q1: Which of the items has caused a collision?

Searching for an item

When searching for an item, these steps are followed:

- apply the hashing algorithm
- examine the resulting cell in the list
- if the item is there, return the item
- if the cell is empty, the item is not in the table
- if there is another item in that spot, keep moving forward until either the item is found or a blank cell is encountered, when it is apparent that the item is not in the table

Other hashing algorithms

To be as efficient as possible, the hashing algorithm needs to be chosen so that it generates the least number of collisions. This will depend to some extent on the distribution of the items to be hashed.

Folding method

There are many other algorithms. The **folding** method divides the item into equal parts, and adds the parts to give the hash value. For example, a phone number 01543 677896 can be divided into groups of two, namely 01, 54, 36, 77, 89, 6. Adding these together, we get 263. If the table has fewer spaces than the maximum possible sum generated by this method, say 100 cells, then the extra steps of dividing by 100 and obtaining the remainder needs to be applied.

Q2: Using the folding method and division by 100, complete the hash table below to show where each number will be stored in a table of 100 spaces. (A sample 123456 is done for you.)
(i) 238464   (ii) 188947   (iii) 276084

Item	"Folded" value	Remainder	Location in hash table
123456	12+34+56=102	2	2
238464			
188947			
276084			

Hashing a string

A hash function can be created for alphanumeric strings by using the ASCII code for each character. A portion of the ASCII table is shown below:

Character	ASCII value
A	65
B	66
C	67
D	68
E	69
F	70
G	71

To hash the word CAB, we could add up the ASCII values for each letter and, if there are 11 spaces in the hash table, for example, divide by 11 and take the remainder as its hash value.

$$67 + 65 + 66 = 198 \quad \text{Hash value} = 198 \bmod 11 = 0$$

so CAB goes in location 0 (assuming that location is empty).

> **Q3:** (i) Using the above hashing algorithm, find the hash values of the following: BAG, TEA, EAT, GAB. (ASCII code for 'T' = 84)
>
> (i) What do you notice about the hash values associated with these words?
>
> (iii) Can you suggest a modification of the hashing algorithm that may result in fewer collisions?

7-40

Collision resolution

The fuller the hash table becomes, the more likely it is that there will be collisions, and this needs to be taken into account when designing the hashing algorithm and deciding on the table size. For example, the size of the table could be designed so that when all the items are stored, only 70% of the table's cells are occupied.

Rehashing is the name given to the process of finding an empty slot when a collision has occurred. The rehashing algorithm used above simply looks for the next empty slot. It will loop round to the first cell if the table of the end is reached. A variation on this would be to look at every third cell, for example (the "plus 3" rehash). Alternatively, the hash value could be incremented by 1, 3, 5, 7, ... until a free space is found.

Different hashing and rehashing methods will work more efficiently on different data sets – the aim is to minimise collisions.

Uses of hash tables

Hash tables are primarily used for efficient lookup, so that for example an index would typically be organised as a hash table. A hash table could be used to look up, say a person's telephone number given their name, or vice versa. They can also be used to store data such as user codes and encrypted passwords that need to be looked up and verified quickly.

Hash tables are used in the implementation of the data structure called a **dictionary**, which is discussed below.

Dictionaries

A dictionary is an abstract data type consisting of associated pairs of items, where each pair consists of a **key** and a **value**. It is a built-in data structure in Python and Visual Basic, for example. When the user supplies the key, the associated value is returned. Items can easily be amended, added to or removed from the dictionary as required.

In Python, dictionaries are written as comma-delimited pairs in the format **key:value** and enclosed in curly braces. For example:

```
IDs = {342:'Harry', 634:'Jasmine', 885:'Max',571:'Sheila'}
```

Operations on dictionaries

It is possible to implement a dictionary using either a static or a dynamic data structure. The implementation needs to include the following operations:

- Create a new empty dictionary
- Add a new `key:value` pair to the dictionary
- Delete a `key:value` pair from the dictionary
- Amend the value in a `key:value` pair
- Return a value associated with key `k`
- Return `True` or `False` depending on whether key is in the dictionary
- Return the length of the dictionary

An interactive Python session is shown below:

```
>>> IDs = {342:'Harry', 634:'Jasmine', 885:'Max', 571:'Sheila'}
>>> IDs
{634: 'Jasmine', 571: 'Sheila', 885: 'Max', 342: 'Harry'}
>>> IDs[885]
'Max'
>>> IDs[333] = 'Maria'
>>> IDs
{634: 'Jasmine', 571: 'Sheila', 885: 'Max', 342: 'Harry', 333: 'Maria'}
>>> IDs[885] = 'Maxine'
>>> IDs

{634: 'Jasmine', 571: 'Sheila', 885: 'Maxine', 342: 'Harry', 333:
'Maria'}
>>> del IDs[885]
>>> IDs
{634: 'Jasmine', 571: 'Sheila', 342: 'Harry', 333: 'Maria'}
>>> 634 in IDs
True
>>> len(IDs)
4
```

Note that the pairs are not held in any particular sequence. The key is hashed using a hashing algorithm and placed at the resulting location in a hash table, so that a fast lookup is possible.

7-40

Example 1

Suppose we are given a piece of text, and wish to find the number of occurrences of each word. The results will be held in a dictionary. For example, in the text *"one man went to mow, went to mow a meadow, one man and his dog, went to mow a meadow"* the dictionary would start with the key value pairs in the format *{word:frequency}*: {'one':2, 'man':2, 'went':3, 'to':3, …}.

The procedure is basically as follows:

```
Read the text word by word
Check if the word exists in the dictionary
If No, add the word to the dictionary with the value 1
Otherwise, increase the frequency value of the word by 1
```

Note that if the dictionary is implemented as a hash table, as in the Python built-in data structure, the words will not be in alphabetical sequence in the dictionary.

Exercises

1. Student records held by a school are stored in a database which organises the data in files using hashing.

    (a)   In the context of storing data in a file, explain what a hash function is.   [1]

    (b)   The system allows for a maximum of 1000 unique 6-digit integer student IDs in the file holding current student records. Give an example of a hashing function that could be used to find a particular record. Ignore collisions.   [2]

2. A bank has a number of safety deposit boxes in which customers can store valuable documents or possessions. The details of which box is rented by a customer with a particular account number are held in a dictionary data structure. Sample entries in the dictionary are:

    {0083456: 'C11', 0154368: 'B74', 1178612: 'B6', 0567123: 'A34'}

    (a)   What value will be returned by a lookup operation using the key 1178612?   [1]

    (b)   The dictionary is implemented using a hash table, using the algorithm

    accountNumber mod 500

    What value is returned by the hashing function when it is applied to account number 0093421?   [1]

    (c)   What is the maximum number of entries that can be made in the dictionary?   [1]

    (d)   (i)   Explain what is meant by a collision.   [1]

    (ii)   Give an example of how a collision might occur in this scenario, using sample account numbers.   [2]

    (iii)   Describe **one** way of dealing with collisions in the hash table.   [1]

7-40

Chapter 41 – Graphs

Objectives

- Be aware of a graph as a data structure used to represent complex relationships
- Be familiar with typical uses for graphs
- Be able to explain the terms: graph, weighted graph, vertex/node, edge/arc, undirected graph, directed graph
- Know how an adjacency matrix and an adjacency list may be used to represent a graph
- Be able to compare the use of adjacency matrices and adjacency lists

Definition of a graph

A graph is a set of **vertices** or **nodes** connected by **edges** or **arcs**. The edges may be one-way or two way. In an **undirected graph**, all edges are bidirectional. If the edges in a graph are all one-way, the graph is said to be a **directed graph** or **digraph.**

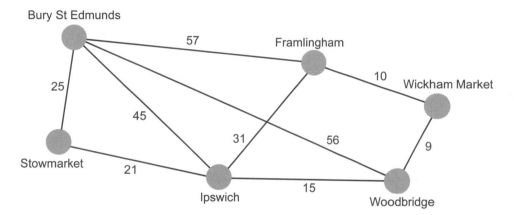

Figure 41.1: An undirected graph with weighted edges

The edges may be **weighted** to show there is a cost to go from one vertex to another as in Figure 41.1. The weights in this example represent distances between towns. A human driver can find their way from one town to another by following a map, but a computer needs to represent the information about distances and connections in a structured, numerical representation.

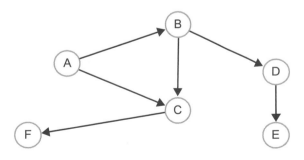

Figure 41.2: A directed, unweighted graph

7-41

Implementing a graph

Two possible implementations of a graph are the **adjacency matrix** and the **adjacency list**.

The adjacency matrix

A two-dimensional array can be used to store information about a directed or undirected graph. Each of the rows and columns represents a node, and a value stored in the cell at the intersection of row i, column j indicates that there is an edge connecting node i and node j.

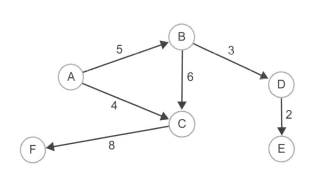

	A	B	C	D	E	F
A		5	4			
B			6	3		
C						8
D					2	
E						
F						

In the case of an **undirected graph**, the adjacency matrix will be symmetric, with the same entry in row 0 column 1 as in row 1 column 0, for example.

An unweighted graph may be represented with 1s instead of weights, in the relevant cells.

7-41

> **Q1:** Draw an adjacency matrix to represent the weighted graph shown in Figure 41.1.

Advantages and disadvantages of the adjacency matrix

An adjacency matrix is very convenient to work with, and adding an edge or testing for the presence of an edge is very simple and quick. However, a sparse graph with many nodes but not many edges will leave most of the cells empty, and the larger the graph, the more memory space will be wasted. Another consideration is that using a static two-dimensional array, it is harder to add or delete nodes.

The adjacency list

An adjacency list is a more space-efficient way to implement a sparsely connected graph. A list of all the nodes is created, and each node points to a list of all the adjacent nodes to which it is directly linked. The adjacency list can be implemented as a list of dictionaries, with the key in each dictionary being the node and the value, the edge weight.

The graph above would be represented as follows:

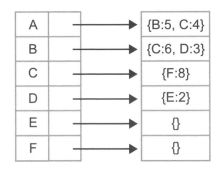

The unweighted graph in Figure 41.2 would be represented as shown below, with the adjacency list containing lists of nodes adjacent to each node. A dictionary data structure is not required here as there are no edge weights.

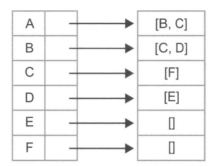

The advantage of this implementation is that is uses much less memory to represent a sparsely connected graph.

Q2: Draw an adjacency list to represent the unweighted graph shown in Figure 41.2, but assuming this time that it is undirected.

Applications of graphs

Graphs may be used to represent, for example:

- computer networks, with nodes representing computers and weighted edges representing the bandwidth between them

- roads between towns, with edge weights representing distances, rail fares or journey times

- tasks in a project, some of which have to be completed before others

- states in a finite state machine

- web pages and links

Google's PageRank algorithm

In the 1990s two postgraduate Computer Science students called Larry Page and Sergey Brin met at Stanford University. Brin was working on data mining systems and Page was working on a system to rank the importance of a research paper according to how often it was cited in other papers.

The pair realised that this concept could be used to build a far superior search engine to the existing ones, and they started to work on a new Search Engine for the Web. The problem they set themselves was how to rank the thousands or even millions of web pages that had a reference to the search term typed in by a user. To make a search engine useful, the most reliable and relevant pages need to appear first in the list of links.

Until that point, pages had generally been ranked simply by the number of times the search term appeared on the page. Page's and Brin's insight was to realise that the usefulness and therefore the **rank** of a given page, say Page X, can be determined by how many visits to Page X result from other web pages containing links to the page. Taking this further, links from a Page Y that itself has a high rank are more significant than those from pages which have themselves only had a few visits. The importance or authority of a page is also taken into account so that a link from a .gov page or a page belonging to the BBC site, for example, may be given a higher PageRank rating.

7-41

An initial version of Google was launched in August 1996 from Stanford University's website. By mid-1998 they had 10,000 searches a day, and realised the potential of their invention.

They represented the Web as a directed graph of pages, using an algorithm to calculate the PageRank (named after Larry Page) of each page. Every web page is a node and any hyperlinks on the page are edges, with the edge weightings dependent on the PageRank algorithm.

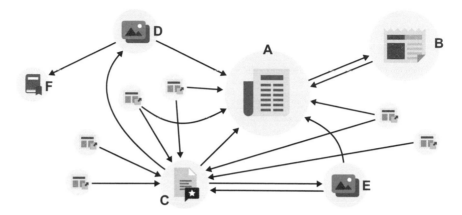

*Using PageRank, **B** has a higher page rank than **C** because it is a more authoritative source.*

By 2015, Google was processing 40,000 search queries every second, worldwide. David Vise, the author of The Google Story noted that "Not since Gutenberg* ... has any new invention empowered individuals, and transformed access to information, as profoundly as Google."

(*Gutenberg invented the printing press in the fifteenth century)

7-41

Exercises

1. The figure below shows an adjacency matrix representation of a directed graph (digraph).

		To				
		A	**B**	**C**	**D**	**E**
From	**A**	0	5	3	10	0
	B	0	0	1	8	0
	C	0	0	0	7	6
	D	0	0	0	0	4
	E	0	0	0	0	0

(a) Draw a diagram of the directed graph, showing edge weights. [3]

(b) Draw an adjacency list representing this graph. [3]

(c) Give **one** advantage of using an adjacency matrix to represent a graph, and **one** advantage of using an adjacency list. Explain the circumstances in which each is more appropriate. [3]

2. Graph algorithms are used with GPS navigation systems, social networking sites, computer networks, computer games, exam timetabling, matching problems and many other applications.

Describe **two** practical applications of graphs. [6]

Chapter 42 – Trees

Objectives

- Know that a tree is a connected, undirected graph with no cycles
- Know that a binary tree is a rooted tree in which each node has at most two children
- Be familiar with typical uses for rooted trees

Concept of a tree

Trees are a very common data structure in many areas of computer science and other contexts. A family tree is an example of a tree, and a folder structure where a root directory has many folders and sub-folders is another example. Like a tree in nature, a **rooted tree** has a root, branches and leaves, the difference being that a rooted tree in computer science has its root at the top and its leaves at the bottom.

Typical uses for rooted trees include:

- manipulating hierarchical data, such as folder structures or moves in a game
- making information easy to search (see binary tree search below)
- manipulating sorted lists of data

The uses of various tree-traversal algorithms are covered in Section 8, Chapter 44.

Generations of a family may be thought of as having a tree structure:

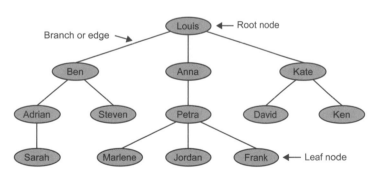

The tree shown above has a **root node**, and is therefore defined as a **rooted tree**. Here are some terms used in connection with rooted trees:

Node: The nodes contain the tree data

Edge: An edge connects two nodes. Every node except the root is connected by exactly one edge from another node in the level above it

Root: This is the only node that has no incoming edges

Child: The set of nodes that have incoming edges from the same node

Parent: A node is a parent of all the nodes it connects to with outgoing edges

Subtree: The set of nodes and edges comprised of a parent and all descendants of the parent. A subtree may also be a leaf

Leaf node: A node that has no children

> **Q1:** Identify the left subtree of the root, the parent of Frank and the children of Kate. How many parent nodes are there in the tree? How many child nodes?

7-42

Note that a rooted tree is a special case of a **connected graph**. A node can only be connected to one parent node, and to its children. It is described as having has no **cycles** because there can be no connection between children, or between branches, for example from Ben to Anna or Petra to Kate.

A more general definition of a tree

A tree is a connected, undirected graph with no cycles. "Connected" implies that it is always possible to find a path from a node to any other node, by backtracking if necessary. "No cycles" means that it is not possible to find a path in the tree which returns to the start node without traversing an edge twice. Note that a tree does not have to have a root.

Q2: Using the above definition of a tree, which of the following diagrams represents a tree? If any of them does not represent a tree, explain why.

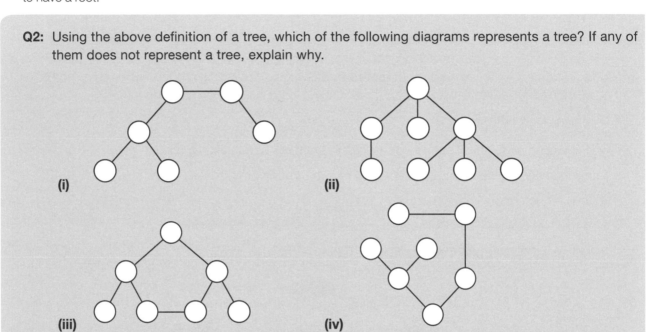

(i)   (ii)

(iii)   (iv)

A binary search tree

A **binary tree** is a rooted tree in which each node has a maximum of two children. A **binary search tree** holds items in such a way that the tree can be searched quickly and easily for a particular item, new items can be easily added, and the whole tree can be printed out in sequence. A binary search tree is a typical use of a rooted tree.

Constructing a binary search tree

Suppose the following list of numbers is to be inserted into a binary tree, in the order given, in such a way that the tree can be quickly searched.

17, 8, 4, 12, 22, 19, 14, 5, 30, 25

The tree is constructed using the following algorithm:

Place the first item at the root. Then for each item in the list, visit the root, which becomes the current node, and branch left if the item is less than the value at the current node, and right if the item is greater than the value at the current node. Continue down the branch, applying the rule at each node visited, until a leaf node is reached. The item is then placed to the left or right of this node, depending on whether it is less than or greater than the value at that node.

Following this algorithm, 17 is placed at the root. 8 is less than 17, so is placed at a new node to the left of the root.

4 is less than 17, so we branch left at the root, branch left at 8, and place it to the left.

12 is less than 17, so we branch left at the root, branch right at 8, and place it to the right.

The final tree looks like this:

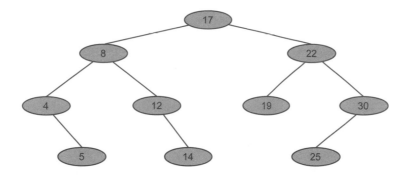

To search the tree for the number 19, for example, we follow the same steps.

19 is greater than 17, so branch right.

19 is less than 22, so branch left. There it is!

Q3: (a) Which nodes will be visited when searching for the number 14?

(b) Which nodes will be visited when searching for the number 21, which is not in the tree?

(c) Where will new nodes 10 and 20 be inserted?

Traversing a binary tree

There are three ways of traversing a tree:

- Pre-order traversal
- In-order traversal
- Post-order traversal

The names refer to whether the root of each sub-tree is visited before, between or after both branches have been traversed.

Pre-order traversal

Draw an outline around the tree structure, starting to the left of the root. As you pass to the left of a node (where the red dot is marked), output the data in that node.

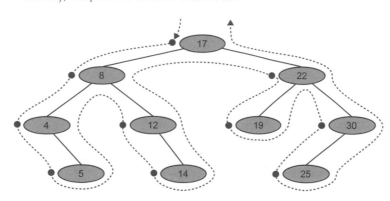

The nodes will be visited in the sequence 17, 8, 4, 5, 12, 14, 22, 19, 30, 25

A pre-order traversal may be used to produce prefix notation, used in functional programming languages. A simple illustration would be a function statement, `x = sum a,b` rather than `x = a + b`, in which the operation comes before the operands rather than between them, as in infix notation.

In-order traversal

Draw an outline around the tree structure, starting to the left of the root. As you pass underneath a node (where the red dot is marked), output the data in that node.

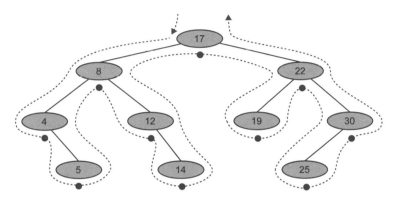

The nodes will be visited in the sequence 4, 5, 8, 12, 14, 17, 19, 22, 25, 30.

The in-order traversal visits the nodes in sequential order.

> **Q4:** Construct a binary search tree to hold the names Mark, Stephanie, Chigozie, Paul, Anne, Hanna, Luke, David, Vincent, Tom. List the names, in the order they would be checked, to find David.
>
> **Q5:** List the names in the order they would be output when an in-order traversal is performed.

Post-order traversal

Draw an outline around the tree structure, starting to the left of the root. As you pass to the right of a node (where the red dot is marked), output the data in that node.

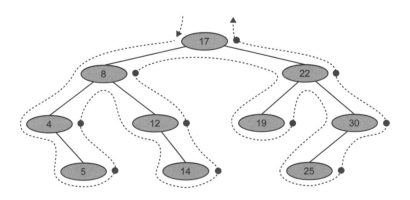

The nodes will be visited in the sequence 5, 4, 14, 12, 8, 19, 25, 30, 22, 17.

Post-order traversal is used in program compilation to produce **Reverse Polish Notation** (Chapter 55).

Algorithms for implementing a binary tree and each of these traversals will be covered in Chapter 44.

Implementation of a binary search tree

A binary search tree can be implemented using an array of records, with each node consisting of:

- left pointer
- data item
- right pointer

Alternatively, it could be held in a list of tuples, or three separate lists or arrays, one for each of the pointers and one for the data items.

The numbers 17, 8, 4, 12, 22, 19, 14, 5, 30, 25 used to construct the tree above could be held as follows:

	left	data	right
tree[0]	1	17	4
tree[1]	2	8	3
tree[2]	-1	4	7
tree[3]	-1	12	6
tree[4]	5	22	8
tree[5]	-1	19	-1
tree[6]	-1	14	-1
tree[7]	-1	5	-1
tree[8]	9	30	-1
tree[9]	-1	25	-1

7-42

For example, the left pointer in tree[0] points to tree[1] and the right pointer points to tree[4]. The value -1 is a 'rogue value' which indicates that there is no child on the relevant side (left or right).

Q6: Show how the search tree below could be implemented in an array with left and right pointers.

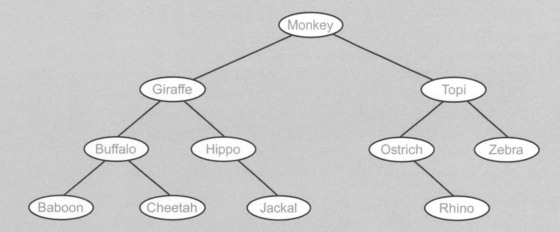

Names were inserted in the tree in the following order: Monkey, Topi, Ostrich, Giraffe, Hippo, Zebra, Buffalo, Cheetah, Rhino, Baboon, Jackal

Exercises

1. Figure 1 shows an adjacency matrix representation of a directed graph (digraph).

Figure 1

		To				
		1	**2**	**3**	**4**	**5**
From	**1**	0	1	0	1	0
	2	0	0	1	1	0
	3	0	0	0	0	0
	4	0	0	0	0	1
	5	0	1	0	0	0

(a) Complete this unfinished diagram of the directed graph.   [2]

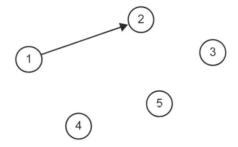

(b) Directed graphs can also be represented by an adjacency list.

Explain under what circumstances an adjacency matrix is the most appropriate method to represent a directed graph, and under what circumstances an adjacency list is more appropriate.   [2]

(c) A tree is a particular type of graph.

What properties must a graph have for it to be a tree?   [2]

(d) Data may be stored as a binary tree.

Show how the following data may be stored as a binary tree for subsequent processing in alphabetic order by drawing the tree. Assume that the first item is the root of the tree and the rest of the data items are inserted into the tree in the order given.

Data items: Jack, Bramble, Snowy, Butter, Squeak, Bear, Pip   [3]

(e) A binary tree such as the one created in part (d) could be represented using one array of records or, alternatively, using three one dimensional arrays.

Describe how the data in the array(s) could be structured for one of these two possible methods of representation.   [3]

AQA Comp 3 Qu 7 2010

7-42

Chapter 43 – Vectors

Objectives

- Be familiar with the concept of a vector and notations for specifying a vector as a list of numbers, as a function or as a geometric point in space

- Represent a vector using a list, dictionary or array data structure

- Perform operations on vectors: addition, scalar vector multiplication, convex combination, dot or scalar product

- Describe applications of dot product of two vectors

Vector notation

A **vector** can be represented as:

- a list of numbers

- a function

- a way of representing a geometric point in space

There are several different notations for specifying a given vector.

1. A list of numbers may be written as [2.0, 3.14159, -1.0, 2.71828].

2. A 4-vector over $\mathbb{R}$ such as [2.0, 3.14159, -1.0, 2.71828] may be written as $\mathbb{R}^4$

3. A vector may be interpreted as a function, $f : S \mapsto \mathbb{R}$ where S is the set {0, 1, 2, 3} and $\mathbb{R}$ the set of real numbers

   For example

   $0 \mapsto 2.0$

   $1 \mapsto 3.14159$

   $2 \mapsto 1.0$

   $3 \mapsto 2.71828$ where $\mapsto$ means "maps to"

   Note that all the entries must be drawn from the same field, e.g. $\mathbb{R}$.

Vectors in up to 3 dimensions, ie up to $\mathbb{R}^3$ can also be conveniently represented geometrically, and this will be explained later in the chapter.

Implementation of vectors in a programming language

In Python, for example, a vector may be represented as a list: [2.0, 3.14159, -1.0, 2.71828]

In a different language, it could be represented in a one-dimensional array.

The 4-vector example could be represented as a dictionary: {0:2.0, 1:3.14159, 2: -1.0, 3: 2.71828}

Vectors in computer science

Many applications in Computing involve processing spatial information. For example:

- a computer controlling a robot arm needs to keep track of its current coordinates, and work out how to move it to its next location

- computer games and simulations need to work out how objects moving in 3-D space can be represented on the screen; for example, how does a ball move when it is struck by a golf club?

- on-board computers in fly-by-wire aircraft need to take into account wind speed and direction when setting and holding a course in three dimensions.

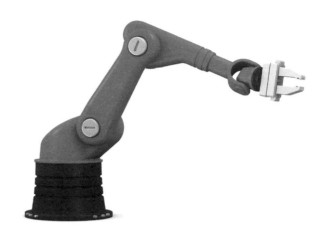

In order to perform these tasks, the computer must represent spatial information and movement in a numerical way. In mathematics, **vectors** and **matrices** are used to do this, and these concepts are crucial for any computer application which involves spatial movement.

Vectors in mathematics

In mathematics, a very common use of vectors is as a numerical way of describing and processing spatial information such as **position**, **velocity**, **acceleration** or **force**.

Velocity may be represented by a vector showing both speed and direction. This can be shown graphically by an arrow with its tail at the origin and its head at coordinates (x,y). Speed is represented by length **a**, and direction by the angle between **A** and the x-axis.

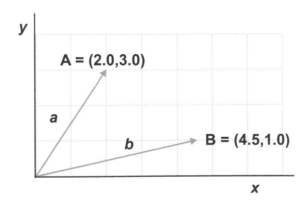

The graphical representation shows how a vector consisting of just two numbers can represent both **magnitude** and **direction**.

Adding and subtracting vectors

Vectors may be added by adding the x and y coordinates separately:

C = A + B = (2.0 + 4.5, 3.0 + 1.0) = (6.5, 4.0)

The resultant vector can be represented graphically by moving the vector **b** so that it joins on to the end of **a**. The resulting vector **c** will represent the new magnitude and direction. Physically, you can imagine an aeroplane flying at speed **b**, with a wind **a** blowing at an angle to the direction of flight: the aeroplane will actually travel with the combined speed and direction shown by the vector **c** in the graph below.

7-43

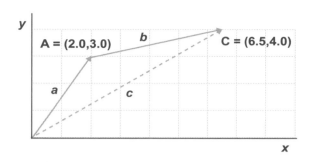

Q1: How can we calculate the lengths of the lines marked **a** and **c**?

We can also subtract the vector **a** from the vector **b**, to get a vector **d** = (2.5, -2.0). This might represent a wind **a** blowing in the opposite direction.

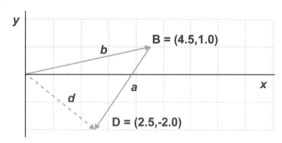

Example

A vector **Current** represents the speed (in km/hr) and direction of a current. A swimmer, who swims at 8km/hr, has to swim to a buoy at B, and we need to find the direction he should swim in (marked Swimmer).

7-43

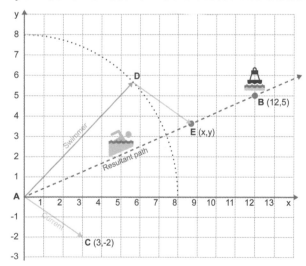

The vector **Swimmer** must lie on the arc of radius 8 shown in red, since any point on this arc represents the distance the swimmer will travel in one hour. To find the direction he must swim in, we need to transpose the current vector so that it its tail is on the arc and its head on the desired resultant path. If he keeps swimming in direction AD he will eventually reach the buoy at B.

```
swimmer = resultant path - current
        = (x,y) - (3,-2)
        = (x-3,y+2)
```

Scaling vectors

A vector can be scaled by multiplying it by a value. In the figure below, B = 3 * A.

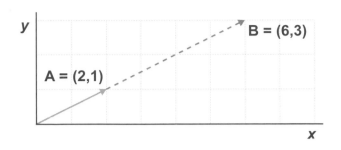

Convex combination of two vectors

A **convex combination of vectors** is an expression of the form

$\alpha u + \beta v$ where $\alpha + \beta = 1$ and $\alpha, \beta \geq 0$

e.g.   0.7 *(5.0, 3.0) + 0.3 * (4.0 ,2.0) = (3.5, 2.1) + (1.2, 0.6) = (4.7, 2.7)

In the diagram below, if A and B represent two vectors, any vector C represented by (αA + βB) must lie within the shaded area between A and B.

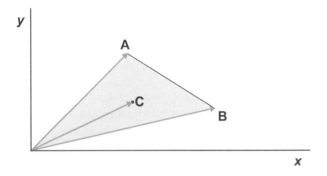

7-43

Q2: If two vectors P and Q are defined as P = (0,4) and Q = (6,0), draw the vector space represented by

R = αP + βQ   where $\alpha + \beta = 1$ and $\alpha, \beta \geq 0$

Mark on the diagram the position of vector R = 0.75P + 0.25Q

Dot product of two vectors

To find the **dot product** (sometimes called the **scalar product**) of two vectors, each component of the first vector is multiplied by the corresponding component of the second vector, and the products are added together.

The dot product of two vectors u and v where u = [u_1, ..., u_n] and v = [v_1, ..., v_n] is

$u \bullet v = u_1 v_1 + u_2 v_2 + ... + u_n v_n$

Thus [2, 3, 4] $\bullet$ [5, 2, 1] = 10 + 6 + 4 = 20

Notice that the result of the dot product is **a number**, not a vector, and it can be used as a way to compare two vectors.

Finding the angle between two vectors

Graphics programmers often need to find the angle between two vectors, and the dot product may be used to do this. Consider the two vectors u and v in the figure below:

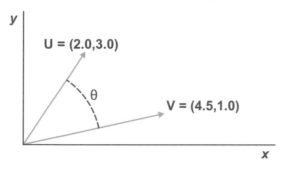

The lengths of the vectors u and v can be written in mathematical notation as ‖u‖ and ‖v‖.

The formula for finding the angle θ between u and v is:

$$\cos \theta = \frac{(u \bullet v)}{(\|u\| \bullet \|v\|)}$$

The steps to find the angle are:

1. Calculate the dot product of the two vectors

    u • v = (2.0 x 4.5) + (3.0 x 1.0)

    = 9 + 3 = 12

2. Calculate the values of ‖u‖ and ‖v‖ (i.e. the length of each vector)

    $\|u\|^2 = 2.0^2 + 3.0^2 = 13$ (using Pythagoras' theorem)

    $\|u\| = \sqrt{13} = 3.6$

    $\|v\|^2 = 4.5^2 + 1.0^2 = 20.25 + 1 = 21.25$

    $\|v\| = \sqrt{21.25} = 4.6$

3. Calculate   ‖u‖ • ‖v‖

    ‖u‖ • ‖v‖ = 3.6 x 4.6 = 16.56

4. Calculate   cos θ = 12 / 16.56

    = 0.72

5. Look up value of θ in tables or use a calculator

    θ = 44° (approximately)

Q3: Calculate the angle between two vectors A and B where A = (3, 4) and B = (6, 0).

Since cos 90° = 0, two vectors u and v are orthogonal (at right angles to each other) if and only if u • v = 0.

Q4: Calculate the dot product of the two vectors (3, 4) and (-2, -1.5).

(a) Are these vectors at right angles to each other? Draw these vectors on squared paper.

(b) What is the value of cos θ, where θ is the angle between the two vectors (3, 4) and (7.5, 10)?

(c) What is the angle between the two vectors?

7-43

Exercises

1. Two vectors A and B are defined as A = (1, 3) and B = (10, 4). Calculate:

    (a) A + B [1]

    (b) A • B [1]

    (c) 3 * A [1]

2. (a) A and B are two vectors implemented as lists. Trace through the following pseudocode and state what is printed. What does the program calculate? [3]

```
SUB calcX(A,B)
    calcAB ← 0
    for i ← 0 TO len(A) - 1
        calcAB ← calcAB + (A[i] + B[i])
    END FOR
    RETURN calcAB
ENDSUB

#main
A ← [3,4]
B ← [2,1]
x ← calc(A,B)
OUTPUT x
```

    (b) (i) What are the coordinates (x, y) of the normalised vector B in the following diagram?

    (Note: A normalised vector always has length 1.)

    [2]

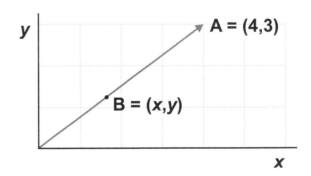

    (ii) Write a pseudocode subroutine `normalise(A)` to normalise a vector A(x, y). [4]

3. (a) Calculate the dot product of the vectors u = (3, 4) and v = (-1.5, -2) [1]

    (b) Use the formula

$$\cos \theta = \frac{(u \bullet v)}{(\|u\| \bullet \|v\|)}$$

    to calculate the cosine of the angle θ between the two vectors. [2]

    (c) Plot the points roughly to verify that u and v point in opposite directions. [2]

Section 8

Algorithms

In this section:

8

Chapter 44 – Recursive algorithms

Objectives

- Be familiar with the use of recursive techniques in programming languages

- Be able to solve simple problems using recursion

- Be able to trace recursive tree-traversal algorithms: pre-order, post-order, in-order

- Be able to describe uses of tree-traversal algorithms

Definition of a recursive subroutine

A subroutine is **recursive** if it is defined in terms of itself. The process of executing the subroutine is called **recursion**.

A recursive routine has three essential characteristics:

- A stopping condition or **base case** must be included which when met means that the routine will not call itself and will start to 'unwind'

- For input values other than the stopping condition, the routine must call itself

- The stopping condition must be reached after a finite number of calls

Recursion is a useful technique for the programmer when the algorithm itself is essentially recursive.

Example

A simple example of a recursive routine is the calculation of a factorial, where **n!** (read as **factorial n**) is defined as follows:

If n = 0 then n! = 1

otherwise n! = n x (n-1) x (n-2) ... x 3 x 2 x 1

Thus for example 5! = 5 x 4 x 3 x 2 x 1

If we were calculating this manually, we probably calculate 5 x 4 =20, then multiply 20 by 3 and so on. The calculation could be written as

5! = ((((5 x 4) x 3) x 2) x 1) = (((20 x 3) x 2) x 1) = ((60 x 2) x 1) = 120 x 1 = 120

This is essentially how recursion works. In pseudocode, it can be written like this:

```
SUB calcFactorial(n)
    IF n = 0 THEN
       factorial ← 1
    ELSE
       factorial ← n * calcFactorial(n-1)
       OUTPUT factorial      #LINE A
    ENDIF
    RETURN factorial
ENDSUB
```

Nothing will be printed until the routine has stopped calling itself. As soon as the stopping condition is reached, in this case n = 0, the variable factorial is set equal to 1, the return statement at the end of the subroutine is reached and control is passed back (for the first time, but not the last) to the next statement after the last call to calcFactorial, which is the OUTPUT statement marked LINE A.

> **Q1:** How many times is the `OUTPUT` statement executed? What is printed by the statement `OUTPUT`
> `factorial` when the routine is called with the statement: x ← `calcFactorial(4)`?

Use of the call stack

In Chapter 39 the use of the **call stack** was discussed. Each time a subroutine is called, the return address, parameters and local variables used in the subroutine are held in a **stack frame** in the call stack. Consider the following example:

```
1. SUB printList(num)
2.    num ← num - 1
3.    if num > 1 then printList(num)
4.    print("At B, num = ", num)     //Line B
5. ENDSUB
6. #main program
7. x ← 4
8. printList(x)
9. print("At A, x = ", x)                //Line A
```

Return addresses, parameters and local variables (not used here) are put on the stack each time a subroutine is called, and popped from the stack each time the end of a subroutine is reached. At Line 8, for example, Line 9 (referred to here as Line A) is the first return address to be put on the stack with the parameter 4 when `printlist(x)` is called from the main program, with the parameter 4.

Representations of the current state of the stack each time a recursive call is made, and the subsequent "unwinding" are shown below.

The output from the program is:

At B, num = 1   (printed at Line B)

At B, num = 2   (printed at Line B)

At B, num = 3   (printed at Line B)

At A, x = 4   (printed at Line A)

> **Q2:** Write iterative and recursive routines to sum the integers held in a list `numbers`.
> Show how each routine will be called.

Tree traversal algorithms

In the previous chapter, three tree traversal algorithms were described: in-order, pre-order and post-order. The pseudocode algorithm for each of these traversals is recursive.

The algorithm for an in-order traversal is

```
traverse the left subtree
visit the root node
traverse the right subtree
```

Example of in-order traversal

An algebraic expression is represented by the following binary tree. It could be represented in memory as, for example, three 1-dimensional arrays or as a list with each list element holding the data and left and right pointers to the left and right subtrees. The value of the root node is stored as the first element of the list.

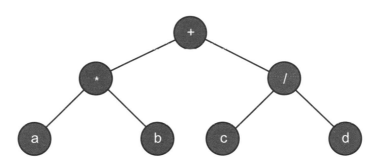

Figure 1

Suppose this data is held as shown below:

	left	data	right
tree[0]	1	+	2
tree[1]	3	*	4
tree[2]	5	/	6
tree[3]	-1	a	-1
tree[4]	-1	b	-1
tree[5]	-1	c	-1
tree[6]	-1	d	-1

8-44

In pseudocode:

```
SUB inorderTraverse(p)
   IF tree[p].left <> -1 THEN
      inorderTraverse(tree[p].left)
   ENDIF
   OUTPUT (tree[p].data)
   IF tree[p].right <> -1 THEN
      inorderTraverse(tree[p].right)
   ENDIF
ENDSUB
```

The routine is called with a statement `inorderTraverse(0)`

Tracing through the algorithm, the nodes are output in the order **a * b + c / d**.

Use of in-order traversal algorithm

An in-order traversal may be used to output the values held in the nodes in alphabetic or numerical sequence. An example is given in Chapter 42.

Algorithm for post-order traversal

The algorithm for a post-order traversal is

```
traverse the left subtree
traverse the right subtree
visit the root node
```

In pseudocode:

```
SUB postorderTraverse(p)
   IF tree[p].left <> -1 THEN
      postorderTraverse(tree[p].left)
   ENDIF
   IF tree[p].right <> -1 THEN
      postorderTraverse(tree[p].right)
   ENDIF
   OUTPUT (tree[p].data)
ENDSUB
```

The nodes are output in the sequence **a b * c d / +**. This is the sequence in which algebraic expressions are written using **Reverse Polish Notation**, which is covered in Chapter 55.

Algorithm for pre-order traversal

The algorithm for a pre-order traversal is

```
visit the root node
traverse the left subtree
traverse the right subtree

SUB preorderTraverse(p)
   OUTPUT (tree[p].data)
   IF tree[p].left <> -1 THEN
      preorderTraverse(tree[p].left)
   ENDIF
   IF tree[p].right <> -1 THEN
      preorderTraverse(tree[p].right)
   ENDIF
ENDSUB
```

8-44

A pre-order traversal may be used for copying a tree, and for producing a prefix expression from an expression tree such as the one shown in Figure 1, where the nodes will be output in the order **+ * a b / c d**. Prefix is used in some compilers and calculators.

Exercises

1. (a) Explain briefly the main features of a recursive procedure from the programmer's point of view. What is required from the system in order to enable recursion to be used? [3]

(b) The following recursive subroutine carries out a list operation.

```
SUB listProcess(numList)
    IF length(numlist) > 0 THEN
        Remove first element of numlist and store in first
        listProcess (numList)
        append first to end of numList
    ENDIF
    RETURN numList
ENDSUB
```

(i) Complete the following trace table if the list numbers is defined in the main program as

numbers ← [3,5,10,2]

and the subroutine is called with the statement

new ← listProcess(numbers)

length (numlist)	numlist				first	new
	0	1	2	3	first	new
4	3	5	10	2	3	

[6]

(ii) Explain what the subroutine does. [1]

2. The routine stars(n) is called from the main program with the statement stars(4).

```
1. SUB stars(n)
2.    IF n = 1 THEN
3.        RETURN "*"
4.    ELSE
5.        RETURN stars(n-1) + "*"
6.    ENDIF
7. ENDSUB

   #main program
8. line ← stars(4)
9. OUTPUT line
```

(a) How many times is the subroutine stars called? Explain your answer. [4]

(b) What is printed by the final line of the program (line 9)? [1]

(c) What will be printed at line 9 if line 5 is replaced with the following statement?

RETURN stars(n-1) + str(n)

[1]

8-44

Chapter 45 – Big-O notation

Objectives

- Be familiar with the concept of a function as a mapping from one set of values to another
- Be familiar with the concept of linear, polynomial, exponential and logarithmic functions
- Be familiar with the notion of permutation of a set of objects or values
- Be familiar with the Big-O notation to express time complexity
- Be able to derive the time complexity of an algorithm

Comparing algorithms

Algorithms may be compared on how much time they need to solve a particular problem. This is referred to as the **time complexity** of the algorithm. The goal is to design algorithms which will run quickly while taking up the minimal amount of resources such as memory.

In order to compare the efficiency of different algorithms in terms of execution time, we need to quantify the number of basic operations or steps that the algorithm will need, in terms of the number of items to be processed.

For example, consider these two algorithms, which both calculate the sum of the first n integers.

```
SUB sumIntegersMethod1(n)
    sum ← 0
    FOR i ← 1 TO n
        sum ← sum + n
    ENDFOR
    RETURN sum
ENDSUB
```

The second algorithm computes the same sum using a different algorithm:

```
SUB sumIntegersMethod2(n)
    sum ← n * (n+1)/2
    RETURN sum
ENDSUB
```

Q1: Which algorithm is more efficient? Why?

The first algorithm performs one operation (sum ← 0) outside the loop and n operations inside the FOR loop, a total of n + 1 operations. As n increases, the extra operation to initialise sum is insignificant, and the larger the value of n, the more inefficient this algorithm is. Its **order of magnitude** or **time complexity** is basically n. The second algorithm, on the other hand, takes the same amount of time whatever the value of n. Its time complexity is a constant.

We will return to this idea later in the Chapter, but first, we need to look at some of the maths involved in calculating the time complexity of different algorithms.

Introduction to functions

The order of magnitude, or time complexity of an algorithm can be expressed as a **function** of its size.

A function maps one set of values onto another.

INPUT x

FUNCTION f: OUTPUT f(x)

A linear function

A linear function is expressed in general terms as **f(x) = ax + c**

Values of the function f(x) = 3x + 4 are shown below for x = 1, 10, 100, 10,000

x	3x	4	y = f(x)
1	3	4	7
10	30	4	34
100	300	4	304
10,000	30,000	4	30,004

8-45

Notice that the constant term has proportionally less and less effect on the value of the function as the value of x increases. The only term that is significant is 3x, and f(x) increases in a straight line as x increases.

A polynomial function

A polynomial expression is expressed as **f(x) = ax^m + bx + c**

Values of the function f(x) = 2x^2 + 10x + 50 are shown below for x = 1, 10, 100, 10,000

x	x^2	2x^2	10x	50	y = f(x)
1	1	2	10	50	62
10	100	200	100	50	350
100	10,000	20,000	1,000	50	21,050
10,000	100,000,000	200,000,000	100,000	50	200,100,050

The values of b and c have a smaller and smaller effect on the answer as x increases, compared with the value of a. The only term that really matters is the term in x^2, if we are approximating the value of the function for a large value of x.

An exponential function

An exponential function takes the form **f(x) = ab^x**. This function grows very large, very quickly!

Q2: What is the value of f(x) = 2^x when x = 1? When x = 10? When x = 100?

A logarithmic function

A logarithmic function takes the form **f(x) = a log$_n$ x**

"The logarithm of a number is the power that the base must be raised to make it equal to the number."

Values of the function f(x) = log$_2$ x are shown below for x = 1, 8, 1,024, 1,048,576.

x	y = log$_2$ x
1	0
8 (2^3)	3
1024 (2^{10})	10
1,048,576 (2^{20})	20

Permutations

The permutation of a set of objects is the number of ways of arranging the objects. For example, if you have 3 objects A, B and C you can choose any of A, B or C to be the first object. You then have two choices for the second object, making 3 x 2 = 6 different ways of arranging the first two objects, and then just one way of placing the third object. The six permutations are ABC, ACB, BAC, BCA, CAB, CBA.

> **Q3:** How many permutations are there of four objects? How many ways are there of arranging six students in a line?

The formula for calculating the number of permutations of four objects is 4 x 3 x 2 x 1, written 4! and spoken as "four factorial". (Note that 10! = 3.6 million... so don't try getting 10 students to line up in all possible ways!)

Big-O notation

Now that we have got all the maths out of the way and hopefully understood, we can study the so-called **Big-O notation** which is used to express the **time complexity**, or performance, of an algorithm. ('O' stands for 'Order'.)

The best way to understand this notation is to look at some examples.

O(1) (Constant time)

O(1) describes an algorithm that takes **constant time** (the same amount of time) to execute regardless of the size of the input data set.

Suppose array a has n items. The statement

```
length ← len(a)
```

will take the same amount of time to execute however many items are held in the array.

O(n) (linear time)

O(n) describes an algorithm whose performance will grow in **linear time**, in direct proportion to the size of the data set. For example, a linear search of an array of 1000 unsorted items will take 1000 times longer than searching an array of 1 item.

O(n²) (Polynomial time)

O(n^2) describes an algorithm whose performance is directly proportional to the square of the size of the data set. A program with two nested loops each performed n times will typically have an order of time complexity O(n^2). The running time of the algorithm grows in **polynomial time**.

O(2ⁿ) (Exponential time)

O(2^n) describes an algorithm where the time taken to execute will double with every additional item added to the data set. The execution time grows in **exponential time** and quickly becomes very large.

O(log n) (Logarithmic time)

The time taken to execute an algorithm of order O(log n) (**logarithmic time**) will grow very slowly as the size of the data set increases. A **binary search** is a good example of an algorithm of time complexity O(log n). Doubling the size of the data set has very little effect on the time the algorithm takes to complete. (Note that in Big-O notation the base of the logarithm, 2 in this case, is not specified because it is irrelevant to the time complexity, being a constant factor.)

O(n!) (Factorial time)

The time taken to execute an algorithm of order O(n!) will grow very quickly, faster than O(2^n). Suppose that the problem is to find all the permutations of n letters. If n=2, there are 2 permutations to find. If n=6, there are 720 permutations – far more than 2^n, which is only 64.

8-45

Q4: A hacker trying to discover a password starts by checking a dictionary containing 170,000 words. What is the maximum number of words he will need to try out?

This procedure fails to find the password. He now needs to try random combinations of the letters in the password. He starts with 6-letter combinations of a-z, A-Z.

Explain why the second procedure will take so much longer than the first.

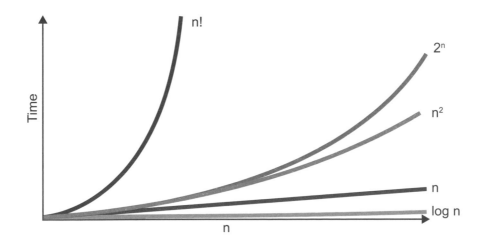

Graphs of log n, n, n^2, 2^n, n!

Calculating the time complexity of an algorithm

Here are two different algorithms for finding the smallest element in an array called `arrayX` of size `n`. Assume the index starts at 0.

The first algorithm puts the first value in the array equal to a variable called `minimum`. It then compares each subsequent item in the array to the first item, and if it is smaller, replaces minimum with the new lowest value.

```
minimum ← arrayX[0]
FOR k ← 1 TO n - 1
   IF arrayX[k] < minimum THEN
      minimum ← arrayX[k]
   ENDIF
ENDFOR
```

To calculate the time complexity of the algorithm in Big-O notation, we need to count the number of basic operations relevant to the size of the problem that it performs. The basic operation here is the `IF` statement, and as this is performed n times, the time complexity is O(n).

The second algorithm compares each value in the array to all the other values of the array, and if the current value is less than or equal to all the other values in the array then it is the minimum.

```
FOR k ← 0 TO n - 1
   isMinimum ← True
   FOR j ← 0 TO n - 1
      IF arrayX[k] > arrayX[j] THEN
         isMinimum ← false
      ENDIF
   ENDFOR
   IF (isMinimum) THEN
      minimum ← arrayX[k]
   ENDIF
ENDFOR
```

To calculate the time complexity of this algorithm, we count the number of basic operations it performs.

There are two basic operations in the outer loop, (`isMinimum ← true` and the final `IF` statement) which are each performed n times. The inner loop has one basic operations performed n^2 times.

This gives us a time complexity of $2n + n^2$, but as discussed earlier, the only significant term is the one in n^2. The time complexity is therefore O(n^2).

> **Q5:** What is the time complexity of each of the two subroutines `sumIntegerMethod1` and `sumIntegerMethod2` discussed at the beginning of this chapter?

8-45

Exercises

1. Assuming a is an array of n elements, compute the time complexity of the following algorithm.

Explain how you arrive at your answer.

```
duplicate ← False
FOR i ← 0 TO n - 2
    FOR j ← i + 1 TO n - 1
        IF a[i] = a[j] THEN duplicate ← True
    ENDFOR
ENDFOR
```
[3]

2. (a) Complete the following table showing values of f(n):

n	1	2	4	8	12
$f(n) = n^2$	1	4			
$f(n) = 2^n$	2	4			
$f(n) = \log_2 n$	0	1			3.585
$f(n) = n!$	1				479,001,600

[4]

(b) Place the following algorithms in order of time complexity, with the most efficient algorithm first. [2]

Algorithm A of time complexity $O(n)$

Algorithm B of time complexity $O(2^n)$

Algorithm C of time complexity $O(\log n)$

Algorithm D of time complexity $O(n^2)$

Algorithm E of time complexity $O(n!)$

(c) Explain why algorithms with time complexity $O(n!)$ are generally considered not to be helpful in solving a problem. Under what circumstances would such an algorithm be considered? [3]

(d) The merge sort algorithm has time complexity $O(n \log n)$. For a list of 1,024 items in random sequence, is this algorithm more or less efficient than a sort algorithm of time complexity $O(n^2)$? Explain your answer, with the aid of an example. [3]

Chapter 46 – Searching and sorting

Objectives

- Know and be able to trace and analyse the time complexity of the linear search and binary search algorithms
- Be able to trace and analyse the time complexity of the binary tree search algorithm
- Know and be able to explain and trace and analyse the time complexity of the bubble sort algorithm
- Be able to trace and analyse the time complexity of the merge sort algorithm

Linear search

Sometimes it is necessary to search for items in a file, or in an array in memory. If the items are not in any particular sequence, the data items have to be searched one by one until the required one is found or the end of the list is reached. This is called a **linear search**.

The following algorithm for a linear search of a list or array `alist` (indexed from 0) returns the index of `itemSought` if it is found, -1 otherwise.

```
SUB linearSearch(alist,itemSought)
   index ← -1
   i ← 0
   found ← False
   WHILE i < length(alist) AND NOT found
      IF alist[i] = itemSought THEN
         index ← i
         found ← True
      ENDIF
      i ← i + 1
   ENDWHILE
   RETURN index
ENDSUB
```

8-46

> **Q1:** What is the maximum number of items that would have to be examined to find a particular item in a linear search of one million items? What is the average number that would have to be searched?

Time complexity of linear search

We can determine the algorithm's efficiency in terms of execution time, expressed in Big-O notation. To do this, you need to compute the number of basic operations that the algorithm will require for n items. The loop is performed n times for a list of length n, and the basic operation in the loop is the `IF` statement, giving a total of n steps in the algorithm. The time complexity of the algorithm basically depends on *how often the loop has to be performed in the worst-case scenario*.

Therefore, the time complexity of the linear search is O(n).

Binary search

The binary search is a much more efficient method of searching a list for an item than a linear search, but crucially, the items in the list must be sorted. If they are not sorted, a linear search is the only option.

Suppose the items to be searched are held in an ordered array. The ordered array is divided into three parts; a middle item, the first part of the array starting at `aList[0]` up to the middle item and the second part starting after the middle item and ending with the final item in the list. The middle item is examined to see if it is equal to the sought item.

If it is not, then if it is greater than the sought item, the second half of the array is of no further interest. The number of items being searched is therefore halved and the process repeated until the last item is examined, with either the first or second half of the array of items being eliminated at each pass. A subroutine for a binary search on an array of n items in an array `aList` is given below.

`first`, `last` and `midpoint` are integer variables used to index elements of the array. The variable `first` will start at 0, the beginning of the array. The variable `last` starts at `len(aList) - 1`, the last array index.

```
SUB binarySearch(aList, itemSought)
   found ← False
   index ← -1
   first ← 0
   last ← len(aList) - 1
   WHILE first <= last AND found = False
      midpoint ← Integer part of ((first + last) / 2)
      IF aList[midpoint] = itemSought THEN
         found ← True
         index ← midpoint
      ELSE
         IF aList[midpoint] < itemSought THEN
            first ← midpoint + 1
         ELSE
            last ← midpoint - 1
         ENDIF
      ENDIF
   ENDWHILE
   RETURN index      #index = -1 if key not found
ENDSUB
```

Time complexity of binary search

The binary search halves the search area with each execution of the loop – an excellent example of a **divide and conquer** strategy. If we start with n items, there will be approximately n/2 items left after the first comparison, n/4 after 2 comparisons, n/8 after 3 comparisons, and $n/2^i$ after i comparisons. The number of comparisons needed to end up with a list of just one item is i where $n/2^i = 1$. One further comparison would be needed to check if this item is the one being searched for or not.

Solving this equation for i, $\qquad n = 2^i$

Taking the logarithm of each side, $\qquad \log_2 n = i \log_2 2$ giving $i = \log_2 n$ (since $\log_2 2 = 1$)

Therefore, the binary search is O(log n).

Q2: An array contains 12 numbers 5, 13, 16, 19, 26, 35, 37, 57, 86, 90, 93, 98

Trace through the binary search algorithm to find how many items have to be examined before the number 90 is found. The first row of the trace table is filled in below.

itemSought	index	found	first	last	midpoint	aList(midpoint)
90	-1	false	0	11	5	35

Q3: What is the maximum number of items that would have to be examined to find a particular item in a binary search of one million items?

A recursive algorithm

The basic concept of the binary search is in fact recursive, and a recursive algorithm is given below. The procedure calls itself, eventually "unwinding" when the procedure ends. When recursion is used there must always be a condition that if true, causes the program to terminate the recursive procedure, or the recursion will continue forever.

Once again, `first`, `last` and `midpoint` are integer variables used to index elements of the array, with `first` starting at 0 and `last` starting at the upper limit of the array index.

```
SUB binarySearch (aList, itemSought, first, last)
   IF last < first THEN
      RETURN -1
   ELSE
      midpoint ← integer part of (first + last)/2
      IF aList[midpoint] > itemSought THEN #key is in first half of list
         RETURN binarySearch(aList, itemSought, first, midpoint-1)
      ELSE
         IF aList[midpoint] < itemSought THEN
            RETURN binarySearch(aList, itemSought,  midpoint+1, last)
         ELSE
            RETURN midpoint
         ENDIF
      ENDIF
   ENDIF
ENDSUB
```

Q4: What condition(s) will cause a value to be returned from the subroutine to the calling program?

8-46

Binary tree search

The recursive algorithm for searching a binary tree is similar to the binary search algorithm above, except that instead of looking at the midpoint of a list, or a subset of the list, on each pass, half of the tree or subtree is eliminated each time its root is examined. In the tree below, a maximum of 4 nodes has to be examined to find a value or return "not found". The time complexity is the same as the binary search, i.e. O(log n).

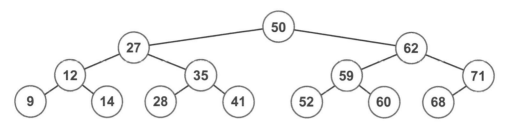

```
SUB binarySearchTree(itemSought,currentNode)
   IF currentNode = None THEN
      RETURN False
   ELSE
      IF itemSought = item at currentNode THEN
         RETURN True
      ELSE
         IF itemSought < item at currentNode THEN
            IF left child exists THEN
               RETURN binarySearchTree (itemSought, left child)
            ELSE
               RETURN False
            ENDIF
            IF right child exists THEN
               RETURN binarySearchTree (itemSought, right child)
            ELSE
               RETURN False
            ENDIF
         ENDIF
      ENDIF
   ENDIF
ENDSUB
```

8-46

Sorting algorithms

The **bubble sort** (see Chapter 9) is the simplest but by far the most inefficient sorting algorithm. It uses two nested loops to sort n items:

```
FOR i = 0 to n-2
   FOR j = 0 to n-i-2
      IF item[j] > item[j+1] THEN swap the items
   ENDFOR
ENDFOR
```

The IF statement in the inner loop is performed (n-1) + (n-2) + ... + 2 + 1 times. This is equal to ½n(n-1), or $\frac{1}{2}n^2 - \frac{1}{2}n$, using the formula for an arithmetic progression. Its time complexity is therefore a quadratic function involving n^2, i.e. $O(n^2)$, ignoring the coefficient of n and the less dominant term in n.

Merge sort

The merge sort uses a **divide and conquer** approach and is far more efficient for a large number of items. The list is successively divided in half, forming two sublists, until each sublist is of length one. The sublists are then sorted and merged into larger sublists until they are recombined into a single sorted list. The basic steps are:

- Divide the unsorted list into n sublists, each containing one element

- Repeatedly merge sublists to produce new sorted sublists until there is only one sublist remaining. This is the sorted list.

The merge process is shown graphically below for a list is in the initial sequence 5 3 2 7 9 1 3 8.

Initial sequence split into sublists each of length 1

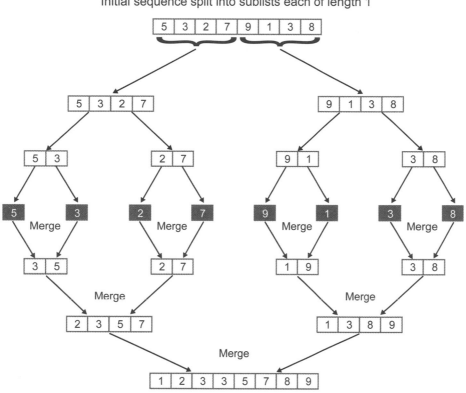

Final merged and sorted list

The list is first split into sublists each containing one element.

The merge process merges each pair of sublists into the correct sequence. Taking for example two lists: `leftlist = [2, 3]` and `rightlist = [1, 3]`, the merge process works like this:

1. Compare the first item in `leftlist` with the first element in `rightlist`

2. If item in `leftlist` < item in `rightlist`, add item from `leftlist` to `mergedlist` and read the next item from `leftlist`

3. Otherwise, add item from `rightlist` to `mergedlist` and read the next item from `rightlist`

4. Once one list is empty, any remaining items are copied into the merged list

5. Repeat from Step 2 until all items are in `mergedlist`

The process is then repeated for each pair of sublists until the lists are merged into the final sorted list.

An algorithm for the merge sort is given below.

```
SUB mergeSort(mergelist)
   IF len(mergelist) > 1 THEN
      mid ← len(mergelist) div 2  #performs integer division
      lefthalf ← mergelist[:mid]   #left half of mergelist into lefthalf
      righthalf ← mergelist[mid:] #right half of mergelist into righthalf
      mergeSort(lefthalf)
      mergeSort(righthalf)
      i ← 0
      j ← 0
      k ← 0
      WHILE i < len(lefthalf) and j < len(righthalf)
         IF lefthalf[i] < righthalf[j] THEN
            mergelist[k] ← lefthalf[i]
            i ← i + 1
         ELSE
            mergelist[k] ← righthalf[j]
            j ← j + 1
         ENDIF
         k ← k + 1
      ENDWHILE
      #check if left half has elements not merged
      WHILE i < len(lefthalf)
         mergelist[k] ← lefthalf[i]    #if so, add to mergelist
         i ← i + 1
         k ← k + 1
      ENDWHILE
      #check if rt half has elements not merged
      WHILE j < len(righthalf)
         mergelist[k] ← righthalf[j]  #if so, add to mergelist
         j ← j + 1
         k ← k + 1
      ENDWHILE
   ENDIF
ENDSUB
#****** MAIN PROGRAM *******
mergelist ← [5, 3, 2, 7, 9, 1, 3, 8]
mergeSort(mergelist)
print(mergelist)
```

8-46

Q5: The following list of numbers is to be sorted using a merge sort.

[54, 36, 66, 78, 64, 19, 42, 44, 51, 89, 72, 62, 22, 67, 81, 79]

Which answer below shows the first two lists to be merged?

a. [44] and [51]

b. [54] and [36]

c. [54, 36] and [66, 78]

d. [19, 36, 42, 44, 54, 64, 66, 78] and [22, 51, 62, 67, 72, 79, 81, 89]

Q6: Draw a graphical representation of how a list [5, 3, 9, 4, 2, 6, 1] is first split into halves until each sublist contains one item, and then the sublists are merged to become the sorted list.

Time complexity of merge sort

The merge sort is another example of a divide and conquer algorithm, but in this case, there are n sublists to be merged, so the time complexity has to be multiplied by a factor of n.

The time complexity is therefore O(nlog n).

Space complexity

The amount of resources such as memory that an algorithm requires, known as the **space complexity**, is also a consideration when comparing the efficiency of algorithms. The bubble sort, for example, requires n memory locations for a list of size n. The merge sort, on the other hand, requires additional memory to hold the left half and right half of the list, so takes much more memory space.

8-46

Exercises

1. There are many methods of sorting a set of records into ascending order of key. What factors would you consider in deciding which of these methods is the most suitable for a particular application?   [2]

2. The binary search method can be used to search for an item in an ordered list.

(a) Show how the binary search method works by writing numbers on Figure 1 below to indicate which values would be examined to determine if the name "Richard" appears in the list.

Write the number "1" by the first value to be examined, "2" by the second value to be examined and so on.

Figure 1

Position	Value	Order examined in
1	Adam	
2	Alex	
3	Anna	
4	Hon	
5	Mohammed	
6	Moonis	
7	Niraj	
8	Philip	
9	Punit	
10	Ravi	
11	Richard	
12	Timothy	
13	Tushara	
14	Uzair	
15	Zara	

[3]

(b) A different list contains 137 names.

What is the maximum number of names that would need to be accessed to determine if the name "Rachel" appears in the list?   [1]

(c) Which of the following is the order of time complexity of the binary search method?

$O(\log_2 n)$ $O(n)$ $O(n^2)$ [1]

AQA Unit 3 Qu 1 June 2011

8-46

Chapter 47 – Graph-traversal algorithms

Objectives

- Be able to trace depth-first and breadth-first algorithms

- Describe typical applications of each

Graph traversals

There are two ways to traverse a graph so that every node is visited. Each of them uses a supporting data structure to keep track of which nodes have been visited, and which node to visit next.

- A **depth-first** traversal uses a **stack**, which is implemented automatically during execution of a recursive routine to hold local variables, parameters and return addresses each time a subroutine is called (see Chapter 39). Alternatively, a non-recursive routine could be written and the stack maintained as part of the routine.

- A **breadth-first** traversal uses a **queue.**

Depth-first traversal

In this traversal, we go as far down one route as we can before backtracking and taking the next route.

The following recursive subroutine `dfs` is called initially from the main program, which passes it a graph, defined here as an **adjacency list** (see Chapter 41) and implemented as a dictionary with nodes A, B, C,… as keys, and neighbours of each node as data. Thus if `"A"` is the current vertex, `graph["A"]` will return the list `["B","D","E"]` with reference to the algorithm below and the graph overleaf.

The calling program also passes an empty list of visited nodes and a starting vertex.

Check the graph in Step 1 on the next page to verify that it corresponds to the nodes and their neighbours. There are different ways of drawing the graph but logically they should all be equivalent!

```
GRAPH = { "A":["B","D","E"],  "B":["A","C","D"],  "C":["B","G"],
          "D":["A","B","E","F"], "E":["A","D"] , "F":["D"], "G":["C"]}
visitedList = []       #an empty list of visited nodes

SUB dfs(graph, currentVertex, visited)
   append currentVertex to list of visited nodes
   FOR vertex in graph[currentVertex]  #check neighbours of currentVertex
      IF vertex NOT IN visited THEN
         dfs(graph, vertex, visited) #recursive call
#stack will store return address, parameters and local variables
      ENDIF
   ENDFOR
   RETURN visited
ENDSUB

#main program
traversal = dfs(GRAPH, "A", visitedList)
OUTPUT "Nodes visited in this order: ", traversal
```

8-47

It is easiest to understand how this works by looking at the graphs below. This shows the state of the **stack** (here it just shows the current node when a recursive call is made), and the contents of the **visited** list. Each visited node is coloured dark blue.

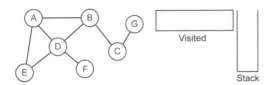

1. Start the routine with an empty stack and an empty list of visited nodes.

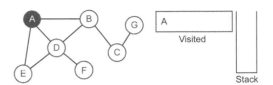

2. Visit A, add it to the visited list. Colour it to show it has been visited.

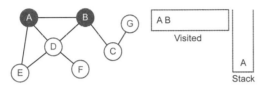

3. Push A onto the stack to keep track of where we have come from and visit A's first neighbour, B. Add it to the visited list. Colour it to show it has been visited.

4. Push B onto the stack and from B, visit the next unvisited node, C. Add it to the visited list. Colour it to show it has been visited.

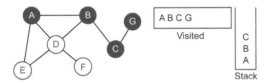

5. Push C onto the stack and from C, visit the next unvisited node, G. Add it to the visited list. Colour it to show it has been visited.

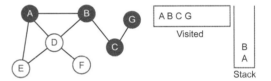

6. At G, there are no unvisited nodes so we backtrack. Pop the previous node C off the stack and return to C

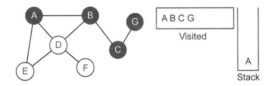

7. At C, all adjacent nodes have been visited, so backtrack again. Pop B off the stack and return to B.

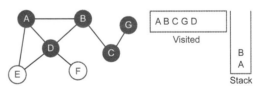

8. Push B back onto the stack to keep track of where we have come from and visit D. Add it to the visited list. Colour it to show it has been visited.

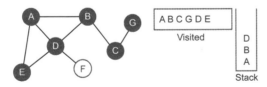

9. Push D onto the stack and visit E. Add it to the visited list. Colour it to show it has been visited.

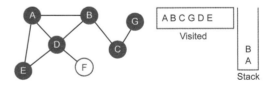

10. From E, A and D have already been visited so pop D off the stack and return to D.

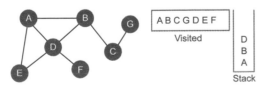

11. Push D back onto the stack and visit F. Add it to the visited list. Colour it to show it has been visited.

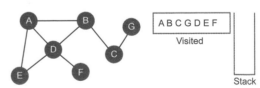

12. At F, there are no unvisited nodes so we pop D, then B, then A, whose neighbours have all been visited. The stack is now empty which means every node has been visited and the algorithm has completed.

8-47

Breadth-first traversal

With a breadth first traversal, starting at A we first visit all the nodes adjacent to A before moving to B and repeating the process for each node at this 'level', before moving to the next level. Instead of a stack, a queue is used to keep track of nodes that we still have to visit. Nodes are coloured pale blue when queued and dark blue when dequeued and added to the list of nodes that have been visited.

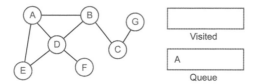

1. Append A to the empty queue at the start of the routine. This will be the first visited node.

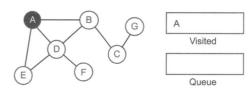

2. Dequeue A and mark it by colouring it dark blue. Add it to the visited list.

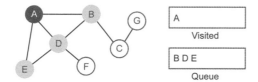

3. Queue each of A's adjacent nodes B, D and E in turn, Colour each node pale blue to show it has been queued.

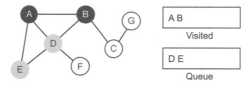

4. We've now finished with A, so dequeue the first item in the queue, which is B. Mark it by colouring it dark blue and add it to the visited list.

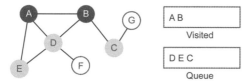

5. Queue B's remaining neighbour C. Colour it pale blue to show it has been queued.

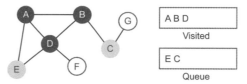

6. B's neighbours are all coloured, so dequeue the first item in the queue, which is D. Mark it by colouring it dark blue and add it to the visited list.

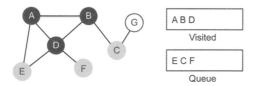

7. D's adjacent node E has already been queued and coloured. Add D's adjacent node F to the queue. Colour it pale blue to show it has been queued.

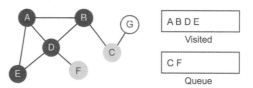

8. Dequeue the first item, E. Mark it by colouring it dark blue and add it to the visited list.

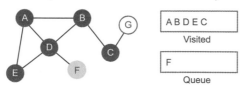

9. E's neighbours are all coloured, so dequeue the next item, C. Mark it by colouring it dark blue and add it to the visited list.

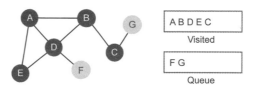

10. Add C's adjacent node G to the queue and colour it pale blue to show it has been queued.

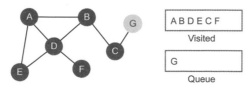

11. C's neighbours are all coloured now, so dequeue F, mark it by colouring it dark blue and add it to the visited list.

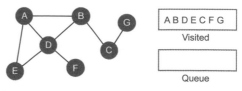

12. Finally, dequeue G, mark it by colouring it dark blue and add it to the visited list. The queue is now empty and all the nodes have been visited.

8-47

Note that we need to distinguish between a *dequeued* vertex that is added to the visited list and whose neighbours we are examining, which we colour dark blue, and *neighbours* of the current vertex, which we put in the queue and colour pale blue to show they have been queued but not visited.

Pseudocode algorithm for breadth-first traversal

The following algorithm assumes you are starting from a vertex `currentVertex`. The queue q is a dynamic data structure implemented for example as a list. A second list called `visitedNodes` holds the nodes that have been visited. Colours Black, Grey and White are more traditional in this algorithm than Dark Blue, Pale Blue and white so are used here – the diagrams are clearer in colour!

The breadth-first traversal is an iterative, rather than a recursive routine. The first node ('A' in this example), is appended to the empty queue as soon as the subroutine is entered. A Python definition of the graph as a dictionary is given below for interest, but is not directly used in the pseudocode, as implementations will vary in different languages.

```
GRAPH = {
   "A": {"colour": "White", "neighbours": ["B", "D", "E"]},
   "B": {"colour": "White", "neighbours": ["A", "D", "C"]},
   "C": {"colour": "White", "neighbours": ["B", "G"]},
   "D": {"colour": "White", "neighbours": ["A", "B", "E", "F"]},
   "E": {"colour": "White", "neighbours": ["A", "D"]},
   "F": {"colour": "White", "neighbours": ["D"]},
   "G": {"colour": "White", "neighbours": ["C"]}
}
```

8-47

```
SUB bfs(graph, vertex)
   queue  ← []      #an empty queue
   visited ← []     #an empty list of visited nodes
   enqueue vertex
   WHILE queue NOT empty
      dequeue item and put in currentNode
      set colour of currentNode to "Black"
      append currentNode to visited
      FOR each neighbour of currentNode
         IF colour of neighbour = "White" THEN
            enqueue neighbour
            set colour of neighbour to "Grey"
         ENDIF
      ENDFOR
   ENDWHILE
   RETURN visited
ENDSUB

#main
visited ← bfs(GRAPH, "A")
OUTPUT "List of nodes visited: ", visited
```

Applications of depth-first search

Applications of the depth-first search include the following:

- In scheduling jobs where a series of tasks is to be performed, and certain tasks must be completed before the next one begins.

- In solving problems such as mazes, which can be represented as a graph

Finding a way through a maze

A depth-first search can be used to find a way out of a maze. Junctions where there is a choice of route in the maze are represented as nodes on a graph.

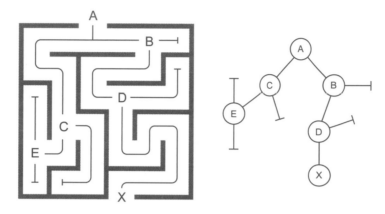

Q1: (a) Redraw the graph without showing the dead ends.

(b) State the properties of this graph that makes it a tree.

(c) Complete the table below to show how the graph would be represented using an adjacency matrix.

	A	B	C	D	E	X
A						
B						
C						
D						
E						
X						

Q2: Draw a graph representing the following maze. Show the dead ends on your graph.

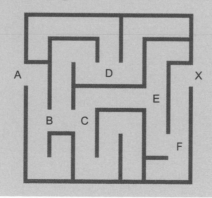

8-47

Applications of breadth-first search

Breadth-first searches are used to solve many real-life problems. For example:

- A major application of a breadth-first search is to find the *shortest* path between two points A and B, and this will be explained in detail in the next chapter. Finding the shortest path is important in, for example, GPS navigation systems and computer networks.

- Facebook. Each user profile is regarded as a node or vertex in the graph, and two nodes are connected if they are each other's friends. This example is considered in more depth in Chapter 72, Big Data.

- Web crawlers. A web crawler can analyse all the sites you can reach by following links randomly on a particular website.

Exercises

1. (a) Name the supporting data structure which is commonly used when traversing a graph

      (i)   depth-first   [1]

      (ii)   breadth-first   [1]

  (b) Show the order in which vertices in the following graph are visited, starting at A, using

      (i)   depth-first traversal   [3]

      (ii)   breadth-first traversal   [3]

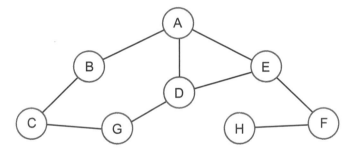

  (c) (i)   Explain why the graph above is not a tree. Which edges would need to be removed for it to be a tree?   [2]

      (ii)   Show, by traversing the tree below using a pre-order traversal and writing the nodes in the order that they are visited, that a pre-order tree traversal is equivalent to a depth-first graph traversal.   [2]

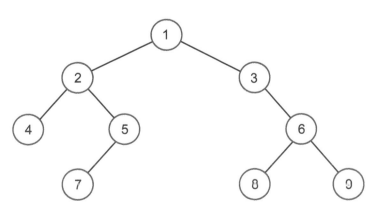

Chapter 48 – Optimisation algorithms

Objectives

- Understand and be able to trace Dijkstra's shortest path algorithm

- Be aware of applications of shortest path algorithm

Optimisation problems

We increasingly rely on computers to find the optimum solution to a range of different problems. For example:

- scheduling aeroplanes and staff so that air crews always have the correct minimum rest time between flights

- finding the best move in a chess problem

- timetabling classes in schools and colleges

- finding the shortest path between two points – for building circuit boards, route planning, communications networks and many other applications

Finding the shortest path from A to B has numerous applications in everyday life and in computer-related problems. For example, if you visit a site like Google Maps to get directions from your current location to a particular destination, you probably want to know the shortest route. The software that finds it for you will use representations of street maps or roads as **graphs**, with estimated driving times or distances as **edge weights**.

Dijkstra's shortest path algorithm

Dijkstra (pronounced dike-stra) lived from 1930 to 2002. He was a Dutch computer scientist who received the Turing award in 1972 for fundamental contributions to developing programming languages. He wrote a paper in 1968 which was published under the heading "GO TO Statement Considered Harmful" and was an advocate of **structured programming**.

Dijkstra's algorithm is designed to find the shortest path between one particular start node and every other node in a weighted graph. The algorithm is similar to a breadth first search, but uses a priority queue rather than a FIFO queue.

The weights could represent, for example, distances or time taken to travel between towns, or the cost of travel between airports.

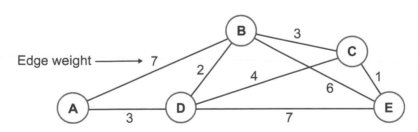

8-48

The algorithm

The algorithm works as follows:

```
Assign a temporary distance value to every node, starting with zero for
the initial node and infinity for every other node
Add all the vertices to a priority queue, sorted by current distance.
(This puts the initial node at the front, the rest in random order.)
WHILE the queue is not empty
      remove the vertex u from the front of the queue
      FOR each unvisited neighbour w of the current vertex u
         newDistance ← distanceAtU + distanceFromUtoW
         IF newDistance < distanceAtW THEN
            distanceAtW ← newDistance
            change position of w in priority queue to reflect new
                                                       distance to w
         ENDIF
      ENDFOR
ENDWHILE
```

Example

In the figure below, A is the start node. A temporary distance value has been assigned to every node, starting with zero for the start node and infinity for every other node.

The priority queue is shown beside the graph, and it is kept in order of vertices with the shortest known distance from A. To start with, A is at the front, and the other nodes are in random order, in this case alphabetical.

The vertices are coloured.

- White vertices have not been visited and their distances remain at infinity.

- Pale blue vertices have been partially explored. A tentative distance to them has been found but all possible paths to them have not yet been explored, so this distance cannot be guaranteed to be the shortest one and they remain in the queue.

- Dark blue vertices have been removed from the queue and their minimum distance from A has been found. These vertices are described as having being visited.

Start at A, remove it from the front of the queue and shade it dark blue to show it has been visited

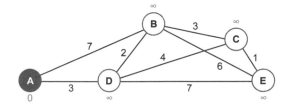

Priority queue

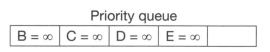

B = ∞	C = ∞	D = ∞	E = ∞	

Node A has two neighbours B and D. Shade each of these pale blue to show they have been partially explored, and calculate new distance values for nodes B and D by taking the distance value at A (i.e. zero) and adding it to the edge weight between A and B, A and D.
Since all these values are less than infinity, update the distances at B and D. Distance at D is less than distance at B, so move D to the front of the priority queue.

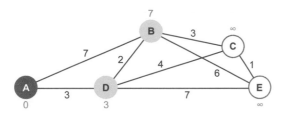

| D = 3 | B = 7 | C = ∞ | E = ∞ | |

Remove D from the front of the queue. Shade it dark blue to show it has been visited. Shade D's neighbours C and E pale blue to show they have been partially explored.

Now calculate new values for the unvisited neighbours of D, namely B, C and E. The distance between D and B is 2, and this is added to the edge weight between D and A. 3 + 2 = 5 so the distance value at B is changed to the new lowest value, 5.

The current tentative distance ∞ at C is replaced with 3 + 4 = 7, at E is replaced with 3 + 7 = 10.

The order of nodes in the priority queue does not need to be changed since B, the node with the smallest current distance from A, is already at the front.

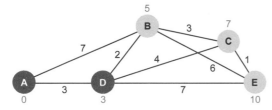

| B = 5 | C = 7 | E = 10 | | |

Remove B from the priority queue. Shade B dark blue to show it has been visited.

At B, the values at C and E are calculated as 5 + 3 = 8 and 5 + 6 = 11 respectively, but these are both greater than the tentative values already there, so these values are not changed.

8-48

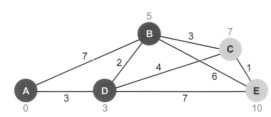

| C = 7 | E = 10 | | | |

Remove C from the queue and shade it dark blue to show it has been visited. The distance to E via C will be calculated as 7 + 1 = 8. This is less than current tentative distance to E (10) so will replace it.

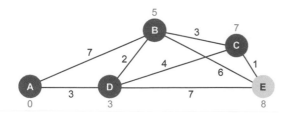

| E = 8 | | | | |

Remove E from the queue. It has no unvisited neighbours, so there are no new distances to calculate. Shade E dark blue.

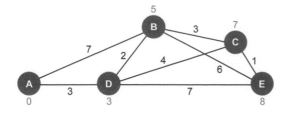

| | | | | |

The queue is empty, all the nodes have now been visited so the algorithm ends.

We have found the shortest distance from A to every other node, and the shortest distance from A is marked in blue at each node.

Q1: Copy the graph below and use the method above to trace the shortest path from A to all other nodes. Write the shortest distance at each node.

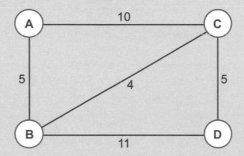

Q2: Use a similar method to trace the shortest path from A to all other nodes. Write the shortest distance at each node. What is the shortest distance from A to G?

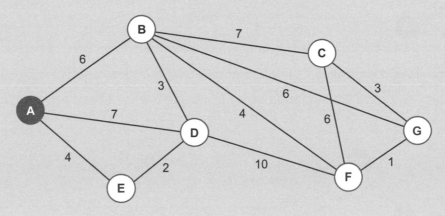

8-48

Exercises

1. (a) What is the purpose of Dijkstra's shortest path algorithm? [2]

(b) Describe briefly **two** applications of the algorithm. [4]

(c) The weighted graph (Figure 1) shows distances between each of the graph's vertices.

Copy Figure 1 and show the tentative distances from the starting node A allocated to each node after nodes B and D have been visited (dequeued and finished with) using Dijkstra's algorithm. [4]

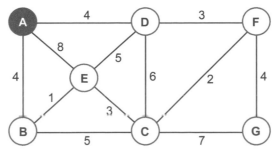

Figure 1

2. The following graph shows distances between five cities. Dijkstra's shortest path algorithm is used to find the shortest distance between Liverpool and each of the other cities. The algorithm is given below.

```
Assign a temporary distance value to every node, starting with zero
for the initial node and infinity for every other node

Add all the vertices to a priority queue, sorted by current
distance. (This puts the initial node at the front, the rest, which
all start with temporary distances of infinity, in random order.)

WHILE the queue is not empty
    remove the vertex u from the front of the queue
    FOR each unvisited neighbour w of the current vertex u
        newDistance ← distanceAtU + distanceFromUtoW
        IF newDistance < distanceAtW THEN
            distanceAtW ← newDistance
            change position of w in priority queue to reflect new
                                              distance to w
        ENDIF
    ENDFOR
ENDWHILE
```

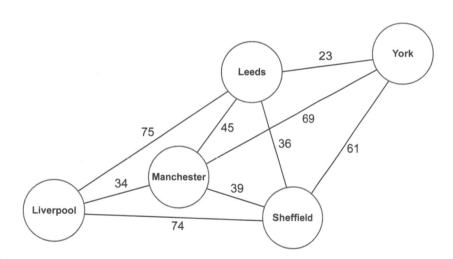

The following table represents the distances after the first statement in the algorithm is executed.

Liverpool	Leeds	Manchester	Sheffield	York
0	∞	∞	∞	∞

(a) Complete the following table after **one** iteration of the WHILE loop in the above algorithm.   [3]

Liverpool	Leeds	Manchester	Sheffield	York

(b) Complete the table after the **second** iteration of the WHILE loop.   [2]

Liverpool	Leeds	Manchester	Sheffield	York

8-48

Chapter 49 – Limits of computation

Objectives

- Be aware that algorithmic complexity and hardware impose limits on what can be computed

- Know that algorithms may be classified as being either tractable or intractable

- Be aware that some problems cannot be solved algorithmically

- Describe the Halting problem, and understand its significance for computation

Does every computational problem have a solution?

In this chapter we will look at the limits of computation. Some problems may be theoretically soluble by computer but if they take millions of years to solve, they are in a practical sense, insoluble. Cracking a password of 10 or more characters consisting of a random mix of upper and lowercase letters, numbers and symbols is one example.

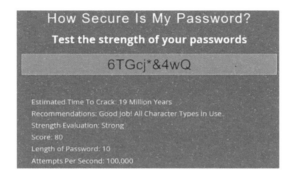

How secure is my password? www.roboform.com

The travelling salesman problem

This is a very well-known optimisation problem. It poses the question "Given a list of towns and the distances between each pair of towns, what is the shortest possible route that the salesman can use to visit each town exactly once and return to the starting point?" This is different from finding the shortest path from A to B. This problem has many applications in fields such as planning, logistics, the manufacture of microchips and DNA sequencing.

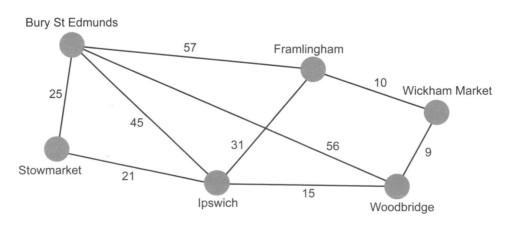

To solve the problem, we could look first at a **brute-force** method, testing out every combination of routes.

With just five cities, the number of possible routes is: 4! = 4 x 3 x 2 x 1 = 24.

A computer could calculate the best route in a fraction of a second.

Q1: How many different routes are there for (a) 10 cities? (b) 20 cities? (c) 50 cities?

The problem is **computationally difficult** because it will take a long time for a fast computer to find the optimal solution for even a relatively small number of cities, and using the brute force algorithm, the problem rapidly becomes impossible to solve within a reasonable time as the number of cities increases.

Another approach is needed, and later in this chapter we will discuss **heuristic** solutions to problems such as this one.

Tractable and intractable problems

Computer scientists are interested in the efficiency of algorithms, and whether or not it is possible, for example, to find an algorithm that will solve a problem in a "reasonable amount of time" using only a "reasonable amount of memory". Some problems in fact cannot be solved at all, however much time and memory is available. This chapter looks at how we can categorise algorithms.

A problem that has a **polynomial-time solution** or better is called a **tractable problem**. A polynomial-time solution is one of time complexity $O(n^k)$. So for example, problems which have solutions with time complexities of $O(n)$, $O(n \log n)$ and $O(n^{10})$ are all tractable.

An **intractable problem** is one that does not have a polynomial-time solution. Problems of time complexity $O(2^n)$ and $O(n!)$ are examples of intractable problems. In other words, although these problems have a theoretical solution, it is very hard to solve such a problem for a value of n of any size greater than something very small. Note that "intractable" does not mean "insoluble".

Q2: Show that for a very small value of n, a problem defined as intractable can be solved in a relatively short time.

An example of a tractable problem is: "Find the shortest path between two vertices in a given weighted graph." We saw in the last chapter that this is relatively easy to solve efficiently.

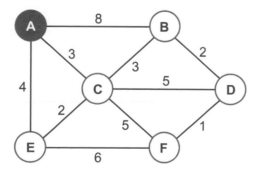

However, if we wanted to find the *longest* path between two vertices, this is a problem which can only be solved by exhaustive search – in other words, trying every option.

Comparing time complexities

The table below shows what a huge difference there is in algorithms with different orders of time complexity for different values of n.

	10	**50**	**100**	**1000**
n	10	50	100	1000
$\log_2 n$	3.3	5.64	6.65	9.97
n^2	100	2500	10,000	1 million
n^3	1000	125000	1 million	1 billion
2^n	1024	A 16-digit number	A 31-digit number	A 302-digit number
n!	3.6 million	A 65-digit number	A 161-digit number	A very, very large number!

Q3: Algorithms for problems A, B and C have time complexities $O(n^3)$, $O(2^n)$, $O(n!)$. Using the table above, which of A, B, C are tractable and which are intractable?

Intractable problems, which have no efficient algorithms to solve them, are in fact quite common; so how can solutions to these problems be found?

Heuristic methods

Not all intractable problems are equally hard, and not all instances of a given intractable problem are equally hard. Brute-force algorithms are not the only option. It may be quite simple to get an approximate answer, or an answer that is good enough for a particular purpose. One approach is to find a solution which has a high probability of being correct.

Another approach is to solve a simpler or restricted version of the problem, if that is possible. This may give useful insights into possible solutions.

An approach to problem solving which employs an algorithm or methodology not guaranteed to be optimal or perfect, but is sufficient for the purpose, is called a **heuristic** approach. An adequate solution may be achieved by trading optimality, completeness, accuracy or precision for speed.

Returning to the **Travelling Salesman Problem** (TSP), a large number of heuristic solutions have been developed, the best of which (developed in 2006) can compute a solution within two or three percent of an optimal tour for as many as 85,000 "cities" or nodes.

In fields other than computer science, individuals and organisations frequently use heuristic methods in reaching decisions, and researchers have found that ignoring part of the information at hand can actually lead to more accurate decisions. Examples of a heuristic approach include using a rule of thumb, making an educated guess or an intuitive judgement, or simply using common sense.

Many **virus scanners** use heuristic rules for detecting viruses and other forms of malware. The heuristic algorithm looks for code and behaviour patterns indicative of a class or family of viruses.

Computable and non-computable problems

There are some problems which cannot be solved algorithmically. In fact, the number of things which can be computed is tiny compared with the number of things we would like to be able to compute! In the 1920s, a mathematician named David Hilbert proposed that any problem, defined properly, could be solved by writing an appropriate algorithm – i.e. that every problem was computable. In 1936 Turing was able to prove him wrong. Some problems are simply non-computable.

8-49

The fact that some problems have no solution is of significance to computer scientists. One definition of Computer Science is "the study of problems that are and that are not computable", or the study of the existence and the nonexistence of algorithms.

A non-computable problem sometimes appears in the form of a paradox. For example:

Suppose in a certain town there is just one barber, who is male. Every man in the town is clean-shaven, and he keeps himself this way by doing either of the following (but not both):

1. shaving himself, or

2. going to the barber

Another way of putting this is to say that the barber is a man in town who shaves only those men in the town who do not shave themselves.

Who shaves the barber?

Q4: Can you think of some categories of non-computable problem?

The Halting problem

The Halting problem is the problem of determining whether for a given input, a program will finish running or continue for ever. The problem can be represented graphically:

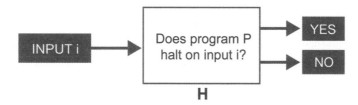

H

Alan Turing proved in 1936 that a machine **H** to solve the Halting problem for all possible programs and their inputs, cannot exist. It is not possible to devise a program H which can show that, given any program and its inputs, it will halt or continue for ever. It is, however, often possible to show that given a specific algorithm, it will halt for any input.

What the Halting problem shows is that there are some problems that cannot be solved by computer.

8-49

Exercises

1. The figure below illustrates the time complexity of three different algorithms, A, B and C.

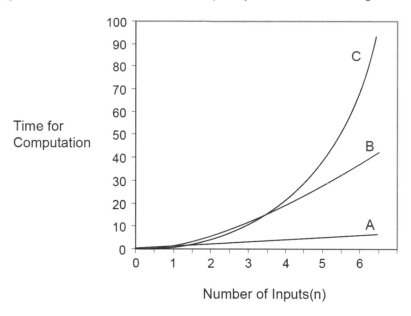

(a)   The three algorithms have orders of time complexity $O(n^2)$, $O(n)$ and $O(a^n)$.

   (i)   What is the order of time complexity of algorithm C?   [1]

   (ii)   Which of the algorithms, A, B or C, is the most time efficient?   [1]

(b)   The Travelling Salesman problem is intractable.

   (i)   What is meant by an intractable problem?   [2]

   (ii)   What approach might a programmer take if asked to 'solve' an intractable problem?   [2]

AQA Unit 3 Qu 5 June 2010

2. (a)   Complete the missing parts of the question posed by the Halting problem in the Figure below.

Is it possible in general to ....

that can tell, given any program and its inputs and without

.... whether the

given program with the given inputs will halt?

                                                                                               [2]

(b)   What is the significance of the Halting problem?   [1]

AQA Unit 3 Qu 11 June 2012

8-49

Section 9

Regular languages

In this section:

9

Chapter 50 – Mealy machines

Objectives

- Be able to draw and interpret simple state transition diagrams for FSMs with no output and with output

- Be able to draw and interpret simple state transition tables for FSMs with no output and with output

Finite state machines

A finite state machine (FSM) which does not have output is sometimes referred to as a **finite state automaton.** (These were covered in Chapter 12 and you should refer back to this chapter for more detail.) An FSM is an abstract representation or model of computation used in designing computer systems and logic circuits, and one which can also be used to check the syntax of programming languages.

This chapter gives a brief revision of the concepts previously covered in Chapter 12 before moving on to a specific type of FSMs *with output*, known as **Mealy machines**.

State transition diagrams

State transition diagrams use circles to represent the states that a system may be in, and arrows to represent the transitions between states. One of the states is a **start state**, shown with an arrow pointing to it, and one or more of the states is an **accept state**, shown as a double circle.

The finite state automaton produces a Yes or No answer to the question: does the input sequence move from the start state to an accept state by any of the possible paths?

Example 1

The finite state diagram below accepts certain combinations of the letters a and b, and rejects others. Which of the following combinations of letters are accepted?

baabb   aaabb   aaaa   abba   abb   baa

Answer: aaabb, abb, baa. These are the only three combinations that end at an accept state, S3 or S4.

State transition tables

A state transition table is an alternative way of representing an FSM, showing in tabular form the current state and the next state for each input. Here is the state transition table for the example above.

Current state	Next state	
	Input = a	Input = b
S0	S1	S2
S1	S1	S3
S2	S4	S2
S3	S5	S3
S4	S4	S5
S5	S5	S5

Mealy machines

A **Mealy machine** is a type of FSM with an output, named after its inventor George Mealy. A Mealy machine has outputs that are determined **both by its current state and the current input**. For each state and input, no more than one transition is possible.

Example 2

The controller for a vending machine is implemented as a Mealy machine as shown in the finite state diagram below. The initial state is shown with an arrow, and each transition shows both the input and the output. A packet of crisps will be dispensed when the customer has inserted three 10p coins or a 10p coin and a 20p coin. If two 20p coins are inserted, the machine will give 10p change. For example, 10p/00 means that 10p has been input and the controller does not dispense the packet of crisps and does not give change. 20p/11 means that 20p has been inserted and the machine dispenses the crisps and gives change. A Reset button gives change if the customer presses it when they have entered less than 30p.

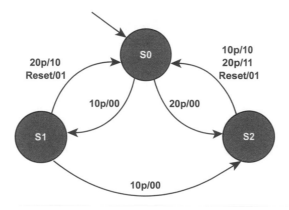

The transition table representing this Mealy machine is as follows:

Input	Current state	Output	Next state
10p	S0	00	S1
20p	S0	00	S2
10p	S1	00	S2
20p	S1	10	S0
10p	S2	10	S0
20p	S2	11	S0
Reset	S1	01	S0
Reset	S2	01	S0

Q1: What does an output of 10 mean?

Example 3

The FSM below represents a Mealy machine which accepts any number of inputs of 0 or 1. If the last two symbols input are 00 or 11, the final output is **y** (yes), otherwise the final output is **n** (no).

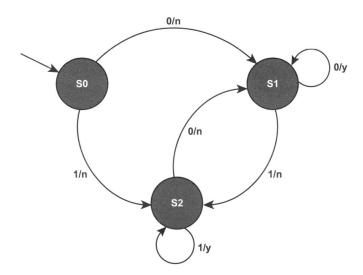

The corresponding state transition table is shown below.

Input	Current state	Output	Next state
0	S0	n	S1
1	S0	n	S2
0	S1	y	S1
1	S1	n	S2
0	S2	n	S1
1	S2	y	S2

You can show the output for any input string. Suppose you input the string 0 0 1 0 1 1.

9-50

Write these inputs down and underneath them, complete the state sequence and the output rows, column by column. Working along the row, for each input, write down the next state arrived at and the output.

Input =   0   0   1   0   1   1
State sequence = S0   S1   S1   S2   S1   S2   S2
Output =   n   y   n   n   n   y

The final output from this string is y, at the final state S2.

> **Q2:** Write out the state sequence for the input 1 0 1 1 0 1. What is the final state and what is the final output?

Applications of Mealy machines

Mealy machines can provide a simple model for cipher machines. Given a string of letters (a sequence of inputs), a Mealy machine can be designed to give a ciphered string (a sequence of outputs). They can also be used to represent traffic lights, timers, vending machines, and basic electronic circuits.

Example 4

This example shows a Mealy machine that represents an exclusive OR of the two most recent values input.

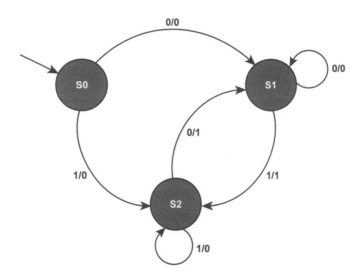

> **Q3:** Complete the state transition table for the FSM given above.
>
> | Input | Current state | Output | Next state |
> |-------|---------------|--------|------------|
> | 0 | S0 | 0 | S1 |
> | 1 | | | |
> | 0 | | | |
> | 1 | | | |
> | 0 | | | |
> | 1 | | | |
>
> **Q4:** Write out the state sequence for the input string 001001.

Exercises

1. A Mealy machine is to be designed so that its final output is a 1 when at least three ones have been entered in sequence.

    (a) With the aid of the state transition table below, draw the finite state diagram representing the Mealy machine. [3]

Input	Current state	Output	Next state
0	S0	0	S0
1	S0	0	S1
0	S1	0	S0
1	S1	0	S2
0	S2	0	S0
1	S2	1	S2

    (b) Write the state sequence showing the output for each of the following input sequences:

    (i)   110111 [2]

    (ii)   101101 [2]

2. The following Mealy machine accepts as input a string of binary digits. The output is the remainder, given in decimal, when the string of binary digits is divided by 5. Thus for example an input string of binary digits 10 will give an output of 2, and an input string of 1011 will output 1.

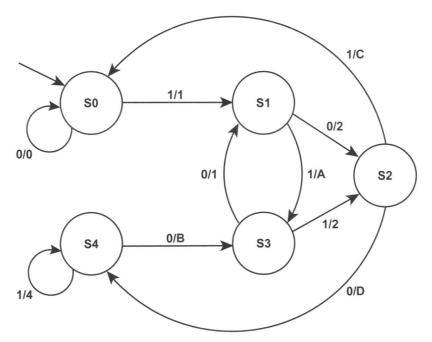

    (a) What are the outputs **A**, **B**, **C** and **D**? [4]

    (b) (i)   The binary string 1010011 is input. List the state sequence. [2]

        (ii) What is the output from the string? [1]

9-50

264

Chapter 51 – Sets

Objectives

- Be familiar with the concept of a set and the notations used for specifying a set and set comprehension

- Be familiar with the compact representation of a set

- Be familiar with the concept of finite and infinite sets, countably infinite sets, cardinality of a finite set, Cartesian product of sets

- Be familiar with the meaning of the terms subset, proper subset, countable set

- Be familiar with set operations: membership, union, intersection, difference

Definition of a set

A **set** is an unordered collection of values or symbols in which each value or symbol occurs at most once.

A set may be defined in one of three ways, and the notation used for each of these is explained below.

Defining a set by listing each member

The list of members is enclosed in curly brackets:

e.g. A = {2, 4, 6, 8}

Q1: Define a set A consisting of all prime numbers between 1 and 20.

Common sets

There are some sets that are used so often that they have special names and notational conventions to identify them. These include:

- The empty set {} or ∅, which has no elements.

- The (infinite) set of natural numbers, including zero, referred to as $\mathbb{N}$ in mathematics.

   N or $\mathbb{N}$ = {0, 1, 2, 3, …}

A **natural** number is a whole number that is used in counting. For example, five gold rings, four calling birds, three French hens. (This is sometimes defined as {1, 2, 3, …} without including zero.)

Note that the ellipsis ("…") indicates that the set continues in the obvious way, and can be used to indicate an infinite set.

- The set of all **integers** whether positive, negative or zero:

   Z or $\mathbb{Z}$ = {…, -2, -1, 0, 1, 2, …}

- The set of all **rational numbers Q** or $\mathbb{Q}$, i.e. any value that can be expressed as a ratio, or fraction. This includes all integer values since each can simply be expressed as 7/1 or 1076/1, to use the examples above.

- The set **R** or $\mathbb{R}$ of **real numbers** is defined as 'the set of all possible real world quantities'. This includes, for example, -10, -6.456, 0 4, 6.0, $\sqrt{2}$ and π. It does not include 'imaginary' numbers such as $\sqrt{-1}$, or infinity (∞).

Q2: Define a set B of all positive integers divisible by 2.

Finite and infinite sets

A **finite set** is one whose elements can be counted off by natural numbers up to a particular number. For example, 10 is the fourth and final element of the set A = {1, 4, 6, 10}.

Another example of a finite set is the set of all odd numbers from 1 to 99, which may be specified as:

A = {1, 3, 5, …, 99}

Again, the ellipsis (…) indicates that the list continues in the obvious way.

The **cardinality** of a finite set is the number of elements in the set.

An **infinite set** may be countable or uncountable. For example, $\mathbb{N}$ (the set of natural numbers) and $\mathbb{R}$ (the set of real numbers) are examples of infinite sets, because they cannot be counted off against the set of natural numbers up to a certain number.

$\mathbb{N}$ is a **countably infinite set** because you can count the elements off against the set of natural numbers; 0, 1, 2, 3 and so on. This is in contrast to the set $\mathbb{R}$ which is not countable; you cannot list all the numbers in the set or say which is the next number.

A **countable** set is a set which can be counted off against a subset of the natural numbers, i.e. all of the natural numbers up to a fixed limit. A countably infinite set is one which can be counted off against the natural numbers but without ever stopping.

Defining a set by set comprehension

A set may be defined by **set comprehension**, using the notation shown in the example below:

B = $\{n^2 \mid n \in \mathbb{N} \wedge n < 5\}$

- The vertical bar | means "such that"

- The $\in$ symbol indicates membership, so $x \in \mathbb{N}$ is read as "x belongs to $\mathbb{N}$"

- $\wedge$ means "and"

Another way of writing the set B, therefore, is

B = {0, 1, 4, 9, 16}

Q3: Given that A = $\{x \mid x \in \mathbb{N} \wedge x \geq 1\}$, complete the sentence
"A is the set consisting of those elements *x* such that …"

Q4: Define set A = {0, 1, 8, 27, 64} using set comprehension.

Q5: List the numbers in the following set: A = $\{\{2x \mid x \in \mathbb{N} \wedge x \geq 1 \wedge x \leq 4\}\}$

Defining a set using the compact representation

A set may be defined using the **compact representation**, as in the following example:

A = $\{0^n 1^n \mid n\}$

In this notation, A is the set containing all strings with an equal number of 0s and 1s.

Another way of writing this set is A = {01, 0011, 000111, 00001111, …}

Q6: Using set comprehension or compact representation, define:

(a) the set A consisting of all the positive integers divisible by 5.

(b) the set B consisting of all positive integers between 1 and 9.

(c) the set C consisting of all positive integer powers of 2.

Cartesian product of two sets

The Cartesian product of two sets A and B, written A x B and spoken "A cross B", is the set of all ordered pairs (a, b) where a is a member of A and b is a member of B.

Example: The set A is defined as A = {1, 3, 5} and the set B as B = {12, 25, 40}. The definition of set C, which is defined as A x B is written:

C = {(1, 12), (1, 25), (1, 40), (3, 12), (3, 25), (3, 40), (5, 12), (5, 25), (5, 40)}

Q7: What is the Cartesian product C of sets S1 and S2, where S1 = {4, 8, 3} and S2 = {8}?

Subsets

If every member of set A is also a member of set B, then A is a **subset** of B, written

$A \subseteq B$

An equivalent statement is "B is a superset of A" or "B contains A", written

$B \supseteq A$

If A is a subset of, but not equal to B, then A is called a **proper subset** of B.

$A \subset B$ e.g. $\{0, 1, 2\} \subset \mathbb{N}$

Q8: If A is the set of prime numbers less than 10, B is the set of odd numbers less than 10 and C is the set of even numbers less than 10, which of the following statements are true?

$A \subseteq B$ $B \subseteq A$ $A \subseteq C$ $C \subseteq A$ $B \subseteq C$ $C \subseteq B$

9-51

Set membership

If A is a set and x is one of the elements of A, then x is a member of A, denoted by $x \in A$.

Set operations

There are several operations which can be used to construct new sets from given sets.

Union

Two sets A and B can be "added together", resulting in the set that contains everything in either A or B. The **union** of A and B is denoted by

$A \cup B$

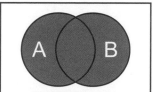

Examples: A = {1, 3, 5} B = {3, 4, 8}

A ∪ B = {1, 3, 4, 5, 8}

Q9: If A = {1, 3, 5}, what is in set A ∪ A?

Intersection

The **intersection** of two sets contains all the members that both sets have in common. Thus the intersection of the two sets

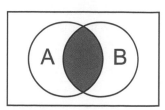

A = {1, 2, 3, 4, 5} and B = {1, 3, 5, 7, 9} is the set {1, 3, 5}

This is written as A ∩ B = {1, 3, 5}

Q10: If A is defined as {1, 2, 3} and B = Ø (the empty set), define the set A ∩ B.

Difference

The **difference** of two sets is denoted by A \ B (or alternatively A − B) and is defined by

A \ B = {x : x ∈ A and x ∉ B}

If A = {1, 2, 3, 4} and B = {1, 3, 5}, then A \ B = {2, 4}. "Subtracting" a member that is not in set A has no effect.

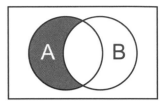

Q11: If A is the set of prime numbers less than 10 and B is the set of odd numbers less than 12, what numbers are in set C = B \ A?

Exercises

1. Give an equivalent definition of the set A = {x | x = x^2} which shows the values in the set. [1]

2. (a) What is the meaning of

    (i) A ⊆ B

    (ii) A ⊇ B?

    Give an example of each. [4]

    (b) Given that A = {2x | x ∈ ℕ} and B = {4x | x ∈ ℕ}, which of the following is true?

    (i) A ⊆ B

    (ii) A ⊇ B

    Explain how you reached this conclusion. [3]

3. The following is a list of sets.

    S1 = {1, 2, 3, 4}

    S2 = {3, 1}

    S3 = {3, 4, 5}

    S4 = {1, 2, 3, 4}

    S5 = {1}

    S6 = {2, 4}

    (a) (i) State the name of **three** proper subsets of S1. [3]

    (ii) State the name of a subset of S1 which is not a proper subset of S1. [1]

    (b) What is the Cartesian product of sets S1 and S2? [1]

    (c) Show how the set S6 can be created using the difference set operator together with two of the other sets listed. [1]

    (d) Define the following sets:

    (i) S7, which is the union of sets S1 and S3. [1]

    (ii) S8, which is the intersection of sets S1 and S3. [1]

Chapter 52 – Regular expressions

Objectives

- Understand that a regular expression is a way of describing a set
- Understand that regular expressions allow particular types of languages to be described in convenient shorthand notation
- Be able to form and use simple regular expressions for string manipulation and matching
- Be able to describe the relationship between regular expressions and finite state machines
- Be able to write a regular expression to recognise the same language as a given FSM and vice versa

What is a regular expression?

Regular expressions are a tool that enables programmers and computers to work with text patterns. They are used, for example,

- to match patterns in text files (for example when searching for a particular word in a word processing program)
- by compilers to recognise the correct form of a variable name or the syntax of a statement
- by programmers to validate user input (for example to check that a postcode or an email address is in the correct format)

Many programming languages including Python and Java support regular expressions.

A regular expression, often called a **pattern**, is an expression used to specify a set of strings that satisfy given conditions.

The most common symbols used in regular expressions are described below.

- | A vertical bar separates alternatives
- ? A question mark indicates that there are zero or one of the preceding element
- * An asterisk indicates that there are zero or more of the preceding element
- + A superscript plus sign indicates that there is one or more of the preceding element

Regular expression	Meaning	Matching strings
(Edward)|(Eddie)|(Ed)	Boolean OR; a vertical bar separates alternatives	Edward, Eddie, Ed
(D|d)is(c|k)	Parentheses are used to define the scope and precedence of the operators	"Disc", "disc", "Disk" and "disk"
Dialog(ue)?	? indicates zero or one of the preceding element	Dialog, Dialogue
ab*	* indicates there are zero or more of the preceding element	a, ab, abb, abbb, ...
a$^+$b	$^+$ indicates there are one or more of the preceding element	ab, aab, aaab ...

269

Regular language

A language is called **regular** if it can be represented by a regular expression. A regular language can also be defined as any language that a **finite state machine** will accept. Any finite language (one containing only a finite number of words) is a regular language, since a regular expression can be created that is the union of every word in the language.

Example 1

A regular language consists of all words beginning and ending in *a*, with zero or more instances of *b* in between, e.g. aa, aba, abba, abbba.

Write a regular expression that describes this language, and draw the corresponding finite state machine (FSM).

Answer: R = ab*a. Note that the FSM is drawn with an outgoing transition from every state for every possible input symbol.

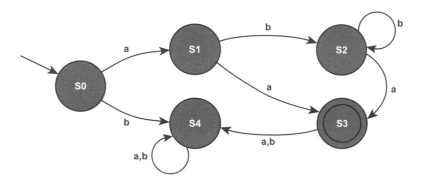

Example 2

Describe the set of strings found by 0⁺1⁺0 and draw the FSM.

Answer: It would find all strings with one or more zeros followed by one or more ones followed by one zero. e.g. 010, 0010, 00010, 0010, 00110

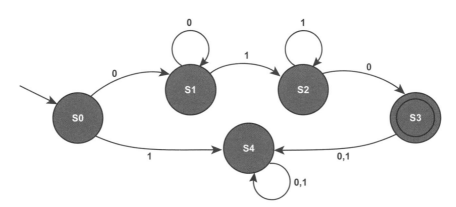

Q1: Write a regular expression to find all the occurrences of "color" or "colour" in a document.

Q2: Write a regular expression that matches any non-empty string that starts with zero or more "a"s, followed by one or more "b"s.

Q3: Which of the following strings is matched by the regular expression Sc(o⁺)(b|d)*y?

Scooby   Scoby   Scddy   Scobby   Scoobdbdbdy

Draw an FSM that recognises the same language.

Finding a regular expression to express an automaton

The set of strings accepted by a language can be expressed either in graphical form as a finite state diagram, or as a regular expression. Given the regular expression, it is usually not too difficult to draw the FSM, as we have seen. The examples below give practice in writing the regular expression corresponding to a given FSM.

Example 1

Consider the FSM shown below, which has four states.

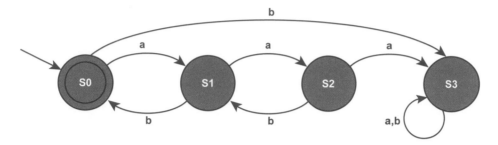

This allows an empty string and strings of the form ab, aabb and all combinations of these such as abab, aabb, aababb.

The corresponding regular expression is (a(ab)*b)*.

Q4: Write the regular expression which represents the finite state machine shown below.

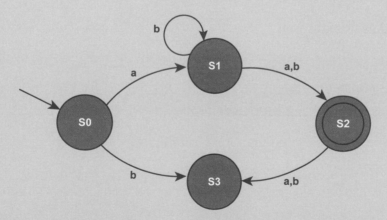

Q5: Write the regular expression which represents the finite state machine shown below.

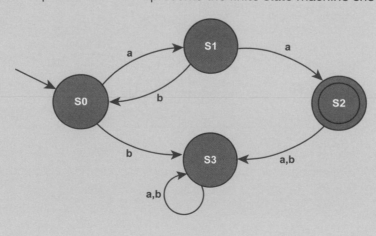

Exercises

1. Regular expressions can be used to search for strings. For example, de(f|g)*h+ matches any string that starts with *de* and is followed by zero or more instances of either *f* or *g* followed by one or more instances of *h*.

    Write regular expressions that will match:

    (a) any string that starts with a letter a, ends with a letter c and has one or more occurrences of the letter b in the middle of it, ie the expression should match the strings abc, abbc, abbbc and so on.   [1]

    (b) any string that starts with either a 0 or a 1, followed by zero or more occurrences of the digit 1, ie the expression should match the strings 0, 1, 01, 11, 011 and so on.   [1]

    AQA Unit 3 Qu 12 June 2012

2. Regular expressions can be used to search for strings.

    (a) For each of the following regular expressions, describe the set of strings that they would find.

        (i)   a+b   [1]

        (ii)   a?b   [1]

        (iii) (ab)*   [1]

    (b) Write regular expressions that match:

        (i)   either Clare or Claire.   [1]

        (ii)   any non-empty string that:

    - starts with 10

    - has zero or more occurrences of any combination of 0 or 1 in the middle

    - ends with 01

    Example strings that the expression should match are 1001, 100010101, 101111010101001.   [2]

    AQA Unit 3 Qu 9 June 2011

3. (a) Which of the following strings will be accepted by the finite state automaton shown below?   [3]

    11001   01000   101111   000110

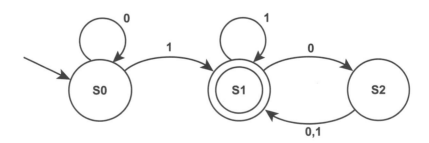

    (b) Write a regular expression to describe the language that the FSA will accept.   [3]

4. Draw a four-state FSM that represents the regular expression b*ab*a.   [3]

Chapter 53 – The Turing machine

Objectives

- Know that a Turing machine can be viewed as a computer with a single fixed program, expressed using
  - a finite set of states in a state transition diagram
  - a finite alphabet of symbols
  - an infinite tape with marked off squares
  - a sensing read-write head that can travel along the tape, one square at a time
- Understand the equivalence between a transition function and a state transition diagram
- Be able to:
  - represent transition rules using a transition function
  - represent transition rules using a state transition diagram
  - hand-trace simple Turing machines
- Explain the importance of Turing machines and the Universal Turing machine to the subject of computation

Alan Turing

Alan Turing (1912–1954) was a British computer scientist and mathematician, best known for his work at Bletchley Park during the Second World War. While working there, he devised an early computer for breaking German ciphers, work which probably shortened the war by two or more years and saved countless lives.

Turing was interested in the question of **computability**, and the answer to the question "Is every mathematical task computable?" In 1936 he invented a theoretical machine, which became known as the **Turing machine**, to answer this question.

The Turing machine

The Turing machine consists of an infinitely long strip of tape divided into squares. It has a read/write head that can read symbols from the tape and make decisions about what to do based on the contents of the cell and its current state.

Essentially, this is a finite state machine with the addition of an infinite memory on tape. The FSM specifies the task to be performed; it can erase or write a different symbol in the current cell, and it can move the read/write head either left or right.

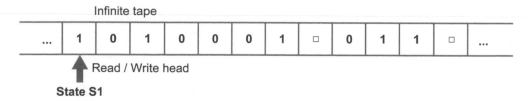

The Turing machine is an early precursor of the modern computer, with input, output and a program which describes its behaviour. Any alphabet may be defined for the Turing machine; for example a binary alphabet of 0, 1 and □ (representing a blank), as shown in the diagram above.

A Turing machine must have at least one state, known as a **halting state** or **stop state** that causes it to halt for some inputs.

Example 1

A Turing machine is designed to find the first blank cell on the tape to the right of the current position of the read/write head.

It has three states S0, S1 and S2, where S0 is the start state and S2 is the stop state. The machine's alphabet is 0, 1 and □ where □ represents a blank.

The finite state transition diagram representing the machine is shown below.

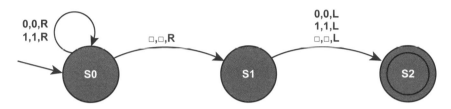

The notation (*input*, *output*, *movement*) is used in this diagram so that for example, (0, 0, R), means "If the input is 0, write a 0 and move right". (0, 1, L) means "If the input is 0, write a 1 and move left."

The string 110□□□ is on the tape, and the read-write head is positioned at the leftmost 1.

The computation of the Turing machine can be traced as follows:

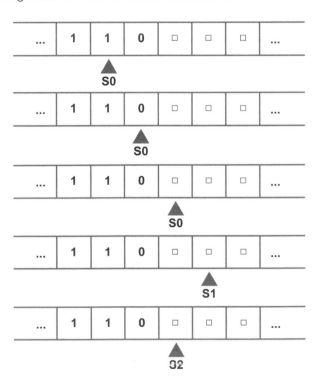

Example 2

The following state transition table shows a procedure for incrementing a binary number by 1.

Current state	Read symbol	Write symbol	Move	Next state
S0	□	□	left	S1
S0	0	0	right	S0
S0	1	1	right	S0
S1	□	1	right	S2
S1	0	1	left	S2
S1	1	0	left	S1
S2	□	□	left	S3
S2	0	0	right	S2
S2	1	1	right	S2

The machine starts in state S0 with the head at the leftmost digit on the tape holding the string 10. Trace the computation of the Turing machine.

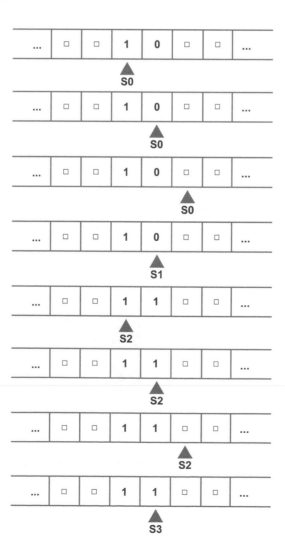

9-53

The finite state machine corresponding to the state transition diagram is given below.

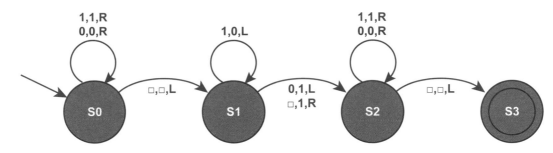

Q1: Trace the computation of the Turing machine if the tape starts with the data 11 as shown below.

| ... | □ | □ | 1 | 1 | □ | □ | ... |

▲
S0

(You will need to draw ten representations of the tape to complete the computation.)

Transition functions

The transition rules for any Turing machine can be expressed as a **transition function** δ. The rules are written in the form

δ (Current State, Input symbol) = (Next State, Output symbol, Movement).

Thus the rule

δ (S1, 0) = (S2, 1, L)

means "IF the machine is currently in state S1 and the input symbol read from the tape is 0, THEN write a 1 to the tape, and move left and change state to S2".

Q2: Looking at the state transition diagram above, write the transition rules for inputs of 0, 1 and □ when the machine is in state S0.

The universal Turing machine

A Turing machine can theoretically represent any computation.

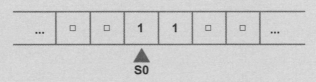

Each machine has a different program to compute the desired operation. However, the obvious problem with this is that a different machine has to be created for each operation, which is clearly impractical.

Turing therefore came up with the idea of the **Universal Turing machine**, which could be used to compute any computable sequence. He wrote: "If this machine **U** is supplied with the tape on the beginning of which is written the string of quintuples separated by semicolons of some computing machine **M**, then **U** will compute the same sequence as **M**."

U is essentially an interpreter that reads the description <M> of any arbitrary Turing machine **M** and faithfully executes operations on data precisely as **M** does. The description <M> is written at the beginning of the tape, followed by the data **D**.

Anything that a Turing machine can compute, a real computer can also compute, and so it provides a definition of what is computable. The universal machine reads both the description of the machine to be simulated, and the input to the machine, from its own tape. This model of computation is considered by some computer scientists to have been the fundamental theoretical breakthrough that led to the idea of the **stored program computer**, in which both the program and its data are held in memory.

Exercises

1. A particular Turing machine has states S1, S2, S3, and S4. S1 is the start state and S4 is the stop state. The machine uses one tape which is infinitely long in one direction to store data. The machine's alphabet is 1, □. The symbol □ is used to indicate a blank cell on the tape.

   The transition rules for this Turing machine can be expressed as a transition function δ. Rules are written in the form

   δ (Current State, Input symbol) = (Next State, Output symbol, Movement).

   So, for example, the rule

   δ (S1, 1) = (S1, 1, →)

   means

   IF   the machine is currently in state S1 and the input symbol read from the tape is 1

   THEN   the machine should remain in state S1, write a 1 to the tape and move the read/write head one cell to the right.

   The machine's transition function is defined by:

   δ (S1, 1) = (S1, 1, →)

   δ (S1, □) = (S2, □, ←)

   δ (S2, 1) = (S3, □, ←)

   δ (S3, 1) = (S4, □, ←)

   (a) The Turing machine is carrying out a computation. The machine starts in state S1 with the string 1111 on the tape. All other cells contain the blank symbol □. The read/write head is positioned at the leftmost 1, as indicated by the arrow.

   Trace the computation of the Turing machine, using the transition function δ. Show the contents of the tape, the current position of the read/write head and the current state as the input symbols are processed. [6]

   (b) Explain what this Turing machine does. [1]

   (c) Explain what a Universal Turing machine is. [2]

   AQA Unit 3 Qu 11 June 2011

Chapter 54 – Backus-Naur Form

Objectives

- Explain why BNF can represent some languages that cannot be represented using regular expressions
- Use Backus-Naur Form (BNF) to represent language syntax and formulate simple production rules
- Draw a syntax diagram to represent a BNF expression

Meta-languages

In order for a computer language such as Python or Pascal to be translated into machine code, all the rules of the language must be defined unambiguously. Languages such as English, Spanish and Arabic are not at all precise, which is one reason why it is hard to get computers to understand 'natural language'.

> **Q1:** What are the possible meanings of each of the following sentences?
>
> Peter and Anna are married.
>
> A salesman visited every house in the area.
>
> Look at that dog with one eye.

Not only is English too imprecise to be used as a computer language, it is not even suitable for defining unambiguously the syntax or grammar of a computer language.

Defining the syntax of a language

In Chapter 52 we saw that regular expressions can be used to describe simple 'languages' and to match patterns in text by specifying sets of strings that satisfy given conditions.

In computer science, the syntax of a language is defined as the set of rules that define what constitutes a valid statement. It would be possible, but lengthy and time-consuming, to define a valid identifier in a given programming language using a regular expression. However, some programming language constructs involving, for example, nested brackets, cannot be defined in this way.

For this reason, special languages called **meta-languages** have been devised, and **Backus-Naur Form** (named after its two originators) is an example of one such meta-language. Many constructs that could be written using a regular expression can be expressed more succinctly using BNF.

Backus-Naur form (BNF)

The structure of BNF is composed of a list of statements of the form

     LHS ::= RHS   where ::= is interpreted as 'is defined by'.

::= is known as a **meta-symbol**.

Example: `<point> ::= .`

<point> is called a **meta-component**, or sometimes a **syntactic variable**, and is distinguished by being enclosed in angle brackets.

The other important meta-symbol is **|** which means 'or'.

Thus, for example, **<digit>** can be defined as

     <digit> ::= 0|1|2|3|4|5|6|7|8|9

Example1

Write the BNF definition of a variable name which, in a certain computer language, may consist of a single letter or a letter followed by a digit.

       \<variable name\> ::= \<letter\>|\<letter\>\<digit\>

       \<letter\> ::= A|B|C|D|E|F|G|H|I|J|K|L|M|N|O|P|Q|R|S|T|U|V|W|X|Y|Z

       \<digit\> ::= 0|1|2|3|4|5|6|7|8|9

Each of these individual rules is known as a **production**.

Using recursion in a BNF definition

BNF often makes use of recursion, where a statement is defined in terms of itself. e.g.

       \<variable list\> ::= \<variable\>|\<variable\>, \<variable list\>

Using this definition, is A, B, C a variable list? We can show that it is, using the following reasoning:

       C is a \<variable\>, and is therefore a \<variable list\>.

       B is a \<variable\>, therefore B,C is \<variable\>,\<variable list\>, i.e. a \<variable list\>

       A,B,C is \<variable\>,\<variable list\>

       Therefore, A, B, C is a \<variable list\>

> **Q2:** Write the definition of a positive integer in BNF. (A positive integer must start with a digit 1-9.)
>
> **Q3:** The syntax of a real number in Pascal is defined as one or more digits, followed by a decimal point, followed by one or more digits. Write this definition using BNF.

The process of ascertaining whether a given statement is valid, given the BNF definition, is called **parsing**. The procedure is to work from left to right, replacing meta-variables with more comprehensive meta-variables at each stage.

Example 2

The following production rules have been used to define the syntax of a valid mathematical expression in a particular programming language.

       \<expression\> ::= \<factor\>|\<factor\> * \<factor\>|\<factor\> / \<factor\>

       \<factor\> ::= \<term\>|\<term\> + \<term\>|\<term\> - \<term\>

       \<term\> ::= \<expression\>|\<number\>

       \<number\> ::= \<digit\>|\<digit\>\<number\>

       \<digit\> ::= 0|1|2|3|4|5|6|7|8|9

Show, using these production rules, that 4 + 75 * 3 is a valid expression.

Answer

4 is a \<digit\>, therefore a \<number\>, therefore a \<term\>

75 is \<digit\>\<number\> and is therefore a \<number\>, therefore a \<term\>

4 + 75 is a \<term\> + \<term\> therefore a \<factor\>

3 is a \<digit\>, therefore a \<number\>, therefore a \<term\>, therefore a \<factor\>

4 + 75 * 3 is a \<factor\> * \<factor\> and therefore an \<expression\>

Q4: An arithmetic expression is defined in BNF as follows:

<expression> ::= <term>|<expression> + <term>|<expression> - <term>

<term> ::= <variable>|<term> * <variable>|<term> / <variable>

<variable> ::= a|b|c|d

(a) Show that a - b is a syntactically correct expression in this language.

(b) Show that a + b * c is also syntactically correct.

(c) Is a * b * c syntactically correct?

When a compiler checks a statement written in a high-level language to see if it is syntactically correct, it will parse each statement in a similar manner to that shown above.

Syntax diagrams

Syntax diagrams are a graphical method of representing the syntax of a language, and map directly to BNF.

The following symbols are used:

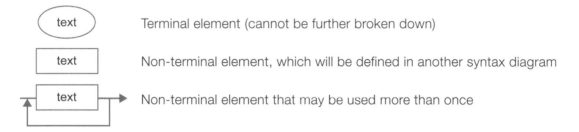

Terminal element (cannot be further broken down)

Non-terminal element, which will be defined in another syntax diagram

Non-terminal element that may be used more than once

Example 3

The syntax diagram representing a positive integer is as follows:

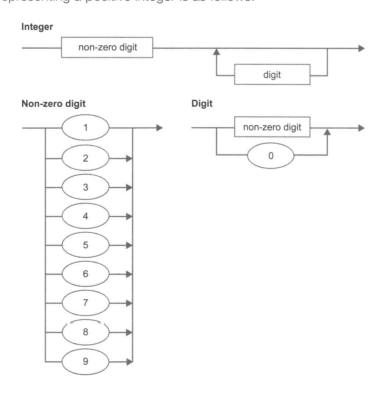

Example 4

The format of a person's initials is defined by the following syntax diagram:

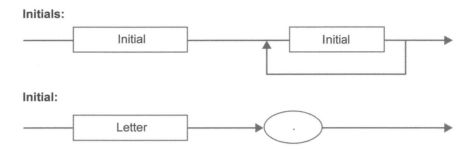

A **letter** is any alphabetic character from "A" to "Z".

(a) Write the corresponding BNF definition.

(b) Which of the following is a valid format for a person's initials?

D.C.T.B   T.K.   W.   D.R.a.M.   A.B.C.D.

Answers

(a) <initials> ::= <initial><initial>|<initial><initials>

   <initial> ::= <letter><dot>

   <letter> ::= A|B|C|D|E|F|G|H|I|J|K|L|M|N|O|P|Q|R|S|T|U|V|W|X|Y|Z

   <dot> ::= .

(b) T.K. and A.B.C.D. are valid initials.

Exercises

1. The following BNF definitions describe the terms **sum**, **value** and **digit**.

   <sum> ::= <value> + <value>

   <value> ::= <digit>|<digit><value>

   <digit> ::= 1|2|3|4|5|6|7|8|9|0

(a) Explain whether each of the following is a sum, a value, a digit or not defined.

   (i)   4686

   (ii) 7 + 8

   (iii) 05 + 170   [3]

(b) Write a BNF definition for **hex**, a hexadecimal number which consists of at least one digit, one letter or a mixture of digits and letters. Your definition must use digit, letter and hex only.

   For example, 5, A, 2B8, FFFF are all valid examples of **hex**.   [3]

(c) The definition for **value** is

   <value> ::= <digit>|<digit><value>

   Draw a syntax diagram to show the definition of **value**.

   You may assume that the correct syntax diagram for **digit** already exists.   [2]

9-54

2. A vowel-string in a high-level programming language has its syntax described in BNF as follows:

    <vowel-string> ::= <vowel>|a<vowel>a|e<vowel>e|i<vowel>i|o<vowel>o|u<vowel>u

    vowel ::= a|e|i|o|u

    (a) State, with reasons, whether each of the following character strings is a valid vowel-string.

    aea   uuu   AEA   aeae   sds   oooaeio

    (b) The word **level** is palindromic because its letters in reverse order give the same word.

    Make simple changes to the rules given above so that a vowel-string of any length is valid if and only if it is palindromic.   [5]

3. The following BNF definition describes a registration number.

    <reg-no> ::= <code><space><number>

    <number> ::= <pos digit><digit><digit>|<pos digit><digit><digit><digit>

    <pos digit> ::= 1|2|3|4|5|6|7|8|9

    <digit> ::= 0|<pos digit>

    <code> ::= AX|AC|BB

    <space> ::= ' '

    State, with reasons, whether each of the following is a valid or invalid registration number.

    AC 234   AB 13   AX 099   BB 2345   AX 6   [5]

Chapter 55 – Reverse Polish notation

Objectives

- Convert simple expressions in infix form to Reverse Polish notation (RPN) and vice versa
- Be aware of why and where RPN is used

Reverse Polish notation

Reverse Polish (also called **postfix**) notation was developed by a Pole called Jan Lukasiewicz. It is a method of writing arithmetic expressions that is particularly suited to computerised methods of evaluation. It has the following advantages and uses:

- It eliminates the need for brackets in sub-expressions
- It produces expressions in a form suitable for evaluation using a stack
- It is used in interpreters based on a stack; for example, Postscript and bytecode

The way in which we normally write arithmetic expressions is called **infix** notation, and it is not easy for a computer to evaluate such an expression directly. Consider for example the expression

        (a + b) * c

The sequence of instructions needed to evaluate this is

1. get a
2. get b
3. add them together and store the intermediate result
4. get c
5. multiply by the result of step 3.

In other words, the computer really needs the operands (a, b and c) and operators in the sequence

        a b + c *

> **Q1:** What would be the sequence of instructions needed to evaluate the expression b * c?
>
> **Q2:** What would be the sequence of instructions needed to evaluate the expression b * (c + d)?

In reverse Polish notation, the operator follows the operands – which is the logical sequence, if you are a computer.

Precedence rules

In order to translate from infix to Reverse Polish notation, we need to define the order of precedence of operators. This is shown below, in increasing order of precedence.

    =
    (
    + -)
    * /
    ^   (exponentiation, where 3^2 means 3^2)
    ~   (unary minus, as in -3 + 2)

9-55

Infix and postfix expressions

An expression such as (6 * 7) + 4 is known as an **infix** expression, because the operator is written between the operands.

The equivalent Reverse Polish form, 6 7 * 4 + is known as a **postfix** expression, as the operator follows the operands.

Translation from infix to Reverse Polish

A computer will use a fairly complex algorithm using a stack to translate from infix to reverse Polish notation. However, it is quite simple to do it manually with the benefit of common sense, a knowledge of the rules of precedence and a few simple rules, given below:

1. Starting from the left-hand side of the expression, allocate numbers 1, 2, 3 … to operands and operators as follows:

   - If the next symbol is an operand, allocate the next number (1, 2, 3…) to it. If it is an operator, move to the next operand.

   - Ignore parentheses except in so far as they affect the order of calculation.

   - Bearing in mind the rules of precedence, decide which is the next operation that should be performed, and as soon as its operands have been allocated numbers, back up and allocate it the next number.

   e.g.   a + b * c

        1 5 2 4 3

        a + b * c

   Working from the left, allocate 1 to a, 2 to b. Multiplication is done before addition, so keep going and allocate 3 to c. Then back up and allocate 4 to *, and finally 5 to +.

2. Write down the tokens (operators and operands) in the order of the numbers you have allocated.

   The Reverse Polish Form of the expression is a b c * +

Example 1

Convert the following expression to Reverse Polish notation: 8 + ((7 + 1) * 2) – 6

Following the rules above, taking into account order of precedence and brackets where they affect this:

  1 7   2 4 3   6 5   9 8

  8 + ((7 + 1) * 2) - 6

Note that taking the brackets into account, 7 + 1 is the first thing to be calculated, and then this is multiplied by 2. Keep backing up every time you have one or two operands which need to be evaluated next.

The Reverse Polish Form of the expression is 8 7 1 + 2 * + 6 -

> **Q3:** Translate into Reverse Polish Notation:
>
> (a)   (a + b) - x ^ y * 3
>
> (b)   x = - a + (c - d) / e

Translation from Reverse Polish to infix

To translate from RPN to infix, we need to perform this process in reverse.

Example 2

Convert the following RPN expression to infix notation: 25 16 18 + * 12 -

Visually scan the operands, writing them down until you find two operands followed by an operator. The unpaired operand, 25 is written down.

Bracket the next two operands with the operator between them and add them to the expression that is building up. We now have 25   (16 + 18)

Continue writing down operands until you find the next operator, which will operate on the two preceding operands, in this case * operates on 25 and (16 + 18). This gives us 25 * (16 + 18)

The next symbol is an operand, so the following operator will operate on the two operands

 25 * (16 + 18) and 12, giving the final result: 25 * (16 + 18) – 12

> **Q4:** Convert the following expression from postfix (Reverse Polish) notation to infix notation.
>
>   6 3 + 7 2 – *

Evaluation of Reverse Polish notation expressions using a stack

Once a compiler has translated an arithmetic expression into reverse Polish notation, each symbol in the expression may be held in a string or array. The expression may then be evaluated using a stack, scanning the elements of the string (or array) from left to right as follows:

* If the next token is an operand, place it on the stack

* If the next token is an operator, remove the required number of operands from the stack, (two except in the case of a unary minus or exponentiation), perform the operation, and put the result on the stack.

Example 3

Convert the following expression to Reverse Polish notation, and show how the resulting expression may be evaluated using a stack.

   (7 + 10 / 5) + (6 * 2)

First convert to Reverse Polish:

```
     1   5   2   4   3       9         6   8   7
  (   7   +   10 /   5   )   +   (   6   *   2   )
```

i.e. 7 10 5 / + 6 2 * + in Reverse Polish notation

Using a stack to evaluate the expression, the contents of the stack will change as follows:

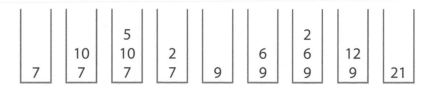

> **Q5:** Convert the expression (5 + 9) / 2 – (2 * 3) to Reverse Polish notation and show how it may be evaluated using a stack.

A binary expression tree

A binary tree can be constructed to represent the expression (7 + 10 / 5) + (6 * 2) as follows:

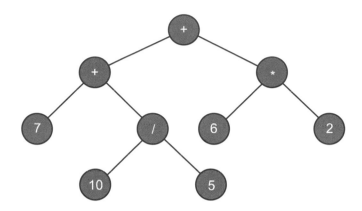

An **in-order traversal** of the tree will give the corresponding algebraic expression in **infix** format.

The nodes are visited in the sequence: 7 + 10 / 5 + 6 * 2

A **post-order traversal** of the tree will give the algebraic expression in **postfix** (reverse Polish) format.

The nodes are visited in the sequence: 7 10 5 / + 6 2 * +

> **Q6:** Draw a binary tree representing the infix expression (a + b) * (c – d)
>
> What is the result of performing a post-order traversal of the tree?

9-55

Exercises

1. At an intermediate stage of compilation, the compiler holds the following expression in reverse Polish form.

   a b * c d - - e + f g * /

   (a) Write down the original infix expression which was translated into this form.   [3]

   (b) Why is reverse Polish used as an intermediate stage during compilation?   [3]

2. (a) The following binary tree represents an algebraic expression. Write down the results of performing

   (i)   an in-order tree traversal   [2]

   (ii) a post-order tree traversal   [2]

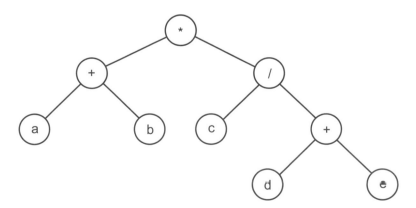

   (b) What names are given to each of these representations of the expression?   [2]

Section 10

The Internet

In this section:

10

Chapter 56 – Structure of the Internet

Objectives

- Understand the structure of the Internet

- Describe the term 'Uniform Resource Locator' in the context of networking

- Explain the terms 'domain name' and 'IP address'

- Describe how domain names are organised

- Understand the purpose and function of the Domain Name Server (DNS) system

- Explain the service provided by Internet registries and why they are needed

A short history of the Internet and the World Wide Web

The Internet is a network of networks set up to allow computers to communicate with each other globally. A United States defence project in the 1960s (ARPA) created **ARPANET** to enable distant departments working on the same project to communicate without the need for physical travel. The project developed, as did their means of communication and the Internet idea was born. In 1995 the Internet became a public hit when the World Wide Web emerged and user numbers began to climb, reaching roughly 2.5 billion users worldwide in 2015 – roughly one third of the world's population. The **World Wide Web** (WWW) is a collection of web pages that reside on computers connected to the Internet. It uses the Internet as a service to communicate the information contained within these pages. The concept of the WWW and using a browser to search the information contained within it was first developed by **Sir Tim Berners-Lee**, a British scientist working at CERN in Geneva, Switzerland. The World Wide Web is not the same as the Internet and even today, the Internet is frequently used without using the WWW.

10-56

Q1: Give one example of where the Internet can be used without the World Wide Web.

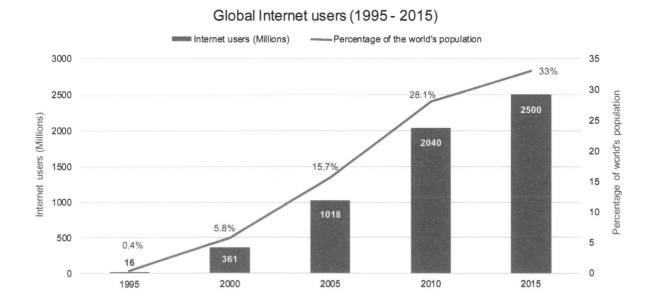

The physical structure of the Internet

Each continent uses backbone cables connected by trans-continental leased lines fed across the sea beds. National **Internet Service Providers** (ISPs) connect directly to this backbone and distribute the Internet connection to smaller providers who in turn provide access to individual homes and businesses.

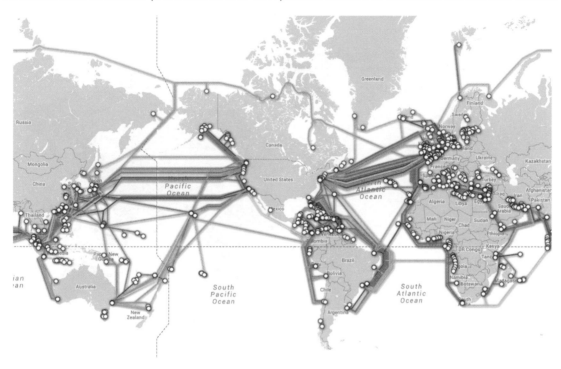

Trans-continental Internet connections, TeleGeography

10-56

Uniform Resource Locators (URLs)

A **Uniform Resource Locator** is the full address for an Internet resource. It specifies the location of a resource on the Internet, including the name and usually the file type, so that a browser can go and request it from the website server.

Internet registries and registrars

Internet registrars are needed to ensure that a particular domain name is only used by one organisation, and they hold records of all existing website names and the details of those domains that are currently available to purchase. These are companies that act as resellers for domain names and allow people and companies to purchase them. All registrars must be accredited by their governing registry.

Internet registries are five global organisations governed by the **Internet Corporation for Assigned Names and Numbers** (ICANN) with worldwide databases that hold records of all the domain names currently issued to individuals and companies, and their details. These details include the registrant's name, type (company or individual), registered mailing address, the registrar that sold the domain name and the date of registry. The registries also allocate IP addresses and keep track of which address(es) a domain name is associated with as part of the **Domain Name System** (DNS).

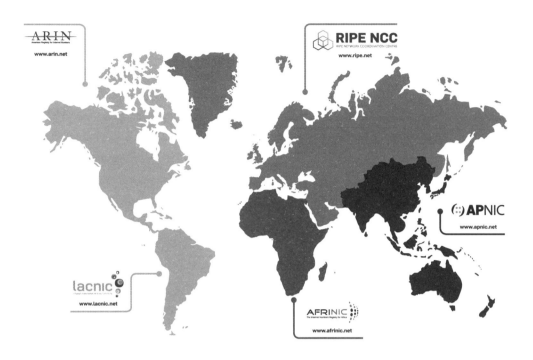

The five global Internet Registries

10-56

Domain names and the Domain Name System (DNS)

A domain name identifies the area or domain that an Internet resource resides in. These are structured into a hierarchy of smaller domains and written as a string separated by full stops as dictated by the rules of the **Domain Name System** (DNS).

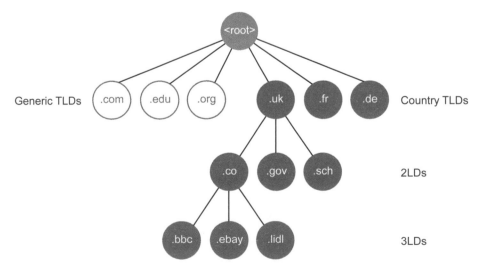

Each domain name has one or more equivalent **IP addresses**. The DNS catalogues all domain names and IP addresses in a series of global directories that domain name servers can access in order to find the correct IP address location for a resource. When a webpage is requested using the URL a user enters, the browser requests the corresponding IP address from a local DNS. If that DNS does not have the correct IP address, the search is extended up the hierarchy to another larger DNS database. The IP address is located and a data request is sent by the user's computer to that location to find the web page data. A webpage can be accessed within a browser by entering the IP address if it is known. Try entering 74.125.227.176 into a browser.

Fully Qualified Domain Name (FQDN)

Q2: Why are IP addresses not used to access websites instead of alphanumeric addresses?

Fully Qualified Domain Names (FQDN)

A **fully qualified domain name** is one that includes the host server name, for example **www**, **mail** or **ftp** depending on whether the resource being requested is hosted on a web, mail or ftp server. This would be written as **www**.websitename.co.uk or **mail**.websitename.co.uk for example.

IP addresses

An IP or **Internet Protocol** address is a unique address that is assigned to a network device. An IP address performs a similar function to a home mailing address.

130.142.37.108

The **IP address** indicates where a packet of data is to be sent or has been sent from. **Routers** can use this address to direct the data **packet** accordingly. If a domain name is associated with a specific IP address, the IP address is the address of the server that the website resides on.

Exercises

1. A Uniform Resource Locator (URL) is the address of a resource on the Internet. For example, http:// www.pgonline.co.uk/courses/alevel/computing_test.html.

   Explain the different parts of the address.

   (a) www.   [1]

   (b) pgonline.co.uk   [1]

   (c) /courses/alevel/computing_test.html   [1]

2. A village hall committee is considering purchasing a lease on a web domain to set up a new website to advertise their events. They have been advised to contact an Internet registrar.

   (a) Explain the role of an Internet registrar.   [3]

   (b) What is the primary role of an Internet Service Provider (ISP)?   [1]

10-56

Chapter 57 – Packet switching and routers

Objectives

- Understand the role of packet switching and routers
- Know the main components of a packet
- Consider where and why routers and gateways are used
- Explain how routing is achieved across the Internet

Packet switching

Packet switching is a method of communicating packets of data across a network on which other similar communications are happening simultaneously. The communications cables are shared between many communications to allow efficient use of them, in contrast to the older circuit-switched telephone network which allowed only one two-way communication at a time along a single cable. Website data that you receive arrives as a series of packets and an email will leave you in a series of packets.

Data packets

Data that is to be transmitted across a network is broken down in more manageable chunks called **packets**. The size of each packet in a transmission can be fixed or variable, but most are between 500 and 1500 bytes. Each packet contains a **header** and a **payload** containing the body of data being sent. Some packets may also use a trailer section with a **checksum** or **Cyclical Redundancy Check** (CRC) to detect transmission errors by creating and attaching a hash total calculated from the data contained in the packets. The CRC checksum is recalculated for each packet upon receipt and a match is used to help verify that the payload data has not changed during transmission. If the CRC totals differ, the packet is refused with suspected data corruption and a new copy is requested from the sender.

The header (much like the box(es) of a consignment you might send or receive through the post) includes the sender's and the recipient's IP addresses, the protocol being used with this type of packet and the number of the packet in the sequence being sent, e.g. packet 1 of 8. They also include the **Time To Live** (TTL) or **hop limit**, after which point the data packet expires and is discarded.

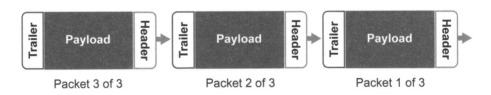

| Packet 3 of 3 | Packet 2 of 3 | Packet 1 of 3 |

Data packets queueing to be sent

> **Q1:** Why is the sender's IP address included in the packet header?

The payload of the packet contains the actual data being sent. Upon receipt, the packets are reassembled in the correct order and the data is extracted.

Routing packets across the Internet

The success of packet switching relies on the ability of packets to be sent from sender to recipient along entirely separate routes from each other. At the moment that a packet leaves the sender's computer, the fastest or least congested route is taken to the recipient's computer. They can be easily reassembled in the correct order at the receiving end and any packets that don't make it can be requested again.

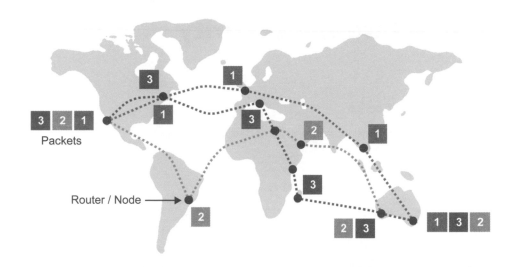

Packets

Router / Node →

> **Q2:** What information is included in the packet header to enable the receiving computer to reassemble packets in the correct order?

Routers

Each node in the diagram above represents a **router**. Routers are used to connect at least two networks, commonly two LANs or WANs, or to connect a LAN and its ISP's network. The act of traversing between one router and the next across a network is referred to as a **hop**. The job of a router is to read the recipient's IP address in each packet and forward it on to the recipient via the fastest and least congested route to the next router, which will do the same until the packet reaches its destination. Routers use routing tables to store and update the locations of other network devices and the most efficient routes to them. A routing algorithm is used to find the optimum route. The routing algorithm used to decide the best route can become a bottleneck in network traffic since the decision making process can be complicated. A common shortest path algorithm used in routing is **Dijkstra's algorithm**. (See Chapter 48.)

When a router is connected to the Internet, the IP address of the port connecting it must be registered with the Internet registry because this IP address must be unique over the whole Internet.

Gateways

Routing packets from one network to another requires a router if the networks share the same protocols, for example TCP/IP. Where these protocols differ between networks, a **gateway** is used rather than a router to translate between them. All of the header data is stripped from the packet leaving only the raw data and new header data is added in the format of the new network before the gateway sends the packet on its way again. Gateways otherwise perform a similar job to routers in moving data packets towards their destination.

Exercises

1. Major parts of the Internet run on a packet switched network that relies on routers and gateways to communicate.

   (a) What is meant by the term packet switching?   [2]

   (b) A data packet contains a header and a payload. The header contains data that it used to route the packet to its destination.

   State **three** data items that might be contained in a data packet's header.   [3]

   (c) Explain the difference between a router and a gateway.   [2]

10-57

Chapter 58 – Internet security

Objectives

- Understand how a firewall works

- Explain symmetric and asymmetric encryption and key exchange

- Explain how digital signatures and certificates are obtained and used

- Discuss worms, Trojans and viruses and the vulnerabilities that they exploit

- Discuss how improved code quality, monitoring and protection can be used against such threats

Firewalls

A **firewall** is a security checkpoint designed to prevent unauthorised access between two networks, usually an internal trusted network and an external, deemed untrusted, network; often the Internet. Firewalls can be implemented in both hardware and/or software. A router may contain a firewall.

A typical firewall consists of a separate computer containing two **Network Interface Cards** (NICs), with one connected to the internal network, and the other connected to the external network. Using special firewall software, each data packet that attempts to pass between the two NICs is analysed against preconfigured rules (**packet filters**), then accepted or rejected. A firewall may also act as a **proxy server**.

Packet filtering

Packet filtering, also referred to as **static filtering**, controls network access according to network administrator rules and policies by examining the source and destination IP addresses in packet headers. If the IP addresses match those recorded on the administrator's 'permitted' list, they are accepted. Static filtering can also block packets based on the protocols being used and the port numbers they are trying to access. A **port** is similar to an airport gate, where an incoming aircraft reaches the correct airport (the computer or network at a particular IP address) and is directed to a particular gate to allow passengers into the airport, or in this case to download the packet's payload data to the computer.

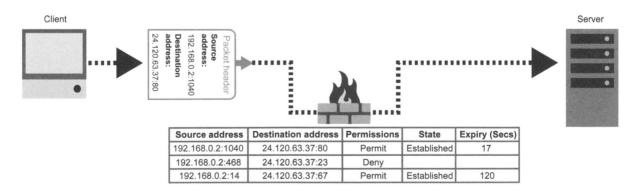

Source address	Destination address	Permissions	State	Expiry (Secs)
192.168.0.2:1040	24.120.63.37:80	Permit	Established	17
192.168.0.2:468	24.120.63.37:23	Deny		
192.168.0.2:14	24.120.63.37:67	Permit	Established	120

Certain protocols use particular ports. Telnet, for example, is used to remotely access computers and uses port 23. If Telnet is disallowed by a network administrator, any packets attempting to connect through port 23 will be dropped or rejected to deny access. A dropped packet is quietly removed, whereas a rejected packet will cause a rejection notice to be sent back to the sender.

Stateful inspection

Rather than relying on the IP addresses, protocols and port numbers to govern a packet's safe passage, **stateful inspection** or **dynamic filtering** can also examine the payload contents of a data packet to better assess it for safety. It can also create temporary contextual rules based on the passage of previous packets in a 'conversation'. This is to ensure that incoming responses (to your outgoing packets) arriving through the same port numbers, and with the same IP addresses, can be temporarily allowed during that communication stream. Routers usually keep the 'conversation' data in a Connection Table which is dynamically updated and referred to in conjunction with rules created by administrators of the network. An example of this would be when a browser makes a request to a specific web server for a web page. The packets containing the web page data returning from the web server would be allowed since the dynamic filter knows that these are in response to the recent request. This provides an added security measure against port scanning for covert access to a computer, since ports are closed off until connection to the specific port is requested by a computer on the protected side of the firewall.

Proxy servers

A **proxy server** intercepts all packets entering and leaving a network, hiding the true network addresses of the source from the recipient. This enables privacy and anonymous surfing. A proxy can also maintain a cache of websites commonly visited and return the web page data to the user immediately without the need to reconnect to the Internet and re-request the page from the website server. This speeds up user access to web page data and reduces web traffic. If a web page is not in the cache, then the proxy will make a request of its own on behalf of the user to the web server using its own IP address and forward the returned data to the user, adding the page to its cache for other users going through the same proxy server to access. A proxy server may serve hundreds, if not thousands of users.

10-58

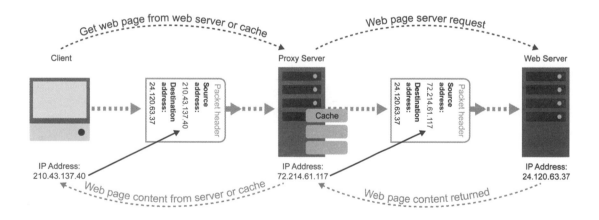

Proxy servers are often used to filter requests providing administrative control over the content that users may demand. A common example is a school web-proxy that filters undesirable or potentially unsafe online content in accordance with their school usage policies. Such proxies may also log user data with their requests.

Encryption

Encryption is the process of scrambling data so that it becomes very difficult to unscramble and interpret without the correct key. Encrypted data is known as **ciphertext**, and the original interpretable data is known as **plaintext**. The process of encryption is carried out using a cryptographic algorithm and a key.

Symmetric (Private key) encryption

Symmetric encryption, also known as **private key** encryption, uses the same key to encrypt and decrypt data. This means that the key must also be transferred (known as **key exchange**) to the same destination as the ciphertext which causes obvious security problems. The key can be intercepted as easily as the ciphertext message to decrypt the data. For this reason **asymmetric** encryption can be used instead.

> **Q1:** What are the risks associated with using private key encryption?

Asymmetric (Public key) encryption

Asymmetric encryption uses two separate, but related keys. One key, known as the **public key**, is made public so that others wishing to send you data can use this to encrypt the data. This public key cannot decrypt data. Another **private key** is known only by you and only this can be used to decrypt the data. It is virtually impossible to deduce the private key from the public key. It is possible that a message could be encrypted using your own public key and sent to you by a malicious third party impersonating a trusted individual. To prevent this, a message can be digitally 'signed' to authenticate the sender.

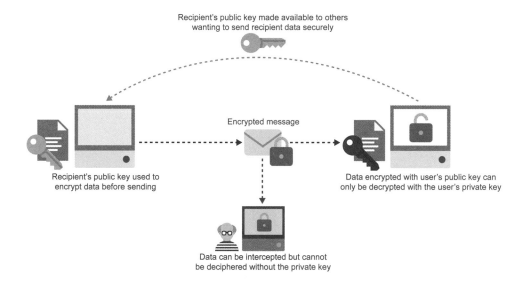

Recipient's public key made available to others wanting to send recipient data securely

Encrypted message

Recipient's public key used to encrypt data before sending

Data encrypted with user's public key can only be decrypted with the user's private key

Data can be intercepted but cannot be deciphered without the private key

> **Q2:** Governments sometimes demand copies of encryption keys in order to decrypt messages if necessary. What reasons are there for and against governments doing this?

Digital signatures

A **digital signature** is the equivalent of a handwritten signature or security stamp, but offers even greater security. First of all, a mathematical value is calculated from the unencrypted message data. This value is also referred to as a **hash total**, **checksum** or **digest**. Since the hash total is generated from the entire message, even the slightest change in the message will produce a different total. The sender of the message uses their own **private key** to encrypt the hash total. The encrypted total becomes the digital signature since only the holder of the private key could have encrypted it. The signature is attached to the message to be sent and the whole message including the digital signature is encrypted using the recipient's **public key** before being sent. The recipient then decrypts the message using their private key, and decrypts the digital signature using the sender's public key. The hash total is then reproduced based on the message data and if this matches the total in the digital signature, it is certain that the message genuinely came from the sender and that no parts of the message were changed during transmission.

10-58

To ensure that the message could not be copied and resent at a later date, the time and date can be included in the original message, which if altered, would cause a different hash total to be generated.

Digital signatures can be used with any kind of message regardless of whether encryption has also been used. They can be used with most email clients or browsers making it easy to sign outgoing communication and validate signed incoming messages. If set up to use digital signatures, your browser should warn you if you download something that does not have a digital signature. This would also mean that anything sent by you including online commercial and banking transactions can be verified as your own.

Q3: Assuming their private key has not been compromised, a digital signature authenticates the sender beyond legal doubt. How might this help protect against viruses?

Hoax digital signatures could be created using a bogus private key claiming to be that of a trusted individual. In order to mitigate against this, a **digital certificate** verifies that a sender's public key is formally registered to that particular sender.

Digital certificates

While digital signatures verify the trustworthiness of message content, a **digital certificate** is issued by official **Certificate Authorities** (CAs) such as Symantec or Verisign and verifies the trustworthiness of a message sender or website. This certificate allows the holder to use the **Public Key Infrastructure** or PKI. The certificate contains the certificate's serial number, the expiry date, the name of the holder, a copy of their public key, and the digital signature of the CA so that the recipient can authenticate the certificate as real. Digital certificates operate within the Transport layer of the TCP/IP protocol stack using TLS (Transport Layer Security), which is beginning to supersede SSL (Secure Sockets Layer) security. TCP/IP is covered in more detail in the following chapter.

10-58

Worms, Trojans and viruses

Worms, Trojans and viruses are all types of **malware** or **malicious software**. They are all designed to cause inconvenience, loss or damage to programs, data or computer systems.

Viruses and worm subclasses

Viruses and **worms** have the ability to self-replicate by spreading copies of themselves. A worm is a sub-class of virus, but the difference between the two is that viruses rely on other host files (usually executable programs) to be opened in order to spread themselves, whereas worms do not. A worm is standalone software that can replicate itself without any user intervention. Viruses come in various types but most become memory resident when their host file is executed. Once the virus is in memory, any other uninfected file that runs becomes infected when it is copied into memory. Other common viruses reside in macro files usually attached to word processing and spreadsheet data files. When the data file is opened, the virus spreads to infect the template and subsequently other files that you create. Macro viruses are usually less harmful than other viruses but can still be very annoying.

The Cascade virus caused text characters to fall from the top of the screen

A worm does not generally hide itself inside another file, but will usually enter the computer through a vulnerability or by tricking the user into opening a file; often an attachment in an email. Rather than simply infecting other files like a virus on your own machine, a worm can replicate itself and send copies to other users from your computer; commonly by emailing others in your electronic address book.

Owing to the ability of a worm to copy itself, worms are often responsible for using up bandwidth, system memory or network resources, causing computers to slow and servers to stop responding.

> **Q4:** Look up the ILOVEYOU, Melissa, Blaster and Cascade viruses or worms. Why should you exercise caution in opening attachments in emails or data files containing macro code?

Trojans

A Trojan is so called after the story of the great horse of Troy, according to which soldiers hid inside a large wooden horse offered as a gift to an opposition castle. The castle guards wheeled the wooden horse inside their castle walls, and the enemy soldiers jumped out from inside the horse to attack. A Trojan is every bit as cunning and frequently manifests itself inside a seemingly useful file, game or utility that you want to install on your computer. When installed, the payload is released, often without any obvious irritation. A common use for a Trojan is to open a back door to your computer system that the Trojan creator can exploit. This can be in order to harvest your personal information, or to use your computer power and network bandwidth to send thousands of spam emails to others. Groups of Internet-enabled computers used like this are called botnets. Unlike viruses and worms, Trojans cannot self-replicate.

The Procession of the Trojan Horse in Troy - Giovanni Domenico Tiepolo, c.1760

System vulnerabilities

Malware exploits vulnerabilities in our systems, be they human error or software bugs. People may switch off their firewalls or fail to renew virus protection which will create obvious weaknesses in their systems. Administrative rights can also fail to prevent access to certain file areas which may otherwise be breached by viral threats. Otherwise cracks in software where data is passed from one function, module or application to another (which is often deemed to have been checked and trusted somehow by the source) may open opportunities for attackers.

Protection against viral threats

Code quality is a primary vulnerability of systems. Many malware attacks exploit a phenomenon called 'buffer overflow' which normally occurs when a program accidentally writes values to memory locations too small to handle them, and inadvertently overwrites the values in neighbouring locations that it is not supposed to have access to. As a result of a buffer overflow attack, overflow data is often interpreted as instructions. The virus could be written to take advantage of this by forcing the program to write something to memory which may consequently alter its behaviour in a way that benefits the attacker.

Social engineering, including phishing, is a confidence trick used to persuade individuals to open files, Internet links and emails containing malware. Spam filtering and education in the use of caution is the most effective method against this sort of vulnerability.

Regular operating system and antivirus software updates will also help to reduce the risk of attack. Virus checkers usually scan for all other malware types and not just viruses, and since new variants are created all the time to exploit vulnerabilities in systems software, it is vital that your system has the latest protection. In the worst cases, a lack of monitoring and protection within a company can make national headlines.

Exercises

1. Software is being developed to allow secure transmission of data over the Internet.

   The two computers involved in a communication will be known as A and B.

   (a) What is *encryption*? [1]

   (b) The data being transmitted will be encrypted using public and private keys. A and B will each have a public key and a private key.

   A will encrypt the data that it is sending using B's public key.

   Explain why the data should not be encrypted using:

   (i) A's public key [1]

   (ii) A's private key [1]

   (c) The communication will be made more secure by the use of a digital signature attached to the end of the message.

   • State the purpose of a digital signature

   • Explain how it will be created and used in the data transmissions process from A to B.

   In your answer you will be assessed on your ability to use good English, and to organise your answer clearly in complete sentences, using specialist vocabulary where appropriate. [6]

   AQA Unit 3 Qu 5 Jun 2012

2. Malicious attacks on systems are frequently identified and blocked by various systems.

   (a) How might a proxy server reduce the risks of malware attacks on a network? [1]

   (b) Explain how stateful inspection provides greater security against port scanning than simple packet filtering. [1]

   (c) Give **three** methods that school systems administrators can use to reduce the threat of malware. [3]

Chapter 59 – TCP/IP, standard application layer protocols

Objectives

- Describe the roles of the four layers in the TCP/IP protocol stack
- Describe the role of sockets in the TCP/IP stack
- Be familiar with MAC addresses
- Explain and differentiate between the common protocols and the well-known ports they use
- Be familiar with transferring files using FTP as an anonymous and non-anonymous user
- Know how Secure Shell (SSH) is used for remote management including the use of application level protocols for sending and retrieving email
- Explain the role of an email server in sending and retrieving email
- Explain the role of a web server in serving up web pages in text form
- Understand the role of a web browser in retrieving web pages and web page resources and rendering these accordingly

The TCP/IP protocol stack

10-59

The **Transmission Control Protocol / Internet Protocol (TCP/IP)** protocol stack is set of networking protocols that work together as four connected layers, passing incoming and outgoing data packets up and down the layers during network communication. The four layers are the:

- Application layer
- Transport layer
- Network layer
- Link layer

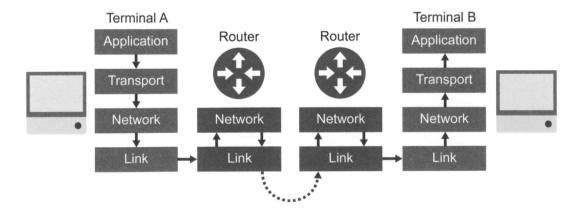

Figure 59.1

The role of the four layers in the stack

Various protocols operate at each layer of the stack, each with different roles. In each layer, the data to be sent is wrapped, or encapsulated in an envelope containing new packet data as it descends the layers and is unwrapped again at the receiving end in a networking equivalent of a game of pass the parcel.

The application layer

The **application layer** sits at the top of the stack and uses protocols relating to the application being used to transmit data over a network, usually the Internet. If this application is a browser, for example, it would select an appropriate higher-level protocol for the communication such as HTTP, POP3 or FTP.

Imagine the following text data is to be sent via a browser using the **Hypertext Transfer Protocol** (HTTP):

> "Only two things are infinite, the universe and human stupidity, and I'm not sure about the former."
>
> *Albert Einstein*

The transport layer

The **transport layer** uses the **Transmission Control Protocol** (**TCP**) to establish an **end-to-end connection** with the recipient computer. The data is then split into packets and labelled with the packet number, the total number of packets and the **port** number through which the packet should route. This ensures it is handled by the correct application on the recipient computer. In the example below, port 80 is used as this is a common port used by the HTTP protocol, called upon by the destination browser.

If any packets go astray during the connection, the transport layer requests retransmission of lost packets. Receipt of packets is also acknowledged.

Packet 1 of 3	Packet 2 of 3	Packet 3 of 3
"Only two things are infinite,	the universe and human stupidity,	and I'm not sure about the former."
Port: 80	Port: 80	Port: 80

The network layer

The **network layer**, sometimes referred to as the **IP layer** or **Internet layer**, adds the source and destination **IP addresses. Routers** operate on the network layer and will use these IP addresses to forward the packets on to the destination. The addition of an **IP address** to the **port** number forms a **socket**, e.g. 42.205.110.140:80, in the same way that the addition of a person's name is added to a street address on an envelope in order to direct the letter to the correct person within a building. A socket specifies which device the packet must be sent to and the application being used on that device.

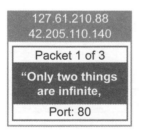

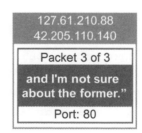

The link layer

The link layer is the physical connection between network nodes and adds the unique **Media Access Control** (**MAC**) addresses identifying the **Network Interface Cards** (**NIC**s) of the source and destination devices. These means that once the packet finds the correct network using the IP address, it can then locate the correct piece of hardware. MAC addresses are changed at each hop, the source MAC address being the address of the device sending the packet for that specific hop and the destination MAC address that of the device receiving the packet for that particular hop. Unless the two computers are on the same network, the destination MAC address will initially be the MAC address of the first router that the packet is sent to.

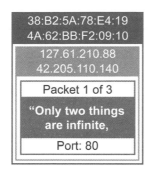
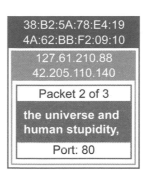
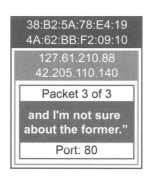

At the receiving end, the MAC address is stripped off by the link layer, which passes the packets on to the network layer. The IP addresses are then removed by the network layer which passes them on to the transport layer. The transport layer uses the port number to determine which application to pass the data to in the application layer, then removes the port numbers and reassembles the packets in the correct order. The resulting data is then passed to the application which presents the data for the user. Since routers operate on the network layer, source and destination MAC addresses are changed at each router node. Packets, therefore, move up and down the lower layers in the stack as they pass through each router or switch between the client and the server as shown in Figure 59.1.

> **Q1:** Imagine you are sending a friend a consignment of 5000 widgets in five boxes via a shipping agent. What information would you, the shipping agent, an intermediary depot and the delivery drivers write on the boxes or on a cover note inside? How does this relate to the TCP/IP stack?

10-59

Media Access Control (MAC) addresses

A **MAC** address is a unique 12-digit hexadecimal code that is hardcoded on every **Network Interface Card** (NIC) during manufacture. This uniquely identifies a particular printer, mobile phone, computer or router, wireless or wired, anywhere in the world so that data packets can be routed directly to them.

MAC: 00-71-5B-A9-38-4A

Well-known server ports and standard application level protocols

A **port** determines which application may deal with a data packet as it enters your computer. Several common application level **protocols** use standard ports on the server.

Server port number	Protocol
20	File Transfer Protocol (FTP) data
21	File Transfer Protocol (FTP) control instructions
22	Secure Shell (SSH) remote login
23	Telnet (unencrypted) remote login
25	Simple Mail Transfer Protocol (SMTP)
80 & 8080	Hypertext Transfer Protocol (HTTP)
110	Post Office Protocol v3 (POP3)
143	Interim Mail Access Protocol (IMAP)
443	Hypertext Transfer Protocol Secure (HTTPS)

Connecting a database to a browser with HTTP request methods

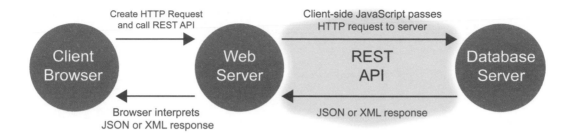

1. A browser makes a client server request from a web server to load a standard web page and all of its resources.

2. The web page HTML file contains some JavaScript which is executed on the client-side.

3. The browser JavaScript calls the RESTful API which enables communication with the server-side database using HTTP requests.

4. The database server responds to the client's HTTP requests with the data in JSON or XML format.

5. The browser renders the JSON or XML data in its own user interface.

Using HTTP methods for RESTful services

Consider the following data stored in a table named `planets` on an online database server:

name	distanceFromSunKM	gravityMS2
Mars	227900000	3.71
Earth	149600000	9.798
Jupiter	778500000	0

An HTTP request treats all of the data as objects and references it in standard URL notation.

HTTP request	Effect
`GET http://solarsystem.com/planets/`	Return all records in the Planets table
`PUT http://solarsystem.com/planets/Jupiter/gravity/24.79`	Update the value for Jupiter's gravity to 24.79
`DELETE http://solarsystem.com/planets/Jupiter`	Remove the record for Jupiter

Q3: What would be the HTTP request to create a new record for Venus? (Tip: Refer to Figure 61.1.)

Comparing JSON (JavaScript Object Notation) with XML (EXtensible Markup Language)

JSON and XML are the two standard methods for transferring data between the server and the web application. Assuming the HTTP requests in the table above had been made upon the data objects on the server, a GET request of `GET http://solarsystem.com/planets/` would now return the values for Mars and Earth. (Jupiter has been deleted.)

In JSON format, this would look like this:

```
{"planets":[
    {"name": "Mars", "distanceFromSunKM": 227900000, "gravityMS2": 3.71},
    {"name": "Earth", "distanceFromSunKM": 149600000, "gravityMS2": 9.798}
]}
```

In XML format, the response would be defined as:

```
<planets>
    <planet>
      <name>Mars</name>
      <distanceFromSunKM>227900000</distanceFromSunKM>
      <gravityMS2>3.71</gravityMS2>
    </planet>
    <planet>
      <name>Earth</name>
      <distanceFromSunKM>149600000</distanceFromSunKM>
      <gravityMS2>9.798</gravityMS2>
    </planet>
</planets>
```

Q4: Write out the JSON response code for the following GET request:

```
GET http://solarsystem.com/planets/Mars/
```

10-61

Advantages of JSON over XML code format

Whilst XML is still very widely used, having its own advantages over JSON, it is widely agreed that JSON provides a neater solution to data-interchange for the reasons outlined in the table below:

JSON is:	Reason:
Easier for a human to read	JSON code is tidier and easier for a human to read in the data oriented format: `{"object": "value"}`
More compact	Shorter code with fewer characters. Quicker to transmit. XML fieldnames need to be written out twice
Easier to create	Simpler syntax and structure. Can also use arrays
Easier for computers to parse and therefore quicker to parse	Can be parsed by a standard JavaScript function. Numeric values (1) are easier to differentiate from alphanumeric strings ("1")

Despite many advantages of JSON over XML, XML is more flexible that JSON in terms of the structure and the data types that it can be used with.

Thin- versus thick-client computing

The 'thickness' of a client computer refers to the level of processing and storage that it does compared with the server it is connected to. The more processing and storage that a server does, the 'thinner' the client becomes. If all the processing and storage is done by the server, then all that is required for the thinnest-client computer is a very basic machine with very little processor power and no storage. This is often known as a dumb terminal. The decision to go 'thick' or 'thin' rather depends on your specific requirements and each option comes with its own advantages and disadvantages.

Q5: How might you design a mobile GPS navigation app in order to optimise its use, given the advantages and disadvantages of thin- and thick-client systems?

	Advantages	Disadvantages
Thin-client	Easy to set up, maintain and add terminals to a network with little installation required locally Software and updates can be installed on the server and automatically distributed to each client terminal More secure since data is all kept centrally in one place	Reliant on the server, so if the server goes down, the terminals lose functionality Requires a very powerful, and reliable server which is expensive Server demand and bandwidth increased Maintaining network connections for portable devices consumes more battery power than local data processing
Thick-client	Robust and reliable, providing greater up-time Can operate without a continuous connection to the server Generally better for running more powerful software applications	More expensive, higher specification client computers required Installation of software required on each terminal separately and network administration time is increased Integrity issues with distributed data

Exercises

1. The following SQL statement returns the Type, Weight and Habitat data for an Aardvark.
   (a) How could this request be written as a URL using CRUD and REST principles? [2]

   ```
   SELECT Type, WeightKG, Food
   FROM Animal
   WHERE Type='Aardvark';
   ```

   (b) Which of the following responses to the request is written in JSON format? [1]

   Response A
   ```
   {"animals":[
      {"type": "Aardvark",
       "weightKG": 50,
       "food": "Termites"}
   ]}
   ```

   Response B
   ```
   <animals>
     <animal>
        <type>Aardvaak</type>
        <weightKG>50</weightKG>
        <food>Termites</food>
     </animal>
   </animals>
   ```

   (c) Give **two** advantages of using JSON over XML for web responses. [2]

2. A travel agency is looking to install a new computer system based on the client-server model for its agents to use for flight and hotel bookings and enquiries at multiple workstations.
   (a) What is meant by the client-server model? [2]

   After some consideration, the company has decided to use a thin-client network.

   (b) Explain how a thin-client network operates. [3]
   (c) How would the decision to use a thin- rather than thick-client network affect the choice of hardware? [2]

3. WebSockets upgrade the HTTP protocol following a handshake between the client cand the server.
   Give **one** feature of the WebSocket protocol and justify an application where it might be used. [3]

10-61

Section 11

Databases and software development

In this section:

11

Chapter 62 – Entity relationship modelling

Objectives

- Produce a data model from given data requirements for a simple scenario involving multiple entities

- Produce entity descriptions representing a data model in the form
  Entity1 (Attribute1, Attribute2…)

- Produce entity relationship diagrams representing a data model

- Be able to define the terms attribute, primary key, composite primary key, foreign key

Modelling data requirements

When a systems designer begins work on a new proposed computer system, one of the first things they need to do is to examine the data that needs to be input, processed and stored and determine what the data **entities** are.

Definition: An **entity** is a category of object, person, event or thing of interest to an organisation about which data is to be recorded.

Examples of entities are: Employee, Film, Actor, Product, Recipe, Ingredient.

Each entity in a database system has **attributes**.

Example 1: A dentist's surgery employs several dentists, and an appointments system is required to allow patients to make appointments with a particular dentist.

Entities in this system include **Dentist**, **Patient** and **Appointment**. The attributes of **Dentist** may include Title, Firstname, Surname, Qualification.

Attributes of **Patient** may include Title, Firstname, Surname, Address, Telephone.

Q1: Can you suggest any more attributes for **Patient**?

Q2: What attributes might the entity **Appointment** have?

Entity descriptions

An entity description is normally written using the format

> Entity1 (Attribute1, Attribute2…)

The entity description for **Dentist** is therefore written

> Dentist (Title, Firstname, Surname, Qualification)

Entity identifier and primary key

Each entity needs to have an **entity identifier** which uniquely identifies the entity. In a relational database, the entity identifier is known as the **primary key** and it will be referred to as such in this section. Clearly none of the attributes so far identified for **Dentist** and **Patient** is suitable as a primary key. A numeric or string ID such as D13649 could be used. In the entity description, the primary key is underlined.

> Dentist (DentistID, Title, Firstname, Surname, Qualification)

Q3: Is National Insurance Number a suitable primary key for Patient? If not, why not?

11-62

Relationships between entities

The different entities in a system may be linked in some way, and the two entities are said to be related.

There are only three different 'degrees' of relationship between two entities. A relationship may be

- **One-to-one**   Examples of such a relationship include the relationship between Husband and Wife, Country and Prime Minister.

- **One-to-many**   Examples include the relationship between Mother and Child, Customer and Order, Borrower and Library Book.

- **Many-to-many** Examples include the relationship between Student and Course, Stock Item and Supplier, Film and Actor.

Entity relationship diagrams

An entity relationship diagram is a diagrammatic way of representing the relationships between the entities in a database. To show the relationship between two entities, both the degree and the name of the relationship need to be specified. E.g. In the first relationship shown below, the degree is one-to-one, the name of the relationship is *in charge of*.

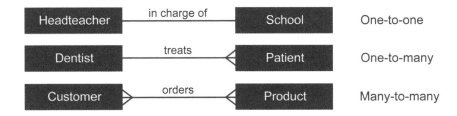

The concept of a relational database

In a relational database, a separate **table** is created for each entity identified in the system. Where a relationship exists between entities, an extra field called a **foreign key** links the two tables.

Foreign key

A foreign key is an attribute that creates a join between two tables. It is the attribute that is common to both tables, and the primary key in one table is the foreign key in the table to which it is linked.

Example 1

In the one-to-many relationship between Dentist and Patient, the entity on the 'many' side of the relationship will have **DentistID** as an extra attribute. This is the foreign key.

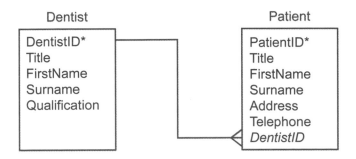

Note that the primary key is indicated by an asterisk, and the foreign key is shown in italics.

Linking tables in a many-to-many relationship

When there is a many-to-many relationship between two entities, tables cannot be directly linked in this way. For example, consider the relationship between **Student** and **Course**. A student takes many courses, and the same course is taken by many students.

In this case, an extra table is needed to link the **Student** and **Course** tables. We could call this **StudentCourse**, or **Enrolment**, for example.

The three tables will now have attributes something like those shown below:

Student (StudentID, Name, Address)

Enrolment (StudentID, CourseID)

Course (CourseID, Subject, Level)

In this data model, the table linking **Student** and **Course** has two foreign keys, each linking to one of the two main tables. The two foreign keys also act as the primary key of this table. A primary key which consists of more than one attribute is called a **composite primary key**.

Drawing an entity relationship diagram

A database system will frequently involve many different entities linked to each other, and an entity relationship diagram can be drawn to show all the relationships.

Example 2

A hospital inpatient system may involve entities **Ward**, **Nurse**, **Patient** and **Consultant**. A ward is staffed by many nurses, but each nurse works on only one ward. A patient is in a ward and has many nurses looking after them, as well as a consultant, who sees many patients on different wards.

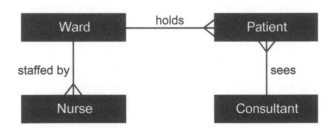

11-62

Q4: Is there a relationship between **Patient** and **Nurse**?

Q5: Draw entity-relationship diagrams to illustrate the relationships between

(a) **Product** and **Component**

(b) **Customer, Order** and **Product** (An order may be for several different products.)

Exercises

1. An estate agent keeps a database of all the properties it has for sale, the owners of the properties, and all the prospective buyers.

Details about the properties for sale include address, number of bedrooms, type of property, asking price.

Data on prospective buyers include name, telephone, address, type of property required, lower and upper limit for price.

Data on vendors include name, address, telephone.

A fourth entity, **Viewing** holds data about all viewings.

(a) Suggest **three** attributes for the entity **Viewing**. [3]

(b) Write entity descriptions for each of the entities **Property**, **Vendor**, **Buyer** and **Viewing**. In each case, identify any primary and foreign keys. [8]

(c) Draw an entity relationship diagram showing relationships between these four entities. [4]

2. A library plans to set up a database to keep track of its members, books and loans. Entities are defined as follows:

Member (<u>MemberID</u>, Surname, FirstName, Address)

Book (<u>BookID</u>, ISBN, Title, Author)

Loan (<u>MemberID</u>, <u>BookID</u>, loanDate, dueDate)

When the book is returned the loan record is deleted.

(a) Draw an entity relationship diagram showing the relationships between the entities. [3]

(b) A relational database is created with tables for each of these entities. The key in the Loan table is made up of two fields.

What is the name given to a key that is made up of multiple attributes? [1]

(c) What is meant by a **foreign** key? Identify a foreign key in one of the tables. [3]

3. An exam board wants to set up a database to hold data about its courses, exam papers, exam entries, candidates and results. For the purpose of this exercise, assume that each candidate can sit each exam once only. A course may have several exam papers (Comp 1, Comp 2, etc.). You may assume that a candidate enrolled for a course will sit every exam paper associated with that course.

The data to be stored for the candidate are CandidateNumber, FirstName, Surname, DateOfBirth.

The data to be stored for the course are CourseID, Subject, Level

The data held for each individual exam paper includes CourseID, ExamPaperID, DateOfExam, Title, TotalMarks, ExamPaperWeighting.

(a) State an identifier for the entity **ExamPaper**. [1]

(b) Write an entity description for another entity which will be required to show which courses each student is taking. [3]

(c) Draw an entity relationship diagram showing the relationships between the entities. [5]

(d) Write an entity description for a **Results** entity which will store the exam mark that candidates receive for each exam paper. [2]

Chapter 63 – Relational databases and normalisation

Objectives

- Explain the concept of a relational database
- Normalise relations to third normal form
- Understand why databases are normalised

Relational database design

In a relational database, data is held in tables (also called **relations**) and the tables are linked by means of common attributes.

A **relational database** is a collection of tables in which relationships are modelled by shared attributes.

Conceptually then, one row of a table holds one record. Each column in the table represents one attribute.

e.g. A table holding data about an entity **Book** may have the following rows and columns:

Book

BookID	DeweyCode	Title	Author	DatePublished
88	121.9	Mary Berry Cooks the Perfect	Berry, M	2014
123	345.440	The Paying Guests	Waters, S	2014
300	345.440	Fragile Lies	Elliot, L	2015
657	200.00	Learn French with stories	Bibard, F	2014
777	001.602	GCSE ICT	Barber, A	2010
etc				

To describe the table shown above, you would write

Book (BookID, DeweyCode, Title, Author, DatePublished)

Note that:

The **entity name** is shown outside the brackets

The **attributes** are listed inside the brackets

The **primary key** is underlined

The primary key is composed of one or more attributes that will uniquely identify a particular record in the table. (When describing an entity this is called an **entity identifier**.)

In order that a record with a particular primary key can be quickly located in a database, an **index** of primary keys will be automatically maintained by the database software, giving the position of each record according to its primary key.

11-63

Linking database tables

Tables may be linked through the use of a common attribute. This attribute must be a primary key of one of the tables, and is known as a **foreign key** in the second table.

We saw in the last chapter that there are three possible types of relationship between entities: one-to-one, one-to-many and many-to-many.

Normalisation

Normalisation is a process used to come up with the best possible design for a relational database. Tables should be organised in such a way that:

- no data is unnecessarily duplicated (i.e. the same data item held in more than one table)

- data is consistent throughout the database (e.g. a customer is not recorded as having different addresses in different tables of the database). Consistency should be an automatic consequence of not holding any duplicated data. This means that anomalies will not arise when data is inserted, amended or deleted.

- the structure of each table is flexible enough to allow you to enter as many or as few items (for example, components making up a product) as required

- the structure should enable a user to make all kinds of complex queries relating data from different tables

There are three basic stages of normalisation known as first, second and third normal form.

First normal form

A table is in **first normal form (1NF)** if it contains no repeating attribute or groups of attributes.

Example 1

A company manufacturing soft toys buys the component parts (fake fur, glass eyes, stuffing, growl etc.) from different suppliers. Each component may be used in the manufacture of several different toys (teddy bear, dog, duck etc.) Each component comes from a sole supplier.

Sample data to be held in the database is shown in the table:

ProductID	ProductName	CostPrice	Selling Price	CompID	CompName	CompQty	SupplierID	SupplierName
123	Small monkey	2.50	5.95	ST01	Stuffing	30	ABC	ABC Ltd
				G56	Eye (small)	2	BH Glass	Brown & Hill
				FF77	Brown Fur	0.3	FineFur	Fine Toys Ltd
156	Pink kitten	3.10	6.00	ST01	Stuffing	45	ABC	ABC Ltd
				G120	Eye (medium)	2	XYZ Glass	XYZ Ltd
				FF88	Pink Fur	0.35	FineFur	Fine Toys Ltd
				S34	Soundbox	1	Ping Toys	Ping & Co

Table 1

As the first stage in normalization, we need to note that there are repeating groups of attributes in this table; for example, ProductID 123 has three components with IDs ST01, G56 and FF77. We need to split the data into two tables to get rid of the repeating groups.

Note that a table in a relational database may be referred to as a **relation**.

Two entities, **Product** and **Component**, can be identified. These have the following relationship:

These two entities could be represented in standard notation:

    Product (<u>ProductID</u>, ProductName, CostPrice, SellingPrice)

    Component (<u>CompID</u>, CompName, SupplierID, SupplierName)

We have not yet put CompQty (the amount or number of each component that is needed to make a particular product) in either table, but we will come to that.

The two tables need to be linked by means of a common attribute, but the problem is that because this is a many-to-many relationship, whichever table we put the link attribute into, there needs to be *more than one* attribute.

e.g.   Product (<u>ProductID</u>, ProductName, CostPrice, SellingPrice, CompQty, ComponentID)

is no good because each toy has several components, so which one would be mentioned?

Similarly, Component (<u>CompID</u>, CompName, SupplierID, SupplierDetails, ProductID)

is no good either because each component is used in a number of different products.

One obvious solution (and unfortunately a bad one) springs to mind. How about allowing space for four components in the record for each product?

    Product (<u>ProductID</u>, ProductName, CostPrice, SellingPrice, CompID1, CompQty1,
            CompID2, CompQty2, CompID3, CompQty3, CompID4, CompQty4)

11-63

Q1: Why is this not a good idea?

This table contains repeating attributes, which are not allowed in first normal form. The attributes ComponentID and CompQty are repeated four times. The table is therefore NOT in first normal form.

It would be represented in standard notation with a line over the repeating attributes:

    Product (<u>ProductID</u>, ProductName, CostPrice, SellingPrice, CompID, CompQty)

To put the data into first normal form, the repeating attributes must be removed.

Introducing the link table

At this stage it becomes clear why we need a third table to link the two tables **Product** and **Component**.

The three tables now have attributes as follows:

    Product (<u>ProductID</u>, ProductName, CostPrice, SellingPrice)

    ProductComp (<u>ProductID</u>, <u>CompID</u>, CompQty)

    Component (<u>CompID</u>, CompName, SupplierID, SupplierName)

The design is now in 1NF because it contains no repeating attribute or groups of attributes.

Q2: Draw three tables representing these three entities and put the test data from Table 1 in the correct tables.

Q3: Which of the primary keys is a composite key?

Dealing with a Many-to-Many relationship

As you get more practice in database design, you will notice that *whenever* two entities have a many-to-many relationship, you will *always* need a link table 'in the middle'. Thus:

will become:

Second normal form - Partial key dependence test

A table is in **second normal form (2NF)** if it is in first normal form and contains no **partial dependencies**. A partial dependency would mean that one or more of the attributes depends on only part of the primary key, which can only occur if the primary key is a composite key.

The only table in which this could arise is **ProductComp** as this is the only table with a composite primary key. However, the only attribute in this table apart from the primary key is CompQty, which depends both on both parts of the primary key – which product and which particular component in that product.

The tables are therefore now in second normal form.

(To demonstrate tables which are not in second normal form, we'll look at Example 2 shortly.)

11-63

Third normal form - Non-key dependence test

A table is in **third normal form (3NF)** if it is in second normal form and contains no 'non-key dependencies'. A non-key dependency is one where the value of an attribute is determined by the value of another attribute which is not part of the key. 3NF means that:

All attributes are dependent on the key, the whole key, and nothing but the key.

Looking at the **Component** table, the SupplierName attribute is dependent on CompID and not on the SupplierID. It therefore needs to be removed from this relation and a new relation created.

The database, now in third normal form, consists of the following tables:

Product (<u>ProductID</u>, ProductName, CostPrice, SellingPrice)

ProductComp (<u>ProductID</u>, <u>CompID</u>, CompQty)

Component (<u>CompID</u>, CompName, *SupplierID*)

Supplier (<u>SupplierID</u>, SupplierName)

The entity relationship diagram showing the relationships between these four tables in third normal form is shown below. Each entity has its own table.

Example 2

A school plans to keep records of Sports Day events for different years in a database. The data that needs to be held for each event in a particular year is illustrated in the following table:

EventID	Year	EventName	Winner	TimeOrDistance
GA100	2015	Girls Under 14 100m	Claire Gordon	16.1
BJ100	2015	Junior Boys 100m	Marc Harris	13.1

The entity description is:

Event (EventID, Year, EventName, Winner, TimeOrDistance)

The composite primary key is composed of EventID and Year. Winner and TimeOrDistance depend on the whole key.

However, EventName depends only on EventID, not on Year, so this is a partial dependency. This table is therefore not normalised. It does not satisfy the requirement of a table in second normal form, namely that there are no partial dependencies.

Q4: Show how the database may be normalised by writing entity descriptions for each relation. Draw an entity relationship diagram.

The importance of normalisation

A normalised database has major advantages over an un-normalised one.

Maintaining and modifying the database

It is easier to maintain and change a normalised database.

Data integrity is maintained since there is no unnecessary duplication of data. For example, a customer with a particular customer ID will have their personal details stored only once. If the customer changes address, the update needs only to be made to a single table, so there is no possibility of inconsistencies arising with different addresses for the customer being held on different files.

It will also be impossible to insert transactions such as details of an order, for a customer who is not recorded in the database.

Faster sorting and searching

Normalisation will produce smaller tables with fewer fields. This results in faster searching, sorting and indexing operations as there is less data involved.

A further advantage is that holding data only once saves storage space.

Deleting records

A normalised database with correctly defined relationships between tables will not allow records in a table on the 'one' side of a one-to-many relationship to be deleted accidentally. For example, a customer who still has unresolved transactions on file cannot be deleted. This will prevent accidental deletion of a customer who has an unpaid invoice recorded, for example.

Exercises

1. A collector of popular music compact discs (CDs) wishes to store details of the collection in a database in a way that will allow information about the CDs to be extracted.

The data requirements are defined as follows.

- Each compact disc is assigned a catalogue number (unique) and labelled with a title, record company and type of popular music.

- Each compact disc contains one or more tracks.

- A track stores a recording.

- The recording may be a song or some other piece of music.

- A particular track recording features just one named artist.

- The name of each artist to be recorded together with a unique identifier, ArtistID.

- Each song and piece of music may be recorded on different CDs and by different artists.

- A particular CD will never have more than one recording of a particular song or piece of music but may contain tracks featuring the same artist or different artists.

- The title of every song and piece of music in the collection is to be recorded together with the name of the composer of the music and a unique identifier, SongMusicID.

- Each track on a particular CD is assigned a different number with the first always numbered one, the next two and so on.

- The duration of a track recording is recorded.

A single table, CDTable, was constructed initially in a relational database. The figure below shows the structure of this table and a few entries.

Catalogue No	Title	Record Company	Music Type	Track No	Track Duration	SongMusic ID	SongMusic Title	Composer Name	ArtistID	Artist Name
1	Quiet Time	ABC	Grunge	1	120	5	Action Man	Smith	1	Eric Ant
				2	150	8	Dedicated Woman	Williams	1	Eric Ant
								Brown	2	Rick Bana
				3	300	23	Last waltz			
				4	360	45	Shout	Nichols	2	Rick Bana
2	Running Scared	ABC	Rock	1	150	8	Dedicated Woman	Williams	2	Rick Bana
				2	140	4	Glad Tidings	Fox	2	Rick Bana
				3	280	12	Zulu	Vermouth	3	Rick Bana
				...	300	...	...	...	...	...
3	Sunshine Blues	BCD	Grunge	1	120	26	Jaded	Orchard	5	Yana Smit
				...	...	...	...	...	...	...
...	...	...	...	1	...	120	...	...	...	...
				...	...	...	...	...	...	...
...	...	...	...	1	...	45	Shout	...	...	...
				...	...	...	...	...	...	...
...	...	...	...	1	...	3	...	...	...	...
				...	...	...	...	...	...	...

(a) Which of the column headings in CDTable would be suitable as a primary key? [2]

(b) CDTable is not in first normal form. Explain. [2]

11-63

After normalisation the database contains the four tables based on the entities:

CompactDisc, CD-Track, SongMusic, Artist

(c) Using a copy of the partially complete entity relationship diagram below as an aid, show the degree of **four** more relationships which exist between the given entities.

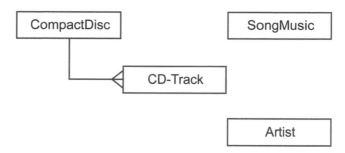

(d) Using the following format

TableName(PrimaryKey, Non-key Attribute 1, Non-key Attribute 2, etc)

Describe tables, stating all attributes, for the following entities underlining the primary key in each case.

(i)   CompactDisc   [2]

(ii) SongMusic   [2]

(iii) Artist   [2]

(iv) CD-Track   [4]

(e) Using the SQL commands **SELECT**, **FROM**, **WHERE**, write an SQL statement to query the database tables for the track numbers, SongMusicIDs and ArtistIDs for a given CD catalogue number, 15438.[3]

(Leave part (e) until you have completed the next chapter.)

AQA Computing Paper 3 Qu 13 Summer 2001

2. A college department wishes to create a database to hold information about students and the courses they take. The relationship between students and courses is shown in the following entity relationship diagram.

Each course has a tutor who is in charge of the course.

Sample data held on the database is shown in the table below.

Student Number	Student Name	DateOfBirth	Gender	Course Number	CourseName	TeacherID	Teacher Name
1111	Bell, K	14-01-1998	M	COMP23	Java1	8563	Davey,A
2222	Cope, F	12-08-1997	F	COMP23	Java1	8563	Davey,A
				COMP16	Intro to OOP	2299	Ross,M
				G101	Animation	1567	Day,S
3333	Behr,K	31-07-1996	M	Comp16	Intro to OOP	2299	Ross,M
				Comp34	Database Design	3370	Blaine, N

(a) Show how the data may be rearranged into relations which are in third normal form.   [6]

(b) State **two** properties that the tables in a fully normalised database must have.   [2]

Chapter 64 – Introduction to SQL

Objectives

- Be able to use SQL to retrieve data from multiple tables of a relational database

SQL

SQL, or **Structured Query Language** (pronounced either as S-Q-L or Sequel) is a **declarative language** used for querying and updating tables in a relational database. It can also be used to create tables. In this chapter, we will look at SQL statements used in querying a database.

The tables shown in Tables 1, 2 and 3 below will be used to demonstrate some SQL statements. The tables are part of a database used by a retailer to store details of CDs in a database that will allow information about the CDs to be extracted. This is a simplified version of the database described in Exercise 1 in the previous chapter.

The four entities **CD**, **CDSong**, **Song** and **Artist** are connected by the following relationships:

Figure 1

The **CD** table is shown below.

CDNumber	CDTitle	RecordCompany	DatePublished
CD14356	Shadows	ABC	06/05/2014
CD19998	Night Turned Day	GHK	24/03/2015
CD25364	Autumn	ABC	11/10/2015
CD34512	Basic Poetry	GHK	01/02/2016
CD56666	The Lucky Ones	DEF	16/02/2016
CD77233	Lucky Me	ABC	24/05/2014
CD77665	Flying High	DEF	31/07/2015

Table 1: CD table

SELECT .. FROM .. WHERE

The SELECT statement is used to extract a collection of fields from a given table. The basic syntax of this statement is

SELECT	*list of fields to be displayed*
FROM	*list the table or tables the data will come from*
WHERE	*list of search criteria*
ORDER BY	*list the fields that the results are to be sorted on (default is Ascending order)*

11-64

Example 1

```
SELECT CDTitle, RecordCompany, DatePublished
FROM CD
WHERE DatePublished BETWEEN #01/01/2015# AND #31/12/2015#
ORDER BY CDTitle;
```

This will return the following records:

CDTitle	RecordCompany	DatePublished
Autumn	ABC	11/10/2015
Flying High	DEF	31/07/2015
Night Turned Day	GHK	24/03/2015

Conditions

Conditions in SQL are constructed from the following operators:

Symbol	Meaning	Example	Notes
=	Equal to	CDTitle = "Autumn"	Different implementations use single or double quotes
>	Greater than	DatePublished > #01/01/2015#	The date is enclosed in quote marks or, in Access, # symbols
<	Less than	DatePublished < #01/01/2015#	
<>	Not equal to	RecordCompany <> "ABC"	
>=	Greater than or equal to	DatePublished >= #01/01/2015#	
<=	Less than or equal to	DatePublished <= #01/01/2015#	
IN	Equal to a value within a set of values	RecordCompany IN ("ABC", "DEF")	
LIKE	Similar to	CDTitle LIKE "S*"	Finds Shadows (wildcard operator varies and can be %)
BETWEEN...AND	Within a range, including the two values which define the limits	DatePublished BETWEEN #01/01/2015# AND #31/12/2015#	
IS NULL	Field does not contain a value	RecordCompany IS NULL	
AND	Both expressions must be true for the entire expression to be judged true	DatePublished > #01/01/2015# AND RecordCompany = "ABC"	
OR	If either or both of the expressions are true, the entire expression is judged true	RecordCompany = "ABC" OR RecordCompany = "DEF"	Equivalent to RecordCompany IN ("ABC", "DEF")
NOT	Inverts truth	RecordCompany NOT IN ("ABC", "DEF")	

Q1: SQL statements are written in the format

```
SELECT *
FROM table
WHERE condition
```

Write a query which will display all fields of records in the CD table published by the ABC or GHK record company in 2014-2015. (Note that the * means 'Display all fields in the record'.) Referring to the data in *Table 1*, what are the CDNumbers of the records returned by this query?

Specifying a sort order

`ORDER BY` gives you control over the order in which records appear in the Answer table. If for example you want the records to be displayed in ascending order of RecordCompany and within that, descending order of DatePublished, you would write, for example:

```
SELECT *
FROM CD
WHERE DatePublished < #31/12/2015#
ORDER BY RecordCompany, DatePublished Desc
```

This would produce the following results:

CDNumber	CDTitle	RecordCompany	DatePublished
CD25364	Autumn	ABC	11/10/2015
CD77233	Lucky Me	ABC	24/05/2014
CD14356	Shadows	ABC	06/05/2014
CD77665	Flying High	DEF	31/07/2015
CD19998	Night Turned Day	GHK	24/03/2015

Extracting data from several tables

So far we have only taken data from one table. The **Song** and **Artist** tables in the database have the following contents:

SongID	SongTitle	ArtistID	MusicType
S1234	Waterfall	A318	Americana
S1256	Shake it	A123	Heavy Metal
S1258	Come Away	A154	Americana
S1344	Volcano	A134	Art Pop
S1389	Complicated Game	A318	Americana
S1392	Ghost Town	A123	Heavy Metal
S1399	Gentle Waves	A134	Art Pop
S1415	Right Here	A134	Art Pop
S1423	Clouds	A315	Art Pop
S1444	Sheet Steel	A334	Heavy Metal
S1456	Here with you	A154	Art Pop

Table 2: **Song** table

ArtistID	ArtistName
A123	Fred Bates
A134	Maria Okello
A154	Bobby Harris
A315	Jo Morris
A318	JJ
A334	Rapport

Table 3: **Artist** table

Using SQL you can combine data from two or more tables, by specifying which table the data is held in. For example, suppose you wanted SongTitle, ArtistName and MusicType for all *Art Pop* music. When more than one table is involved, SQL uses the syntax tablename.fieldname. (The table name is optional unless the field name appears in more than one table.)

```
SELECT Song.SongTitle, Artist.ArtistName, Song.MusicType
FROM Song, Artist
WHERE (Song.ArtistID = Artist.ArtistID) AND (Song.MusicType = "Art Pop")
```

The condition `Song.ArtistID = Artist.ArtistID` provides the link between the Song and Artist tables so that the artist's name corresponding to the ArtistID in the **Song** table can be found in the Artist table. This will produce the following results:

SongTitle	ArtistName	MusicType
Volcano	Maria Okello	Art Pop
Gentle Waves	Maria Okello	Art Pop
Right Here	Maria Okello	Art Pop
Clouds	Jo Morris	Art Pop
Here with you	Bobby Harris	Art Pop

Q2: Write an SQL query which will give the SongTitle, ArtistName, MusicType of all songs by *JJ* or *Rapport*, sorted by ArtistName and SongTitle.

The fourth table in the database is the table **CDSong** which links the songs to one or more of the CDs.

CDNumber	SongID
CD14356	S1234
CD14356	S1258
CD14356	S1415
CD19998	S1234
CD19998	S1389
CD19998	S1423
CD19998	S1456
CD25364	S1256
CD25364	S1392
CD34512	S1392
CD34512	S1234
CD34512	S1389
CD34512	S1444
CD77233	S1256
CD77233	S1344
CD77233	S1399
CD77233	S1456

Table 4: **CDSong** table

Example 2

We can make a search to find the CDNumbers and titles of all the CDs containing the song *Waterfall*, sung by JJ.

```
SELECT Song.SongID, Song.SongTitle, Artist.ArtistName, CDSong.CDNumber,
CD.CDTitle
FROM Song, Artist, CDSong, CD
WHERE CDSong.CDNumber = CD.CDNumber
   AND CDSong.SongID = Song.SongID
   AND Artist.ArtistID = Song.ArtistID
   AND Song.SongTitle = "Waterfall"
```

11-64

This will produce the following results:

SongID	SongTitle	ArtistName	CDNumber	CDTitle
S1234	Waterfall	JJ	CD14356	Shadows
S1234	Waterfall	JJ	CD19998	Night Turned Day
S1234	Waterfall	JJ	CD34512	Basic Poetry

Note that in the **SELECT** statement, it does not matter whether you specify `Song.SongID` or `CDSong.SongID` since they are connected. The same is true of `CDSong.CDNumber` and `CD.CDNumber`. The three Boolean conditions `CDSong.CDNumber = CD.CDNumber`, `CDSong.SongID = Song.SongID` and `Artist.ArtistID = Song.ArtistID` are required to specify the relationships between the data tables. See the Entity Relationship Diagram in Figure 1 above.

Exercises

1. Customers placing orders with ABC Ltd for ABC's products have their orders recorded by ABC in a database.

The data requirements for the database system are defined as follows:

- Each product is assigned a unique product code, ProductId and has a product description.
- The quantity in stock of a particular product is recorded.
- Each customer is assigned a unique customer code, CustomerId and has their name, address and telephone number recorded.
- An order placed by a customer will be for one or more products.
- ABC Ltd assigns a unique code to each customer order, ABCOrderNo.
- A customer placing an order must supply a code, CustomerOrderNo, which the customer uses to identify the particular order.
- A customer may place one or more orders.
- Each new order from a particular customer will have a different customer order code but two different customers may use, independently, the same values of customer order code.
- Whether an order has been despatched or not will be recorded.
- A particular order will contain one or more lines.
- Each line is numbered, the first is one, the second is two, and so on.
- Each line will reference a specific product and specify the quantity ordered.
- A specific product reference will appear only once in any particular order placed with ABC Ltd.

After normalisation the database contains four tables based on the entities:

Customer, Product, Order, OrderLine

(a) The figure below is a partially complete entity relationship diagram. Show the degree of **three** more relationships which exist between the given entities.

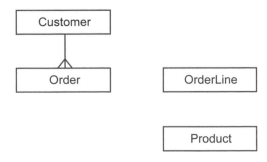

[3]

11-64

(b) Using the following format:

> **TableName (Primary Key, Non-key Attribute1, Non-key Attribute2, etc)**

describe tables, stating all attributes, for the following entities underlining the primary key in each case.

(i) Product [2]

(ii) Customer [2]

(iii) Order [3]

(iv) OrderLine [4]

(c) Using the SQL commands SELECT, FROM, WHERE, ORDER BY, write an SQL statement to query the database tables for all customer names where the orders have been despatched.

The result of the query is to be ordered in ascending order of ABCOrderNo. [6]

AQA CPT5 Qu 8 June 2002

2. A school keeps records of school trips on a database. There are four tables on the database named PUPIL, TRIP, TEACHER, PUPILTRIP, defined as follows:

PUPIL (PupilID, PupilSurname, PupilFirstName)

TRIP (TripID, Description, StartDate, EndDate, Destination, NumberOfStudents, TeacherID)

TEACHER (TeacherID, Title, FirstName, Surname)

PUPILTRIP (PupilID, TripID)

(a) Draw an entity relationship diagram showing the relationship between the entities. [4]

(b) Write SQL statements for each of the following operations:

(i) find the first name and surname of all pupils who went on a trip with TripID 14. [4]

(ii) find all the trips for which the teacher with surname "Black" has been in charge, giving teacher's title and surname, trip description and start date, sorted in descending order of start date. [4]

(iii) find the firstnames and surnames of all the pupils who went on any trip with "Year 7" in the description (e.g. "Year 7 Geography field trip" in May 2015, showing the firstname and surname of the teacher in charge. [6]

11-64

Chapter 65 – Defining and updating tables using SQL

Objectives

- Be able to use SQL to define a database table

- Be able to use SQL to update, insert and delete data from multiple tables of a relational database

- Know that a client server database system provides simultaneous access to the database for multiple clients

- Know how concurrent access can be controlled to preserve the integrity of the database

Defining a database table

The following example shows how to create a new database table.

Example 1

Use SQL to create a table named **Employee**, which has four columns: EmpID (a compulsory *int* field which is the primary key), EmpName (a compulsory *character* field of length 20), HireDate (an optional *date* field) and Salary (an optional *real number* field).

```
CREATE TABLE Employee
(
EmpID      INTEGER NOT NULL, PRIMARY KEY,
EmpName    VARCHAR(20) NOT NULL,
HireDate   DATE,
Salary     CURRENCY
)
```

Data types

Some of the most commonly used data types are described in the table below. (The data types vary depending on the specific implementation.)

Data type	Description	Example
CHAR(n)	Character string of fixed length n	ProductCode CHAR(6)
VARCHAR(n)	Character string variable length, max. n	Surname VARCHAR(25)
BOOLEAN	TRUE or FALSE	ReviewComplete BOOLEAN
INTEGER, INT	Integer	Quantity INTEGER
FLOAT	Number with a floating decimal point	Length FLOAT (10,2) (maximum number of digits is 10 and maximum number after decimal point is 2)
DATE	Stores Day, Month, Year values	HireDate DATE
TIME	Stores Hour, Minute, Second values	RaceTime TIME
CURRENCY	Formats numbers in the currency used in your region	EntryFee CURRENCY

11-65

Altering a table structure

The ALTER TABLE statement is used to add, delete or modify columns (i.e. fields) in an existing table.

To add a column (field):

```
ALTER TABLE Employee
ADD Department VARCHAR(10)
```

To delete a column:

```
ALTER TABLE Employee
DROP COLUMN HireDate
```

To change the data type of a column:

```
ALTER TABLE Employee
MODIFY COLUMN EmpName VARCHAR(30) NOT NULL
```

Q1: Use SQL to create a table called **Student** which is defined as follows:

StudentID	6 characters	(Primary key)
Surname	20 characters	
FirstName	15 characters	
DateOfBirth	Date	

Q2: Write an SQL statement to add a new column named YearGroup, of type Integer.

Defining linked tables

11-65

If you set up several tables, you can link tables by creating foreign keys.

Example 2

Suppose that an extra table is to be added to the Employee database which lists the training courses offered by the company. A third table shows which date an employee attended a particular course.

The structure of the **Employee** table is:

EmpID	Integer (Primary key)
Name	30 characters maximum
HireDate	Date
Salary	Currency
Department	30 characters maximum

The structure of the **Course** table is:

CourseID	6 characters, fixed length (Primary key)
CourseTitle	30 characters maximum (must be entered)
OnSite	Boolean

The structure of the **CourseAttendance** table is:

CourseID	6 characters, fixed length (foreign key)
EmpID	Integer (foreign key) Course ID and EmpID form a composite primary key
CourseDate	Date (note that the same course may be run several times on different dates)

337

The **CourseAttendance** table is created using the SQL statements:

```
CREATE TABLE CourseAttendance
(
CourseID       CHAR(6) NOT NULL,
EmpID          INTEGER NOT NULL,
CourseDate     DATE,
FOREIGN KEY CourseID REFERENCES Course(CourseID),
FOREIGN KEY EmpID REFERENCES Employee(EmpID),
PRIMARY KEY (CourseID, EmpID)
)
```

Q3: Write the SQL statements to create the Course table.

Inserting, updating, and deleting data using SQL

The SQL INSERT INTO statement

This statement is used to insert a new record in a database table. The syntax is:

```
INSERT INTO tableName (column1, column2, ...)
VALUES (value1, value2, ...)
```

Example: add a record for employee number 1122, Bloggs, who was hired on 1/1/2001 for the technical department at a salary of £18000.

```
INSERT INTO Employee (EmpID, Name, HireDate, Salary, Department)
VALUES (1122, "Bloggs", #1/1/2001#, 18000, "Technical")
```

Note that if all the fields are being added in the correct order you would not need the field names in the brackets above to be specified. `INSERT INTO Employee` would be sufficient

Example: add a record for employee number 1125, Cully, who was hired on 1/1/2001. Salary and Department are not known.

```
INSERT INTO Employee (EmpID, Name, HireDate)
VALUES (1125, "Cully", #1/1/2001#)
```

The SQL Update statement

This statement is used to update a record in a database table. The syntax is:

```
UPDATE tableName
SET column1 = value1, column2 = value2, ...
WHERE columnX = value
```

Example: increase all salaries of members of the Technical department by 10%

```
UPDATE Employee
SET Salary = Salary*1.1
WHERE Department = "Technical"
```

Example: Update the record for the employee with ID 1122, who has moved to Administration.

```
UPDATE Employee
SET Department = "Administration"
WHERE EmpID = 1122
```

11-65

The SQL Delete statement

This statement is used to delete a record from a database table. The syntax is:

```
DELETE FROM tableName
WHERE columnX = value
```

Example: Delete the record for Bloggs, Employee ID 1122.

```
DELETE FROM Employee
WHERE EmpID = 1122
```

Q4: The table Student is defined below:

StudentID	6 characters	(Primary key)
Surname	20 characters	
FirstName	15 characters	
DateOfBirth	Date	

(a) Use SQL to add a record for Jennifer Daley, StudentID AB1234, Date of Birth 23/06/2005.

(b) Update this record, the student's name is Jane, not Jennifer.

(c) Add a new column DateStarted to the table, of type DATE.

Client-Server databases

Many modern database management systems provide an option for client-server operation. Using a client-server Database Management System (DBMS), DBMS server software runs on the network server, and DBMS client software runs on individual workstations. The server software processes requests for data searches and reports that originate from individual workstations running DBMS client software. For example, a car dealer might want to search the manufacturer's database to find out whether there are any cars of a particular specification available. The DBMS client refers this request to the DBMS server, which searches for the information and sends it back to the client workstation. Once the information is at the workstation, the dealer can sort the list and produce a customised report. If the DBMS did not have client-server capability, the entire database would be copied to the workstation and software held on the workstation would search for the requested data – involving a large amount of time being spent on transmitting irrelevant data and probably a longer search using a less powerful machine.

The advantages of a client-server database are, therefore:

- the consistency of the database is maintained because only one copy of the data is held (on the server) rather than a copy at each workstation

- an expensive resource (powerful computer and large database) can be made available to a large number of users

- Access rights and security can be managed and controlled centrally

- Backup and recovery can be managed centrally

Potential problems with client-server databases

Allowing multiple users to simultaneously update a database table may cause one of the updates to be lost unless measures are taken to prevent this.

When an item is updated, the entire record (indeed the whole **block** in which the record is physically held) will be copied into the user's own local memory area at the workstation. When the record is saved, the block is rewritten to the file server. Imagine the following situation:

11-65

User A accesses a customer record, thereby causing it to be copied into the memory at his/her workstation, and starts to type in a new address for the customer.

User B accesses the same customer record, and alters the credit limit and then saves the record and calls up the next record that needs updating.

User A completes the address change, and saves the record.

> **Q5:** What state will the record be in? (i.e. which address and credit limit will it hold?)

There are several methods which may be employed to avoid updates being lost.

Record locks

Record locking is the technique of preventing simultaneous access to objects in a database in order to prevent updates being lost or inconsistencies in the data arising. In its simplest form, a record is locked whenever a user retrieves it for editing or updating. Anyone else attempting to retrieve the same record is denied access until the transaction is completed or cancelled.

Problems with record locking

If two users are attempting to update two records, a situation can arise in which neither can proceed, known as **deadlock**. Suppose a bank clerk is updating Customer A's record with a transfer to Customer B's account. Meanwhile a second bank clerk is trying to update Customer B's record, as he needs to transfer money to Customer A's account.

User1	User2
locks Customer A's record	locks Customer B's record
tries to access Customer B's record	tries to access Customer A's record
waits ..	waits ..
DEADLOCK!	

The DBMS must recognise when this situation has occurred and take action. **Serialisation**, **timestamp ordering** or **commitment ordering** may be used.

Serialisation

This is a technique which ensures that transactions do not overlap in time and therefore cannot interfere with each other or lead to updates being lost. A transaction cannot start until the previous one has finished. It can be implemented using **timestamp ordering**.

Timestamp ordering

Whenever a transaction starts, it is given a timestamp, so that if two transactions affect the same object (for example record or table), the transaction with the earlier timestamp should be applied first.

In order to ensure that transactions are not lost, every object in the database has a **read timestamp** and a **write timestamp**, which are updated whenever an object in a database is read or written.

When a transaction starts, it reads the data from a record causing the read timestamp to be set. Before it writes the updated data back to the record it will check the read timestamp. If this is not the same as the value that was saved when this transaction started, it will know that another transaction is also taking place on the record. A range of potential problems can thus be identified and avoided.

Commitment ordering

This is another serialisation technique used to ensure that transactions are not lost when two or more users are simultaneously trying to access the same database object. Transactions are ordered in terms of their dependencies on each other as well as the time they were initiated. It can be used to prevent deadlock by blocking one request until another is completed.

Exercises

1. A company sells furniture to customers of its store. The store does not keep furniture in stock. Instead, a customer places an order at the store and the company then orders the furniture required from its suppliers. When the ordered furniture arrives at the store a member of staff telephones or emails the customer to inform them that it is ready for collection. Customers often order more than one type of furniture on the same order, for example a sofa and two chairs.

   Details of the furniture, customers and orders are to be stored in a relational database using the following four relations:

   Furniture (<u>FurnitureID</u>, FurnitureName, Category, Price, SupplierName)

   CustomerOrder (<u>OrderID</u>, CustomerID, Date)

   CustomerOrderLine (<u>OrderID</u>, <u>FurnitureID</u>, Quantity)

   Customer (<u>CustomerID</u>, CustomerName, EmailAddress, TelephoneNumber)

   (a) These relations are in Third Normal Form (3NF).

       (i) What does this mean? [2]

       (ii) Why is it important that the relations in a relational database are in Third Normal Form? [2]

   (b) On the incomplete Entity Relationship diagram below show the degree of any **three** relationships that exist between the entities. [3]

   (c) Complete the following Data Definition Language (DDL) statement to create the Furniture relation, including the key field.

   ```
   CREATE TABLE Furniture (
   ```
   [3]

   (d) A fault has been identified with the product that has FurnitureID number 10765. The manager needs a list of the names and telephone numbers of all the customers who have purchased this item of furniture so that they can be contacted. This list should contain no additional details and must be presented in alphabetical order of the names of the customers.

   Write an SQL query that will produce this list. [6]

   AQA Unit 3 Qu 9 June 2013

2. (a) Explain how, in a client-server database with multiple users, an update made by one user may not be recorded if the DBMS does not have measures in place to ensure the integrity of the database. [3]

   (b) Explain what is meant by deadlock and how this can arise. [2]

   (c) Name and describe briefly a method of preventing this from happening. [2]

Chapter 66 – Systematic approach to problem solving

Objectives

- Describe aspects of software development
- Explain the prototyping/agile approach that may be used in the analysis, design and implementation of a system
- Understand what is meant by data modelling
- Know the criteria for evaluating a computer system

Aspects of software development

There is an infinite variety of different types of problem that can be solved using a computer. Whether you are developing a website for a new company selling goods or services, designing a simulation of a physics experiment, building a control system using a microprocessor or something else, all software projects have certain aspects in common.

Analysis

Before a problem can be solved, it must be defined. The requirements of the system that solves the problem must be established. In the case of a data processing system, or for example the construction of a website, this could cover:

- the **data** – its origin, uses, volumes and characteristics
- the **procedures** – what is done, where, when and how, and how errors and exceptions are handled
- the **future** – development plans and expected growth rates
- **problems** with any existing system

In the case of a different type of problem such as a simulation or game, the requirements will still need to cover a similar set of considerations.

Agile modelling

At all the stages of analysis, design and implementation, an **agile approach** may be adopted, as the stages of software development may not be completed in a linear sequence. It might be that some analysis is done and then some parts of a system are designed and implemented while other parts are still being analysed and then, for example, implementation and testing may be intermixed. The developer may then go back to design another aspect of the system.

Throughout the process, feedback will be obtained from the user; this is an **iterative process** during which changes made are incremental as the next part of the system is built. Typically the software developers do just enough modelling at the start of the project to make sure that the system is clearly understood by both themselves and the users.

11-66

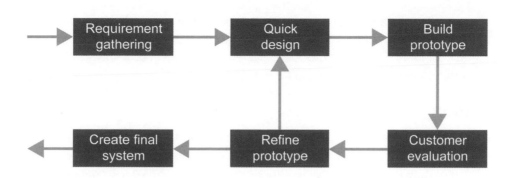

At each stage, a **prototype** is built with user participation to ensure that the system is being developed in line with what the user wants. The success of the software development depends on

- **keeping the model simple**, and not trying to incorporate features which may come in useful at a later date

- **rapid feedback from the user**

- understanding that user requirements may change during development as they are forced to consider their needs in detail

- being prepared to make **incremental changes** as the model develops

Design

Depending on the type of project, the systems designer may consider some or all of the following:

- **processing**: the algorithms and appropriate modular structure for the solution, specifying modules with clear documented interfaces

- **data structures:** how data will be held and how it will be accessed – for example in a dynamic data structure such as a queue or tree, or in a file or database

- **output**: content, format, sequence, frequency, medium (e.g. screen or hard copy) etc.

- **input:** volume, frequency, documents used, input methods;

- **user interface:** screens and dialogues, menus, special-purpose requirements

- **security**: how the data is to be kept secure from accidental corruption or deliberate tampering or hacking

- **hardware**: selection of an appropriate configuration

Modelling data requirements

What exactly is "an abstract representation of a problem"? We cannot easily represent the world as it "really is", but we can make abstractions and simplifications so that we can structure and manipulate relevant data to help us achieve a particular goal.

> **Q1:** How could you model the relationships between several generations of a family so that they can be clearly understood?

Whatever the proposed data structures are, modelling will involve deciding what data needs to be held and how the data items are related to each other.

11-66

In addition to modelling data requirements, a **prototype of the user interface** may be built so that the user can get a clear idea of how they will interact with the system, how data will be input and how arduous this task might be under the proposed system. Once again user involvement is crucial, and at this stage changes to the prototype should be straightforward.

Implementation

Once the design has been agreed, the programs can be coded. A clear focus needs to be maintained on the ultimate goal of the project, without users or programmers being sidetracked into creating extra features which might be useful, or possible future requirements. "*Solve the critical path first!*"

Programmers will need to be flexible in accepting user feedback and making changes to their programs as problems or design flaws are detected. In even a moderately complex system it is hard to envision how everything will work together, so iterative changes at every stage are a normal part of a prototyping/agile approach.

Testing

Testing is carried out at each stage of the development process. Testing the implementation is covered in Chapter 10. Once all the programs have been tested with normal, boundary and erroneous data, unit testing, module testing and system testing will also be carried out.

The system then needs to be tested by the user to ensure that it meets the specification.

This is known as **acceptance testing**. It involves testing with data supplied by the end user rather than data designed especially for testing purposes.

It has the following objectives:

- to confirm that the system delivered meets the original customer specifications

- to find out whether any major changes in operating procedures will be needed

- to test the system in the environment in which it will run, with realistic volumes of data

Testing is an iterative process, with each stage in the test process being repeated when modifications have to be made owing to errors coming to light at a subsequent stage.

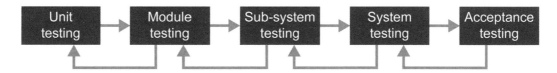

Evaluation

The evaluation may include a post-implementation review, which is a critical examination of the system three to six months after it has been put into operation. This waiting period allows users and technical staff to learn how to use the system, get used to new ways of working and understand the new procedures required. It allows management a chance to evaluate the usefulness of the reports and on-line queries that they can make, and go through several 'month-end' periods when various routine reports will be produced. Shortcomings of the system, if there are any, will be becoming apparent at all levels of the organisation, and users will want a chance to air their views and discuss improvements. The solution should be evaluated on the basis of **effectiveness**, **usability** and **maintainability**.

11-66

The post-implementation review will focus on the following:

- a comparison of the system's actual performance with the anticipated performance objectives

- an assessment of each aspect of the system against preset criteria

- errors which were made during system development

- unexpected benefits and problems

Exercises

1. (a) Explain what is meant by the **prototyping/agile approach** to system analysis and design.   [4]

   (b) What are the advantages of this approach?   [4]

2. A systems analyst/developer is planning a system for the administration of student courses to be used in an office in a college.

   (a) Other than data modelling, describe **three** tasks that may be carried out by the analyst to establish the requirements of the system.   [6]

   (b) A database will be used in the implementation of the system. Describe the steps involved in creating a data model.   [3]

11-66

Section 12

OOP and functional programming

In this section:

12

Chapter 67 – Basic concepts of object-oriented programming

Objectives

- Be familiar with the basic concepts of object-oriented programming, such as class, object, instantiation and encapsulation

Procedural programming

Programming languages have been evolving ever since the development of assembly languages. High level languages such as Basic and Pascal are known as **procedural languages**, and a program written in one of these languages is written using a series of step-by-step instructions on how to solve the problem. This is usually broken down into a number of smaller modules, and the program then consists of a series of calls to procedures or functions, each of which may in turn call other procedures or functions.

In this method of programming, the data is held in separate primitive variables such as integer or char, or in data structures such as array or list. The data may be accessible by all procedures in the program (**global** variables) or **local** to a particular subroutine. Changes made to global data may affect other parts of the program, either intentionally or unintentionally, and may mean other subroutines have to be modified.

Object-oriented programming

In object-oriented programming, the world is viewed as a collection of **objects**. An object might be a person, animal, place, concept or event, for example. It could be something more abstract like a bank account or a data structure such as a stack or queue that the programmer wishes to implement.

An object-oriented program is composed of a number of interacting objects, each of which is responsible for its own data and the operations on that data. Program code in an object-oriented program creates the objects and allows the objects to communicate with each other by sending messages and receiving answers. All the processing that is carried out in the program is done by objects.

12-67

Object attributes and behaviours

Each object will have its own **attributes**. The attributes of a car might include its make, engine size, colour, etc. The attributes of a person could include first name, last name, date of birth.

An object has a **state**. A radio, for example, may be on or off, tuned to a particular station, set to a certain volume. A bank account may have a particular balance, say £54.20 and a credit limit of £300.

Q1: What attributes might be assigned to the following objects?

    (a)   Cat

    (b)   Rectangle

    (c)   Hotel booking

An object has **behaviours**. These are the actions that can be performed by an object; for example, a cat can walk, pounce, catch mice, purr, miaow and so on.

Classes

A **class** is a blueprint or template for an object, and it defines the **attributes** and **behaviours** (known as **methods**) of objects in that class. An attribute is data that is associated with the class, and a method is a functionality of the class – something that it can do, or that can be done with it.

For example, a stock control system might be used by a bookshop for recording the items that it receives into stock from suppliers and sells to customers. The only information that the stock class will hold in this simplified system is the stock ID number, stock category (books, stationery, etc.), description, and quantity in stock.

Part of a sample definition of a class named `StockItem` is defined below. Program coding will vary according to the language used.

```
* Stock class used to model a simple stock control system,
* allowing stock to be added and sold.

StockItem = Class
* A function may take one or more parameters. It returns a value
* A procedure may take one or more parameters. It does not return a value
        Public
            Function GetQtyInStock
            Procedure StockItem(String aStockID,
                String aCategory, String aDescription, Integer aQty)
            Procedure ReceiveStock (Integer aQty)
            Procedure SellStock (Integer aQty)
* instance variables (properties/attributes)
        Private
            StockID:String
            Category: String
            Description: String
            QtyInStock: Integer
    End
```

In this part of the class definition, each of the attributes is given a variable type – here the first three attributes are of type `String` and `QtyInStock` is `Integer`.

As a general rule, instance variables or attributes are declared **private** and most methods **public**, so that other classes may use methods belonging to another class but may not see or change their attributes. This principle of **information hiding**, where other classes cannot directly access the attributes of another class when they are declared private, is an important feature of object-oriented programming.

A **constructor** is used to create objects in a class. In the above example the constructor is called `StockItem`; in many programming languages the constructor must have the same name as the class. In the pseudocode used here, methods are defined as either procedures, which are "setter" methods, or functions, which are "getter" methods. (See below "Sending messages")

Instantiation (creating an object)

Once the class and its constructor have been defined, and each of the methods coded, we can start creating and naming actual objects. The creation of a new object (an instance of a class) is known as **instantiation**. Multiple instances of a class can be created which each share identical methods and attributes, but the values of those attributes will be unique to each instance.

This means that multiple enemy objects (zombies, for example) can be created in a computer game by programming just one zombie class, with health, position and speed attributes; but each individual zombie could operate independently with different attribute values.

Suppose we want to create a new stock item called `book1`. The type of variable to assign to `book1` has to be stated. This will be the class name, `StockItem`. The word `new` is typically used (e.g. in Java) to **instantiate** (create) a new object in the class.

```
book1 = new StockItem("PT123", "Book", "Computer Science", 35)
```

`book1` is called **a reference type variable**, or simply a **reference variable**. Note that this is a different type of variable from `stockID` or `qtyInStock`, which are `String` or `Integer` variables.

Like primitive variables of type `integer`, `double`, `char` (and the special case `String`), reference variables are named memory locations in which you can store information. However, a reference variable does not hold the object – it holds a pointer or reference to where the object itself is stored.

A **variable reference diagram** shows in graphical form the new `StockItem` object referenced by the variable `book1`. In the diagram, reference variables are shown as circles and primitive data types (and `string` variables) are shown as rectangles.

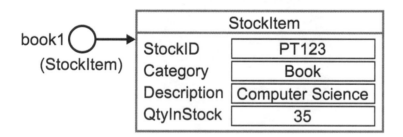

12-67

Sending messages

Messages can be categorised as either "getter" or "setter" messages. In some languages, "getter" messages are written as **functions** which return an answer, and "setter" messages as **procedures** which change the state of an object. This is reflected in the pseudocode used in this book.

The state of an object can be examined or changed by sending it a message, for example to get or increase the quantity in stock. To get the quantity in stock of `book1`, for example, you could write:

```
quantity ← book1.GetQtyInStock
```

To record the sale of 3 `book1` objects, you could write

```
book1.SellStock(3)
```

Q2: Complete the class definition for `Radio` shown in the figure below. Include the instance variables and appropriate method headers written as functions or procedures.

```
Radio = Class
    Public
        Procedure SetVolume(Integer aVolume)
        Function GetVolume
        * insert more methods here
    * instance variables
    Private
        Volume: Integer
        * insert more instance variables here
```

Write pseudocode to instantiate two new radio objects named `robertsRadio` and `philipsRadio`.

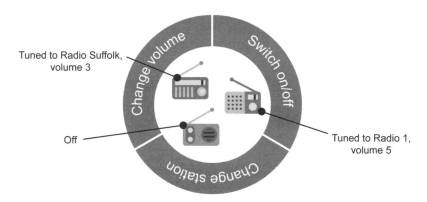

Tuned to Radio Suffolk, volume 3

Change volume

Switch on/off

Off

Change station

Tuned to Radio 1, volume 5

A radio modelled as a software object

Each object belongs to a class, and all the objects in the same class have the same structure and methods but they each have their own data. Objects created from a class are called **instances** of the class.

Q3: Draw a variable reference diagram to show the two new radio objects.

Encapsulation

An object **encapsulates** both its state (the values of its instance variables) and its behaviours or methods. All the data and methods of each object are wrapped up into a single entity so that the attributes and behaviours of one object cannot affect the way in which another object functions. For example, setting the volume of the `philipsRadio` object to 5 has no effect on any other `radio` object.

Encapsulation is a fundamental principle of object-oriented programming and is very powerful. It means, for example, that in a large project different programmers can work on different classes and not have to worry about how other parts of the system may affect any code they write. They can also use methods from other classes without having to know how they work.

Related to encapsulation is the concept of **information hiding**, whereby details of an object's instance variables are hidden so that other objects must use messages to interact with that object's state.

To invoke the method `ReceiveStock`, for example, we might write:

```
book1.ReceiveStock(50);
```

This would have the effect of updating the quantity in stock of `book1` by 50. A programmer using the method does not need to know how this is achieved. The documentation of each method will specify the number and variable type of any arguments that need to be passed to the method, and what value, if any, is returned by the method.

> **Q4:** Write statements to invoke the procedures to switch on the `philipsRadio`, and tune the `robertsRadio` to BBC2.

Inheritance

Classes can **inherit** data and behaviour from a parent class in much the same way that children can inherit characteristics from their parents. A "child" class in object-oriented program is referred to as a **subclass**, and a "parent" class as a **superclass**.

For example, we could draw an inheritance hierarchy for animals that feature in a computer game. Note that the inheritance relationship in the corresponding **inheritance diagram** is shown by an unfilled arrow at the "parent" end of the relationship.

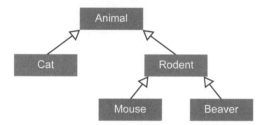

Class diagram involving inheritance

All the animals in the superclass `Animal` share common attributes such as `colour` and `position`. Animals may also have common procedures (methods), such as `moveLeft`, `moveRight`. A `Cat` may have an extra attribute `hungry`, and an extra method `pounce`. A `Rodent` may have an extra method `gnaw`. A `Beaver` has an extra method, `makeDam`.

> **Q5:** What extra methods might `Mouse` have?

When to use inheritance

There is a simple rule to determine whether inheritance is appropriate in a program, called the "**is a**" rule, which requires an object to have a relationship to another object before it can inherit from the object. This rule asks, in effect, "Is object A an object B"? For example, "Is a `Cat` an `Animal`?" "Is a `Mouse` a `Rodent`?" Technically, there is nothing to stop you coding a program in which a man inherits the attributes and methods of a mouse, but this is going to cause confusion for users!

Coding inherited classes

Common behaviour can be defined in a **superclass** and inherited into a **subclass**.

To code the class header for `Cat`, which is a subclass of `Animal`, in pseudocode we could write something like

```
Cat = Subclass(Animal) or
Class Cat(Animal)
```

or in Java, for example,

```
public class Cat extends Animal
```

12-67

Q6: Complete the following pseudocode class definitions for `Animal`, `Rodent` and `Beaver`.

An `Animal` has methods `MoveLeft`, `MoveRight` and attributes `Colour` and `Position`

A `Rodent` has an additional method `Gnaw`

A `Beaver` has additional methods `CutTree`, `MakeDam` and additional attributes `TreesCut`, `DamComplete`

```
Animal = Class
    Public
        Procedure MoveLeft(Integer Steps)
        insert code  for procedures
        Function GetPosition
        insert functions
    Private
        Position: Integer
        insert attributes


Rodent = Subclass(Animal)
    Public
```

Exercises

1. A sports club keeps details of its members. Each member has a unique membership number, first name, surname and telephone number recorded. Three classes have been identified:

   ```
   Member
   JuniorMember
   SeniorMember
   ```

   The classes `JuniorMember` and `SeniorMember` are related, by single inheritance, to the class `Member`.

   (a) Draw an inheritance diagram for the given classes. [2]

   (b) Programs that use objects of the class `Member` need to add a new member's details, delete a member's details, and show a member's details. No other form of access is to be allowed.

   Complete the class definition for this class.

   ```
   Member = Class



                    End
   ```
   [4]

   (c) In object-oriented programming, what is meant by **encapsulation**? [1]

2. (a) In an object-oriented computer game there is a class called `Crawlers`. Two sub-classes of `Crawlers` are `Spiders` and `Bugs`. Draw an inheritance diagram for this. [2]

   (b) For the sub-class `Spiders` suggest:

   (i) **one** property;

   (ii) **one** method. [2]

Chapter 68 – Object-oriented design principles

Objectives

- Understand concepts of association, composition and aggregation

- Understand the use of polymorphism and overriding

- Be aware of object-oriented design principles:
    - encapsulate what varies
    - favour composition over inheritance
    - program to interfaces, not implementation

- Be able to draw and interpret class diagrams

Association, aggregation and composition

Recall that inheritance is based on an "is a" relationship between two classes. For example, a cat "is a(n)" animal, a car "is a" vehicle. In a similar fashion, **association** may be loosely described as a "**has a**" relationship between classes. Thus a railway company may be associated with the engines and carriages it owns, or the track that it maintains. A teacher may be associated with a form bi-directionally – a teacher "has a" student, and a student "has a" teacher. However, there is no **ownership** between objects and each has their own lifecycle, and can be created and deleted independently.

Aggregation is a special type of more specific association. It can occur when a class is a collection or container of other classes, but the contained classes do not have a strong lifecycle dependency on the container. For example, a player who is part of a team does not cease to exist if the team is disbanded.

Aggregation may be shown in class diagrams using a hollow diamond shape between the two classes.

Class diagram showing aggregation

Composition is a stronger form of association. If the container is destroyed, every instance of the contained class is also destroyed. For example if a hotel is destroyed, every room in the hotel is destroyed.

Composition may be shown in class diagrams using a filled diamond shape. The diamond is at the end of the class that owns the creational responsibility.

Class diagram showing composition

Q1: Specify whether each of the following describe aggregation or composition.

    (a)   Zoo and ZooAnimal

    (b)   RaceTrack and TrackSection

    (c)   Department and Teacher

12-68

Polymorphism

Polymorphism refers to a programming language's ability to process objects differently depending on their class. For example, in the last chapter we looked at an application that had a superclass Animal, and subclasses Cat and Rodent. All objects in subclasses of Animal can execute the methods moveLeft, moveRight, which will cause the animal to move one space left or right.

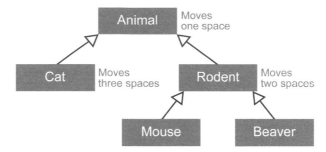

We might decide that a cat should move three spaces when a moveLeft or moveRight message is received, and a Rodent should move two spaces. We can define different methods within each of the classes to implement these moves, but keep the same method name for each class.

Defining a method with the same name and formal argument types as a method inherited from a superclass is called **overriding**. In the example above, the moveLeft method in each of the Cat and Rodent classes overrides the method in the superclass Animal.

12-68

Q2: Suppose that tom is an instance of the Cat class, and jerry is an instance of the Mouse class. What will happen when each of these statements is executed?

tom.moveRight()

jerry.moveRight()

Q3: Looking at the diagram above, what changes do you need to make so that bertie, an instance of the Beaver class, moves only one space when given a moveRight() message?

Class definition including override

Class definitions for the classes Animal and Cat will be something like this:

```
Animal = Class
        Public
            Procedure moveLeft
            Procedure moveRight
        Protected
            Position: Integer
        End
Cat = Subclass (Animal)
        Public
            Procedure moveLeft (Override)
            Procedure moveRight (Override)
            Procedure pounce
        Private
            Name: String
        End
```

Note: The 'Protected' access modifier is described on page 356.

"Favour composition over inheritance"

Composition is generally considered preferable to inheritance for implementing the desired functionality of a system. The main reason for this is that it allows greater flexibility, because composition is a less rigid relationship between two objects than that between two objects with an inheritance relationship. Also, in some cases, an object may be composed of several other objects but cannot be said in a real-world sense to "inherit" their characteristics.

For example, suppose a class house has walls, windows and a door.

We can define classes for House, Wall, Door, Window and Roof. Each of these classes will need attributes of height, width and colour. The House class will need attributes Wall, Door, Window, Roof and a method to draw and position the house.

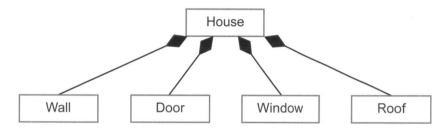

Class diagram showing composition aggregation

The class definition for the House and Wall classes will be written in pseudocode something like this, with similar definitions for Door, Window and Roof.

```
House = Class
    Public
        Procedure drawHouse
        Procedure setHousePosition
        Procedure getHousePosition
    Private
        TheWall: Wall
        TheDoor: Door
        WindowLeft: Window
        WindowRight: Window
        TheRoof: Roof
  End
Wall = Class
    Public
        Procedure drawWall
    Private
        WallHeight: Real
        WallWidth: Real
        WallColour: Integer
  End
```

12-68

Public, private and protected access modifiers (specifiers)

Related to encapsulation is the concept of **information hiding**, meaning that an object's instance variables (e.g. wall, door, etc. in the above example) are hidden so that other objects must use messages (i.e. invoke a procedure or function) to interact with that object's state. (Compare this with the use of local variables in subroutines in a procedural language.) The access modifiers **public**, **private** and **protected** are included in a class definition to implement data hiding.

- If a method or instance variable is declared **private**, only code within the class itself can access it.

- If a method or instance variable is declared **public**, code within any class can access it.

Most commonly, instance variables are declared private and methods public, so that other classes cannot change the values of variables in another class but they can use their methods.

There is a third specifier, **protected**, the definition of which varies between languages. In some languages this restricts access to members of a subclass, in others to members in the same package or library of classes. For example, the classes `Rectangle`, `Triangle`, `Circle` etc. may all be part of a `Shapes` package.

The table below summarises the three types of access modifier.

Member is accessible...	Public	Protected	Private
Within the defining class	Yes	Yes	Yes
Via inheritance	Yes	Yes	No
Via a reference to an object of the class	Yes	Only if it is in a subclass/in the same package (definition varies between languages)	No

Class diagram with access specifiers

Example 1

Animal is an abstract class, with methods that are overridden in the Bird and Mammal classes. It is not possible to create an Animal object.

The class diagram below shows inheritance, with private (-) and public (+) specifiers. (A protected specifier would be shown with #.)

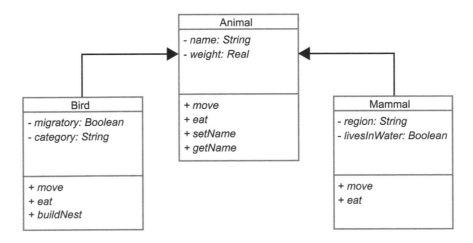

12-68

Programming to an interface

In many situations, a number of different classes of object all need to understand a particular set of messages even though there is no relationship between them. A simple set of messages `switchOn` and `setTimer` could be sent to a wide variety of objects such as `microwave`, `lamp`, `oven`, `watch` etc. How each object responds to the message will vary depending on their class.

In this context, an **interface** is a collection of abstract methods that a group of unrelated classes may implement. Although the methods are specified in the interface, they will only be implemented by a class that implements the interface, and not in the interface itself. The programmer constructing the list of messages or methods does not need to know how the instances of objects in each class will respond to each message.

The programming will be something like this:

```
Public interface Switches
    Procedure SwitchOn
    Procedure SwitchOff
    Procedure SetTimer(aTime)
    Function GetTimer
    etc
End
```

A programmer who wants class `Microwave` to implement the `Switches` interface then includes the name of the interface in the class header:

```
Class Microwave implements Switches
```

The objects in class microwave must be able to receive messages `SwitchOn`, `SetTimer`, etc.

Objects in a class implementing an interface must be able to receive all the messages corresponding to the methods listed in the interface. One advantage of using such an interface is that new classes can be added which use the interface without in any way affecting existing classes.

Encapsulate what varies

The strategy of **encapsulating what varies** is used in order to reduce maintenance and testing effort. It means that when something changes in a program, (such as different specifications for reserving library books or calculating customer discounts in an online store) if the concept in question is encapsulated in a single module, only that module will need to change. At the design stage, consideration should be given to requirements that are most likely to change in the future. It is these aspects of the system that are most important to encapsulate so that if they are changed in the future, the overall amount of code that needs to be modified is minimised.

Furthermore, if a module for calculating customer discounts, for example, contains code for checking a customer's credit status, all that code could itself be encapsulated in a separate module.

Using an interface class encapsulating the varying concept is one way of implementing this concept, since the interface is implemented differently by different classes and code that relies on the interface can handle any class implementing the interface. Thus for example if a different type of electronic gadget is introduced which uses a different procedure to switch on and off, a new module can be introduced and no other module needs to change.

Advantages of the object-oriented paradigm

Building code into objects has a number of advantages, including:

- The object-oriented methodology forces designers to go through an extensive planning phase, which makes for better designs with fewer weaknesses.

- Encapsulation: the source code for an object can be written, tested and maintained independently of the code for other objects

- Once an object is created, knowledge of how its methods are implemented is not necessary in order for a programmer to use it.

- New objects can easily be created with small differences to existing ones

- Re-usability: objects that are already defined, coded and tested may be used in many different programs. OOP provides a good framework for code libraries with a range of software components that can easily be adapted by a programmer.

- Software maintenance: an object oriented program is much easier to maintain than one written in a procedural language because of its rigidly enforced modular structure.

Exercises

12-68

1. An object-oriented program is being written to store details of and play digital media files that are stored on a computer. A class **MediaFile** has been created and two subclasses, **VideoFile** and **MusicFile** are to be developed.

   The classes **VideoFile** and MusicFile are related to **MediaFile** by single inheritance.

   (a) Explain what is meant by *inheritance*.   [1]

   (b) Draw an inheritance diagram for the three classes.   [2]

   (c) One important feature of an object-oriented programming language is the facility to override methods (functions and procedures).

   Explain what is meant by *overriding* when writing programs that involve inheritance.   [2]

   (d) The **MediaFile** class has data fields **Title** and **Duration**.

   The class definition for **MediaFile** is:

   ```
   MediaFile = Class
       Public
           Procedure PlayFile
           Function GetTitle
           Function GetDuration
       Private
           Title: String
           Duration: Real
   End
   ```

   Note that the class does not have procedures to set the values of the variables as these are read automatically from data stored within the actual media file.

   The **MusicFile** class has the following additional data fields:

   - **Artist**: Stores the name of the band or singer that recorded the music.

   - **SampleRate**: Stores the rate at which the music has been sampled

   - **BitDepth**: Stores the number of bits in which each sampled value is represented.

   Write the class definition for **MusicFile**.   [4]

AQA Unit 3 Qu 11 June 2010

2. (a) In object-oriented programming, what is meant by **polymorphism**? [2]

(b) An object-oriented program stores details of a class `Bird` and a subclass `Seagull`, defined as follows:

```
Class Bird
   Public
      Procedure move
         system.print("Birds can fly")
      End
   End

   Class Seabird extends Bird
      Public
         Procedure move (override)
            system.print("Seabirds can fly and swim")
         End
      End
```

Two new objects are instantiated with the lines:

```
Bird bird1 = new Bird()
Bird bird2 = new Seabird()
```

(i)   What will be printed when the following lines are executed?

```
bird1.move
bird2.move
```
[2]

(ii) Explain your answer. [2]

3. (a) In object-oriented programming, what is meant by **aggregation**? [1]

(b) An object-oriented program has been written for a company selling garden furniture. The furniture includes tables, chairs and sets of furniture which include a table and several chairs.

Draw a class diagram for the classes `Table`, `Chair`, `GardenSet`. [2]

(c) Some instance variables (fields) required for the `GardenSet` class are

```
TableType, ChairType, NumberOfChairs
```

A method required for the `GardenSet` class is

```
DisplayDetails
```

The instance variables are declared as `Private`, and the method `Public`.

Explain the effect of the access modifiers `Private` and `Public`. Why is it common to make instance variables `Private` and methods `Public`? [3]

Chapter 69 – Functional programming

Objectives

- Understand what is meant by a programming paradigm
- Define function type, domain and co-domain
- Understand what is meant by a first-class object and how such an object may be used
- Be able to evaluate simple functions
- Use functional composition to combine two functions

Programming paradigms

A **programming paradigm** is a style of computer programming. Different programming languages support tackling problems in different ways, and there are four major programming paradigms each supported by a number of diffferent languages:

- **Procedural** programming is supported by languages such as Python or Pascal, which have a series of instructions that tell the computer what to do with the input in order to solve the problem. They are widely used in educational environments, being relatively easy to learn and applicable to a wide variety of problems. **Structured programming** is a type of procedural programming which uses the programming constructs of sequence, selection, iteration and recursion. It uses modular techniques to split large programs into manageable chunks.

- **Object-oriented** programming is supported by languages such as Java, Python and Delphi. OOP was developed to make it possible to abstract details of implementation away from the user, make code reusable and programs easy to maintain. It is to a great extent taking over from procedural programming.

- **Declarative** programming is supported by languages such as SQL, where you write statements that describe the problem to be solved, and the language implementation decides the best way of solving it. SQL (covered in more detail in Chapter 18) is used to query databases.

- **Functional** programming is supported by languages such as Haskell, as well as languages such as Python, C# and Java. Functions, not objects or procedures, are used as the fundamental building blocks of a program. Statements are written as a series of functions which accept input data as arguments and return an output. Functional programming is not covered in this course.

What is a function?

A function is a mapping from a set of inputs, called the **domain**, to a set of possible outputs, known as the **co-domain**.

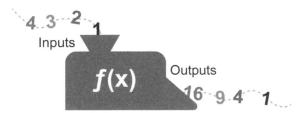

The function machine illustrated above could be defined in more mathematical terms as:

$$f: A \rightarrow B \text{ where } f(x) = x^2$$

That is to say that the *input in domain A produces output in co-domain B*.

The domain and co-domain are always subsets of objects in some data type. In the above function, we could define the domain A as the set of integers, for example. The co-domain B is then the set of all positive integers that are greater than or equal to zero.

> **Q1:** A function f is defined as f: A → B where $f(x) = x^2 + 5$. The domain A is the set of all real numbers. What is the co-domain B?

A function does not have to be an algebraic formula. For example, we could map names to ID numbers using a function:

$$f: \{Ben, Anna, Michael, Gerri\} \rightarrow \{34, 26, 74, 12\}$$

Ben maps to 34, Anna to 26 and so on. Notice that the domain and co-domain are of different data types.

Functional programming in Haskell

Haskell is a functional programming language which will be useful for gaining some practical experience in functional programming. If you want to do some practical work in Haskell to accompany the theory in the next three chapters, you will need access to a text editor such as Notepad for writing programs, and the Haskell platform which uses GHC (**G**lasgow **H**askell **C**ompiler) for compiling your programs. This is available free from https://www.haskell.org/platform.

Once Haskell is installed, you can compile and run a program which you have saved, or use the interactive mode which allows you to type in a function and apply it directly by passing it appropriate **parameters** or **arguments**.

Note that the terms *parameter* and *argument* are often used interchangeably, though the distinction can be made that an *argument* is a value or expression passed to a function, and a *parameter* is a reference declared in a function declaration.

Haskell notation is used in these chapters, and instructions for running each program from a script or in interactive mode are given as each new statement is introduced. If you are not using Haskell, you will still be able to grasp the general principles of functional programming.

Starting Haskell

We will use a text editor to write a simple program consisting of one function.

- Open Notepad or any other text editor and type the following lines:

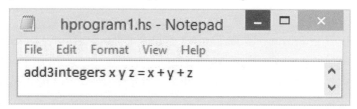

Notice that the function name, `add3integers`, is followed by its three parameters `x y z` separated by spaces. No parentheses or commas are used in Haskell, unlike in, for example, Python or Visual Basic.

- Save this program as `hprogram1.hs` in a convenient folder.
- Now load Haskell (the program name is WinGCHi.exe)
- In the Haskell window, use the file menu to navigate to your folder and load the file `hprogram1.hs`
- The prompt changes from `Prelude>` to `*Main>`

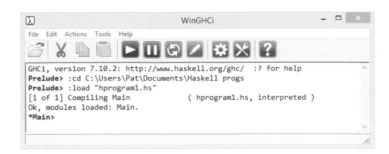

Function application

The process of giving particular inputs to a function is known as **function application**.

We can **apply** or **call** the function `add3integers` to find the sum of three integers 5, 6 and 7 by writing

```
add3integers 5 6 7
```

The function name is followed by the parameters, separated by spaces.

The result, 18, will be displayed.

The type of the function is *f: integer x integer → integer* where *integer x integer* is the Cartesian product of the set integer with itself. (Spoken *integer cross integer maps to integer* – See Chapter 51.)

Instead of typing function definitions into a text document, saving and loading the program, we can type function definitions directly in the Haskell window in interactive mode. The function definition must be preceded by the word `let` in interactive mode or Haskell will give an error message.

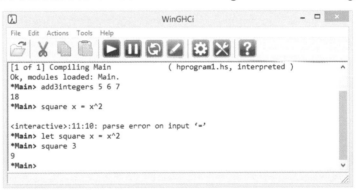

> **Q2:** What do you think the following function does?
>
> ```
> product x y z = x * y * z
> ```
>
> Apply the function to find the product of 2, 3 and 4. What are the parameters of the function?
>
> **Q3:** Write a function called sumOfSquares which calculates the sum of the squares of two numbers. Apply the function to calculate the sum of the squares of 3 and 4. (Use the notation x^2 for x^2.)

First-class objects

In a functional programming language, a **first-class object** is an object which may:

- appear in expressions

- be assigned to a variable

- be assigned as an argument

- bo returned in a function call

For example, integers, floating point values, characters and strings are first-class objects. **Functions** are also first-class objects so may themselves be passed as arguments.

What's special about functional programming languages?

There are some major differences between procedural and functional programming languages. The importance and significance of these features will become apparent when you reach the chapter on Big Data. Here are some of these features listed and explained.

Statelessness

When you execute a procedural program such as Python or Pascal, the computer's memory changes state as it goes along. You could execute the following statements, for example:

```
x = 5
x = x + 1
```

In a functional programming language, the value of a variable cannot change. Variables are said to be **immutable**, and the program is said to be **stateless**.

Try this out now. In Notepad or any text editor, type the following lines:

```
a = 4
a = 5
b = 10
addTwoNumbers x y = x + y
```

Save this program as `variables.hs`, and try to load it. You will get an error message:

```
Prelude> :load "variables.hs"
[1 of 1] Compiling Main            ( variables.hs, interpreted )

variables.hs:2:1:
    Multiple declarations of 'a'
    Declared at: variables.hs:1:1
                 variables.hs:2:1
Failed, modules loaded: none.
Prelude>
```

Remove the second assignment statement a = 5 from the program, save and reload. This time it should load with no problem. Now try typing `addTwoNumbers a b`.

No side effects

The only thing a function can do is calculate something and return a result, and it is said to have no **side effects**.

A consequence of not being able to change the value of an object is that a function that is called twice with the same parameters will always return the same result. This is called **referential transparency** and makes it relatively easy for programmers to write correct, bug-free programs. A simple function can be proved to be correct, and then more complex functions can be built using these functions.

Try this out by adding some more lines to your program `variables.hs` as shown:

```
a = 4
b = 10
addTwoNumbers x y = x + y
doubleSmallNumber x = if x < 10
                      then x * 2
                      else x
```

12-69

Save and load the program.

Notice that we have used an IF statement in the function `doubleSmallNumber`. An IF statement in Haskell must include an ELSE clause. Try out the functions in Haskell:

```
Prelude> :load "variables.hs"
[1 of 1] Compiling Main              ( variables.hs, interpreted )
Ok, modules loaded: Main.
*Main> addTwoNumbers a b
14
*Main> doubleSmallNumber a
8
*Main> doubleSmallNumber b
10
```

Now try using a function as an argument:

```
*Main> addTwoNumbers (doubleSmallNumber a) b
18
```

You can even use a function in the definition of a new function. Add the following function to your program `variables.hs` in the text editor, save and load.

addAndDouble x y = addTwoNumbers (doubleSmallNumber x) y

Q4: What will be the result returned by applying the function with the following parameters:

(a)   a, b

(b)   5, 20

(c)   20, 5

Composition of functions

Since a function may be used as an argument, we can combine two functions to get a new function. This is called **functional composition**.

Given two functions

f: A → B and g: B → C

the function **g o f** (called *the composition of f and g*) is a function whose domain is A and co-domain is C.

Example 1

Consider the two functions f(x) = x + 3 and g(x) = $2x^2$

g o f could be written as g(f(x)) = g(x+3) = 2 (x+3) ^{2}

f is applied first and then g is applied to the result returned by f.

In Haskell notation, we would write

f x = x + 3   (f)

g x = 2 * x^2   (g)

Applying the function g(f(x)) or **g o f** with argument 4, in Haskell we write

(g.f) 4

which will return the value 98, since f(4) = 7, g(7) = 2*49 = 98

(f.g) 4 will return the value 35, since g(4) = 32, f(32) = 32 + 3 = 35)

Q5: What value will be returned if we apply the function with the following statement?

(g.f) 5

Q6: Using Haskell notation write two functions f(a) = a + 1 and g(a) = a³. What will be the value of each of these functions if a = 4? Write a statement to evaluate the composition of g and f, i.e. **g o f** when passed the argument 4.

Q7: The function **doubleNum** is defined as `doubleNum x = 2 * x`. Write a function **quadruple** which uses the function **doubleNum** in its definition.

Types and typeclasses

In Haskell, **types** are sets of values, and **typeclasses** are sets of types. So for example:

Type `Integer` includes values 1, 2, 3 ...

Type `Float` includes 3.142, 2.5

Type `Bool` includes True and False

Type `Char` includes a, b, c ...

`Integer`, `Int`, `Double` and `Float` are all in Typeclass Num. `Integer` is unbounded to represent really big numbers. `Int` is restricted to minimum and maximum value.

Note that Type and Typeclass names always start with uppercase letters.

Functions also have types. It is considered good practice to always give functions explicit type declarations. These take the form shown in the example below (colour coded to show the relationship between the declaration and the function arguments):

    sumOfSquares :: Integer -> Integer -> Integer

    sumOfSquares x y = x^2 + y^2

The types of the two arguments x and y are both declared as integer, and the result is also an integer. The three types are written one after the other separated by ->.

The value returned by a function does not necessarily have the same type as the arguments. For example, the function `isEqual x y = x == y` will return `True` if x and y are equal, `false` otherwise. Note the **equality operator** == used here.

    isEqual :: Int -> Int -> Bool
    isEqual x y = x == y

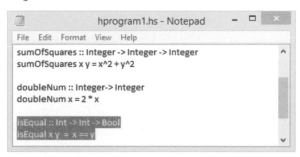

To try this out – type the statements as shown in the screenshot above into your text editor, save the file and load it again using **File, Load...** from the menu.

You can check the function type in Haskell by typing

:type isEqual *or*

:t isEqual

```
*Main> isEqual 4 5
False
*Main> :t isEqual
isEqual :: Int -> Int -> Bool
```

Q8: A function cuboidVol takes 3 arguments l, b, h representing the length, breadth and height of a cuboid as floating point numbers (real) numbers of type `Float`. Write a type statement followed by the function definition. What will be returned if the function is applied to parameters 4, 2, 0.5?

Type variables

Using interactive mode in Haskell, you may see something like the following:

```
*Main> let sumOfTwo x y = x + y
*Main> sumOfTwo 2 3
5
*Main> :t sumOfTwo
sumOfTwo :: Num a => a -> a -> a
```

12-69

Here, no type declaration has been written, and Haskell cannot tell what the variable types are – they could be Integer or Float, for example. As shown by the fact that it does not begin with an uppercase letter, a is neither a type nor a typeclass; it is in fact a **type variable**, which represents any type.

Exercises

1. (a)   Use functional programming notation to write a type declaration and define a function

$$f(x) = 2x + 1$$

Assume all values are integers, and name the function `doublePlusOne`.   [4]

(b)   Write a second function named `square` which returns the value of $g(x) = x^2$.   [2]

(c)   Combine the two functions in **(a)** and **(b)** to write a function h(x) which returns the value of

$$h(x) = g(x) + f(x)$$

Name the function `squarexPlusf`. What will be returned when this function is applied to the parameter 3?   [3]

2. (a)   Explain what is meant by the following statements:

(i)   "In a functional programming language, variables are **immutable**."   [1]

(ii)   "Functional programming is **stateless**, and has **no side effects**."   [2]

(b)   Explain why these features help programmers to create programs that do not contain hard-to-find bugs.   [3]

Chapter 70 – Function application

Objectives

- Understand what is meant by partial function application
- Know that a function takes only one argument which may itself be a function
- Define and use higher-order functions, including map, filter and fold

Higher-order functions

A **higher-order function** is one which either takes a function as an argument or returns a function as a result, or both. Later in this chapter we will be looking at the higher-order functions **map**, **filter** and **fold**, in which the first argument is a function and the second argument is a list on which the function operates, returning a list as a result.

Every function in Haskell takes only one argument. This may seem like a contradiction because we have seen many functions, such as the one below which adds three integers,

```
add3Integers x y z = x + y + z
```

which appear to take several arguments. So how can this be true?

Any function takes only one parameter at a time

Taken at face value and assuming the function takes three integer parameters and returns an integer result, the type declaration for this function would normally be written

```
add3Integers :: integer -> integer -> integer -> integer
```

It could also be written

```
add3Integers :: integer -> (integer -> (integer -> integer))
```

How the function is evaluated

What happens when you write `add3Integers 2 4 5`?

The function `add3Integers` is applied to the arguments. It takes the first argument 2 and produces a new function (shown in blue above) which will add 2 to its arguments, 4 and 5.

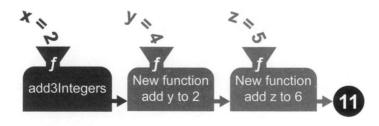

This function (shown in blue) produces a new function (shown in green) that takes the argument 5 and adds it to 6, returning the result, 11.

Our function `add3Integers` takes an integer argument (2) and returns a function of type

```
(integer -> (integer -> integer))
```

This function takes an integer argument (4) and returns a function of type `(integer -> integer)`

This function takes an integer argument (5) and returns an integer (11).

Partial function application

Partial function application takes advantage of this by decomposing multi-argument functions into smaller functions with fewer arguments. For example, suppose we have a function `add` that takes two integers and returns their sum:

```
add :: Integer -> Integer -> Integer
add x y = x + y
```

Remember that `add 3 4` actually means `(add 3) 4`. If we write

```
add 3
```

we will get an error message from Haskell saying it doesn't know how to print the resulting value, which is a function of type `Integer -> Integer`.

However, we can now use this partially applied function as an argument of a different function – `addSix`, for example, adds six to the result of the function.

```
addSix :: Integer -> Integer
addSix = add 6
```

We can now use this function, and it adds 6 to the n that replaces `add` in the calling statement.

```
*Main> addSix 10
16
```

12-70

We have a function `add` that takes more than one argument, and we pass it fewer arguments than it wants. It returns a new function that will take the remaining argument and return the result, as demonstrated with the `addSix` function.

Partial application means fixing/binding the values of some inputs to a function to produce another more specific function.

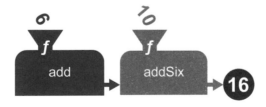

Q1: What will be returned by the following function call?
```
addSix 3
```

Now consider the following code snippet which uses the function add3Integers that we defined earlier. This function takes three arguments.

```
*Main> let addTen = add3Integers 10
*Main> addTen 1 2
13
*Main> addTen 7 8
25
```

Once again we have created a brand new function "on the fly" by using **partial function application**. We have passed two arguments instead of three to add3Integers and the third argument is supplied by `addTen`.

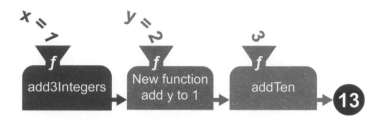

The function `add3Integers` is partially applied to the arguments 1 and 2, giving 3, and the resulting function is applied to 10.

Q2: What is returned as a result of executing the following statements?

```
add3Integers :: Integer -> Integer -> Integer -> Integer
add3Integers x y z = x + y + z
addTen :: Integer -> Integer -> Integer
addTen = add3Integers 10
addTen 40 50
```

Map

Map is a higher-order function that takes a list and the function to be applied to the elements in the list as inputs, and returns a list made by applying the function to each element of the old list.

Lists will be covered in detail in the next chapter, but for now it is enough to know that a list is a collection of elements which can be written in square brackets, e.g. [3, 7, 5, 9].
The empty list is written [].

The function `max x y` is a built-in library function which returns the maximum of two numbers:

e.g.   `max 8 3` will return 8.

We can partially apply `max` to get the maximum of 3 and its argument. We then map that function, which has no name, to a list:

```
map (max 3)[1,2,3,4,5]
```

getting the result

```
[3,3,3,4,5]
```

Here, `max` has been applied to each element of the list in turn. The maximum of 3 and 1 is 3, so the first element of the resulting list is 3. Likewise, the maximum of 2 and 3 is 3, so the second element of the resulting list is 3, and so on.

Here's another example:

```
map (+5) [2,8,4,10]
```

This returns

```
[7,13,9,15]
```

Filter

Filter is another higher-order function which takes a **predicate** (to define a Boolean condition) and a list. This returns the elements within the list that satisfy the Boolean condition.

e.g. `filter (>6)[2,5,6,8,9]`

will return

`[8,9]`

You can write your own predicate to be used in the filter:

e.g.   `isEven n = n `mod` 2 == 0`

(Use the backward quotes on the left of the 1 key on the keyboard to surround the mod operator.)

`filter (isEven)[1,2,3,4,5,6]`

will return `[2,4,6]`

Fold (reduce) function

A fold function reduces a list to a single value, using recursion. For example, to find the sum of all the elements of a list, we write:

`foldl (+) 0 [2, 3, 4, 5]`

this will return the value 14. The initial value 0 is combined with the first element of the list, which is then recursively combined with the first element of the remaining list, and so on. This could be parenthesised as

`(((0 + 2) + 3) + 4) + 5`

(`foldl` stands for fold left, i.e. the recursion starts with the leftmost value. `foldr` or fold right starts with the rightmost value. In this example it would not make any difference which we used.)

Exercises

1. The function `multiply3` is defined as follows:

```
multiply3 :: Integer -> Integer -> Integer -> Integer
multiply3 x y z = x * y * z
```

   (a)   What result is returned by the following statement?

      `multiply3 2 3 5`   [1]

   (b)   A further function `multByTen` is defined as follows:

      `multByTen = multiply3 10`

      (i)   What result is returned by the following statement?

         `multByTen 6 2`   [1]

      (ii)   What is partial function application? Explain, in terms of partial function application, how this result is arrived at.   [3]

2. (a) Explain what the `map` function does in a functional programming language such as Haskell.   [2]

     (b) Use `map` to write a function that trebles each element of the list `[1,2,3,4,5]`   [2]

3. Write statements that will return a list containing only the odd numbers from the list.   [3]

12-70

Chapter 71 – Lists in functional programming

Objectives

- Understand that a list is a concatenation of a head and a tail, where the head is an element of a list and the tail is a list

- Define an empty list

- Describe and apply the following operations:
    - return head of list
    - return tail of list
    - test for empty list
    - return length of list
    - construct an empty list
    - prepend an item to a list
    - append an item to a list

Head and tail of a list

A **list** is a collection of elements of a similar type, such as integers, characters or strings, enclosed in square brackets. For example, in Haskell a list may be created using the keyword **let**:

```
let names = ["Anna", "Bob", "Jo", "Keira", "Tom", "George"]
let numbers = [3, 7, 14, 83, 2, 77]
```

(Alternatively, you can create the list in Notepad, save and load the file.

A list is composed of a **head** and a **tail**. The head is the first element of the list, and the tail is the remainder of the list. In Haskell:

```
Prelude> :load "lists.hs"
[1 of 1] Compiling Main ( lists.hs, interpreted )
Ok, modules loaded: Main.
*Main> names
["Anna","Bob","Jo","Keira","Tom","George"]
*Main> numbers
[3,7,14,83,2,77]
*Main> head names
"Anna"
*Main> tail names
["Bob","Jo","Keira","Tom","George"]
```

Q1: What is the head of the list `numbers`? What is the tail of this list?

We can apply the list argument repeatedly to the function tail. For example:

```
*Main> tail (tail (tail numbers))
[83,2,77]
```

Working from the right, the tail of the list [3, 7, 14, 83, 2, 77] is [7,14,83,2,77]

The tail of this list is [14, 83, 2, 77]

Finally the tail of this list is [83, 2, 77]

Q2: Write a statement which applies the operation `tail` to the list `names` repeatedly until the list consists of a single element.

Note that applying a function such as `head` or `tail` does not change the original list. Lists are **immutable**, which means that they can never be changed.

Defining an empty list

An empty list has no elements and is written []. You can create an empty list directly in Haskell:

```
let newlist = []
```

The function **null** tests for an empty list.

```
*Main> null numbers
False
*Main> null newlist
True
*Main>
```

Prepending and appending to a list

Prepending means adding an element to the front of a list, and **appending** means adding an element to the end of a list.

To add an element to the front of the list, you can either add an element using the : (colon) operator, or add a list using the ++ operator.

```
*Main> 5:numbers
[5, 3, 7, 14, 83, 2, 77]
*Main> [6, 10] ++ numbers
[6, 10, 3, 7, 14, 83, 2, 77]
*Main> 8 : 9 : 10 : numbers
[8, 9, 10, 3, 7, 14, 83, 2, 77]
```

To append an element to the end of a list, one method in Haskell to use the ++ operator and append a list made from the element to be appended.

```
*Main> numbers ++ [100]
[3, 7, 14, 83, 2, 77, 100]
```

Remember this does not alter the original list. We can find the length of `numbers` using the `length` function.

```
*Main> length numbers
6
```

12-71

Q3: (a) Write code to create a new list [1,2,3,4] called newNumbers.

(b) Concatenate the two lists numbers and newNumbers; that is, create a new list called newList containing all the numbers from both lists.

(c) Use the filter function to obtain a list of all the numbers greater than 10 in the concatenated list.

(Tip: look back at the last chapter to remind yourself how the filter function works.)

Exercises

1. The list **animals** contains the following items:

    ["otter", "fox", "deer", "badger", "seal", "dolphin"]

What result is returned by each of the following function calls?

(a) tail animals [1]

(b) head (tail (tail animals)) [2]

(c) null (tail (tail (tail (tail (tail animals)))))) [2]

2. The list **results** contains the following items:

    [56, 78, 45, 62, 68]

What result is returned by applying each of the following functions?

(a) map (*2) results [1]

(b) filter (>50) results [1]

(c) map (*2) (filter (>60) results) [2]

12-71

3. Write code to

(a) add the numbers 2, 6, 8 to the start of a list xs [7,2,4,10] [1]

(b) add the numbers 12,13,14 to the end of xs. [1]

(c) remove the first number from xs [1]

(d) replace the first two numbers from the list xs with 12, 13 [3]

Chapter 72 – Big Data

Objectives

- Understand that Big Data is a term used to describe data whose volume is too large to fit on a single server and is generally unstructured
- Describe examples of Big Data
- Describe features of functional programming which make it suitable for analysing Big Data
- Be familiar with the fact-based model for representing data
- Be familiar with graph schema for capturing the structure of the dataset

What is Big Data?

Big Data analysis is quite probably going to be the most exciting, interesting and useful field of study in the computing world over the next decade or two. We are just at the beginning of exploring its massive benefits in healthcare and medicine, business, communication, speech recognition, banking, and many other fields. Here are some questions it can answer:

- Does cellphone use increase the likelihood of cancer? With six billion cellphones in the world, there is plenty of data to analyse. (The answer turned out to be "No"!)
- How can you improve voice-translation software? By scoring the probability that a given digitised snippet of voice corresponds to a specific word. Google has made use of this data in its speech recognition software.
- How does the Bank of England find out whether house prices are rising or falling? By analysing search queries related to property.
- How can online education programmers use data collection to improve the courses offered? By studying data on the percentage of thousands of students registered who rewatched a segment of the course, suggesting it was not clear, or collecting data on wrong answers to assignments.

The term "Big Data" was first coined in the early 2000s by scientists working in fields such as astronomy and human genome projects, where the amount of data they were collecting was so massive that traditional methods of organising and analysing data, such as relational databases, could no longer be used. Initially, "Big Data" meant that the volume of data was so large that it could not fit into the memory of the computers that were used for processing it, so new tools were needed for analysing it.

Computer scientists and mathematicians soon realised that the most difficult aspect of Big Data was its lack of structure. The data cannot be neatly organised into the rows and columns of a relational database, and it is impossible to use standard query tools such as SQL. Frequently, it is essential to be able to analyse the data in seconds or milliseconds to produce a response.

These three aspects of Big Data can be summarised in terms of:

- **volume** – too big to fit on a single server
- **velocity** – milliseconds or seconds to respond, particularly with streamed data
- **variety** – the data may be in many forms such as structured, unstructured, text or multimedia

Essentially, Big Data collection and processing enables us to detect and analyse relationships within and among individual pieces of information that previously we were unable to grasp.

Examples of Big Data

Healthcare

Doctors and other medical professionals generally use two sets of data when diagnosing ailments and recommending treatments: retrospective data collected from the medical records not only of the patient but from thousands or millions of other people, and real-time clinical data such as blood pressure, temperature, etc. If for example a diabetic patient complains of numbness in their toes, the doctor can measure their blood flow, oxygen levels and so on, and from data gathered on a multitude of other patients with a similar problem, determine if this is a potentially serious situation and what treatment should be offered.

Recently, however, medical science has gone further and in many circumstances can take gene sequencing into account. Gene sequencing is already used to determine the best course of treatment for cancer patients, and as costs fall, it may become a routine part of a patient's medical record. In the case of an infectious disease outbreak, hours and even minutes matter in determining the best course of treatment for an individual patient.

But how much data is involved in sequencing one human genome? It depends on exactly what data is being collected for analysis, but assuming around three billion base pairs for a human genome, one estimate is around 200GB. Another estimate is that the human body contains about 150 trillion gigabytes of information… so there are undoubtedly challenges in analysing this type of data for an entire population!

Google

Google processes more than 24 petabytes of data per day – that's 24×10^{15} bytes of data. They receive more than three billion search queries every day and save every single one. The company can use this data in thousands of different ways. For example, between 2003 and 2008, Google computer scientists identified areas in the US affected by seasonal flu by what people searched for on the Internet. They did this by taking the 50 million most common search terms that Americans type and comparing them with the spread of seasonal flu between 2003 and 2008 and they found 45 search terms that when used together in a mathematical model, produced a strong correlation between their prediction and the official figures nationwide.

When a new flu virus called H1N1 struck in 2009, Google was able to identify its spread far more quickly than government statistics could, and thus arm public health officials with valuable information to contain the outbreak.

Amazon

The online bookseller Amazon uses the huge amounts of customer data that it collects to recommend specific books to its customers. In the early days of the company, they processed their data in a conventional way, by looking at topics and authors that the reader had purchased and recommending more of the same. This was generally more annoying than helpful to customers – if you have bought one book on Python programming, you don't necessarily need a recommendation for five more books on Python every time you log on.

What they then did was to apply Big Data techniques, simply finding associations among the products themselves, regardless of what a particular customer had bought. If huge numbers of customers who bought a book by Dan Brown also purchased a book by Ian McEwan, a customer who bought a book by one of those authors would be recommended a book by the other, even if they had never bought one before.

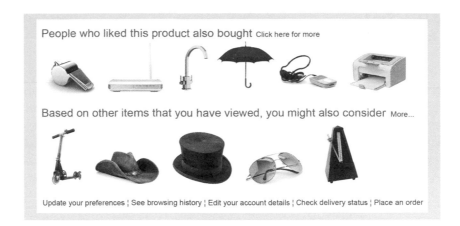

Personalised recommendations generated for users of online shopping websites

Functional programming and Big Data

Functional programming has features which make it useful for working with data distributed across several servers.

Writing correct code

- **Functional languages have no side effects**. A function is said to have a **side effect** if it modifies the state of the calling program in some way. For example, in a procedural language a particular function might modify a global variable, write to or delete data from a file. Functional languages support **statelessness**, meaning that the program's behaviour does not depend on how often a function is called or in what order different functions are called.

  This makes it easier to write correct code, and to understand and predict the behaviour of a program.

- **Functional programming languages support higher order functions**. A higher-order function is one which does at least one of the following:
  - takes one or more functions as input
  - outputs a function

  The **map** function is an example of a higher-order function. It takes as parameters a function f and a list of elements, and as the result, returns a new list with f applied to each element from the list. **Map** and **reduce** operations can be easily parallelised, meaning that many processors can work simultaneously on part of a dataset without changing or affecting other parts of the data. Higher order functions are therefore a very powerful way of solving problems involving massive amounts of data.

- **Functional programming languages forbid assignment**. In a functional programming language such as Haskell, you cannot write statements such as

  ```
  x = 1
  x = 2
  ```

  This property is known as immutability. An **immutable** object is one whose state cannot be modified after it is created.

  Why is this important for processing across many servers? The answer is that it makes parallel processing extremely easy, because the same function always returns the same result. Given two functions f(x), g(x) in sequence, they can be executed in any order without any possibility that g(x) changes the value of x in a way that changes the result of f(x).

Fact-based model

The fact-based model is an alternative to the relational data model in which immutable facts are recorded with timestamps. This means that data is never deleted and the data set just continues to grow. Because of the timestamps, it is always possible to determine what is current from what is past, i.e. if a fact such as a person's surname changes, the current name can be distinguished from previous names. The fact-based model is particularly suitable for big data because it is very simple and database updates are quick. A graph schema shows how data are represented in the fact-based model, but often (as is the case in this book) the time stamps are omitted for clarity, and only the most recent version of facts are shown, even through all historical versions of them are stored.

Graph schema

The enormous volume of data collected by companies such as Google and Facebook, business enterprises and healthcare organisations typically consist of highly connected entities which are not easily modelled using traditional relational database methods. Instead, graph data structures can be used to represent connected data and to perform analyses on very large datasets.

In a graph database, data is stored as **nodes** and **relationships**, and both nodes and relationships have **properties**. Instead of capturing relationships between entities in a join table as in a relational database, a graph database captures the relationships themselves and their properties directly within the stored data.

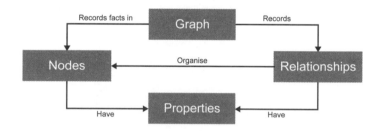

Example 1

A social network is a good example of a densely connected network. Facebook, which was founded in 2004, had 968 million daily active users in June 2015. Worldwide, they had 1.49 billion monthly active users, approximately 38% of the global population.

The flexibility of the graph model allows new nodes and new relationships to be added without compromising the existing data.

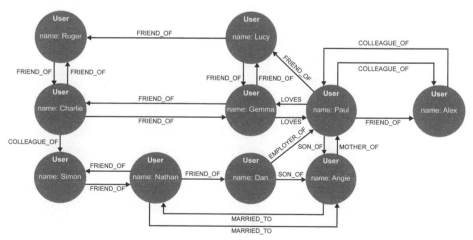

If the data on people and their friends was stored in a relational database, in order to find the answer to the question "Who is friends with Charlie?" we would have to scan the entire dataset looking for friend entries that contained Charlie. With a small dataset, that is straightforward. But now recall the Big O notation, a shorthand way of describing how the performance of the algorithm changes with the size of the dataset. When the dataset doubles, the number of searches doubles – so the algorithm is O(n).

In a graph database, the size of the dataset makes very little difference; we simply have to locate Charlie in the index and follow the links to his friends.

Finding friends-of-friends, or friends-of-friends-of-friends, would be impractical in a relational database, but traversing a graph by following paths makes this task relatively straightforward. Who would know if there is any truth behind the theory of six degrees of separation between any two individuals on earth? Microsoft proved this in 2008 by studying records of 30 billion electronic conversations in 2006, and calculating the chain lengths between 180 billion pairs of users. Any individual user was on average 6.6 hops from another.

Q1: How many degrees of separation are there between Roger and Angie?

Q2: Identify some of the nodes, edges and properties of the above graph. (Tip: See chapter 41.)

A graph database will be able to find in a fraction of a second, all friends-of-friends to a depth of say five, whereas a relational database reliant on looking up indexes will take an unacceptably long time.

Example 2

The purchase history of a user can be modelled using a connected graph. In the graph, the user is linked to her orders, and the orders are linked to provide a purchase history.

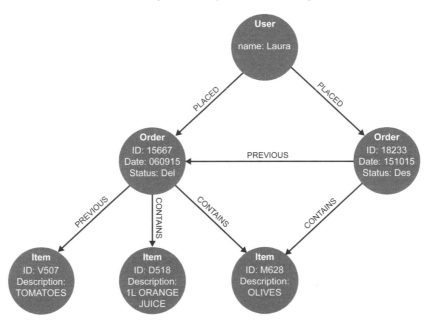

Using the graph, we can see all the orders that a customer has placed, and find what items each order contains. Orders are linked so that order history is easily viewable.

The graph opens up all sorts of useful possibilities. For example, if we find that many users who buy spaghetti also buy coffee beans, we can make a recommendation for coffee beans to purchasers of spaghetti and vice versa. We can add further dimensions to the graph, for example where a customer lives, so that we can find out whether people living in a certain area buy certain products, and then recommend these products to others living in the same area.

Note that there are different ways of drawing these graphs. An alternative way, with the properties written in separate boxes connected to the nodes by dashed lines, is shown in Exercise 4.

12-72

Exercises

1. Describe **two** features of functional programming languages which make it easy to write correct and efficient distributed code. [4]

2. List **three** features of a dataset that indicate that a graph schema would be preferable to a relational database for holding the data. In each case, give a reason why this would be the case. [6]

3. "At its core, big data is about predictions." Using two different examples, justify this statement. [6]

4. Big Data can be represented using a graph schema. Data has been collected on families and their occupations. Part of the graph schema is shown below. Complete the graph to show the following facts:

   (a) Bob is the father of Mark (ID 102) and Emma (ID 103). [2]

   (b) Mark is an actor, and Emma is a doctor. [2]

   (c) Gina has a brother Pete (ID 408) who is married to Emma. Pete is a singer. [3]

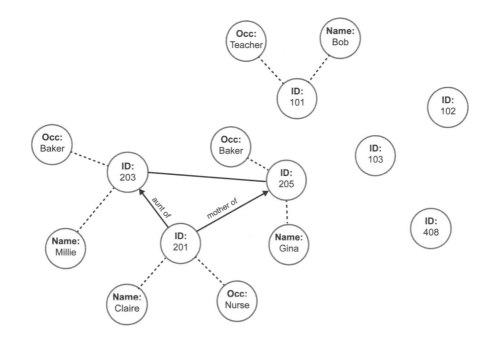

12-72

References

Mayer-Schonberger, Viktor and Cukier, Kenneth, "Big Data: A Revolution that will transform how we live, Work and Think", Houghton Mifflin Harcourt Publishing Company, New York, 2013

Miller, Bradley and Ranum, David "Problem solving with algorithms and data structures using Python", Franklin, Beedle and Associates Inc., USA 2011

Robinson, Ian, Webber, Jim and Eifrem, Emil, "Graph databases, 2nd edition" O'Reilly Media Inc., USA 2015

Big data:

http://blog.softwareabstractions.com/the_software_abstractions/2013/06/big-data-and-graph-databases.html

Appendix A – Floating point form

Objectives

- Know how numbers with a fractional part can be represented in floating point form
- Explain why fixed and floating point representation of decimal numbers may be inaccurate
- Be able to calculate the absolute and relative errors of numerical data stored and processed in computer systems
- Compare absolute and relative errors for large and small magnitude numbers, and numbers close to one
- Compare the advantages and disadvantages of fixed and floating point form in terms of range, precision and speed of calculation
- Be able to normalise un-normalised floating point numbers with positive or negative mantissas
- Explain underflow and overflow and describe the circumstances in which they occur

Revision of fixed point binary numbers

Fixed point binary assumes a pre-determined number of bits before and after the point. This makes fixed point numbers simpler to process but there is a compromise in the range and number of values that can be represented and therefore in the accuracy of representation. Moving the point to the right increases the range but reduces the accuracy of the fractional part and vice versa.

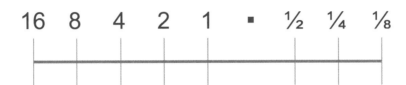

In the example above, only numbers which are multiples of ⅛ can be represented. The value 4.9, for example would be 'rounded' to 4.875 or 00100111 with three fractional bits to the right of the point.

Q1: Using 1 byte to hold each number with the three least significant bits to the right of the point, convert the following binary numbers to decimal:

    (a) 01010100   (b) 01011101   (c) 00111011   (d) 01010111

Q2: Convert the following numbers to 8-bit binary assuming four bits after the point:

    (a) 2.75   (b) 10.875   (c) 7.5625   (d) 3.4375

Q3: What are the largest and smallest unsigned numbers that can be held in two bytes with four bits after the point? See Figure 1.

Figure 1

Floating point binary numbers

Using 32 bits (4 bytes), the largest fixed point number that can be represented with just one bit after the point is only just over two billion. Floating point binary allows very large numbers to be represented.

When ordinary decimal numbers become very large, they are written in a more convenient scientific notation $m \times 10^n$ where m is known as the **mantissa** or **coefficient**, and n is the exponent or order of magnitude. 5000 can therefore written as 0.5×10^4, and 42,750.254 can be written as 0.42750254×10^5, moving the decimal point five places to the left.

This technique can easily be applied to binary numbers too, where the mantissa and exponent are represented for example using 12 bits, with 8 bits for the mantissa and 4 bits for the exponent. The leftmost bit of both the mantissa and the exponent are sign bits, with 0 indicating a positive number, and 1 a negative number. In a computer, of course, many more bits than this will be used to represent a floating point number, with 32-, 64- and 128-bit floating point numbers all being common.

In all the examples below, eight bits are used for the mantissa and four bits for the exponent. The implied binary point is to the right of the sign bit.

Sign bit		Mantissa								Exponent			
0	•	**1**	**0**	**1**	**1**	**0**	**1**	**0**		**0**	**0**	**1**	**1**

$$0 \bullet 1011010\ 0011 = 0.101101 \times 2^3 = 0101.101 = 4+1+0.5+0.125 = 5.625$$

To convert the floating point binary number above to decimal:

- Write down the mantissa, 0.1011010

- Translate the exponent from binary to decimal 0011 = 3. This means that you have to move the point 3 places to the right, as the mantissa has to be multiplied by 2^3.

- The binary number is therefore 101.1010

- Translate this to binary using the table in Figure 1. The number is 5.625.

> **Q4:** Convert the following floating point numbers to decimal: You can use Figure 1 to help you.
>
> (a) 0 • 1101010 0100   (b) 0 • 1001100 0011

Negative exponents

If the exponent is negative, the binary point must be moved left instead of right.

$$0 \bullet 1000000\ 1110 = 0.1 \times 2^{-2} = 0.001 = 0.125$$

The example above has a positive mantissa of 0.1000000 and a negative exponent of -2.

- Find the two's complement of the exponent. (Remember that to convert a positive to negative binary number using two's complement you must flip the bits and add 1.) Exponent = -2

- Move the binary point of the mantissa two places to the left, to make it smaller. The mantissa is therefore 0.001 (You can ignore the trailing zeros)

- Translate this to decimal with the help of Figure 1. The answer is 0.125.

> **Q5:** Convert the following floating point number to decimal: 0 • 1100000 1110

Handling negative mantissas

A negative floating point number will have a 1 as the sign bit or MSB (Most Significant Bit) of the mantissa indicating a negative place value.

$$\textbf{1} \bullet \textbf{0101101 0101} = -0.\underset{\smile\smile\smile\smile}{1010011} \times 2^5 = -10100.11 = -20.75$$

The example above has a negative mantissa of 1.0101101 and a positive exponent of 0101.

- Find the twos complement of the mantissa. It is 0.1010011, so the bits represent -0.1010011

- Translate the exponent to decimal, 0101 = 5

- Move the binary point 5 places to the right to make it larger. The mantissa is -10100.11

- Translate this to binary with the help of Figure 1. The answer is -20.75.

If the exponent and the mantissa are both negative, the same technique applies, but the point moves to the left instead of the right.

$$\textbf{1} \bullet \textbf{0100000 1101} = \textbf{1.0100000} \times 2^{-3} = -0.1100000 \times 2^{-3} = -0.\underset{\smile\smile\smile}{0001100} = -0.09375$$

> **Q6:** Convert the following binary numbers to decimal:
>
> (a) 0 • 1000000 1110   (b) 1 • 0011000 0100   (c) 1• 0011000 1111

Normalisation

Normalisation is the process of moving the binary point of a floating point number to provide the maximum level of precision for a given number of bits. This is achieved by ensuring that the first digit after the binary point is a significant digit. To understand this, first consider an example in decimal.

In the decimal system, a number such as $5,842,130_{10}$ can be represented with a 7-digit mantissa in many different ways

$$0.584213 \times 10^7 = 5,842,130$$

$$0.058421 \times 10^8 = 5,842,100$$

$$0.005842 \times 10^9 = 5,842,000$$

The first representation, with a significant (non-zero) digit after the decimal point has the maximum precision.

A number such as 0.00000584213 can be represented as 0.584213×10^{-5}.

Normalising a positive binary number

In binary arithmetic, the leading bit of both mantissa and exponent represent the sign bit.

In normalised floating point form:

A positive number has a sign bit of 0 and the next digit is always 1.

This means that the mantissa of a positive number in normalised form always lies between ½ and 1.

Example 1

Normalise the binary number 0.0001011 0101, held in an 8-bit mantissa and a 4-bit exponent.

- The binary point needs to move 3 places to the right so that there is a 1 following the binary point.
- Making the mantissa larger means we must compensate by making the exponent smaller, so subtract 3 from the exponent, resulting in an exponent of 0010.
- The normalised number is 0.1011000 0010

Normalising a negative binary number

An unnormalised number will have a sign bit of 1 and one or more 1s after the binary point.

Example 2

Normalise the binary number 1.1110111 0001, held in an 8-bit mantissa and a 4-bit exponent.

- Move the binary point right 3 places, so that it is just before the first 0 digit. The mantissa is now 1.0111000
- Moving the binary point to the right makes the number larger, so we must make the exponent smaller to compensate. Subtract 3 from the exponent. The exponent is now $1 - 3 = -2 = 1110$
- The normalised number is 1.0111000 1110

A normalised negative number has a sign bit of 1 and the next bit is always 0.

The mantissa of a negative number in normalised form always lies between -½ and -1.

Example 3

What does the following binary number (with a 5-bit mantissa and a 3-bit exponent) represent in decimal?

-1	1/2	1/4	1/8	1/16	-4	2	1
0	1	1	1	1	0	1	1

This is the largest positive number that can be held using a 5-bit mantissa and a 3-bit exponent, and represents $0.1111 \times 2^3 = 7.5$

Example 4

The most negative number that can be held in a 5-bit mantissa and 3-bit exponent is:

-1	1/2	1/4	1/8	1/16	-4	2	1
1	0	0	0	0	0	1	1

This represents $-1.0000 \times 2^3 = -1000.0 = -8$

Note that the size of the mantissa will determine the **precision** of the number, and the size of the exponent will determine the **range** of numbers that can be held.

Q7: Normalise the following numbers, using an 8-bit mantissa and a 4-bit exponent

    (a)   0.0000110 0001

    (b)   1.1110011 0011

Converting from decimal to normalised binary floating point

To convert a decimal number to normalised binary floating point, first convert the number to fixed point binary.

Example 5

Convert the number 14.25 to a normalised floating point binary, using an 8-bit mantissa and a 4-bit exponent.

- In fixed point binary, 14.25 = 01110.010

- Remember that the first digit after the sign bit must be 1 in normalised form, so move the binary point 4 places left and increase the exponent from 0 to 4. The number is equivalent to 0.1110010×2^4

- Using a 4-bit exponent, 14.25 = 0 1110010 0100

Example 6

If the decimal number is negative, calculate the two's complement of the fixed point binary:

e.g. Calculate the binary equivalent of -14.25

14.25 = 01110.010

-14.25 = 10001.110 (two's complement)

In normalised form, the first digit after the point must be 0, so the point needs to be moved four places left.

$10001.110 = 1.0001110 \times 2^4 = 10001110\ 0100$

> **Q8:** Convert the following numbers to normalised binary floating point numbers, using an 8-bit mantissa and 4-bit exponent:
>
> (a) 16.75 (b) -4.5

Rounding errors

In the decimal system, ⅓ can never be represented completely accurately as a decimal number.

Similarly, some binary numbers cannot be represented in the finite number of bits used to represent them, and other numbers such as 0.1_{10} can never be represented completely accurately in binary. Their accuracy will depend on the number of bits available in fixed point binary, or the size of the mantissa in floating point binary.

Rounding errors are unavoidable and result in a loss of precision.

Example: Using the number line below, find the closest binary representation for the number 0.7610 that can be held in fixed point binary using 8 bits

0.76 is approximately equal to 0.5 + 0.25 + 0.0078125 = 0.7578125

The **absolute error** is calculated as the difference between the number to be represented, and the actual binary number that is the closest possible approximation in the given number of bits.

Absolute error = 0.76 - 0.7578125 = 0.0021875

The **relative error** is the absolute error divided by the number, and may be expressed as a percentage.

Relative error = (0.0021875/0.76) = 0.002878 or 0.2878% (approximately)

> **Q9:** Using the same number line, find the closest binary representation of
> (a) 0.1 (b) 0.3333̇ Calculate the absolute and relative errors in each case.

In computer systems reliant on the manipulation of fractional numbers such as foreign currency or stock exchange systems, rounding errors can be expensive. In other systems such as missile guidance and timing, such errors can be fatal.

The effect of number magnitude on absolute and relative errors

An international sprinting track must be exactly 100 metres. What degree of tolerance would be accepted here? 1m? 1cm? 0.1cm or 0.001cm? In fact the IAAF recognise that a tolerance of 2cm or 0.02% is acceptable. 2cm is the **absolute error** above or below an actual track length, and 0.02% is the **relative error**, relative to the official length.

Depending on the application and the magnitude of the numbers, the significance or implications of an absolute or relative error can change. A relative margin of error of only 0.0005 on an estimated drilling depth of 32,000ft might seem small, but not when you find you are an absolute 16ft short of drilling pipe on board an oil platform in the middle of the sea. Notice that absolute errors are always a positive difference between the actual or recorded data.

An absolute error of say 0.5 in a number of 10,000 is a relative error of 0.005%. The same error in a number close to 1, say 0.99, is approximately 50.5%; clearly very much more significant.

In a very small number, for example 0.00001, a seemingly very small absolute error of 0.000005 is a relative error of 50%.

Application	Published data	Recorded data	Absolute error	Relative error
Currency exchange rate	1.35264 Euros to GBP	1.35 Euros to GBP	0.00264	0.20%
Train times	18 minutes	19 minutes	1 minute	5.56%
Offshore oil drilling depth	32,000 feet	32,016 feet	16 feet	0.05%

Fixed point vs floating point

Fixed and floating point each have their own advantages and disadvantages in terms of range, precision and the speed of calculation.

- Floating point allows a far greater range of numbers using the same number of bits. Very large numbers and very small fractional numbers can be represented. The larger the mantissa, the greater the precision, and the larger the exponent, the greater the range.

- In fixed point binary, the range and precision of numbers that can be represented depends on the position of the binary point. The more digits to the left of the point, the greater the range, but the lower the precision. For example, referring to Figure 1, if the binary point in a 16-bit number is placed four places from the least significant bit, numbers are only precise to four binary places. A decimal number such as 12.53125 cannot be accurately represented. In floating point, it can be represented with absolute precision as, say, 011001000100 0100.

- Fixed point binary is a simpler system and is faster to process.

Underflow and overflow

Underflow occurs when a number is too small to be represented in the allotted number of bits. If, for example, a very small number is divided by another number greater than 1, underflow may occur and the result will be represented by 0.

Overflow occurs when the result of a calculation is too large to be held in the number of bits allocated.

Exercises

1. A normalised floating point representation uses an 8-bit mantissa and a 4-bit exponent, both stored using **two's complement format**.

(a) In binary, write in the boxes below, the smallest positive number that can be represented using this normalised floating point system.

	.							

Mantissa   Exponent   [2]

(b) This is a floating point representation of a number:

1	.	0	1	1	0	0	0	0

0	0	1	0

Mantissa   Exponent   [2]

Calculate the decimal number. Show your working.   [2]

(c) Write the normalised representation of the decimal value 12.75 in the boxes below:

	.							

Mantissa   Exponent   [2]

(d) Floating point numbers are usually stored in normalised form.

State two advantages of using a normalised representation.   [2]

(e) An alternative **two's complement format** representation is proposed. In the alternative representation **7 bits** will be used to store the mantissa and **5 bits** will be used to store the exponent.

Existing representation (8-bit mantissa, 4-bit exponent):

	.							

Mantissa   Exponent

Proposed alternative representation (7-bit mantissa, 5-bit exponent):

	.						

Mantissa   Exponent   [2]

Explain the effects of using the proposed alternative representation instead of the existing representation.   [2]

AQA Unit 3 Qu 3 June 2011

Appendix B – Adders and D-type flip-flops

Objectives

- Recognise and trace the logic of the circuits of a half-adder and a full-adder
- Construct the circuit for a half-adder
- Be familiar with the use of the edge-triggered D-type flip-flop as a memory unit

Performing calculations using gates

With the right combination of gates, it is possible to output the result of a binary addition or subtraction including the value of any carry bit as a second output.

Half-adders

A half-adder can take an input of two bits and give a two-bit output as the correct result of an addition of the two inputs.

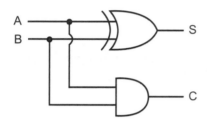

A		B		S	C
0	+	0	=	0	0
0	+	1	=	1	0
1	+	0	=	1	0
1	+	1	=	0	1

This is shown by the diagram above and represented by the truth table where S represents the sum and C represents the carry bit. S can be given as $S = A \oplus B$, and C as $C = A \cdot B$. Although a half-adder can output the value of a carry bit, it only has two inputs so it cannot use the carry from a previous addition as a third input to a subsequent addition in order to add n-bit numbers.

Full adders

A full adder combines two half-adders to add three bits together including the two inputs A and B, and a carry bit C. The logic gate circuit below illustrates how two half-adders have been connected with an additional OR gate to output the carry bit.

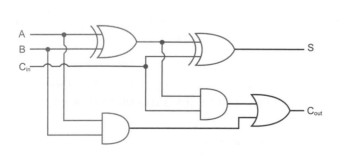

A		B		C_{in}		S	C_{out}
0	+	0	+	0	=	0	0
0	+	0	+	1	=	1	0
0	+	1	+	0	=	1	0
0	+	1	+	1	=	0	1
1	+	0	+	0	=	1	0
1	+	0	+	1	=	0	1
1	+	1	+	0	=	0	1
1	+	1	+	1	=	1	1

Now the Boolean logic becomes $S = A \oplus B \oplus C_{in}$, and $C_{out} = (A \cdot B) + (C_{in} \cdot (A \oplus B))$.

Concatenating full adders

Multiple full adders can be connected together. Using this construct, n full adders can be connected together in order to input the carry bit into a subsequent adder along with two new inputs to create a concatenated adder capable of adding a binary number of n bits.

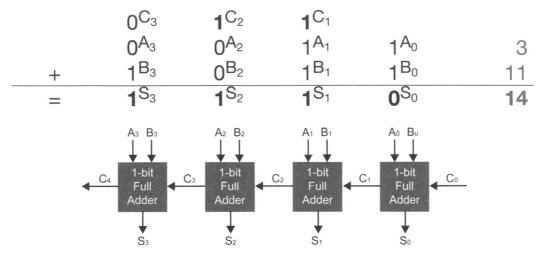

Q1: What would be the output S_4 from a fifth adder connected to the diagram above if the inputs for A_4 and B_4 were 0 and 1? What would be the output C_5?

B

D-type flip-flops

A flip-flop is an elemental **sequential logic circuit** that can store one bit and flip between two states, 0 and 1. It has two inputs, a control input labelled D and a clock signal.

The **clock** or **oscillator** is another type of sequential circuit that changes state at regular time intervals. Clocks are needed to synchronise the change of state of flip-flop circuits.

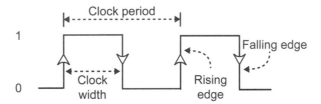

The **D-type flip-flop** (D stands for Data or Delay) is a positive **edge-triggered flip-flop**, meaning that it can only change the output value from 1 to 0 or vice versa when the clock is at a rising or positive edge, i.e. at the beginning of a clock period.

When the clock is not at a positive edge, the input value is held and does not change. **The flip-flop circuit is important because it can be used as a memory cell to store the state of a bit.**

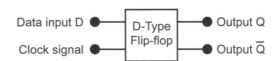

Output Q only takes on a new value if the value at D has changed at the point of a clock pulse. This means that the clock pulse will freeze or 'store' the input value at D until the next clock pulse. If D remains the same on the next clock pulse, the flip-flop will hold the same value.

The use of a D-type flip-flop as a memory unit

A flip-flop comprises several NAND (or AND and OR) gates and is effectively 1-bit memory. To store eight bits, eight flip-flops are required. **Register memories** are constructed by connecting a series of flip-flops in a row and are typically used for the intermediate storage needed during arithmetic operations. Static RAM is also created using D-type flip-flops. Imagine trying to assemble 16GB of memory in this way!

The graph below illustrates how the output Q only changes to match the input D in response to the rising edge on the clock signal. Q therefore delays, or 'stores' the value of D by up to one clock cycle.

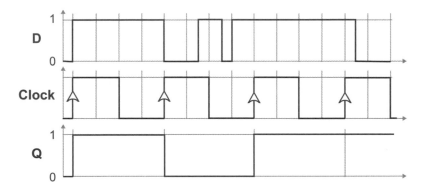

Exercises

1. A half-adder is used to find the sum of the addition of two binary digits.

    (a) Complete the diagram below to construct a half adder circuit. [1]

    (b) Complete the following truth table for a half adder's outputs S and C.

A	B	S	C

    [2]

    (c) How does a full adder differ from a half adder in terms of its inputs? [2]

2. An edge-triggered D-type flip-flop can be used as a memory cell to store the value of a single bit. The following graph shows the clock cycle and the input signals applied to D.

(a) Label each rising edge on the diagram below. [1]

(b) Draw the flip-flop's output Q on the graph. [4]

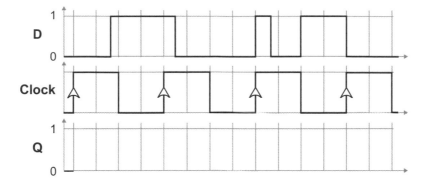

Index

Index

Index

Index

Index

AQA A LEVEL 7516/7517 Specification map

The content in each section of the textbook covers the same specification points as the corresponding downloadable teaching unit, e.g. Section 1 complements Unit 1.

4.1 Fundamentals of programming

	Section 1	Section 2	Section 3	Section 4	Section 5	Section 6	Section 7	Section 8	Section 9	Section 10	Section 11	Section 12	Appendix
4.1.1 Programming	✓							✓					
4.1.2 Programming paradigms	✓	✓										✓	

4.2 Fundamentals of data structures

	Section 1	Section 2	Section 3	Section 4	Section 5	Section 6	Section 7	Section 8	Section 9	Section 10	Section 11	Section 12	Appendix
4.2.1 Data structures and abstract data types	✓												
4.2.2 Queues							✓						
4.2.3 Stacks							✓						
4.2.4 Graphs							✓						
4.2.5 Trees							✓						
4.2.6 Hash tables							✓						
4.2.7 Dictionaries							✓						
4.2.8 Vectors							✓						

4.3 Fundamentals of algorithms

	Section 1	Section 2	Section 3	Section 4	Section 5	Section 6	Section 7	Section 8	Section 9	Section 10	Section 11	Section 12	Appendix
4.3.1 Graph-traversal							✓	✓					
4.3.2 Tree-traversal							✓	✓					
4.3.3 Reverse Polish								✓	✓				
4.3.4 Searching algorithms								✓					
4.3.5 Sorting algorithms								✓					
4.3.6 Optimisation algorithms								✓					

AQA A LEVEL 7516/7517 Specification map

4.4 Theory of computation

	Section 1	Section 2	Section 3	Section 4	Section 5	Section 6	Section 7	Section 8	Section 9	Section 10	Section 11	Section 12	Appendix
4.4.1 Abstraction and automation		✓											
4.4.2 Regular languages		✓							✓				
4.4.3 Context-free languages									✓				
4.4.4 Classification of algorithms								✓	✓				
4.4.5 A model of computation									✓				

4.5 Fundamentals of data representation

	Section 1	Section 2	Section 3	Section 4	Section 5	Section 6	Section 7	Section 8	Section 9	Section 10	Section 11	Section 12	Appendix
4.5.1 Number systems			✓										
4.5.2 Number bases			✓										
4.5.3 Sections of information			✓										
4.5.4 Binary number system			✓										✓
4.5.5 Information coding systems			✓										
4.5.6 Representing images, sound and other data			✓										

4.6 Fundamentals of computer systems

	Section 1	Section 2	Section 3	Section 4	Section 5	Section 6	Section 7	Section 8	Section 9	Section 10	Section 11	Section 12	Appendix
4.6.1 Hardware and software				✓									
4.6.2 Classification of programming languages				✓									
4.6.3 Types of program translator				✓									
4.6.4 Logic gates				✓									✓
4.6.5 Boolean algebra				✓									

AQA A LEVEL 7516/7517 Specification map

4.7 Fundamentals of computer organisation and architecture

	Section 1	Section 2	Section 3	Section 4	Section 5	Section 6	Section 7	Section 8	Section 9	Section 10	Section 11	Section 12	Appendix
4.7.1 Internal hardware components of a computer					✓								
4.7.2 The stored program concept					✓								
4.7.3 Structure and role of the processor and its components					✓								
4.7.4 External hardware devices					✓								

4.8 Consequences of uses of computing

	Section 1	Section 2	Section 3	Section 4	Section 5	Section 6	Section 7	Section 8	Section 9	Section 10	Section 11	Section 12	Appendix
4.8.1 Individual (moral), social (ethical), legal and cultural issues and opportunities						✓							

4.9 Fundamentals of communication and networking

	Section 1	Section 2	Section 3	Section 4	Section 5	Section 6	Section 7	Section 8	Section 9	Section 10	Section 11	Section 12	Appendix
4.9.1 Communication						✓							
4.9.2 Networking						✓							
4.9.3 The Internet										✓			
4.9.4 The Transmission Control Protocol/Internet Protocol (TCP/IP) protocol										✓			

4.10 Fundamentals of databases

	Section 1	Section 2	Section 3	Section 4	Section 5	Section 6	Section 7	Section 8	Section 9	Section 10	Section 11	Section 12	Appendix
4.10.1 Conceptual data models and entity relationship modelling											✓		
4.10.2 Relational databases											✓		
4.10.3 Database design and normalisation techniques											✓		
4.10.4 Structured Query Language (SQL)											✓		
4.10.5 Client server databases											✓		

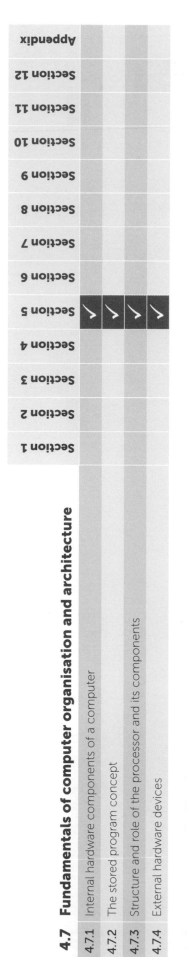

AQA A LEVEL 7516/7517 Specification map

PG ONLINE

	Section 1	Section 2	Section 3	Section 4	Section 5	Section 6	Section 7	Section 8	Section 9	Section 10	Section 11	Section 12	Appendix
4.11 Big Data													
4.11 Big data												✓	
4.12 Fundamentals of functional programming													
4.12.1 Functional programming paradigm												✓	
4.12.2 Writing functional programs												✓	
4.12.3 Lists in functional programming												✓	
4.13 Systematic approach to problem solving													
4.13.1 Aspects of software development		✓									✓		